Income Statement Semantic Models

Building Enterprise-Grade
Income Statement Models
with Power BI

Chris Barber

Apress®

Income Statement Semantic Models: Building Enterprise-Grade Income Statement Models with Power BI

Chris Barber
KINGSTON UPON THAMES, UK

ISBN-13 (pbk): 979-8-8688-0329-1
https://doi.org/10.1007/979-8-8688-0330-7

ISBN-13 (electronic): 979-8-8688-0330-7

Copyright © 2024 by Chris Barber

This work is subject to copyright. All rights are reserved by the Publisher, whether the whole or part of the material is concerned, specifically the rights of translation, reprinting, reuse of illustrations, recitation, broadcasting, reproduction on microfilms or in any other physical way, and transmission or information storage and retrieval, electronic adaptation, computer software, or by similar or dissimilar methodology now known or hereafter developed.

Trademarked names, logos, and images may appear in this book. Rather than use a trademark symbol with every occurrence of a trademarked name, logo, or image we use the names, logos, and images only in an editorial fashion and to the benefit of the trademark owner, with no intention of infringement of the trademark.

The use in this publication of trade names, trademarks, service marks, and similar terms, even if they are not identified as such, is not to be taken as an expression of opinion as to whether or not they are subject to proprietary rights.

While the advice and information in this book are believed to be true and accurate at the date of publication, neither the authors nor the editors nor the publisher can accept any legal responsibility for any errors or omissions that may be made. The publisher makes no warranty, express or implied, with respect to the material contained herein.

>Managing Director, Apress Media LLC: Welmoed Spahr
>Acquisitions Editor: Ryan Byrnes
>Development Editor: Laura Berendson
>Coordinating Editor: Gryffin Winkler

Cover designed by eStudioCalamar
Cover image by adobe stock photos

Distributed to the book trade worldwide by Apress Media, LLC, 1 New York Plaza, New York, NY 10004, U.S.A. Phone 1-800-SPRINGER, fax (201) 348-4505, e-mail orders-ny@springer-sbm.com, or visit www.springeronline.com. Apress Media, LLC is a California LLC and the sole member (owner) is Springer Science + Business Media Finance Inc (SSBM Finance Inc). SSBM Finance Inc is a **Delaware** corporation.

For information on translations, please e-mail booktranslations@springernature.com; for reprint, paperback, or audio rights, please e-mail bookpermissions@springernature.com.

Apress titles may be purchased in bulk for academic, corporate, or promotional use. eBook versions and licenses are also available for most titles. For more information, reference our Print and eBook Bulk Sales web page at http://www.apress.com/bulk-sales.

Any source code or other supplementary material referenced by the author in this book is available to readers on GitHub (https://github.com/Apress). For more detailed information, please visit https://www.apress.com/gp/services/source-code.

If disposing of this product, please recycle the paper

For Gemma and Sophie

Table of Contents

About the Author xv

About the Technical Reviewer xvii

Acknowledgments xix

Preface xxi

Part I: Modelling and the Income Statement 1

Chapter 1: What Is an Income Statement Semantic Model? 3

What Is the Income Statement? 4

    External Income Statement Requirements 5

    Internal Income Statement Requirements 7

What Is a Semantic Model? 9

    An Income Statement Semantic Model As a Navigation Tool 9

    An Income Statement Semantic Model Measures the
Accounting Process 11

Summary 13

Chapter 2: How the Income Statement Is Constructed 15

Building the Income Statement to Net Income 16

    Transaction Entries 18

    Adjusting Entries 20

    Trial Balance 22

    Account Balances 22

    Income Statement to Net Income 24

TABLE OF CONTENTS

    Allocating Net Income to Controlling and Non-controlling Interests 27
        Non-controlling Interest Is Provided by the Finance Team or System 28
        Maintain Analytical Flexibility by Applying Controlling and
        Non-controlling Interests at the Journal Level 29
    Earnings per Share (EPS) 31
        Numerator: Net Income 32
        Denominator: Weighted Average Shares 32
        EPS Presentation 33
    Summary 33

Chapter 3: Building a Reusable Solution 35

    The Sixteen Challenges in Modelling the Income Statement 36
        The Nine Calculation Challenges 36
        The Four Presentation Challenges 37
        The Three Analytical Challenges 38
    The Power BI Semantic Model 39
        Building a Semantic Model 39
        Data Preparation: Transforming the Trial Balance 40
        Data Modelling: Creating Relationships to the Trial Balance 42
        Calculations: Sum of Trial Balance Value 43
        Querying the Semantic Model Using DAX and MDX 43
    The Input-Driven Approach 45
    Summary 47

Chapter 4: Why Model the Income Statement? 49

    Benefits of Modelling the Income Statement 50
        Explain the Income Statement 50
        Improve Decision-Making 51
        Improve Data Quality 53

Gain a Deeper Understanding of Profitability 53
Uncover Insights to Facilitate the Month-End Close Process 53
Why Partially Modelling the Income Statement Is Insufficient............................ 55
Argument 1: Business Intelligence Should Focus on Individual Lines in the Income Statement Rather Than Reproducing Financial Reports in Their Entirety, Which Should Be Managed by the Finance System 56
Argument 2: Visual Calculations Should Overlay Semantic Model Calculations to Create the Income Statement 60
Summary... 64

Part II: Calculating Account Balances 67

Chapter 5: Conceptual Account Balance Models 69
Calculating Account Balances Using the Trial Balance Conceptual Model.......... 70
Account Balances 71
Journal Entry Conceptual Models 74
Why It Is Important to Work at the Atomic Grain.. 75
How Dimensions Are Identified.. 75
Handling Multiple Date Dimensions 77
Working at the Atomic Grain Increases the Number of Rows....................... 77
Increasing Beyond the Atomic Grain... 79
Summary... 81

Chapter 6: Logical Account Balance Models 81
The Trial Balance Logical Model.. 84
An Example Journal Entry Logical Model.. 87
Primary Keys 90
Foreign Keys.. 91
Attributes (AT).. 91
Degenerate Dimensions (DD)... 91
Measures (ME).. 93

TABLE OF CONTENTS

Aggregations 93
    Creating a Single Aggregation 94
    Creating Multiple Aggregations 96
    Journal Entry Aggregation Logical Models 97
Summary 104

Chapter 7: The Trial Balance Semantic Model 107
Semantic Model Inputs 108
Power Query Transformations 108
    Stage 1: Create Shared Expressions 109
    Stage 2: Trial Balance Fact Table 119
    Stage 3: Group Ownership Dimension 123
    Stage 4: Account Dimension 126
    Stage 5: Effective Date Dimension 130
    Stage 6: Measure Table 133
Building the Data Model 137
    Create Relationships 137
    Mark As Date Table 140
    Dates Sort Order 142
DAX 143
    Step 01: Sum 144
    Step 02: Account Type Indicator 144
    Step 03: Line-items 144
Calculating Line-Items, Subtotals, and Subsets 145
Summary 146

TABLE OF CONTENTS

Chapter 8: A Journal Entry Semantic Model 147

Semantic Model Inputs 148

Power Query Transformations 149

    Stage 1: Create Shared Expressions 149

    Stage 2: Journal Entry Fact Tables 165

    Stage 3: Group Ownership dimension 171

    Stage 4: Accounts Dimension 174

    Stage 5: Effective Date Dimension 178

    Stage 6: Customer Dimension 181

    Stage 7: Product Dimension 184

    Stage 8: Posting Date Dimension 186

    Stage 9: Measure Table 190

Building the Data Model 193

    Create Relationships 193

    Mark As Date Table 193

    Date Sort Order 193

DAX 193

    Step 01: Sum 194

    Step 02: Account Type Indicator 196

    Step 03: Lineitems 196

Summary 197

Part III: Producing External Income Statement Semantic Models 199

Chapter 9: The Four Subtotal and Subset Types 201

The Four Subtotal and Subset Options 201

Why Four Options of Subtotal and Subset Are Required 203

Examples of the Four Subtotal and Subset Options 203

ix

TABLE OF CONTENTS

    Subtotal Option 1: Net Credit Less Debit 204

    Subtotal Option 2: All Credit Less Debit 206

    Subtotal Option 3: Net Debit Less Credit 207

    Subtotal Option 4: All Debit Less Credit 209

  Summary 210

Chapter 10: External Reporting Logical Models 213

  The External Layout Table 214

    External Layout Table Overview 214

    Line Name, Income Statement Key, and Is Hidden 217

    Income Statement Line Calculations 217

    Income Statement Line Formatting 219

    Completing the External Layout Table 220

  Extending the Trial Balance Logical Model and a Journal Entry
Logical Model 247

    Extension 1: Adding the Shares Outstanding Fact Table 248

    Extension 2: Creating the Relationship Between Effective Date and
Shares Outstanding 249

    Extension 3: Adding the Layout Snowflake Dimension 250

    Extension 4: Adding a Foreign Key to the Account Dimension 252

    Extension 5: Creating the Relationship Between Layout and Accounts 252

    External Reporting Logical Model 254

  Summary 255

Chapter 11: External Reporting Semantic Models 257

  Semantic Model Inputs 258

  Power Query Transformations 259

    Stage 1: Create Shared Expressions 259

    Stage 2: Shares Outstanding Fact Table 264

> Stage 3: Layout Dimension Table 266
>
> Stage 4: Account Dimension Table 282
>
> Building the Data Model 295
>
> > Creating Relationships 295
> >
> > Sort Hierarchy 296
>
> DAX Actuals Calculation 297
>
> > Step 04: Subtotals 299
> >
> > Step 05: Subset 304
> >
> > Step 06: Controlling and Non-controlling Interests 309
> >
> > Step 07: Weighted Number of Shares 311
> >
> > Step 08: Bespoke Calculations 315
> >
> > Step 09: Divide 315
> >
> > Step 10: Add Blank Rows 320
> >
> > Step 11: Show Values 321
> >
> > Step 12: Combined Calculation 321
>
> Dynamic Format Strings 322
>
> Summary 323

Part IV: Producing Internal Income Statement Semantic Models 325

Chapter 12: Internal Reporting Logical Models 327

> The Internal Layout Table 328
>
> > Internal Layout Table Overview 328
> >
> > Completing the Internal Layout Table 334
>
> Extending the External Reporting Logical Models 360
>
> > Extension 1: Adding the Other Non-general Ledger Information Snapshot Fact Table 361
> >
> > Extension 2: Creating the Relationship Between Effective Date and Other Non-general Ledger Information 363

TABLE OF CONTENTS

    Extension 3: Adding an Additional Foreign Key to the Account Dimension 364

    Extension 4: Creating the Inactive Relationship Between Layout and Account 364

    Extension 5: Adding the Layout Version Attribute 365

    Internal Reporting Logical Model 367

  Summary 368

Chapter 13: Internal Reporting Semantic Models 371

  Semantic Model Inputs 372

  Power Query Transformations 373

    Stage 1: Create Shared Expressions 373

    Stage 2: Other Non-general Ledger Information 378

    Stage 3: Layout Dimension 381

    Stage 4: Accounts Dimension Table 389

  Building the Data Model 395

    Creating Relationships 395

  DAX Actuals Calculation 397

    Step 08: Bespoke Calculations 398

    Step 12: Actuals 401

  Summary 404

Chapter 14: Security and Self-Service Considerations 405

  Security Considerations 405

  Self-Service Considerations 407

    Consideration 1: What Is Relevant to End Users 408

    Consideration 2: How the Semantic Model Should Be Organized 409

    Consideration 3: How the Semantic Model Can Be Enriched 410

  Summary 417

Chapter 15: Review of the 16 Challenges 419

    The Nine Calculation Challenges 419

        Challenges 1–6 419

        Challenges 7–9 421

    The Four Presentation Challenges 422

        Challenges 10–12 422

        Challenge 13: Enabling Multiple Layouts 423

    The Three Analytical Challenges 423

        Challenges 14 and 15 423

        Challenge 16: Drilling from Income Statement Lines to Journal Entries 425

    Summary 426

Index 429

About the Author

Chris Barber is a chartered accountant (ACMA, CGMA) and Microsoft MVP. He has trained over 1,000 people on how to build income statements in Power BI, delivered several public talks on using the Microsoft BI stack within finance, and runs StarSchema.co.uk.

All author proceeds from this book are being donated to Save the Children.

About the Technical Reviewer

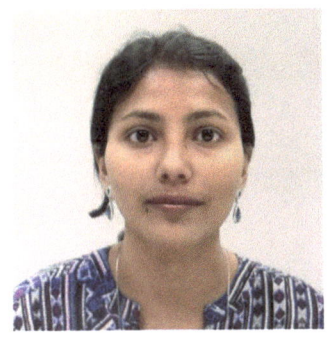

Triparna Ray is a passionate technologist with over two decades of experience in Microsoft Business Intelligence.

She is a well-known Power BI consultant in Microsoft Community specializing in Financial Reporting.

Triparna has worked as an architect in a number of Power BI implementations across domains and geography.

She is a mentor, trainer, and public speaker and has presented in various technical conferences.

Acknowledgments

I have so many people to thank for their contributions that it is impossible to include everyone. So, thank you to everyone who has played a part, even if you did not know you were doing so. The data community has been invaluable with many excellent conferences, user groups, blogs, and other forms of learning. Any presenters, attendees, and those I have spoken to at an event or engaged with through other means, you have all made a significant contribution to the contents of this book.

There are, however, some special mentions I would like to make.

Firstly, to Prathyusha (Prathy) Kamasani who provided the most welcoming and open environment in which to learn and ask questions. Without this, I would not have pursued a change in direction within my career, and this book would never have been written.

I also want to thank Mark Wilcock who has been incredibly supportive. Mark accelerated my involvement in the data community, and without him I would not have received my first Microsoft MVP award.

There are many colleagues and former colleagues I must also thank who provided support or took time to explain the overwhelming process involved in publishing a book. Special mentions to James Dales, Pragati Jain, Rishi Sapra, Mihaly Kavasi, Richard Swinbank, and Lee Englestone. Your help is greatly appreciated.

Finally, a special mention to Triparna Ray (technical reviewer), Ryan Byrnes (acquisitions editor), Laura Berendson (development editor), Gryffin Winkler (coordinating editor), Nirmal Selvaraj (production editor), and all those involved in the publication process. I greatly appreciate all the hours you have spent reviewing this book and working through the various examples.

Preface

For years, I have seen various entities struggle to produce income statement reports that meet modern analytical demands. A quick internet search and you will see a wide variety of methodologies from reputable sources, some which are heavily model focused, others which create a plethora of calculations, and others which use logic within the visual itself to perform calculations. This range of options runs in conflict with what one might intuitively expect if you come from an accounting background; there is a standardized process of building income statements based on the trial balance, and outputs are homogenous because they are regulated by accounting standards such as IAS (International Accounting Standards) 1 Presentation of Financial Statements. This is regardless of whether the company produces semiconductors or sells advertising revenue. Therefore, a valid question is why is there such a lack of consensus on the best way to model income statements?

Part of the reason for the lack of consensus is because the authoritative source on dimensional modelling (*The Data Warehouse Toolkit, Volume 3* by Kimball and Ross) said you should not try to model the entire income statement (I am paraphrasing, but this is the gist of it). While the reasons were conclusive at the time of writing, modern demands and the powerful analytical engines underpinning Microsoft Fabric, Power BI, and Analysis Services Tabular make it possible to produce income statements in their entirety. The, albeit lofty, ambition of this book is to drive consensus on how to achieve this with an approach based on the trial balance that can be reused across entities.

PREFACE

For a semantic model income statement to be widely accepted, this book posits two fundamental criteria. Firstly, the semantic model should be based on the trial balance; the trial balance is the precursory step in the accounting process prior to producing income statements and is thus common across entities. By building a solution based on the trial balance, a base semantic model can be built which can then be customized to the nuances of each particular entity, that is, the ways in which a particular entity explains its income statement. Secondly, the semantic model must adhere to the principles of dimensional modelling as outlined by Kimball and Ross; these principles are widely accepted, and any solution which is in violation is unlikely to be widely adopted within the technology community.

Whom This Book Is For

This book has two primary audiences:

1. Technical (i.e., solution architects, Microsoft Fabric developers, Power BI developers) who are struggling to produce income statement semantic models because of the modelling complexities and knowledge needed of the accounting process
2. Finance (i.e., management accountants) who have hit the limits of Excel and have started using Power BI, but are unsure how income statement semantic models are built

This book covers both finance and technical areas in sufficient depth, without covering areas which are irrelevant to modelling the income statement. For instance, a knowledge of complex group structures is required, but in modelling you do not need to know how to calculate non-controlling interest as this is an output provided by the finance team or system.

If you are coming from a technical background, you may be able to quickly cover the more technical chapters, being familiar with concepts such as role-playing dimensions, surrogate keys, and aggregations. In contrast, you may find you cover the accounting heavy chapters at a slower pace as these introduce concepts such as the qualitative characteristics of financial reports, double-entry bookkeeping, and the accounting process. The reverse is expected to be true of those coming from a finance background.

Assumptions About You

There is an assumption you are aware of Power BI basics including knowledge of Power Query, modelling, DAX (Data Analysis eXpressions), and visualization. This includes a basic understanding of DAX theory such as filter and row context, how to configure security, and amending properties using Power BI Desktop such as adding descriptions, creating folders, and hiding fields. Furthermore, there is an assumption you have a basic grasp of Excel including familiarity with pivot tables and the ability to write formulas.

What Is Not Covered

This book does not cover the data engineering required to go from source systems to semantic model inputs. There are a wide array of ways in which data can be made available for consumption and many excellent resources, such as books and blogs on the topic of data engineering. Some of these resources are technology agnostic and focus on the principles of data engineering, while others focus on specific technologies.

PREFACE

If the data engineering process stores information in delta-parquet, it can immediately be accessed by a semantic model using direct lake mode. However, this is not essential, and all examples in this book use import mode with comma-separated value (CSV) files and thus can be followed along using the free version of Power BI.

Organization of This Book
Parts

This book is divided into four parts, each of which has a specific learning objective:

Part 1, "Modelling and the Income Statement": Learn what modelling the income statement entails, why it is important, and how income statements are constructed.

Part 2, "Calculating Account Balances": Learn how to optimally calculate account balances using a Star Schema.

Part 3, "Producing External Income Statement Semantic Models": Learn how to produce external income statement semantic models which enable income statements to be analyzed from a range of perspectives and drilled into to reveal the underlying accounts and journal entries.

Part 4, "Producing Internal Income Statement Semantic Models": Learn how to create multiple income statement layouts and further contextualize financial information by including percentages and non-financial information. Also, learn about the various security and self-service considerations and how the semantic modelling approach overcomes various challenges in producing income statements.

PREFACE

Chapters

This book is designed to flow from introductory chapters to more advanced concepts. Each chapter assumes the content from the previous chapters has been understood. Once each chapter has been covered, this book is designed to be used as a refresher when building income statement solutions.

At a glance, the chapters are as follows:

Chapter 1, "What Is an Income Statement Semantic Model?," introduces modelling the income statement, covering the core components of statutory reporting, such as net income, controlling interests, non-controlling interests, and earnings per share. It extends the income statement to include internal requirements, such as adding percentages and including non-financial information to contextualize financial information. It also covers two ways of viewing an income statement semantic model, as a way of navigating financial information and a way of measuring the accounting process.

Chapter 2, "How the Income Statement Is Constructed," covers the accounting process which results in the production of the income statement to net income. This introduces key accounting concepts such as double-entry bookkeeping, the accrual method of accounting, the trial balance, and account balances. Also covered is group accounting which can result in net income being attributed to controlling and non-controlling interests. Finally, earnings per share calculations are covered.

Chapter 3, "Building a Reusable Solution," outlines the sixteen challenges in modelling the income statement, divided into nine calculation challenges, four presentational challenges, and three analytical challenges. It breaks down the semantic model into the three stages of data preparation, data modelling, and Data Analysis eXpressions (DAX). It brings the challenges and semantic model process together to highlight

PREFACE

how a reusable solution based on the trial balance can overcome fourteen of the challenges; overcoming the remaining two challenges requires customization from the base solution.

Chapter 4, "Why Model the Income Statement?," covers the benefits of modelling the income statement in its entirety, such as helping to explain the income statement, improve decision-making, improve data quality, gain a deeper understanding of profitability, and uncover insights to facilitate the month-end close process. This also addresses the core arguments against modelling the income statement in its entirety, that (1) business intelligence should focus on individual lines in the income statement rather than reproducing financial reports and (2) the visual – as opposed to the semantic model – should contain the income statement logic.

Chapter 5, "Conceptual Account Balance Models," explains how to calculate account balances using a trial balance Star Schema. It introduces the concept of granularity and increasing the dimensionality of the solution beyond the base trial balance model.

Chapter 6, "Logical Account Balance Models," explains how to convert conceptual models (high-level designs) into logical models (detailed blueprints). It covers the conversion of the trial balance and journal entry conceptual models, including introducing data types, keys, degenerate dimensions, attributes, and measures. Finally, it shows how aggregations can be used to optimize the account balance calculation.

Chapter 7, "The Trial Balance Semantic Model," builds a line-item solution in Power BI based upon trial balances for Tyrell Corp and Weyland Industries. It covers the core stages in building a semantic model of Power Query transformations, data modelling, and DAX. Finally, it shows how the semantic model can be used to re-create external income statements in Excel.

Chapter 8, "A Journal Entry Semantic Model," builds a line-item solution in Power BI based upon journal entries for StarSchema.co.uk. It covers the core stages in building a semantic model of Power Query transformations, data modelling, and DAX.

Chapter 9, "The Four Subtotal and Subset Types," explains how subtotals and subsets can contain a mix of revenue and expense accounts. Consequently, this leads to four drill-down options: net credit less debit, net debit less credit, all credit less debit, and all debit less credit. Examples of all four options are shown exhibiting their different behavior.

Chapter 10, "External Reporting Logical Models," expands the logical account balance models (Chapter 6) to produce logical models which reproduce external reports in their entirety. It introduces, with a worked example, the layout table which contains the logic surrounding the presentation of income statements: what lines appear, in which order they appear, which calculations are performed, and how they are formatted.

Chapter 11, "External Reporting Semantic Models," extends the trial balance semantic model (Chapter 7) and the journal entry semantic model (Chapter 8) to produce external income statements in their entirety. It covers the core stages in expanding the semantic models of Power Query transformations, data modelling, DAX, and dynamic format strings.

Chapter 12, "Internal Reporting Logical Models," expands the external reporting logical models (Chapter 10) adding additional layouts and supporting an additional fact table containing information from departments such as human resources and marketing.

Chapter 13, "Internal Reporting Semantic Models," extends the external reporting semantic models (Chapter 11) to contain multiple layouts and internal metrics. It covers the core stages in expanding the semantic models of Power Query transformations, data modelling, and DAX.

Chapter 14, "Security and Self-Service Considerations," covers various security considerations and ways to make it easier for end users to retrieve information from the semantic model.

Chapter 15, "Review of the 16 Challenges," reviews how the approach to building semantic models outlined in this book overcomes the nine calculation challenges, the four presentational challenges, and the three analytical challenges.

PREFACE

To Get the Most Out of This Book

You will need the latest version of Power BI Desktop downloaded and installed (Download Power BI Desktop from Official Microsoft Download Center). All examples used throughout this book have been tested in the January 2024 release of Power BI Desktop and will work on future versions. It is also advised to turn off default settings for inferring relationships and creating private date tables. At the time of writing, "dynamic format strings for measures" is a preview feature that must be tuned on.

In addition to Power BI Desktop, you will need the latest version of Tabular Editor (https://github.com/TabularEditor/TabularEditor).

In some chapters, you may need to have Excel and a Power BI Service account. You can sign up for a Power BI Service as an individual. Read more here: https://docs.microsoft.com/en-us/power-bi/fundamentals/service-self-service-signup-for-power-bi?WT.mc_id=5003466.

Turning Off Default Settings for Inferring Relationships and Private Date Tables and Enabling Preview Features

To build the solution from scratch, without Power BI inferring any relationships or creating any additional hidden tables in the background, the default settings for relationships and time intelligence are required to be turned off. At the time of writing, *dynamic format string for measures* is a preview feature that should be enabled. All these options can be set in four steps:

Step 1: In Power BI Desktop, select **File (1)**.

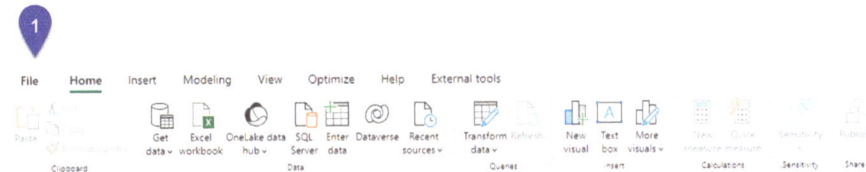

Figure 1. *Select file*

Step 2: Select **Options and settings (1)**. Select **Options (2)**.

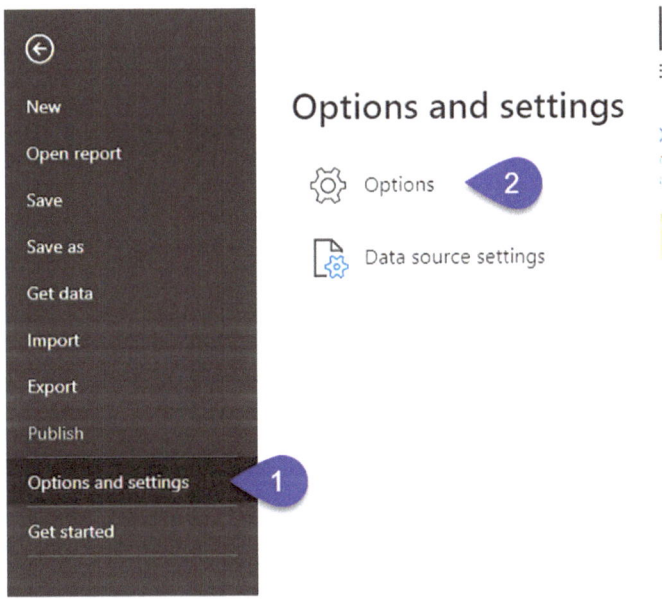

Figure 2. *Select options*

PREFACE

Step 3: In the pop-up box, under current file select **Data Load (1)**, then untick **Import relationships from data sources on first load (2)**, **Autodetect new relationships after data is loaded (3)**, and **Auto date/time (4)**.

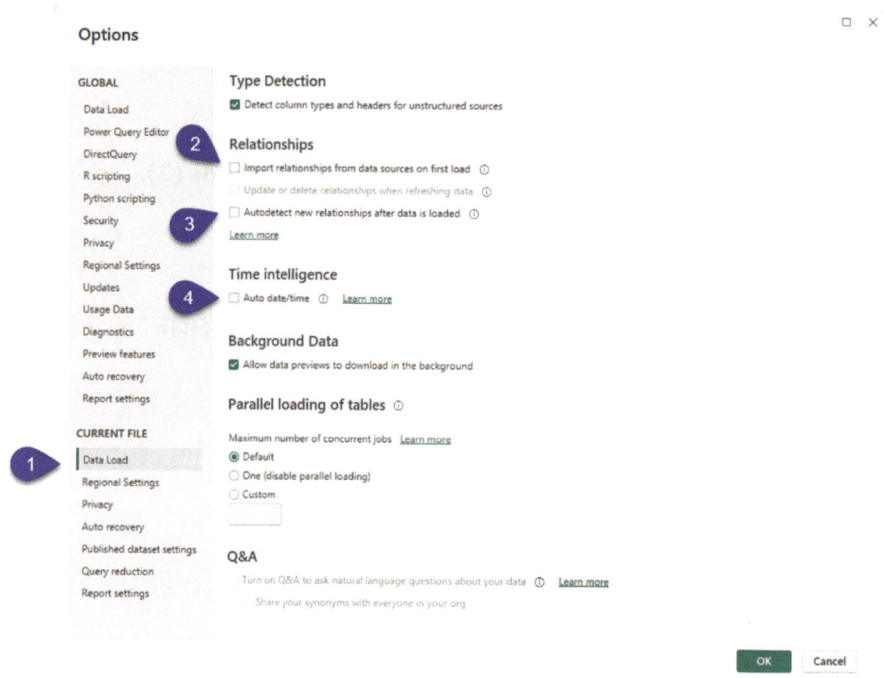

Figure 3. *Data load options*

PREFACE

Step 4: In the pop-up box, under global select **Preview features (1)**, then tick **Dynamic format string for measures (2)**.

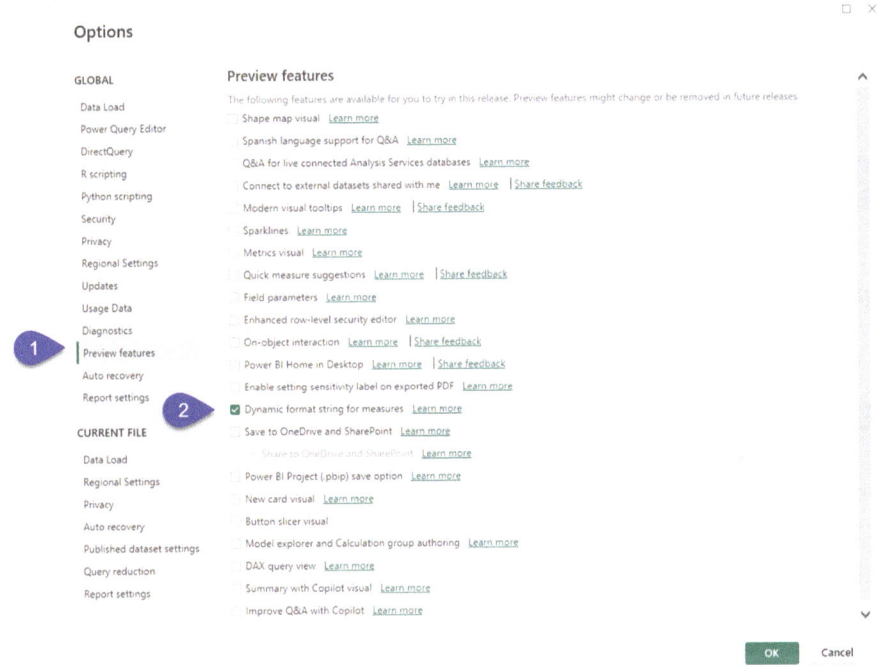

Figure 4. Preview options

Accessing Tabular Editor from Power BI Desktop

Power BI Desktop is catered toward basic to intermediate users from a modelling perspective. While the features available in Power BI Desktop are increasing, third-party tools are still required to access some of the more advanced features, and these tools also drastically speed up development.

xxxi

PREFACE

To open Tabular Editor, click **External tools (1)**, then **Tabular Editor (2)**.

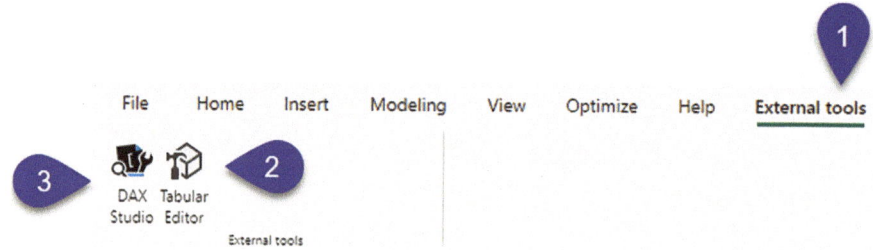

Figure 5. Launch Tabular Editor 2

Resources

You can download the accompanying resources from GitHub at https://github.com/Apress/Income-Statement-Semantic-Models. This includes all the CSV and PBIX files. To use the PBIX files, open Power Query, and in the folder **Parameter (1)**, select **Folder (2)**, then type the path name where it says **TYPE FILE LOCATION (3)**; this is the location CSV files have been downloaded to, that is, "C:\Users\Chris.Barber\OneDrive\Downloads\".

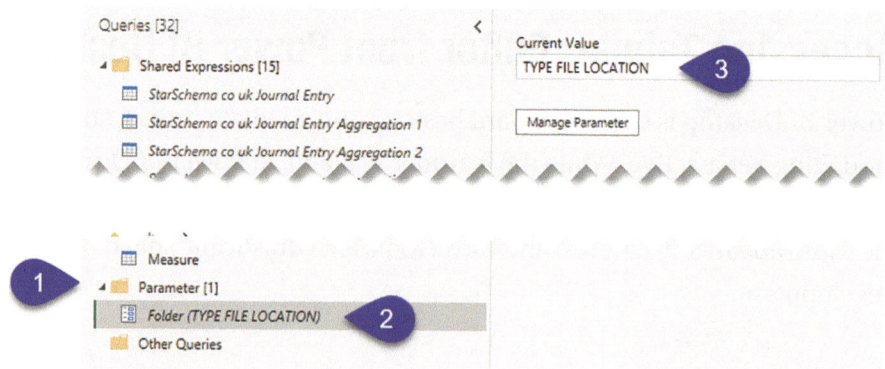

Figure 6. Using parameters

Examples Used

Given financial information is closely guarded, this book uses fictional examples when analyzing income statements down to accounts and individual journal entries. There are three examples used throughout this book:

1. Tyrell Corp
2. Weyland Industries
3. StarSchema.co.uk

The Tyrell Corp and Weyland Industries solutions go down to account level and are used to create trial balance semantic models in Chapter 7, whereas the StarSchema.co.uk solution goes down to individual journal entries in Chapter 8. Chapter 11 builds on any of the three semantic models, creating external reporting semantic models; these contain the logic surrounding the presentation of the income statement. Chapter 13 then covers adding a secondary income statement layout for each example which includes percentages and non-general ledger information, such as the number of full-time equivalent (FTE) employees.

Conventions Used

- Tables are identified using single quotations: 'Table', that is, 'Account'.
- Columns are identified using single quotations for the table and square brackets for the column: 'Table'[Column Name], that is, 'Account'[Account Name].
- Measures are identified using square brackets without a table name: [Measure], that is, [Actuals].

PART I

Modelling and the Income Statement

In this part, the concept of an income statement semantic model is introduced. There is an assumption you are aware of Power BI basics including knowledge of the layers Power Query, data modelling, DAX, and visualization.

In this part, you will learn what modelling the income statement entails, how income statements are constructed, the challenges a reusable solution must overcome, and why it is important to model the income statement in its entirety.

This part comprises the following chapters:

- Chapter 1, "What Is an Income Statement Semantic Model?"
- Chapter 2, "How the Income Statement Is Constructed"
- Chapter 3, "Building a Reusable Solution"
- Chapter 4, "Why Model the Income Statement?"

PART I

Modelling and the biome system

CHAPTER 1

What Is an Income Statement Semantic Model?

An income statement data model is a collection of tables, connected using relationships. These tables and relationships represent the accounting logic surrounding how an income statement is compiled and how it can be analyzed. When combined with calculations, a semantic model is created which tools such as Excel and Power BI can utilize to visualize income statements.

Regardless of whether you are using Excel pivot tables or cube formulas with an Application Programming Interface (API) connection, creating visuals in Power BI Desktop, or viewing reports on your web browser or phone, a request for information is being made to the semantic model. Thus, providing questions are identical, results will also be identical. The semantic model, therefore, creates a shared understanding, allowing users to intuitively uncover insights and retrieve consistent results, regardless of how information is consumed. It is said to be intuitive to use, as the model should accurately represent the accounting process, and thus contain familiar concepts and terminology.

CHAPTER 1   WHAT IS AN INCOME STATEMENT SEMANTIC MODEL?

In this chapter, we will learn what an income statement is, how it contributes to the primary objective of publically listed companies, and the requirements from external and internal perspectives. We will also learn what an income statement semantic model is, viewing the model as a navigation tool and a way of measuring the accounting process.

In this chapter, there are two sections:

1. What Is the Income Statement?
2. What Is a Semantic Model?

What Is the Income Statement?

The statement of comprehensive income is the main source of information about *financial performance* for a given financial period. This comprises

- **An income statement (or profit and loss)**: This shows the revenue and expenses generated by the net assets of an entity.
- **Other comprehensive income**: This shows the gains and losses recorded in reserves such as gains (or losses) on foreign currency fluctuations. These are usually reclassified as profit or loss in a future period.

Net income is the residual amount remaining on the income statement in a specific accounting period after all expenses have been deducted from revenue. Publicly listed companies exist to provide value to their owners (shareholders), and profit (positive net income attributable to controlling interests) is one of the primary methods through which this is achieved. Any profits can be distributed back to shareholders through

1. **Direct methods**: Such as dividend payments
2. **Indirect methods**: Such as repurchasing shares which increases the value of the remaining shares

CHAPTER 1   WHAT IS AN INCOME STATEMENT SEMANTIC MODEL?

In group accounting scenarios where the parent does not own 100% of the subsidiaries, net income can be divided into controlling and non-controlling interests. As group accounts are prepared as if all companies are a single entity, they are prepared against a single accounting standard (that of the parent). Finally, where applicable, earnings per share (EPS) is included; this involves relevant weighted average number of share calculations such as basic or diluted.

External Income Statement Requirements

External income statements are produced to meet statutory requirements, the legal obligations in each jurisdiction. The calculations and presentation of external income statements are tightly regulated, that is, if basic and diluted EPS are both shown, International Accounting Standards (IAS) 33 states both must be calculated according to accounting standards, and one cannot be emphasized over such as using different fonts or italics.

Figure 1-1 shows Microsoft's income statement from their annual report **(1)** and recreated in a Power BI app **(2)**.

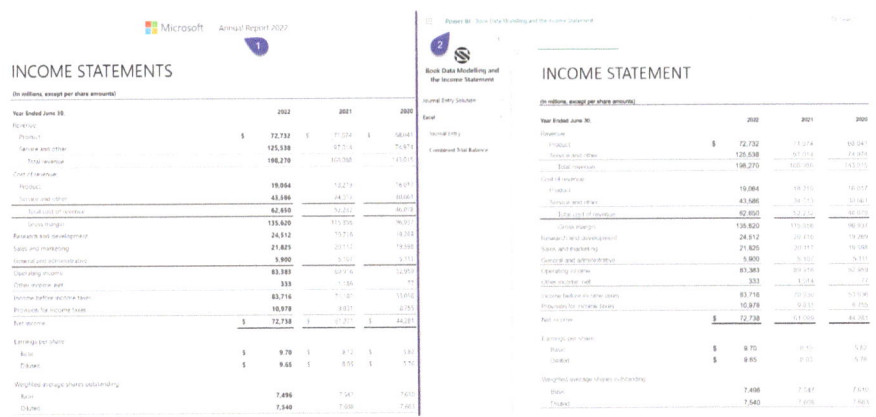

Figure 1-1. *Microsoft income statement from 2022 annual statement*

5

CHAPTER 1 WHAT IS AN INCOME STATEMENT SEMANTIC MODEL?

Standardization of External Outputs

External outputs are similar across entities as the International Accounting Standards Board (IASB) – responsible for International Financial Reporting Standards (IFRS) – and the Financial Accounting Standards Board (FASB) – responsible for US Generally Accepted Accounting Principles (GAAP) – are aligned on qualitative characteristics of financial reports.

Qualitative characteristics ensure a degree of consistency in income statements, that is, an entity cannot show expenses before revenue or redefine net income. This is because the qualitative characteristics underpin the creation of the accounting standards which entities must adhere to. These qualitative characteristics include the

- **Co*mparability* characteristic**: Ensures that users of the financial statements can compare information across entities, that is, the financial performance of an oil company can be compared to an advertising firm.

- ***Verifiability* and *understandability* characteristics**: Ensures formulas in the income statement are intelligible, that is, the subtotal for total revenue is calculated by adding the distinct types of revenue (i.e., product revenue and service revenue).

- ***Materiality* characteristic**: Ensures against omissions; items should be included which could influence the economic decisions of users.

CHAPTER 1 WHAT IS AN INCOME STATEMENT SEMANTIC MODEL?

Internal Income Statement Requirements

Internal income statements build on external requirements. As these are purely for internal purposes, there are no rules surrounding calculations or presentation; the entity can produce any figures it deems necessary and emphasize figures as required.

Internal income statement requirements typically involve calculating percentages by dividing one line on the income statement by another to identify trends – that is, gross margin as a percentage of total revenue – and adding bespoke calculations. Bespoke calculations are required as entities tend to include numbers of strategic importance to contextualize profitability; these vary depending on the entity and are subject to change due to evolving requirements.

Figure 1-2 shows an internal income statement with

- Percentages for gross margin **(1)**, earnings before interest tax depreciation and amortization **(2)**, earnings before interest and tax **(3)**, net income **(4)**, and research as a percentage of research and development **(5)**
- Bespoke calculations for employee attrition rate **(6)**, potential future sales at 75% + probability **(7)**, potential future sales at 50% + probability **(8)**

CHAPTER 1   WHAT IS AN INCOME STATEMENT SEMANTIC MODEL?

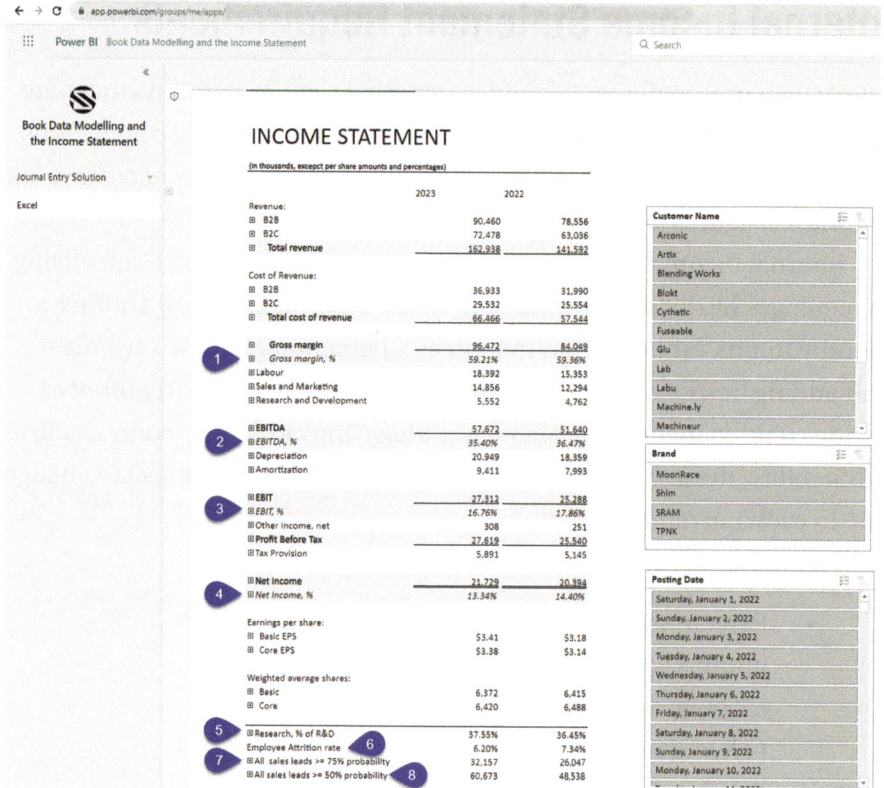

Figure 1-2. Internal income statement

To achieve these external and internal requirements, a robust semantic model is required; fancy reports and visuals are of zero-value if the underlying results are incorrect, or the interacting experience is intolerable to end users.

What Is a Semantic Model?

To understand what a semantic model is, this section provides two perspectives:

1. Viewing the income statement semantic model as a navigation tool
2. Viewing the income statement semantic model as a way of measuring the accounting process

An Income Statement Semantic Model As a Navigation Tool

Financial data can be spread across potentially hundreds of tables in a finance system. Coupled with the need to combine financial data with relevant non-financial data, extracting relevant income statement information can involve navigating a complex landscape. The semantic model provides a way of collating and organizing information so end users can intuitively navigate their way through this complex landscape retrieving their desired information.

Slicing and Dicing

Slicing and dicing involves breaking the income statement down into smaller components and examining it from different viewpoints. Figure 1-3 shows the same data model retrieving an income statement for the entity overall **(1)** and a single brand **(2)**.

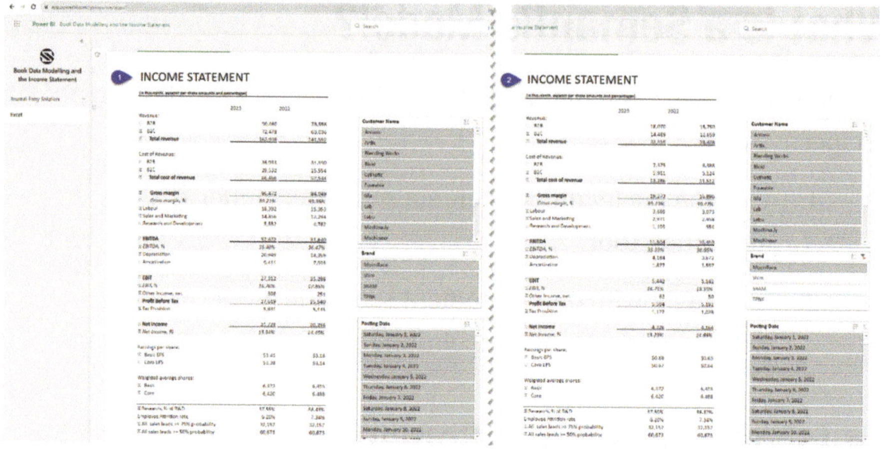

CHAPTER 1   WHAT IS AN INCOME STATEMENT SEMANTIC MODEL?

Figure 1-3. Internal income statement: overall and by brand

Drill Down and Drill Through

Drill down and drill through enable users to go from a more generic view of the income statement down to a more granular view. Figure 1-4 shows how the same model can be used to drill down on individual lines showing the underlying general accounts (**1**) and drill through by right-clicking a number (**2**) and selecting *show details* (**3**) to create a tab containing information about journal entries (**4**).

CHAPTER 1 WHAT IS AN INCOME STATEMENT SEMANTIC MODEL?

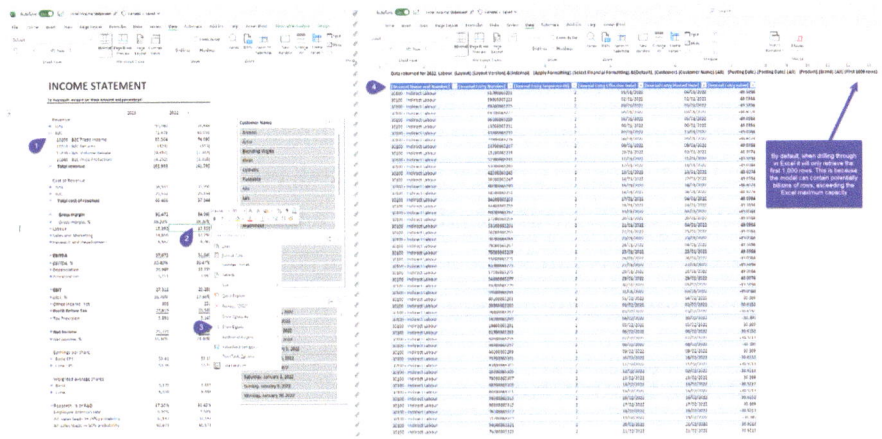

Figure 1-4. Drill down and drill through

An Income Statement Semantic Model Measures the Accounting Process

Semantic models can be thought of as a set of techniques that model the measurement of a business process.[1] Collectively, these are called *dimensional modelling techniques* which, when applied to Power BI, create either a star or snowflake schema.

In the case of the income statement, the business process being measured is the accounting process whereby lines on the income statement consist of accounts, and accounts consist of journal entries (Figure 1-5).

Figure 1-5. Accounting process

---

[1] Adamson: Star Schema the Complete Reference

11

CHAPTER 1   WHAT IS AN INCOME STATEMENT SEMANTIC MODEL?

Dimensional Modelling

Dimensional modelling consists of two components: measurements (facts) and their context (dimensions). The returned result of a measure is dependent on the context in which it is evaluated. For instance, the sum of journal entry values (measure) evaluated by a returns account (context) will produce a different result to the sum of journal entry values (measure) evaluated by a volume rebate account (context).

Evaluation vs. Execution

Dimensional modelling supports the *evaluation* of the income statement – viewing in different contexts – which is different from the model in the finance system which supports the *execution* of the accounting processes, creating journal entries and providing an audit trail.

Precision

Measuring the accounting process involves a high degree of precision; there is zero room for ambiguity in the business definition. For instance, if a user asks for revenue figures for December 2023, this could mean different things, to different people, at different times. For instance, gross revenue, the amount paid for by the customer, or net revenue, the amount which will not be available till all post month-end adjustments have been made for elements such as rebates. Moreover, if users ask for Easter revenue, this could mean

1. **Revenue generated by Easter products**: That is, sales of Easter eggs regardless of when they are sold.

2. **Revenue generated during the Easter weekend**: That is, sales in a specific period.

3. **Revenue generated during Easter holidays**: That is, sales in a specific time period in one geographical area and a different time period in another geographical area; Easter holidays in some regions start with the Easter weekend, in others the Easter weekend is in the middle, and others it is at the end.

Semantic models can contain all definitions using specific terminology and descriptions for each definition; users can then select the appropriate definition.

Summary

- The income statement shows lines down to the *net income* generated by an entity in a given period.
- Depending on the entity, the statutory income statement can also show
  - Net income broken down into controlling and non-controlling interests
  - Earnings per share (EPS) calculations
- The income statement semantic model should also support internal requirements such as
  - The ability to slice and dice
  - The ability to drill down or drill through into the detail
  - Percentages
  - Bespoke calculations such as the number of FTEs (full-time employees) in the organization

CHAPTER 1   WHAT IS AN INCOME STATEMENT SEMANTIC MODEL?

- A semantic model can be viewed as
  - **A navigation tool**: Traversing a complex data landscape to retrieve answers to business questions
  - **Measuring a business process**: Evaluating the income statement in different contexts and enforcing a high degree of precision

CHAPTER 2

How the Income Statement Is Constructed

In the previous chapter, we learned what the income statement is from external and internal perspectives and the two ways of viewing the income statement semantic model, as a navigation tool and as a way of measuring the accounting process.

In this chapter, we will learn how the income statement is constructed. In doing so, we will cover how to build the income statement to net income. This emphasizes that the *account balance* calculation, based on the trial balance, is the standardized step entities undertake prior to producing income statements. As it is standardized, across entities regardless of their nature – that is, it is the same for an organization refining oil and an organization selling advertising revenue – the *account balance* calculation forms the basis of a reusable solution.

In this chapter, we will also learn about group accounting and how this results in the allocation of net income to controlling and non-controlling interests. Finally, we will cover the earnings per share (EPS) calculation which introduces non-journal entry information.

CHAPTER 2   HOW THE INCOME STATEMENT IS CONSTRUCTED

Knowing how the income statement is constructed from an accounting perspective is essential to understanding the solution; to model the measurement of the accounting process, we must first understand the accounting process.

In this chapter, there are three sections:

1. Building the Income Statement to Net Income

2. Allocating Net Income to Controlling and Non-controlling Interests

3. Earnings per Share

Building the Income Statement to Net Income

The fundamental process of building an income statement to net income is shown in Figure 2-1.

Figure 2-1. *Building the income statement*

CHAPTER 2   HOW THE INCOME STATEMENT IS CONSTRUCTED

- **Step 1**: Transactions are recorded; these increase credit and debit values of accounts, either directly or indirectly via subaccounts.

- **Step 2**: Adjusting entries are posted ensuring that all revenue and expenses are captured.

- **Step 3**: A trial balance is produced containing a single row for each account with the associated credit and debit values.

- **Step 4**: Account balances are calculated, subtracting credits from debits or vice versa depending on the account type.

- **Step 5**: The income statement is built to net income. This step is split into three further stages: line-items, subtotals, and subsets.

CHAPTER 2   HOW THE INCOME STATEMENT IS CONSTRUCTED

Transaction Entries

Figure 2-2 shows a receipt from a coffee shop.

Figure 2-2.   *Coffee receipt*

This shows that the shop was Caffe Latte, 802 Kingston, Elm Road **(1)**, the coffee cost £4.00 **(2)**, the date of the transaction was the 29th of September 2023 **(3)**, the time of transaction was 7.43 AM **(4)**, and the tenth coffee bought is free **(5)**.

The principles of double-entry bookkeeping mean that for all financial transactions, such as the one in Figure 2-2, a journal entry is posted consisting of at least one credit and at least one debit, the values of which

CHAPTER 2　HOW THE INCOME STATEMENT IS CONSTRUCTED

offset each other. Transactions are also linked to accounts either directly or via subaccounts. In the coffee example, a journal entry is made to a sales account and a cash account (Table 2-1).

Table 2-1. *Transaction journal entry*

Journal Entry No	Sequence	Account	Effective Date	Time	Shop Code	Credit-Debit Indicator	Journal Entry Amount
32453945	1	Sales	29 Sep 2023	7:43	1582	Credit	4.00
32453945	2	Cash	29 Sep 2023	7:43	3756	Debit	4.00

Compound Journal Entries

More complex transactions (known as compound journal entries) have more than one credit and/or more than one debit; however, these are still required to balance (Table 2-2).

Table 2-2. *Compound transaction journal entry*

Journal Entry No	Sequence	Account	Effective Date	Credit-Debit Indicator	Journal Entry Amount
5173246	1	Trade sales	10 Jan 2023	Credit	50
5173246	2	Cash	10 Jan 2023	Debit	20
5173246	3	Account receivable	10 Jan 2023	Debit	30

CHAPTER 2   HOW THE INCOME STATEMENT IS CONSTRUCTED

Modelling Only Part of the Financial Transaction

While the net balance of credit less debits is always zero, not all journal entries impact the income statement. For instance, cash and account receivables appear directly on the statement of financial position, whereas trade sales appear on the income statement and only indirectly appear on the statement of financial position, that is, via retained earnings. Therefore, producing an income statement solution involves partially modelling individual financial transactions.

Accruals vs. Cash Basis

By using the effective date, it is inferred that the transactions in Tables 2-1 and 2-2 are prepared using the accrual method of accounting; this is the preferred approach by both the Financial Accounting Standards Board (FASB) and the International Accounting Standards Board (IASB). The alternative cash method is generally applicable to small organizations (i.e., those with less than ten employees) and is, therefore, disregarded throughout this book even though it is permissible under both International Financial Reporting Standards (IFRS) and US Generally Accepted Accounting Principles (GAAP). The cash method is the accounting process whereby a transaction is recorded at the point of a cash transfer.

Adjusting Entries

Adjusting entries are made to amend transaction entries, usually after the period has finished. It is not required to understand the details of all types of adjustments for modelling the income statement, but it is important to be aware that adjustments are made as this impacts analytical flexibility.

CHAPTER 2 HOW THE INCOME STATEMENT IS CONSTRUCTED

Provision Adjustments

Building on the coffee example in Figure 2-2, the receipt showed that the tenth cup of coffee bought was free; this amounts to a 10% discount. Based on prior experience, the coffee shop could know that 20% of people claim their free coffee; therefore, an adjustment to revenue of £0.08 is made (£4.00 × 10% discount × 20% claim). This is recorded with an adjustment journal entry (Table 2-3).

Table 2-3. Adjusting journal entry

Journal Entry No	Sequence	Account	Effective Date	Credit-Debit Indicator	Journal Entry Amount
32453967	1	Sales	29 Sep 2023	Debit	0.08
32453967	2	Provision	29 Sep 2023	Credit	0.08

Adjusting Entries Reduce Analytical Flexibility

In practice, adjusting journal entries are usually made at an elevated level. For instance, a provision for future free coffee claims may be made for the entity overall. Adjusting at this elevated level creates discrepancies between the transactional and accounting systems and reduces the grain at which transactions can be analyzed. In the coffee example, there is a debit entry to revenue which is not applicable to a given shop; therefore, when slicing and dicing revenue by shop, an amount is attributable to an *unknown* shop.

This introduces the concept of uniform and non-uniform dimensions. Uniform dimensions are the way all journal entries can be explained and usually refer to dimensions such as the legal entity or effective date.

CHAPTER 2 HOW THE INCOME STATEMENT IS CONSTRUCTED

Non-uniform dimensions are the way some journal entries can be explained, but not others. For instance, in the coffee shop provision example, only part of the entities' overall revenue figure can be explained by the shops.

Trial Balance

Based on the journal entries (transactional and adjusted), a trial balance (Table 2-4) can be produced containing aggregated credit and debit balances for all accounts in a given period.

Table 2-4. Trial balances for three accounts in financial period 1 2023

Account Key	Credit	Debit
30100	100	
30101		5
40100		34

The trial balance is common across entities and thus forms the basis on which a reusable solution is built; conceptual models (Chapter 5), logical models (Chapter 6), and trial balance semantic models (Chapter 7) are all built using a trial balance optimized for calculating account balances as the fact table.

Account Balances

Account balance is the core calculation used when modelling the income statement. For each account on the trial balance, the *account balance* is calculated as either credits less debits or vice versa based on an account type.

The Account Tables

The account table contains a single row for each account in the organization. Typically, this contains at a minimum the account key, account name, and account type (Table 2-5).

Table 2-5. Account table

Account Key	Account Name	Account Type
30100	Trade sales	Revenue
30101	Returns	Revenue
40100	Trade cost of sales	Expense

The two account types used in the income statement are

1. **Revenue**: Used to record income from primary operating activities
2. **Expense**: Used to record costs from primary operating activities

The Account Balance Calculation

Calculating *account balances* involves subtracting debits from credits for revenue accounts and subtracting credits from debits for expense accounts (Table 2-6).

CHAPTER 2   HOW THE INCOME STATEMENT IS CONSTRUCTED

Table 2-6. *Account balance by account key for financial period 1 2023*

Account Key	Account Name	Account Type	Calculation	Credit	Debit	Account Balance
30100	Trade revenue	Revenue	Credit less debit	100		100
30101	Returns	Revenue	Credit less debit		5	(5)
40100	Trade cost of sales	Expense	Debit less credit		34	34

As the *account balance* calculation underpins all statutory reporting, an optimized conceptual model is covered in Chapter 5, and the use of aggregations in Chapter 6 further enhances the query performance of the calculation (the speed at which data is returned following a request to the semantic model).

Income Statement to Net Income

Creating the statutory income statement to net income involves calculating account balances for

1. Line-items
2. Subtotals
3. Subsets

Line-Items

Line-items are those lines on the income statement directly related to accounts. Each line-item can consist of multiple accounts, which must be of the same account type, and each account can only be mapped to one line-item. This ensures against any double counting. For instance, line-items:

- *Product revenue* could consist of all account keys between 30100 and 30200 all of account type revenue.

- *Service and other revenue* could consist of all account keys between 30300 and 30400 all of account type revenue.

- *Product cost of sales* could consist of all account keys between 40100 and 40200 all of account type expense.

When calculating a line-item, the *account balance* is based on the account type of the related accounts; if the accounts are of revenue account type, the calculation is credits less debits, whereas expense lines are debits less credits.

Subtotals

Subtotals combine line-items and thus are indirectly linked to accounts. For instance, a subtotal *total revenue* could comprise line-item *product revenue* (account keys between 30100 and 30200) and line-item *service and other revenue* (account keys between 30300 and 30400). Given *net income* can be calculated based on combining line-items, this is also classed as a subtotal.

When calculating a subtotal line, if all related accounts are of the same account type, the calculation is credits less debits for revenue subtotals and debits less credits for expense subtotals.

CHAPTER 2   HOW THE INCOME STATEMENT IS CONSTRUCTED

Mixed Account Types

When a subtotal combines revenue and expense accounts, the calculation is typically performed as credits less debits for all accounts regardless of their own account type. This creates a profit subtotal, an example of which is gross profit – that is, gross profit (67) as credits (152) less debits (85) – as shown in Table 2-7.

Table 2-7. Subtotal gross profit

	Related Account Type(s)	Credit	Debit	Total	Calculation
Product revenue	Revenue	100	5	95	Credit less debit
Service revenue	Revenue	40	10	30	Credit less debit
Total revenue	Revenue	140	15	125	Credit less debit
Product cost of sales	Expense	7	50	43	Debit less credit
Service cost of sales	Expense	5	20	15	Debit less credit
Total cost of sales	Expense	12	70	58	Debit less credit
Gross profit	Revenue + Expense	152	85	67	Credit less debit

Two Ways of Calculating with Identical Results

Calculating subtotals can be achieved through credits less debits as described. It is, however, more common to explain subtotals based on other lines, that is, gross profit (67) as total revenue (125) less total cost of sales (58). While this is mathematically identical to credits less debits, this approach is disregarded throughout this book. This is because Data

Analysis eXpressions (DAX), which are used for calculations in Power BI, are conceptually unaware of other lines on the income statement; instead, each line is evaluated based on its own context.

Subsets

Subsets are those lines that reference part of a line-item or subtotal. Subsets are used in statutory reporting to calculate *material* items. For instance, an entity could have disposed of an asset in a given period, which is contributing to 20% of the overall gross profit in that fiscal year. As this disposal is a material movement which could influence the economic decision of users, it is required to be separately called out. When subsets contain mixed account types, like subtotals, they are typically treated as credits less debits.

> **Note** While credit less debit is the common behavior for subtotals and subsets of mixed account types, these calculations can occasionally be debit less credit, especially for internal reporting. This leads to four potential options for subtotal and subset calculations as users can drill down from mixed account types to accounts containing a single account type. These options are covered in the four subtotal and subset types (Chapter 9).

Allocating Net Income to Controlling and Non-controlling Interests

Most large entities consist of a network of companies known as a group. Often, the parent company does not outright own each company within the group which can lead to a situation where *net income* is partially

CHAPTER 2   HOW THE INCOME STATEMENT IS CONSTRUCTED

attributable to a non-controlling interest. In these scenarios, the *net income* shown on the income statement is broken down into the amount attributable to non-controlling interest and controlling interest (Table 2-8).

Table 2-8. Non-controlling interest and controlling interest

	Company A	Company B	Total
Net Income	138m	90m	228m
Net income attributable to non-controlling interest	-	18m	18m
Net income attributable to controlling interest	138m	72m	210m

Non-controlling Interest Is Provided by the Finance Team or System

Calculating non-controlling interest involves various adjustments, such as impairment to goodwill; these adjustments are dependent on the accounting standards of the jurisdiction in which the parent company resides, that is, the parent company may reside in the United States and therefore follow US GAAP, even though the subsidiary resides in the United Kingdom and thus follows IFRS. The balancing figure (net income less net income attributable to non-controlling interests) is the net income attributable to controlling interests. To model the income statement, it is not necessary to know the intricacies of how non-controlling interests are calculated, as this is provided by the finance team or finance system and the ownership can evolve over time.

Maintain Analytical Flexibility by Applying Controlling and Non-controlling Interests at the Journal Level

Ownership within a group can evolve over time. For example, partway through a fiscal year a group could

- Directly increase holdings in a subsidiary from 70% to 80%.

- Acquire an 80% controlling interest in a new subsidiary.

- Indirectly increase their holding in a subsidiary via acquiring a new subsidiary; a group could own 80% of a subsidiary A and acquire 70% of a subsidiary B which owns the remaining 20% of subsidiary A, giving the group a 94% controlling interest in subsidiary A (80% + 70% × 20%).

As such, in group scenarios, values are required to be broken down into controlling and non-controlling interests. For instance, Table 2-9 shows how, on the 10th of January 2023, a group has allocated 100% of legal entity A and 80% of legal entity B to controlling interests, with the remaining 20% of legal entity B allocated to non-controlling interests.

CHAPTER 2   HOW THE INCOME STATEMENT IS CONSTRUCTED

Table 2-9. *Allocating journal entry amounts to controlling and non-controlling interests*

Journal Entry No	Account Number	Effective Date	Credit-Debit Indicator	Legal Entity	Controlling or Non-controlling Interest	Total
5173246	30100	10 Jan 2023	Credit	A	Controlling	50
5173247	30100	10 Jan 2023	Credit	A	Controlling	40
5173248	30100	10 Jan 2023	Credit	A	Controlling	80
5173249	30100	10 Jan 2023	Credit	A	Controlling	30
5173250	30100	10 Jan 2023	Credit	B	Controlling	16
5173251	30100	10 Jan 2023	Credit	B	Controlling	40
5173252	30100	10 Jan 2023	Credit	B	Controlling	16
5173253	30100	10 Jan 2023	Credit	B	Controlling	24
5173254	30100	10 Jan 2023	Credit	B	Controlling	24
5173250	30100	10 Jan 2023	Credit	B	Non-controlling	4
5173251	30100	10 Jan 2023	Credit	B	Non-controlling	10

(*continued*)

Table 2-9. (*continued*)

Journal Entry No	Account Number	Effective Date	Credit-Debit Indicator	Legal Entity	Controlling or Non-controlling Interest	Total
5173252	30100	10 Jan 2023	Credit	B	Non-controlling	4
5173253	30100	10 Jan 2023	Credit	B	Non-controlling	6
5173254	30100	10 Jan 2023	Credit	B	Non-controlling	6
Total						350
Controlling						320
Non-controlling						30

Earnings per Share (EPS)

EPS indicates how much income a company makes for each share and is commonly used to estimate the value of a company. The equation for EPS is

$$\text{Earnings per share} = \frac{\text{net income}}{\text{weighted average shares}}$$

The various forms of EPS adjust the numerator (net income) or denominator (weighted average shares).

CHAPTER 2   HOW THE INCOME STATEMENT IS CONSTRUCTED

Numerator: Net Income

Net income can be adjusted, that is, non-GAAP EPS strips out distinct items such as large restructuring costs.

Denominator: Weighted Average Shares

Weighted average shares is the number of shares a company has outstanding in a given period. There are several different versions, such as diluted weighted average shares – the number remaining after all sources of conversion have been exercised.

While weighted average shares is used in EPS calculations, it is sometimes hidden in publicized income statements and explained in the notes to the accounts.

Weighted Average Shares Is Provided by the Finance Team or System

There are several concepts needed to calculate weighted average shares (i.e., treasury shares which are issued and brought back by the entity). Like group accounting, it is not necessary to understand the intricacy of this calculation. This is because weighted average share numbers are provided by the finance team or system.

Relevant to Only a Specific Date Range

Weighted average shares can only be applied to a specified date range. For instance, Table 2-10 contains basic and diluted weighted average shares, and each of the figures is relevant only to that date range.

Table 2-10. *Weighted average shares in millions*

	P1 2022	P2 2022	P3 2022	Q1 2022
Weighted average shares				
Basic	4,235	4,572	4,368	4,478
Diluted	4,012	4,364	4,183	4,346

EPS Presentation

Earnings per share is typically displayed to two decimal places because this is the standard presentation in most currencies. There are, however, exceptions such as the Japanese Yen which is required to be presented with zero decimal places.

Summary

- *Account balance* is the core calculation underpinning all statutory income statement lines and is calculated as either credits less debits or vice versa based on the account type.

- Statutory lines on the income statement can consist of many accounts, and each account can be linked to many journal entries.

- A group consists of a network of companies, and when the group has a controlling interest of less than 100%, the net income usually requires breaking down into a controlling and non-controlling interest.

- Various earnings per share (EPS) calculations can be required, and this involves calculating weighted average shares.

CHAPTER 3

Building a Reusable Solution

In the previous chapters, we have learned what the income statement semantic model is and how the income statement is constructed from the trial balance.

In this chapter, we will bring together learning from the previous two chapters, highlighting the sixteen challenges in modelling the income statement. We will also learn about the semantic model stages and how the semantic model supports queries generated by Data Analysis eXpressions (DAX) and Multidimensional eXpressions (MDX). Finally, we will cover how these challenges are common across entities and, therefore, how an input-driven solution can be created for external reporting, reusing the same semantic model.

In this chapter, there are three sections:

1. The Sixteen Challenges in Modelling the Income Statement
2. The Power BI Semantic Model
3. The Input-Driven Approach

CHAPTER 3 BUILDING A REUSABLE SOLUTION

The Sixteen Challenges in Modelling the Income Statement

To build a semantic model that can support external and internal income statement reporting, sixteen challenges must be overcome. These are categorized into three groups:

- Nine calculation challenges
- Four presentation challenges
- Three analytical challenges

The Nine Calculation Challenges

Calculation challenges cover the required DAX measures which create lines that appear on the income statement:

- **Challenge 1**: Calculating line-items – line-items are those lines on the income statement directly related to accounts. Each line-item can consist of multiple accounts, which must be of the same account type, and each account can only be mapped to a single line-item.

- **Challenge 2**: Calculating subtotals – subtotals combine line-items and thus are indirectly linked to accounts.

- **Challenge 3**: Calculating a subset – subsets are those lines that reference part of a line-item or subtotal, that is, a line-item may consist of accounts between 30100 and 30199, but a subset may be required to call out account 30120 as the figure in this account materially impacts decisions made by users of the income statement.

- **Challenge 4**: Calculating controlling and non-controlling interests – in group accounting, *net income* can be partially attributable to a non-controlling interest.

- **Challenge 5**: Calculating weighted average shares – weighted outstanding shares is the number of shares a company has outstanding in a given period.

- **Challenge 6**: Calculating earnings per share (EPS) – earnings per share indicates how much income a company makes for each share.

- **Challenge 7**: Adding bespoke calculations – adding entity-specific requirements to contextualize financial information, that is, number of employees.

- **Challenge 8**: Calculating percentages – dividing one income statement line by another, that is, gross profit divided by revenue to calculate the gross profit percentage.

- **Challenge 9**: Blank lines – gaps are required between certain lines to separate information and adhere to statutory requirements. This requires a DAX calculation.

The Four Presentation Challenges

Presentation challenges refer to the elements of the semantic model which enable DAX and MDX queries to retrieve data in a way that is conducive to visualizing the information:

- **Challenge 10**: Hide lines – certain lines are required only for the calculation of other lines and, therefore, can be hidden, that is, weighted average shares calculations are frequently hidden on income statements, but are required to calculate EPS.

- **Challenge 11**: Sorting the hierarchy – the income statement has a specific layout that must be adhered to, that is, International Accounting Standards (IAS) 1 contains the guidelines on the presentation of income statements for companies adhering to International Financial Reporting Standards (IFRS).

- **Challenge 12**: Formatting income statement lines individually – each line on the income statement requires its own formatting. For instance, EPS is usually presented in a currency format to two decimal places, whereas net income is displayed in thousands or millions.

- **Challenge 13**: Enabling multiple layouts – layouts are often required to mirror external reporting, for different internal users, and to show potential layouts for the upcoming fiscal year.

The Three Analytical Challenges

Analytical challenges involve how to design a semantic model which users can intuitively navigate to uncover insight:

- **Challenge 14**: Enabling end users to build reports or conduct analysis in Excel or Power BI – the model should be optimized for self-service, including hiding irrelevant technical information, organizing information into folders, and adding descriptions.

CHAPTER 3   BUILDING A REUSABLE SOLUTION

- **Challenge 15**: Slicing and dicing the income statement – view data from multiple perspectives.

- **Challenge 16**: Drilling from income statement lines to journal entries – ability to start at the highest level and delve into the detail.

To overcome these challenges, the Power BI semantic model is required to contain the appropriate logic.

The Power BI Semantic Model
Building a Semantic Model

Producing a semantic model using import mode in Power BI Desktop involves three stages (Figure 3-1).

CHAPTER 3   BUILDING A REUSABLE SOLUTION

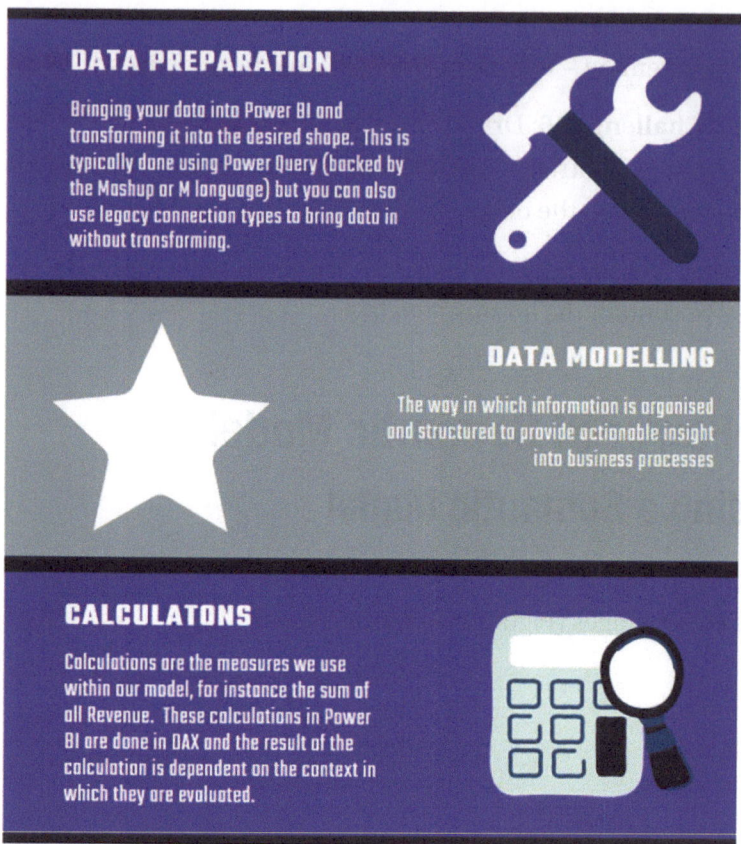

Figure 3-1. The three Power BI semantic model stages

Data Preparation: Transforming the Trial Balance

For an entity using the accrual method of accounting which is the parent of a group that contains non-controlling interests, the trial balance can contain the account key, effective date, whether the amount is attributable to controlling or non-controlling interest, and the credit and debit values (Table 3-1).

CHAPTER 3 BUILDING A REUSABLE SOLUTION

Table 3-1. Example trial balance for financial period 1 2023

Account Key	Effective Date	Controlling or Non-controlling Interest	Credit	Debit
30100	1 Jan 2023	Controlling	100	
30101	1 Jan 2023	Controlling		5
40100	1 Jan 2023	Controlling		34

Power Query can be used to

1. Unpivot the credit and debit values
2. For controlling or non-controlling interests, convert "Controlling" to 1 and "Non-controlling" to 0 and rename to Ownership Key (the use of keys is covered in Chapter 6)
3. Multiply debits by –1

This creates Table 3-2, which can then be loaded into the model.

Table 3-2. Trial balances for financial period 1 2023 transformed

Account Key	Effective Date	Ownership Key	Value
30100	1 Jan 2023	1	100
30101	1 Jan 2023	1	–5
40100	1 Jan 2023	1	–34

This transformation approach creates a *value* column which when summed is *credits less debits* as debits are stored as negatives.

CHAPTER 3 BUILDING A REUSABLE SOLUTION

Data Modelling: Creating Relationships to the Trial Balance

Once all the tables are loaded, physical relationships can be created between the tables. Figure 3-2 shows an example conceptual model of how the trial balance is connected to the account, effective date, and ownership tables by creating relationships between

1. 'Account' [Account Key] to 'Trial Balance' [Account Key]

2. 'Effective Date' [Date] to 'Trial Balance' [Effective Date]

3. 'Group Ownership' [Ownership Key] to 'Trial Balance' [Ownership Key]

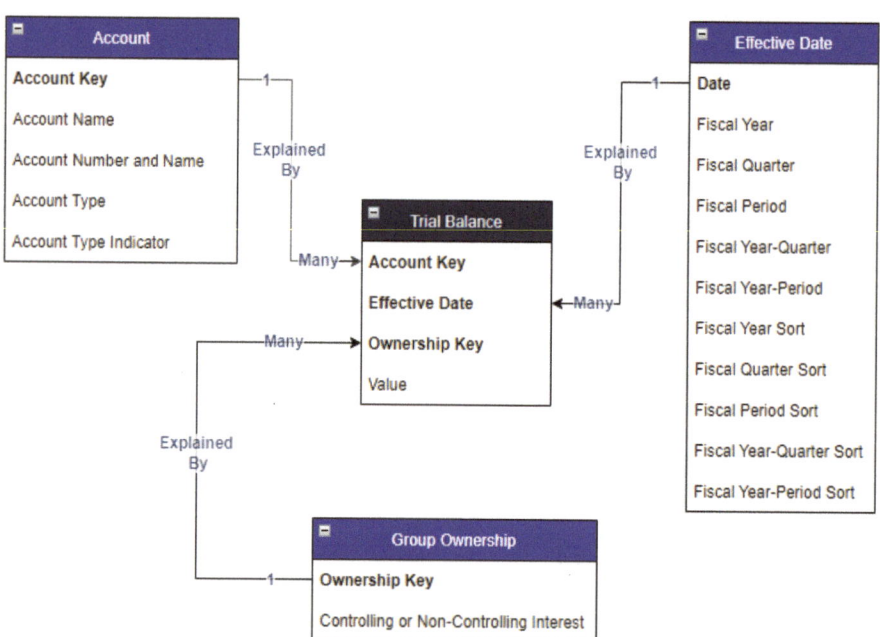

Figure 3-2. *Trial balance conceptual model*

This creates a *star schema*, the optimal modelling approach for calculating *account balances* in a given financial period (see Chapter 5).

In addition to creating physical relationships, modelling also includes amending various properties, such as the sort order of columns, adding descriptions, creating hierarchies, and hiding tables.

Calculations: Sum of Trial Balance Value

Measures are created using DAX. The values returned by the DAX are dependent on the context in which the DAX is evaluated. Given the trial balance value is credits less debits, if all income statement accounts are present in the trial balance table, the sum of this column equates to *net income*. However, if it is analyzed by

- **Account**: The credit less debit amount for each account is returned.
- **Date**: The credit less debit amount for each date is returned.
- **Controlling or non-controlling interests**: The credit less debit amount for controlling and non-controlling interests is returned.

Querying the Semantic Model Using DAX and MDX

A query is a command used to retrieve data from the semantic model. Queries are produced in DAX by Power BI visuals; the visual sends a DAX request to the semantic model, and the semantic model returns data to populate the visual. As well as DAX, queries can also be sent to the semantic model using MDX. Supporting MDX queries is key as several Microsoft and non-Microsoft applications can send MDX requests, that is, Excel and Tableau.

How the Semantic Model Supports MDX

When dimensional modelling techniques are applied to a relational database, a star or snowflake schema is built. At implementation, Power BI is like a relational database and thus a star or snowflake schema is the optimal design, and calculations are built using DAX. Consequently, visuals can produce DAX queries to retrieve data from the semantic model.

When dimensional modelling techniques are applied to a multidimensional database, a cube is built. At implementation, Power BI does not appear like a multidimensional database to users. However, under the hood, the various multidimensional elements are built so the semantic model can be queried using MDX. There are, however, differences that can arise; therefore, it is important to make sure all DAX elements used translate appropriately to MDX. For instance, when sorting columns, DAX and MDX operate differently if the column does not have a unique sort by column.

MDX and Excel

Excel natively supports cube formulas and pivot table connections to multidimensional databases. For instance, Figure 3-3 shows an Excel CUBEVALUE formula which could be used to retrieve 2022 product revenue data for Europe South from Power BI.

CHAPTER 3   BUILDING A REUSABLE SOLUTION

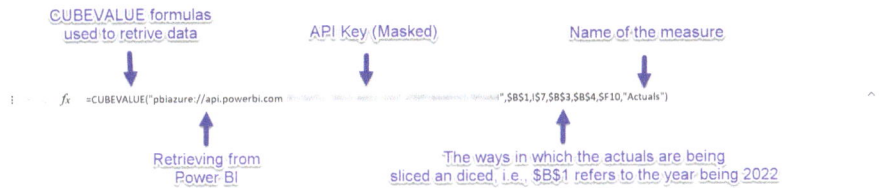

Figure 3-3. *Excel CUBEVALUE formula showing product revenue for 2022, Europe South*

The Input-Driven Approach

When creating a semantic model (either in Power BI, Analysis Services, or Microsoft Fabric), the tabular object model (TOM) exposes tabular metadata. The semantic model contains logic such as the

- Mashup (m) code generated when using Power Query

- Data modelling information such as relationships between tables and sort order of columns

- DAX such as line-item calculations and detailed row expressions used to set the drill through behavior to journal entries in Excel

Because the process of building income statements using trial balances is the same across entities, and outputs are similar because of the adherence to accounting standards, the same logic can be used to overcome 14 of the 16 challenges. For instance, in Figure 3-4, the same semantic model has been used to replicate publicized income statements from Microsoft and Walmart (this can be downloaded from the resources accompanying this book).

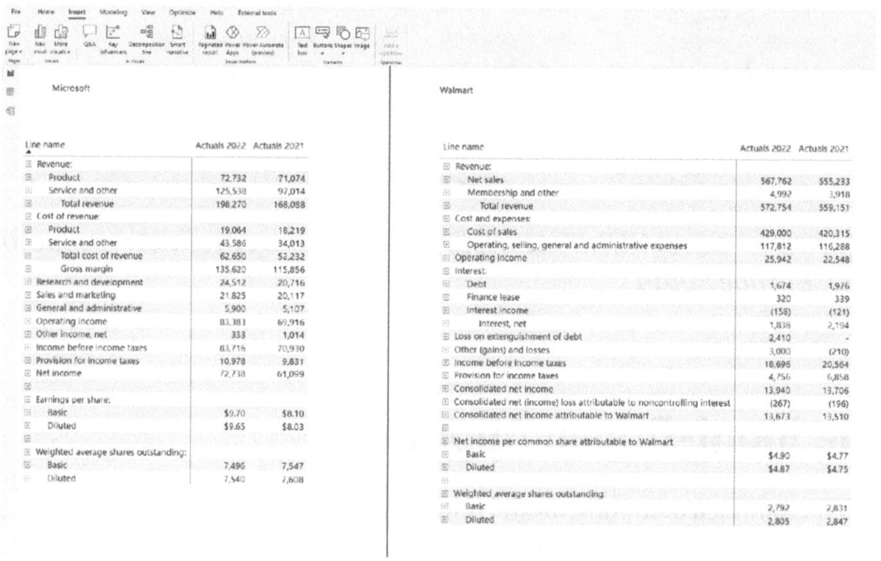

CHAPTER 3 BUILDING A REUSABLE SOLUTION

Figure 3-4. One model used to create two income statements

The two exceptions to the input-driven approach are

- **Challenge 7**: Adding bespoke calculation – by definition, adding bespoke calculations requires customization.

- **Challenge 15**: Slicing and dicing the income statement – each entity can explain its income statement in a bespoke way according to how the entity operates, that is, slice and dice the income statement by legal entity and business unit.

Examples of adaptations to the semantic model to overcome challenges 7 and 15 are covered throughout Parts 2–4.

CHAPTER 3   BUILDING A REUSABLE SOLUTION

Summary

- There are sixteen challenges to be overcome when modelling the income statement:

    - **Nine calculation challenges**: Covers the required DAX measures which create lines that appear on the income statement

    - **Four presentation challenges**: Elements of the semantic model which enable DAX and MDX queries to retrieve data in a way that is conducive to visualizing the information

    - **Three analytical challenges**: Involves designing a semantic model which users can intuitively navigate to uncover insight

- There are three layers to building a Power BI semantic model using import mode:

    - **Data preparation**: Transforming and ingesting data

    - **Data modelling**: Structuring the data such as creating relationships between tables

    - **Calculations**: Writing DAX measures

- Because entities follow the same accounting process based on the trial balance, a semantic model can be built which is reusable across entities.

CHAPTER 4

Why Model the Income Statement?

In the previous chapter, we learned about the sixteen challenges that the income statement semantic model must overcome. Given the extent of these challenges, a valid question is "why model the income statement in its entirety?"

In this chapter, we will learn how modelling the income statement in its entirety benefits an organization by helping to explain the income statement, improve decision-making, improve data quality, increase understanding, and uncover insights to facilitate the month-end close process. We will then cover the two main arguments for partially (rather than fully) modelling the income statement; this includes outlining the position and providing the counterarguments.

In this chapter, two sections are covered:

1. Benefits of Modelling the Income Statement

2. Why Partially Modelling the Income Statement Is Insufficient

CHAPTER 4   WHY MODEL THE INCOME STATEMENT?

Benefits of Modelling the Income Statement

An income statement semantic model enables users to intuitively navigate a complex information landscape. In doing so, the semantic model can be used to

1. Explain the income statement
2. Improve decision-making
3. Improve data quality
4. Gain a deeper understanding of profitability
5. Uncover insights which facilitate the month-end close process

Explain the Income Statement

Using an income statement semantic model, users can clearly see how an entity arrives at net income. Moreover, they can drill into the income statement to see how individual journal entries directly influence overall profitability. This is without having to be exposed to any of the complexities of double-entry bookkeeping, such as credits and debits, or the accrual method of accounting. For instance, Figure 4-1 shows how *sales and marketing* can understand their overall cost (**1**), the breakdown of costs by account (**2**), and breakdown of accounts down to the individual transactions and journal entries (**3**).

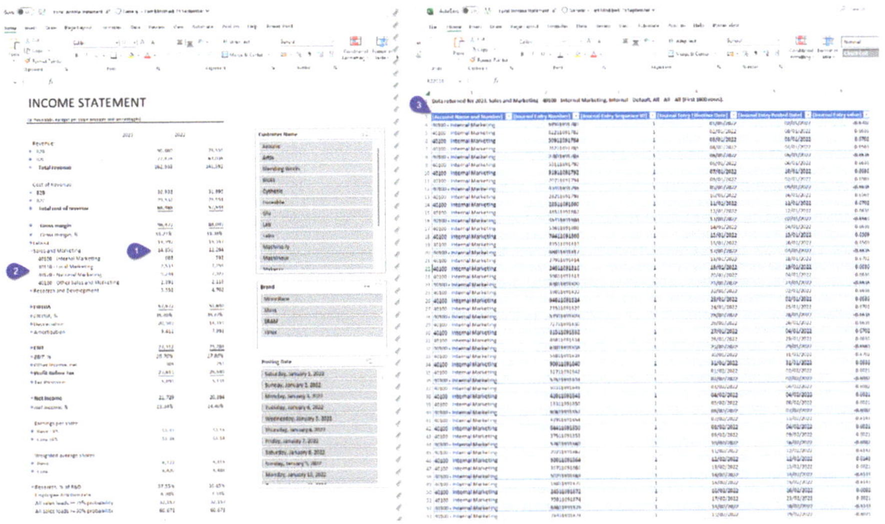

CHAPTER 4   WHY MODEL THE INCOME STATEMENT?

Figure 4-1. Sales and marketing breakdown

By explaining the impact of transactions without resorting to accounting terminology, non-finance teams can view the impact of their actions on profitability.

Improve Decision-Making

Modelling the income statement in its entirety can help users make more informed decisions. For instance, using activity-based costing (see Chapter 5), all lines on the income statement can be allocated to a given customer, meaning net income / (loss) can be shown for each customer. For instance, Figure 4-2 shows net income **(1)** for customer Arconic **(2)**.

51

CHAPTER 4 WHY MODEL THE INCOME STATEMENT?

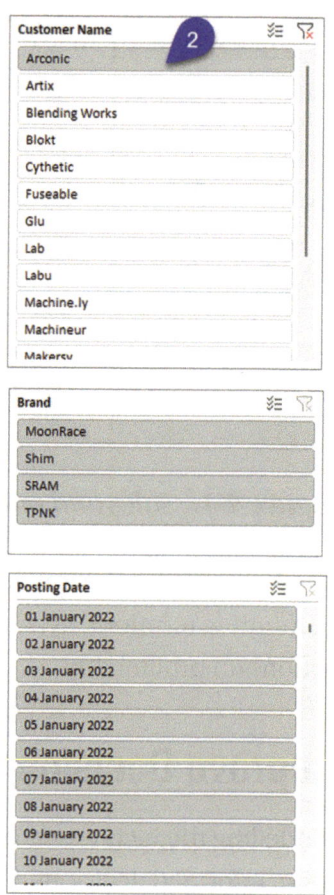

Figure 4-2. *Income statement for Arconic*

Decisions can be made based on this information, such as where to allocate resources and which customers need to be targeted for profitability improvement.

Improve Data Quality

Data held by an entity is a valuable asset. Therefore, like any assets, it is important to maintain the quality. By increasing transparency, more employees can identify errors and request adjustments. For instance, an employee may observe that search engine optimization (SEO) entries are being posted to an account designated for television advertising.

Gain a Deeper Understanding of Profitability

Semantic modelling can indirectly impact shareholder value by facilitating valuable conversations. For instance, analyzing the income statement can lead to questions toward

- The employee who posted an adjusting entry, that is, what is the reasoning for the adjustment?

- The management unit where costs are most volatile, that is, why is there such a significant variation each month in pension contributions?

Conversation facilitated by the semantic model can lead to a deeper understanding of the driving factors behind profitability.

Uncover Insights to Facilitate the Month-End Close Process

Entities are consistently reviewing the month-end close process and are always on the lookout for efficiency improvements. Typically, entities will have multiple cutoff points during a month-end close; journal entries are posted prior to these cutoffs, and results are analyzed. For instance, a cutoff schedule could be

CHAPTER 4   WHY MODEL THE INCOME STATEMENT?

- One day before the period close: workday (WD) – 1
- Three days after the period close: WD + 3
- Seven days after the period close: WD + 7

At the end of each of these workdays, the semantic model can be updated, and all users can then access income statement information. This can

1. Help to identify corrective journals
2. Assist in the preparation of board packs

Identify Corrective Journals: Adjusting Provision Example

At the end of WD + 3, an employee responsible for the income statement line *general and administrative costs* uses the semantic model to examine operating costs. In doing so, the employee notes that these costs are lower than the same period for the prior year and identifies the region concerned. The employee then drills into accounts noting that the money set aside for energy consumed (a financial provision) is lower than expected. It is lower than expected because the user is aware of weather conditions in that region and rising energy costs; therefore, when the bill is received in three months' time, it will be significantly higher than the amount provisioned for. This constitutes a *material* misrepresentation and as such requires an adjustment journal to increase the provision.

Assist in Preparing Board Packs: Commentary Example

At period end, board packs are produced; these contain the financial statements and any associated commentary. Those preparing the board packs can use the semantic model to investigate areas of interest. For instance, if revenue is down 2% vs. prior year, users can navigate the income statement to understand the reasons for this variance. In doing so, a user may note that a particular divisions revenue is down 28%. This

CHAPTER 4   WHY MODEL THE INCOME STATEMENT?

information directs the user to speak to the owner of the region, who informs them this is because of supply issues on a particular component. This information then forms the commentary for the board packs. Typically, this commentary would contain the number stripping out that division, which can be done using the semantic model. For instance, the commentary could read

- *Revenue is down 2% vs. prior year.*

- *The decrease in revenue is due to a 28% year-on-year decrease in Europe South, predominantly because of a supply issue on semiconductors.*

- *Excluding Europe South, revenue is up 6% year-on-year.*

Why Partially Modelling the Income Statement Is Insufficient

Partial modelling is when the semantic model contains all the information up to accounts, but the income statement is not produced in its entirety (Figure 4-3).

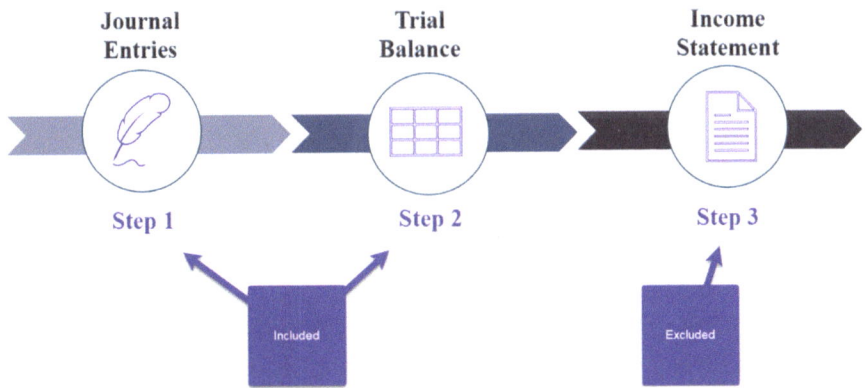

Figure 4-3. *Accounting process excluding income statement stage*

CHAPTER 4   WHY MODEL THE INCOME STATEMENT?

The two core arguments for partially modelling the income statement are

> **Argument 1**: Business intelligence should focus on individual lines in the income statement rather than reproducing financial reports in their entirety, which should be managed by the finance system.
>
> **Argument 2**: Visual calculations should overlay semantic model calculations to create the income statement.

Argument 1: Business Intelligence Should Focus on Individual Lines in the Income Statement Rather Than Reproducing Financial Reports in Their Entirety, Which Should Be Managed by the Finance System

Kimball and Ross are responsible for popularizing dimensional modelling (the advised modelling approach in Power BI) and explicitly advised against modelling the income statement in its entirety in their seminal work *The Data Warehouse Toolkit, Volume 3*. The justification for this conclusion was that

> *The operational system typically handles the production of these reports. You wouldn't want the DW/BI system to attempt to replace the reports published by the operational financial systems*

Instead of focusing on creating financial statements in their entirety, Kimball and Ross focus on *"performance trends for a given line in the financial statement."*

CHAPTER 4   WHY MODEL THE INCOME STATEMENT?

End users can analyze any individual account or group of accounts without having to model the income statement in its entirety. For instance, if interested in overall net income, all income statement accounts can be selected, and any analysis such as drilling down to the journal entries or viewing the accounts for a given business unit can be done.

While analyzing an individual account or a group of accounts provides many benefits, modelling the income statement in its entirety provides the additional benefits of providing a holistic view of profitability and enabling users to focus on value-added activities.

Providing a Holistic View of Profitability

Providing end users with a holistic picture (the entire income statement) enables individual income statement lines to be viewed according to their wider context, how each line compares to another and contributes to overall profitability (net income). This contrasts to analysis starting at the individual income statement line or account, which means users are unaware of the wider picture. For instance, Figure 4-4 shows how the same gross margin for 2022 (84,049k) and 2023 (96,472) can be achieved using a whole income statement **(1)** and an income statement account model **(2)** with the appropriately selected accounts.

CHAPTER 4   WHY MODEL THE INCOME STATEMENT?

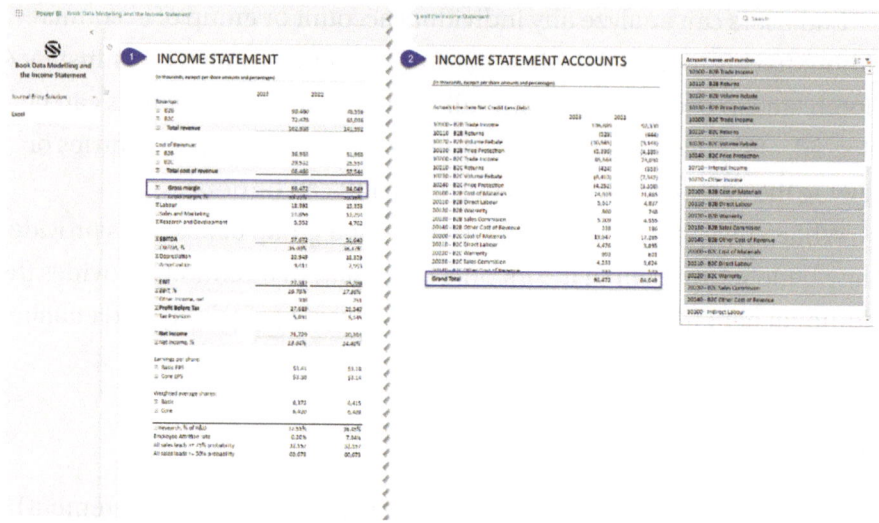

Figure 4-4. Modelling the entire and partial income statement

Both approaches retrieve the same result for gross margin; however, the income statement approach allows users to start at the highest level, viewing each line on the income statement, then progress into the detail (Figure 4-5).

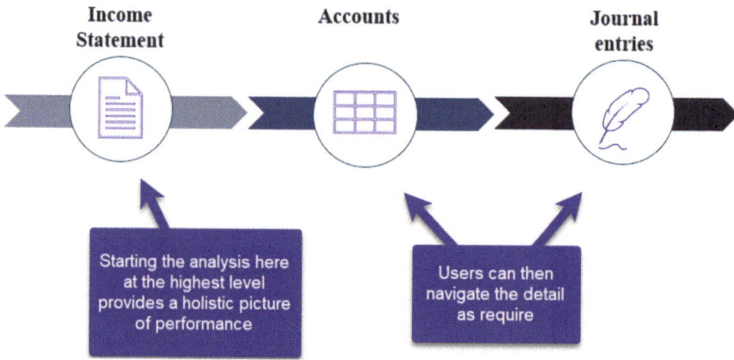

Figure 4-5. Starting analysis at the highest level

CHAPTER 4   WHY MODEL THE INCOME STATEMENT?

This is particularly helpful for non-finance users who can more easily grasp the concept of a single statement showing profitability rather than having to mentally contextualize how selected lines and accounts contribute to the wider picture.

Enabling Users to Focus on Value Added

Reports in Excel and Power BI connected to a semantic model are automatically updated when data becomes available, reducing the time spent on report creation. This allows for greater focus on value-added activities, such as providing insight. Reports might be created for

- The overall income statement
- Various perspectives of the income statement, that is, the income statement for a given management or business unit
- Detailed reports related to a single line on the income statement, that is, marketing cost broken down by accounts such as direct marketing and sales promotions
- Journal entry views by individuals, so they can review their own journal entry postings
- Mobile reports for decision-makers on the go

This approach works as all reports (known as thin reports) can be connected to a single income statement semantic model. This use of a single semantic model creates a powerful combination of dynamic reporting in Power BI alongside Excel(s), all pointing to a single version of the truth (Figure 4-6).

CHAPTER 4   WHY MODEL THE INCOME STATEMENT?

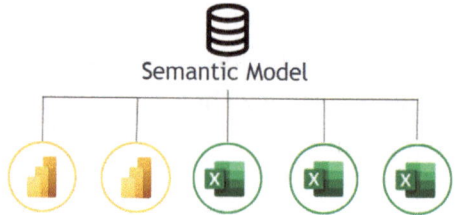

Figure 4-6. *Power BI and Excel pointing to a single semantic model*

Argument 2: Visual Calculations Should Overlay Semantic Model Calculations to Create the Income Statement

The second argument recognizes the need to produce income statements in their entirety. In this approach, the semantic model produces the initial account balances, and visual calculations are overlaid to compile the income statement. Table 4-1 shows an example of visual calculations where

1. The semantic model calculates figures for *product revenue* and *service and other revenue*.

2. Visual calculations combine these lines to calculate *total revenue*.

Table 4-1. *Visual calculations*

Income Statement Line	Value	Calculation	Calculation Type
Product revenue	£7m	Sum of accounts 30100 to 30199	Semantic model
Service revenue	£4m	Sum of accounts 30200 to 30299	Semantic model
Total revenue	£11m	Product revenue + Service revenue	Visual

CHAPTER 4   WHY MODEL THE INCOME STATEMENT?

While the example shown in Table 4-1 is a simple addition, visual calculations can perform a wide array of calculations based on the values in the visual. For instance, a visual calculation could be used to calculate earnings per share (EPS) by dividing *net income* by *number of shares*. These visual calculations are typically

1. **Easier to create**: Visual calculations have an awareness of other lines on the income statement, making it relatively easy to create calculations such as subtotals by referring to lines on the income statement as in the Table 4-1 example.

2. **More performant**

While visual calculations can be beneficial, there are significant downsides when compared to a self-contained semantic model which contains all the logic.

Reduced Integration

Given part of the logic now resides within the visual, the semantic model is no longer able to reproduce the income statement in isolation. Figure 4-7 highlights this diminishing integration, showing how the native Excel no longer contains the business logic.

CHAPTER 4   WHY MODEL THE INCOME STATEMENT?

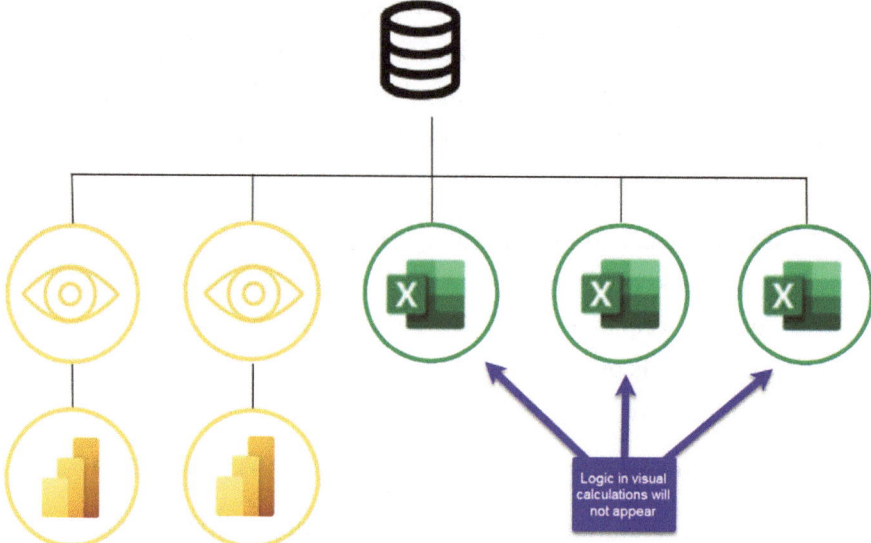

Figure 4-7. *Power BI and Excel pointing to a single semantic model*

If logic is brought separately into these sources, this increases the probability of misalignment, increases the initial workload, and creates an ongoing maintenance overhead for each report.

Inability to Stress Test the Model

Testers cannot stress test the semantic model against outcomes. This is because it does not contain all the required logic. Testing is, therefore, more complicated as there are multiple sources to be validated.

Reduced Functionality

As visual calculations are based on existing model calculations, they do not support drill-down functionality. Figure 4-8 shows how model calculations enable users to drill down on

CHAPTER 4   WHY MODEL THE INCOME STATEMENT?

1. **The *total revenue* subtotal**: Calculated by B2B + B2C revenue

2. ***Basic EPS***: Calculated by dividing net income by basic number of shares

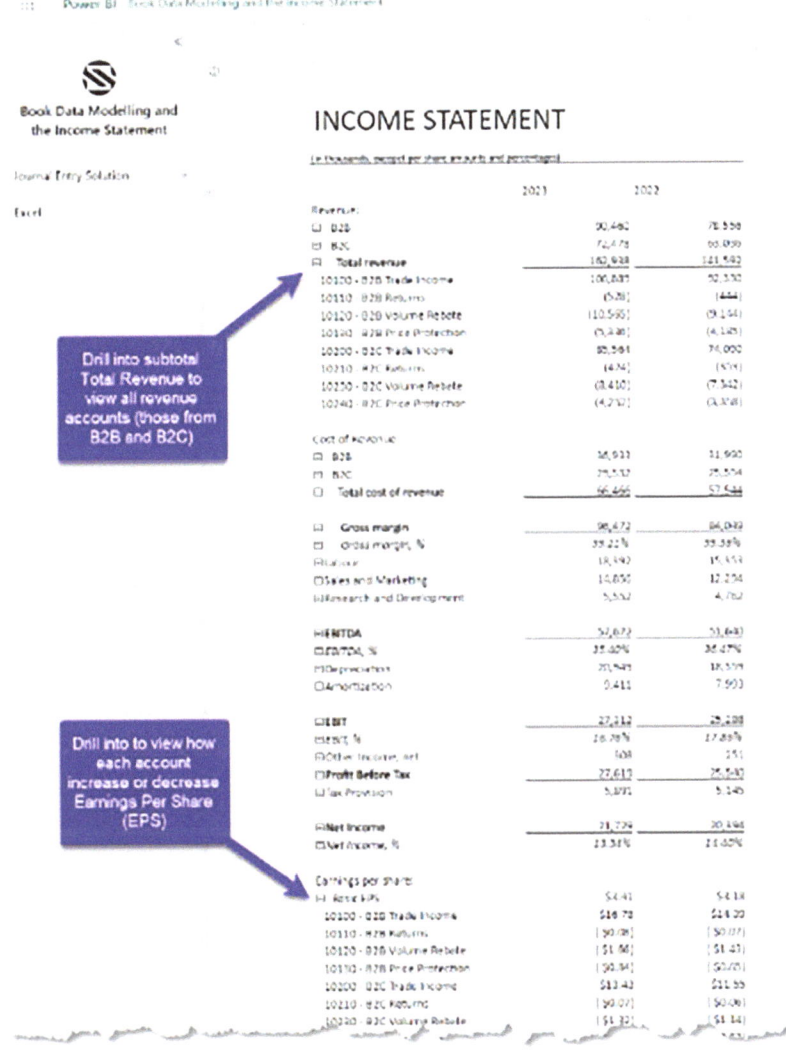

Figure 4-8. Drill down into subtotals

63

Moreover, income statement solutions should support four different drill-down options (Chapter 9), including additive and non-additive subtotals for different use cases.

Multiple Layouts

Multiple layouts of the income statement can exist for several reasons:

1. Condensed vs. expanded views
2. Internal vs. external views
3. Current year layout vs. a proposed future layout

With visual calculations, it is difficult to support multiple layouts as there may be different definitions of where accounts are allocated. In contrast, a modelling approach can be created which supports multiple layouts (see Part 4).

Extendibility

If expanding from the income statement to three-way financial reporting, calculations are needed for use in the Statement of Cash Flows when using the indirect method. This is because the Statement of Cash Flow is based on items from the Statement of Comprehensive Income and the Statement of Financial Position. Once logic exists outside the model, it is difficult to extend these across financial reports.

Summary

- Creating an income statement semantic model benefits an entity as it
  - Helps to explain the income statement
  - Improves decision-making

CHAPTER 4   WHY MODEL THE INCOME STATEMENT?

- Improves data quality
- Facilitates a deeper understanding of profitability
- Helps to uncover insights to facilitate the month-end close process
- Providing users with partial modelling of the income statement is insufficient as
  - Users require a holistic picture of profitability before drilling into the detail
  - It increases the reporting burden on finance teams, rather than allowing them to focus on value-added activities
- Visual calculations are inappropriate for the actuals calculation due to
  - Calculations not being accessible using native analyze in Excel
  - Increased potential for misalignment
  - Increased ongoing maintenance
  - Testing is more complex as part of the logic exists outside the model
  - There is reduced functionality for drill down and drill through
  - Producing multiple layouts for different audiences requires additional logic in the semantic model
  - Extendibility is reduced if there is desire to produce other financial statements

PART II

Calculating Account Balances

In this part, we will learn how to build semantic models optimized for calculating *account balances*. By extension, these semantic models are optimized for calculating line-items, subtotals, and subsets as these comprise accounts (see Chapter 2). In developing a model optimized for calculating *account balances*, we will cover the three stages of modelling:

> **Stage 1**: Conceptual – High-level model designs for senior stakeholders
>
> **Stage 2**: Logical – Detailed blueprint model designs for technical stakeholders
>
> **Stage 3**: Physical – Building semantic models based on the logical model designs

For all three stages, we will build a trial balance model – a base model which is reusable across organizations – and an example journal entry model, which is an extension of the trial balance.

This part comprises the following chapters:

- Chapter 5, "Conceptual Account Balance Models"
- Chapter 6, "Logical Account Balance Models"
- Chapter 7, "The Trial Balance Semantic Model"
- Chapter 8, "A Journal Entry Semantic Model"

PART II

Calculating Account Balances

CHAPTER 5

Conceptual Account Balance Models

At this point in the book, you understand how the income statement is compiled from the trial balance. It is now time to apply this knowledge and model the measurement of this accounting process using dimensional modelling techniques. In doing so, we will create conceptual models, high-level designs that can be used to communicate accounting rules to senior stakeholders.

In this chapter, we will learn how *account balances* can be calculated using the trial balance conceptual model. We will also cover the process of adding additional dimensionality to the trial balance conceptual model, creating journal entry conceptual models which enable *account balances* to be further contextualized.

In this chapter, there are two main sections:

1. Calculating *Account Balances* Using the Trial Balance Conceptual Model
2. Journal Entry Conceptual Models

CHAPTER 5 CONCEPTUAL ACCOUNT BALANCE MODELS

Calculating Account Balances Using the Trial Balance Conceptual Model

Chapter 3 introduced the conceptual model for calculating *credits less debits* (Figure 5-1).

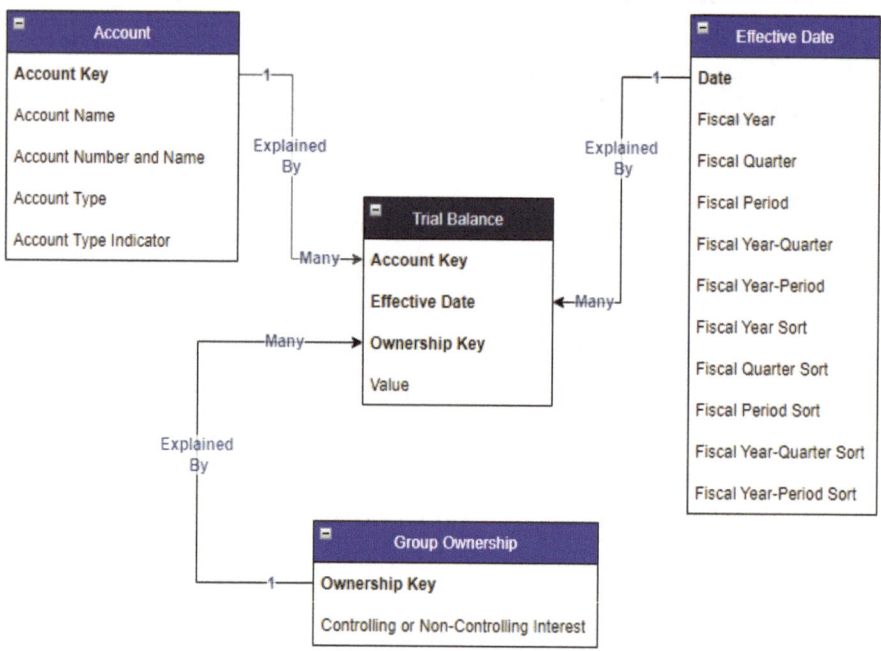

Figure 5-1. Conceptual Star Schema for calculating credits less debits

This high-level model is used to communicate rules to a senior audience. The model shows that credits less debits – the 'Trial Balance'[Value] – can be explained by

1. **'Account'**: For instance, the value of credits less debits where 'Account'[Account Name] equals *product trade revenue*

2. **'Group Ownership'**: For instance, the value of credits less debits for controlling interests

3. **'Effective Date'**: For instance, the value of credits less debits for the first fiscal quarter of 2024

These explanations can be applied simultaneously, for instance, the value of credits less debits for *product trade revenue* accounts attributable to controlling interests for the first fiscal quarter of 2024.

Account Balances

As the 'Trial Balance'[Value] is credits less debits, a sum of this column can be used for

- Line-items, subtotals, and subsets consisting of accounts which are only of account type *revenue*
- Subtotals and subsets consisting of accounts which are of account types *revenue* and *expense*, where credit less debit is the desired calculation, that is, net profit

However, the model must also support debit less credit calculations for

- Line-items, subtotals, and subsets consisting of accounts which are only of account type *expense*
- Subtotals and subsets consisting of accounts which are of account types *revenue* and *expense*, where debit less credit is the desired calculation, that is, net loss

To support all permutations, two calculations are required; *net credit less debit* and *net debit less credit*. These return identical results, except when both revenue and expense accounts are in scope (Table 5-1).

CHAPTER 5   CONCEPTUAL ACCOUNT BALANCE MODELS

Table 5-1. *Trial balance example with account type and effective data*

Calculation	Revenue Accounts Only	Expense Accounts Only	Revenue and Expense Accounts
Net credit less debit	Credit less debit	Debit less credit	Credit less debit
Net debit less credit	Credit less debit	Debit less credit	Debit less credit

Net Credit Less Debit

For the net credit less debit (NCLD) calculation, sometimes an *expense* account is calculated as debit less credit (i.e., when evaluated on its own or with other expense accounts) and sometimes as credit less debit (i.e., when evaluated with revenue accounts). To achieve this, the 'Account' table contains an 'Account'[Account Type Indicator] (Table 5-2).

Table 5-2. *Trial balance example with account type and effective data*

Account Key	Account Name	Account Type	Account Type Indicator
30100	Trade sales	Revenue	1
30101	Returns	Revenue	1
40100	Trade cost of sales	Expense	−1

The 'Account'[Account Type Indicator] is 1 for revenue accounts and −1 for expense accounts. By calculating the maximum of the 'Account'[Account Type Indicator]:

- When revenue accounts are in scope, a value of 1 is returned.

CHAPTER 5 CONCEPTUAL ACCOUNT BALANCE MODELS

- When expense accounts are in scope, a value of –1 is returned.
- When revenue and expense accounts are both in scope, a value of 1 is returned.

The sum of 'Trial Balance'[Value] can then be multiplied by the maximum of the 'Account'[Account Type Indicator]:

$$NCLD = \sum(\text{'Trial Balance'}[Value]) \times \max(\text{'Account'}[\text{Account Type Indicator}])$$

Multiplying the 'Trial Balance'[Value] by 1 has no impact, but multiplying by –1 has the mathematical effect of turning credits less debits into debits less credits:

$$debit - credit = (credit - debit) \times -1$$

Therefore

- When only revenue accounts are in scope, the calculation returns credit less debit.
- When only expense accounts are in scope, the calculation returns debit less credit.
- When both revenue and expense accounts are in scope, the calculation returns credit less debit.

This calculation can, therefore, be used to calculate all line-items, subtotals, and subsets, except those where revenue and expense accounts are in scope and the calculation required is debit less credit (i.e., loss generated by the sale of an asset).

CHAPTER 5   CONCEPTUAL ACCOUNT BALANCE MODELS

Net Debit Less Credit

By calculating the minimum (as opposed to the maximum) of 'Account'[Account Type Indicator], when both revenue and expense accounts are in scope, a value of −1 is returned. For the net debit less credit (NDLC) calculation, the sum of 'Trial Balance'[Value] can then be multiplied by the minimum of the 'Account'[Account Type Indicator]:

$$NDLC = \sum('Trial\ Balance'[Value]) \times \min('Account'[Account\ Type\ Indicator'])$$

Therefore

- When only revenue accounts are in scope, the calculation returns credit less debit.

- When only expense accounts are in scope, the calculation returns debit less credit.

- When both revenue and expense accounts are in scope, the calculation returns debit less credit.

This calculation can, therefore, be used to calculate subtotals and subsets where revenue and expense accounts are in scope and the calculation required is debit less credit.

Journal Entry Conceptual Models

The trial balance conceptual model includes the fundamental elements required to calculate *account balances* for controlling and non-controlling interests on a given date. However, this is a highly restrictive model, and in practice the income statement is required to be sliced and diced by other dimensions (challenge 15 from Chapter 3). These dimensions are unique to each entity, and each dimension added increases the granularity of the fact table, the level of detail by which it can be explained.

CHAPTER 5   CONCEPTUAL ACCOUNT BALANCE MODELS

Why It Is Important to Work at the Atomic Grain

The most granular level of a fact table is known as the atomic grain. It is important to implement a solution at the atomic grain as this offers the greatest degree of analytical flexibility, the number of ways a user can slice and dice the income statement. These can also be used to control security, that is, by adding a legal entity dimension, users can be restricted to certain legal entities.

In accounting terms, the dimensions which all accounts can be explained by are the uniform dimensions. Subaccounts can also be assigned to non-uniform dimensions, dimensions specific to a subaccount or group of subaccounts. For instance, certain revenue accounts could be explained by a customer dimension, but depreciation cannot; thus, customer is a non-uniform dimension. Thoughout this book, when discussing atomic grain, it is with reference to uniform dimensions.

How Dimensions Are Identified

Dimensions are identified by the words *explained by*, that is, explain the income statement by business units. Figure 5-2 shows an example fundamental journal entry conceptual model including explanations by

1. **Legal entity**: These are individual companies with their own rights and legal responsibilities (most medium and large companies are made up of several legal entities).

2. **Business unit**: A division responsible for managing its own income statement.

3. **Posting date**: The date a journal entry posting was made.

CHAPTER 5   CONCEPTUAL ACCOUNT BALANCE MODELS

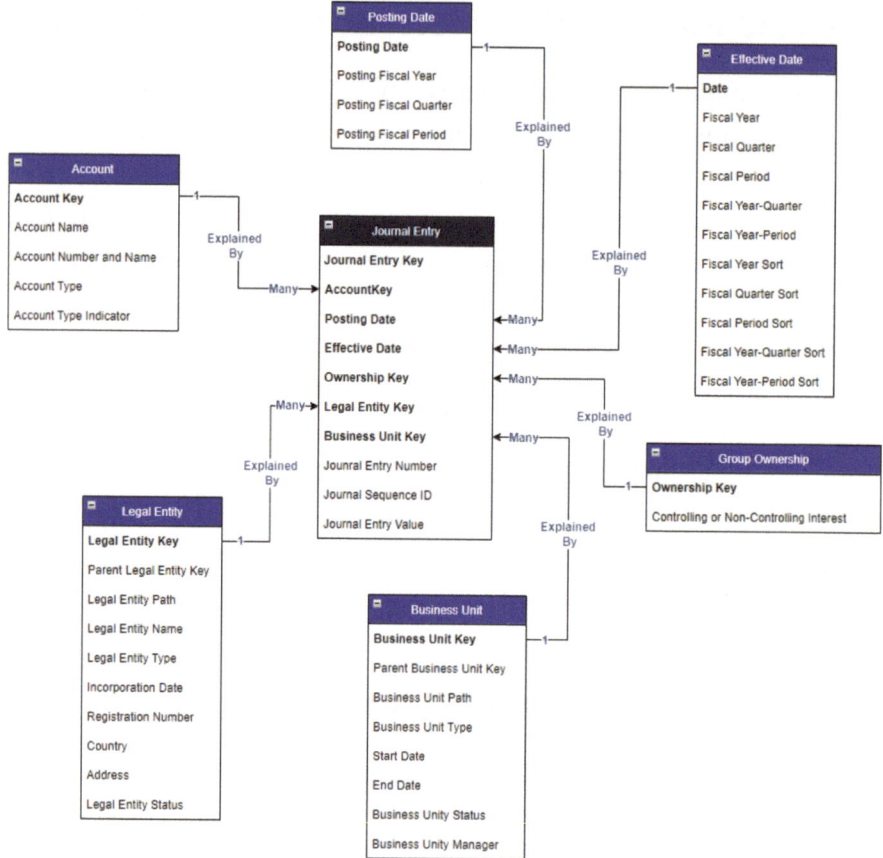

Figure 5-2. *Journal entry conceptual model with legal entity and business unit dimensions*

As well as the dimensions, the journal entry fact table in Figure 5-2 is also *explained by* journal entry number and journal sequence ID (Chapter 2 covered how each journal entry number has at least two records due to the nature of double-entry bookkeeping). Journal entry number and journal sequence ID are stored within the fact table as opposed to a separate dimension. This is because the grain of any dimension containing journal entry number and journal sequence ID would be the same as the fact table; having two tables of the same grain linked with a one-to-one relationship adds unnecessary complexity to the model.

Handling Multiple Date Dimensions

The inclusion of *posting date* alongside *effective date* is a common request. This enables the entity to view journal entries on the day they were entered, as well as the fiscal period to which the transaction belongs; journal entries are frequently posted on different financial periods to the effective date, that is, postings three days after the financial period has closed.

A common pattern in a business intelligence solution is to introduce a role-playing dimension rather than two separate date tables as observed in Figure 5-2. However, this approach is not suitable for income statement solutions. This is because with a role-playing dimension, two (or more) relationships from the date dimension to the journal entry fact table are required, and, to avoid ambiguity, only one relationship can be active at a time; journal entries could, therefore, be viewed by either *effective date* or *posting date*. However, the typical finance requirement is to filter by *effective date* and *posting date* simultaneously with different date selections. For instance, for period 1 of 2024 (effective date), show the entries made on day 7 after the period closed (posting date).

Working at the Atomic Grain Increases the Number of Rows

As a fact table becomes more granular, the number of rows in the table increases. To understand this relationship between dimensionality and the number of rows, Table 5-3 shows a single record for an account key (50100) on a single day (1 January 2024).

CHAPTER 5　CONCEPTUAL ACCOUNT BALANCE MODELS

Table 5-3. *Record for a single account on a single day*

Account Key	Effective Date	Journal Entry Value
50100	1 Jan 2024	100

If the granularity of this table is expanded to include business units, then the total journal entry value remains the same (100), but additional rows are required for each business unit (Table 5-4).

Table 5-4. *Record for a single account on a single day by business unit*

Account Key	Effective Date	Business Unit	Journal Entry Value
50100	1 Jan 2024	A	9
50100	1 Jan 2024	B	22
50100	1 Jan 2024	C	14
50100	1 Jan 2024	D	13
50100	1 Jan 2024	E	33
50100	1 Jan 2024	F	2
50100	1 Jan 2024	G	7

As more dimensions are added, the number of rows increases exponentially. For instance, if account 50100 also required explaining by 23 organizations for the last five years, the number of rows for this one account could be as high as 293,825:

Number of rows (293,825) = business unit (7) X organization (23) X days in year (365) X number of years (5)

CHAPTER 5 CONCEPTUAL ACCOUNT BALANCE MODELS

Increasing Beyond the Atomic Grain

While there are uniform dimensions, there are also dimensions which are only relevant to certain accounts or subaccounts. For instance, amortization is not typically explained by customer, but revenue can often be explained by customer. Moreover, because journal entry adjustments frequently occur at a higher level (see Chapter 2), even if transactional revenue is recorded by customer, overall revenue will typically only partially be explainable by customer (Table 5-5).

Table 5-5. Revenue by customer

Customer	Transaction Entries	Adjusting Entries	Total
Customer A	£24.8m		£24.8m
Customer B	£46.3m		£46.3m
Customer C	£17.0m		£17.0m
Customer D	£16.6m		£16.6m
Unknown		£4.7m	£4.7m
Total	**£104.7m**	**£4.7m**	**£109.4m**

Entities may wish to explain the income statement based on these non-uniform dimensions, that is, create customer income statements. To achieve this, journal entries are allocated based on rules using an accounting process known as Activity-Based Costing (ABC). For instance, adjusting entries could be allocated based on the percentage of transaction entries (Table 5-6).

CHAPTER 5   CONCEPTUAL ACCOUNT BALANCE MODELS

Table 5-6. *Revenue by customer with allocations*

Customer	Transaction Entries	% of Total Transaction Entries	Adjusting Entries Allocated	Total
Customer A	£24.8m	23.7%	£1.1m	£25.9m
Customer B	£46.3m	44.2%	£2.1m	£48.4m
Customer C	£17.0m	16.2%	£0.8m	£17.8m
Customer D	£16.6m	15.9%	£0.7m	£17.3m
Total	**£104.7m**	100%	£4.7m	**£109.4m**

Figure 5-3 shows a journal entry conceptual model for StarSchema.co.uk where all entries not explained by customer or product have been allocated at this grain.

CHAPTER 5   CONCEPTUAL ACCOUNT BALANCE MODELS

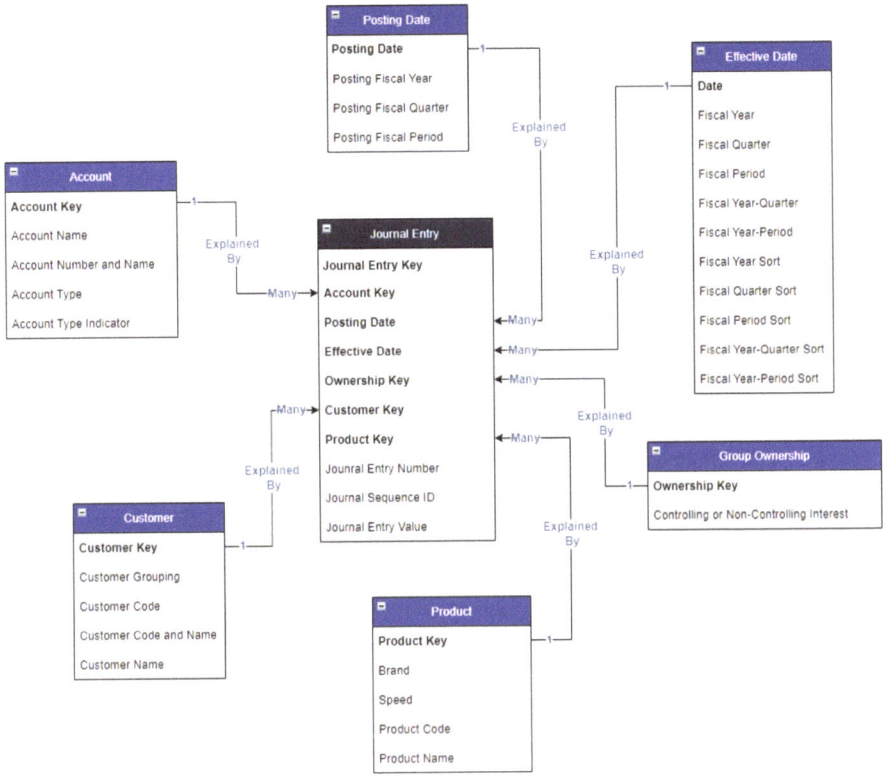

Figure 5-3. *StarSchema.co.uk conceptual model with allocations to customer and product*

Summary

- Dynamic *account balance* calculations can be created that use

  - Credits less debits when analyzing revenue accounts

  - Debits less credits when analyzing expense accounts

  - Either credit less debit or debit less credit when both revenue and expenses are in scope

CHAPTER 5   CONCEPTUAL ACCOUNT BALANCE MODELS

- A reusable conceptual model is based on the trial balance as this is the common output across entities from which income statements are built.

- Working at the atomic grain offers the greatest degree of analytical flexibility.

- Dimensions are identified by the phrase *explained by*.

- Separate date dimension tables are required for effective date and posting date as opposed to a single role-playing date dimension.

- As the number of dimensions increases, so does the number of rows in the fact table.

- Uniform dimensions are dimensions all journal entries can be explained by.

- Non-uniform dimensions, such as customer, can be used to explain certain subaccounts, but not all accounts.

- Activity-Based Costing (ABC) can be used to allocate records to non-uniform dimensions, increasing the analytical flexibility of the solution.

CHAPTER 6

Logical Account Balance Models

In the previous chapter, we learned about the trial balance conceptual model optimized for calculating *account balances*. We also learned how this elevated abstract model, containing data objects and their relationships, can be used to convey business rules to a senior audience. We then expanded upon this foundational trial balance model, creating more complex models with additional dimensionality, including detail down to the individual journal entries and allocations to non-uniform dimensions.

In this chapter, we will learn how to convert conceptual models into logical models; while conceptual models are designed for a senior audience, logical models are designed for a technical audience. The logical models created in this chapter are used as blueprints for the physical models in Chapter 7, the trial balance semantic model, and Chapter 8, a journal entry semantic model. We will also learn about aggregations; these summarizations of fact tables can improve query performance. Because aggregations exist for performance reasons, they are excluded from conceptual models and only form part of a logical data model design.

In this chapter, there are three main sections:

1. The Trial Balance Logical Model
2. An Example Journal Entry Logical Model
3. Aggregations

CHAPTER 6   LOGICAL ACCOUNT BALANCE MODELS

The Trial Balance Logical Model

Chapter 5 covered the trial balance conceptual model which is optimized for calculating *account balances* in a given fiscal period (Figure 6-1).

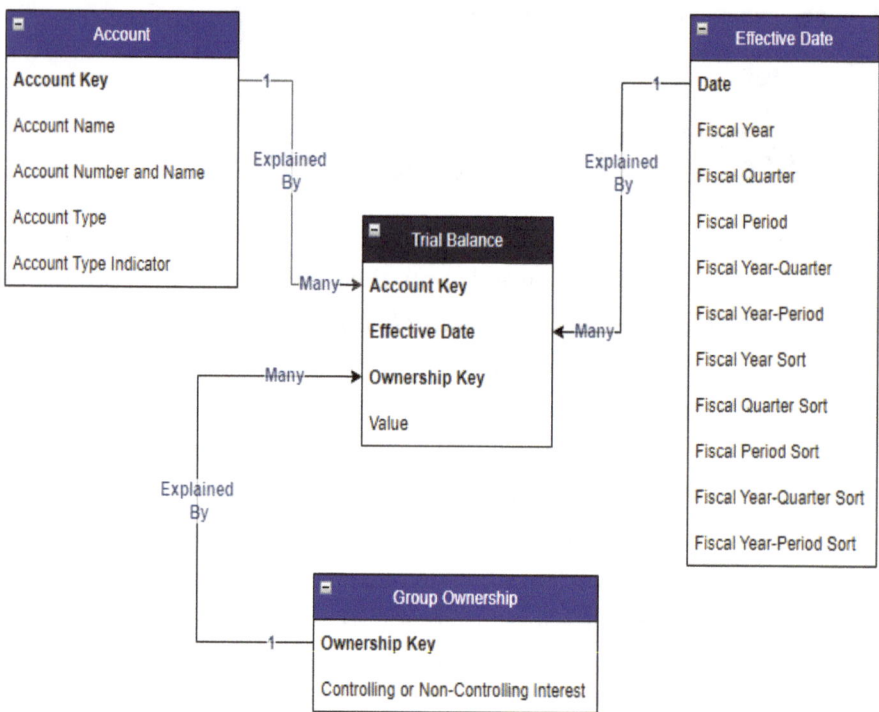

Figure 6-1. *Optimized trial balance conceptual model*

For this elevated abstract model to be converted into a blueprint logical model from which a physical model can be built in Power BI or Microsoft Fabric, the following changes are required:

1. **Add field types**: For instance, 'Account'[Account Name] is an attribute (AT), which is a level of summary in a dimension table.

CHAPTER 6   LOGICAL ACCOUNT BALANCE MODELS

2. **Add data types:** For instance, 'Account'[Account Name] is a string data type which can contain Unicode characters such as letters, dates, or numbers in a text format.

3. **The word *explained by* is removed**: Technical readers understand what the relationship means, and thus the wording is superfluous.

4. The word *many* is replaced with a * to indicate the many sides of the relationship.

Based on this understanding, the optimized trial balance conceptual model (Figure 6-1) is converted into an optimized trial balance logical model (Figure 6-2), creating a detailed blueprint on which the trial balance semantic model (Chapter 7) is based:

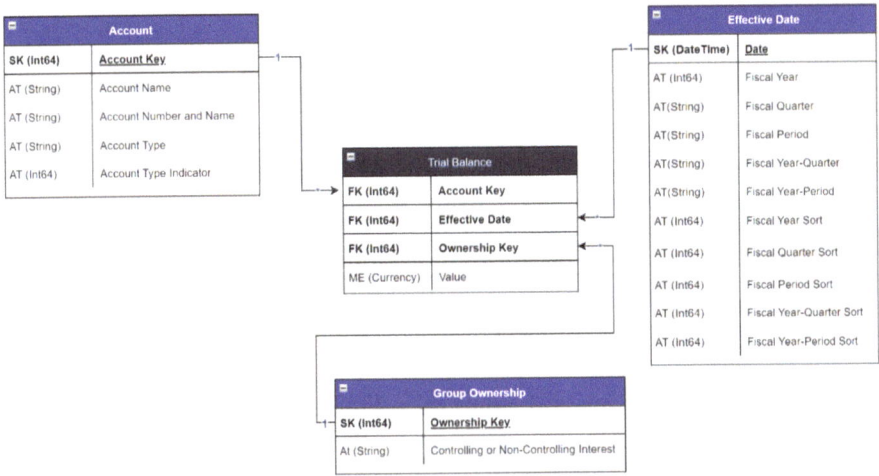

Figure 6-2. Optimized trial balance logical model

CHAPTER 6 LOGICAL ACCOUNT BALANCE MODELS

The first column of each table in Figure 6-2 contains the field and data type. For instance, the first row and column in the account table is SK (Int64); SK is the field type (field types are covered in the next section), and Int64 means the data type is a 64-bit (8-byte) integer. In all, there are seven data types available in Power BI, a summary of which is provided in Table 6-1.

Table 6-1. Power BI data types based on Microsoft official documentation

Data Type in Model	Data Type in DAX (Data Analysis eXpressions)	Description
Whole Number	A 64-bit (8-byte) integer value*	Numbers that have no decimal places. Integers can be positive or negative numbers but must be whole numbers between −9,223,372,036,854,775,807 (−2^63+1) and 9,223,372,036,854,775,806 (2^63−2).
Decimal Number	A 64-bit (8-byte) real number*	Real numbers are numbers that can have decimal places. Real numbers cover a wide range of values: • Negative values from −1.79E + 308 through −2.23E − 308 • Zero • Positive values from 2.23E − 308 through 1.79E + 308 However, the number of significant digits is limited to 15 decimal digits.
Boolean	Boolean	Either a True or False value.

(continued)

Table 6-1. (*continued*)

Data Type in Model	Data Type in DAX (Data Analysis eXpressions)	Description
Text	String	A Unicode character data string. Can be strings, numbers, or dates represented in a text format.
Date	Date/time	Dates and times in an accepted date-time representation. Valid dates are all dates after March 1, 1900.
Currency	Currency	Currency data type allows values between −922,337,203,685,477.5808 to 922,337,203,685,477.5807 with four decimal digits of fixed precision.
N/A	Blank	A blank is a data type in DAX that represents and replaces SQL nulls. You can create a blank by using the BLANK function and test for blanks by using the logical function, ISBLANK.

* DAX formulas do not support data types that are too small to hold the minimum value listed in the description.

An Example Journal Entry Logical Model

In addition to the optimized conceptual trial balance model, Chapter 5 introduced adding further dimensionality. This resulted in a conceptual journal entry model for StarSchema.co.uk (Figure 6-3).

CHAPTER 6 LOGICAL ACCOUNT BALANCE MODELS

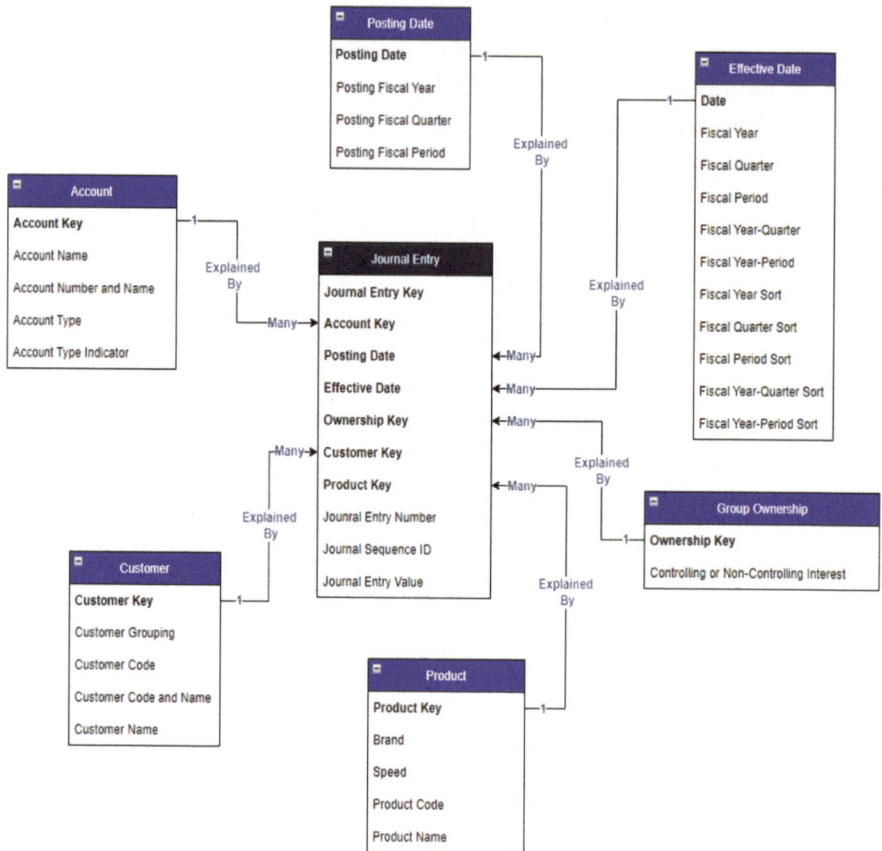

Figure 6-3. *StarSchema.co.uk conceptual model with allocations to customer and product*

As with the optimized trial balance conceptual model, the StarSchema.co.uk conceptual model (Figure 6-3) can be converted into an optimized logical model (Figure 6-4), creating a detailed blueprint on which the StarSchema.co.uk journal entry semantic model (Chapter 8) is based.

CHAPTER 6   LOGICAL ACCOUNT BALANCE MODELS

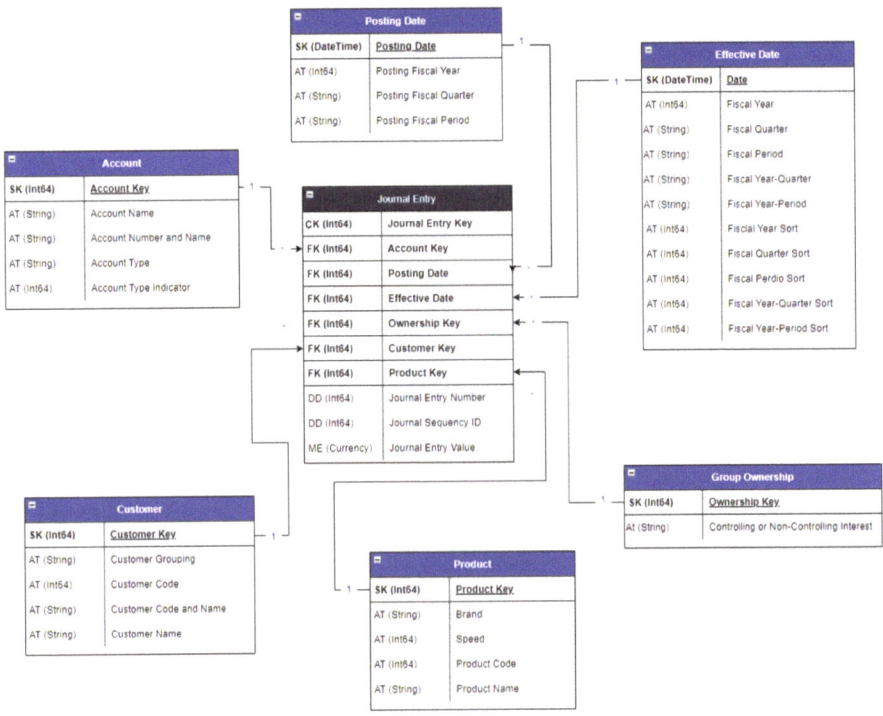

Figure 6-4. *StarSchema.co.uk logical model with allocations to customer and product*

Figure 6-4 contains six field types:

- Surrogate keys (SK)
- Composite keys (CK)
- Foreign keys (FK)
- Attributes (AT)
- Degenerate Dimensions (DD)
- Measures (ME)

89

CHAPTER 6   LOGICAL ACCOUNT BALANCE MODELS

Primary Keys

Primary keys uniquely identify each row within a table. In Figure 6-4, there are two types of primary keys.

Surrogate Keys

Surrogate keys are a type of primary key initiated by the database (not from the source system) to uniquely identify each row. It is considered best practice to create unique keys in the database rather than relying on source systems because

1. Source systems can contain inconsistencies.

2. Business intelligence involves comparing data across multiple source systems, and thus using the database to create the key ensures that a common key is used across systems. For instance, different business unit identifiers may exist in Enterprise Report Planning (ERP) and budgeting systems.

Composite Keys

The process of double-entry bookkeeping (Chapter 2) results in two or more *journal entry numbers* for each transaction; this means that 'Journal Entry'[Journal Entry Number] is not a primary key. Moreover, each journal entry can be further broken down into controlling and non-controlling interests.

To create a unique record for each row in a journal entry fact table, a 'Journal Entry'[Journal Entry Key] is created combining the *journal entry number*, the *journal sequence ID*, and the *ownership ID*. For example:

- A compound journal entry consists of three journal entries, each of which has the same *journal entry number* '456392'.

CHAPTER 6   LOGICAL ACCOUNT BALANCE MODELS

- Each distinct entry is assigned a *journal sequence ID* of ascending numbers. When this is combined with *journal entry number*, identifiers '456392 0001', '456392 0002', and '456392 0003' are created.

- 80% of the entry is then assigned to a controlling interest (0) and 20% to a non-controlling interest (1). When this is combined with *journal entry number* and *journal sequence ID*, unique identifiers '456392 0001 0', '456392 0001 1', '456392 0002 0', '456392 0002 1', '456392 0003 0', and '456392 0003 1' are created.

Foreign Keys

Foreign keys are the representation of a primary key in another table; this is essential for creating relationships between tables. Unlike primary keys, foreign keys can be duplicated; this is central to the star schema design and enables the creation of one-to-many relationships between dimensions and facts.

Attributes (AT)

An attribute describes a desired level of summary within a dimension table. For instance, the date table contains a row for each date, but dates can be grouped by the attribute year.

Degenerate Dimensions (DD)

Degenerate dimensions contain no attributes and are directly stored in the fact table. In the case of the income statement, 'Journal Entry'[Journal Entry Number] and 'Journal Entry'[Journal Entry Sequence ID] are degenerate dimensions.

CHAPTER 6   LOGICAL ACCOUNT BALANCE MODELS

In practice, these degenerate dimensions are available in the model for users to select, and the composite key is not. Figure 6-5 contains an updated logical model for StarSchema.co.uk with the composite key 'Journal Entry'[Journal Entry Key] removed.

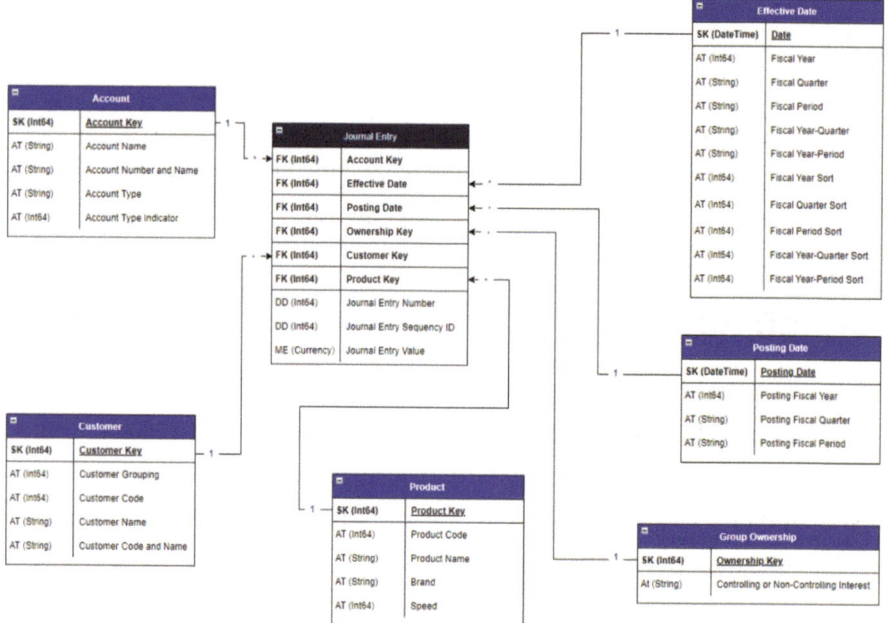

Figure 6-5. *StarSchema.co.uk logical model with the composite key removed*

The 'Journal Entry'[Journal Entry Key] is excluded in the model because

1. **It contains no intuitive business meaning**: It combines three concepts of journal entry number, journal entry sequence, and ownership.

CHAPTER 6   LOGICAL ACCOUNT BALANCE MODELS

2. **Users can derive the same information from the component parts**: The two degenerate dimensions ('Journal Entry'[Journal Entry Number] and 'Journal Entry'[Journal Entry Sequence ID]) and the attribute 'Group Ownership'[Controlling or Non-Controlling Interest].

The 'Journal Entry'[Journal Entry Key] is, however, important for the data engineering as it is the field that uniquely identifies each row in the fact table.

Measures (ME)

Measure is the field type which indicates a calculation is performed. 'Journal Entry'[Journal Entry Value] is the only measure; this stores each credit as a positive and each debit as a negative (see Chapter 2).

Aggregations

The previous chapter highlighted the importance of grain; the more granular the fact table, the more analytically flexible the solution. However, the most granular solution also requires the largest number of rows within the fact table. Conversely, the trial balance model (Figure 6-2) contains a fact table with the fewest possible number of rows required when calculating a group income statement which contains non-controlling interests. As the fact table in the trial balance model contains the fewest possible number of rows, it is thus the most performant; only the essential foreign keys for connecting to dimension tables (account, date, and ownership) are included. The trade-off for this performance is the fact table in the trial balance model is the least analytically flexible solution possible when calculating a group income statement which contains non-controlling interests.

Aggregations is a method by which analytical flexibility is retained; however, queries can also be sent to smaller – thus more performant – tables containing summarized data. In the case of the income statement, aggregations are more straightforward than many other types of models. This is because the calculation performed is always a summation; in other scenarios, there are calculations such as distinct count that are harder to optimize. There may be other more complex calculations, such as the average net income per month; however, these always use the summation as the base measure.

Creating a Single Aggregation

In Figure 6-6, the model contains a single journal entry aggregation, summarizing the journal entry by *account key*, *effective date*, and *ownership key*.

CHAPTER 6   LOGICAL ACCOUNT BALANCE MODELS

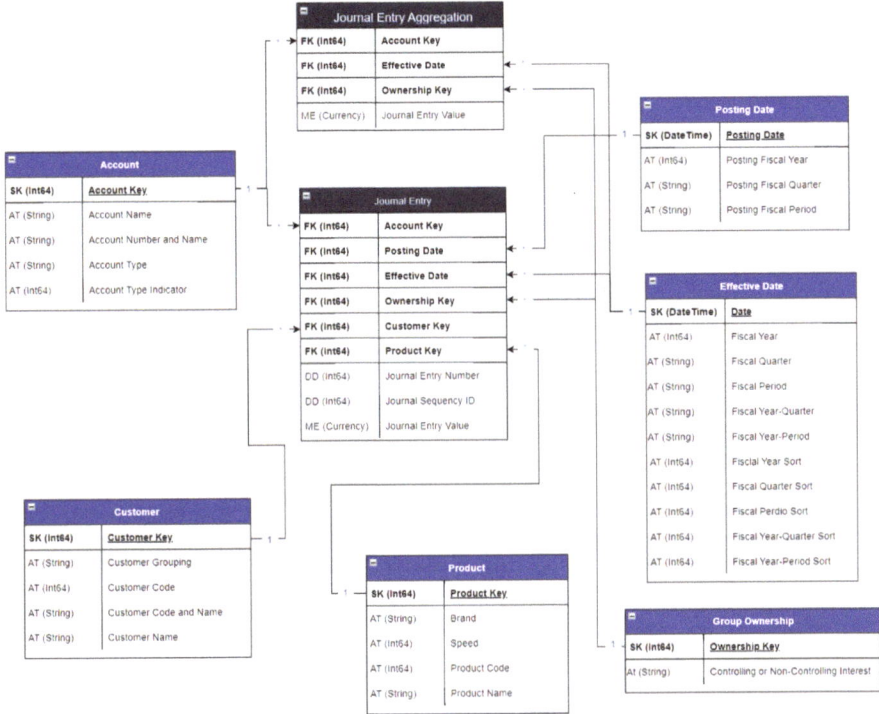

Figure 6-6. *Journal entry logical model with aggregation by account key, effective date, and ownership key*

When end users view accounts related to a line on the income statement for a given date – that is, the accounts used in calculating gross profit for Q1 2023 – the aggregation is used to retrieve the required value. However, if the end user slices and dices by a dimensional attribute which exists in a dimension not covered by the aggregation – that is, 'Customer'[Customer Name] – the model defaults back to retrieving the value from the 'Journal Entry' fact table.

CHAPTER 6 LOGICAL ACCOUNT BALANCE MODELS

Creating Multiple Aggregations

Analytical query patterns are said to be unpredictable; it is unknowable, in advance, how end users will slice and dice the model. Therefore, the advice is to optimize for all eventualities. Aggregations should thus be created for all permutations where the *account key*, *effective date*, and *ownership key* are present, the required dimensions for calculating line-items, subtotals, and subsets. For Figure 6-5, this results in eight aggregations:

- **Aggregation 1**: Account, effective date, and ownership

- **Aggregation 2**: Account, effective date, ownership, and customer

- **Aggregation 3**: Account, effective date, ownership, and posting date

- **Aggregation 4**: Account, effective date, ownership, and product

- **Aggregation 5**: Account, effective date, ownership, customer, and product

- **Aggregation 6**: Account, effective date, ownership, posting date, and customer

- **Aggregation 7**: Account, effective date, ownership, posting date, and product

- **Aggregation 8**: Account, effective date, ownership, posting date, customer, and product

The *journal entry value* is then retrieved from the appropriate table, depending on which dimensions are in scope. For instance, if end users slice and dice by 'Customer'[Customer Name], then *journal entry value* is calculated using aggregation 2: account, effective date, ownership, and customer.

CHAPTER 6   LOGICAL ACCOUNT BALANCE MODELS

From an end-user perspective, these aggregation tables are hidden; these operate in the background to improve query performance.

Journal Entry Aggregation Logical Models

In Chapter 8, a semantic model is built for StarSchema.co.uk. This is based on the StarSchema.co.uk logical model (Figure 6-5) and the eight aggregations covered in this chapter; a logical model for each of these aggregations is shown in Figures 6-7 to 6-14.

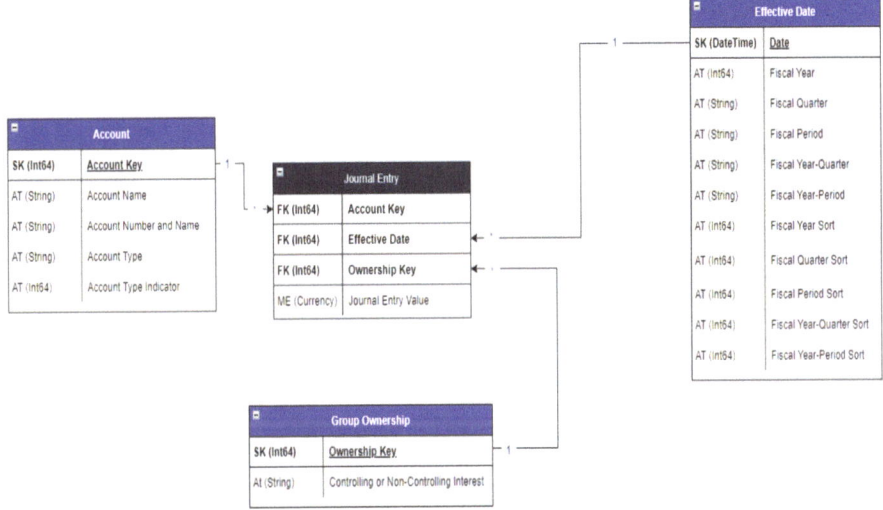

Figure 6-7. *StarSchema.co.uk Aggregation 1 by Effective Date, Account Key, and Ownership Key*

97

CHAPTER 6   LOGICAL ACCOUNT BALANCE MODELS

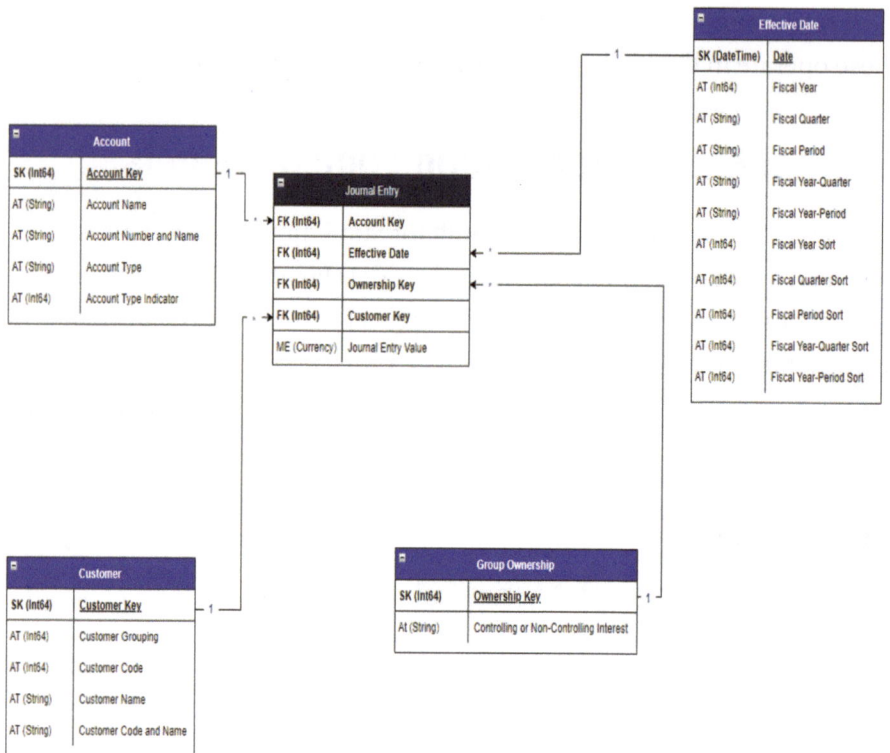

Figure 6-8. *StarSchema.co.uk Aggregation 2 by Effective Date, Account Key, Ownership Key, and Customer Key*

CHAPTER 6 LOGICAL ACCOUNT BALANCE MODELS

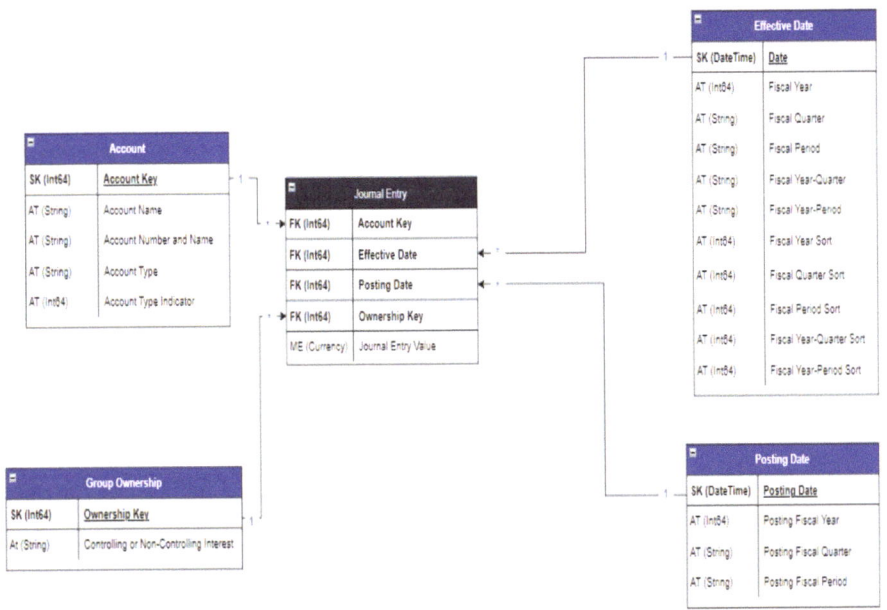

Figure 6-9. *StarSchema.co.uk Aggregation 3 by Effective Date, Account Key, Ownership Key, and Posting Date*

CHAPTER 6   LOGICAL ACCOUNT BALANCE MODELS

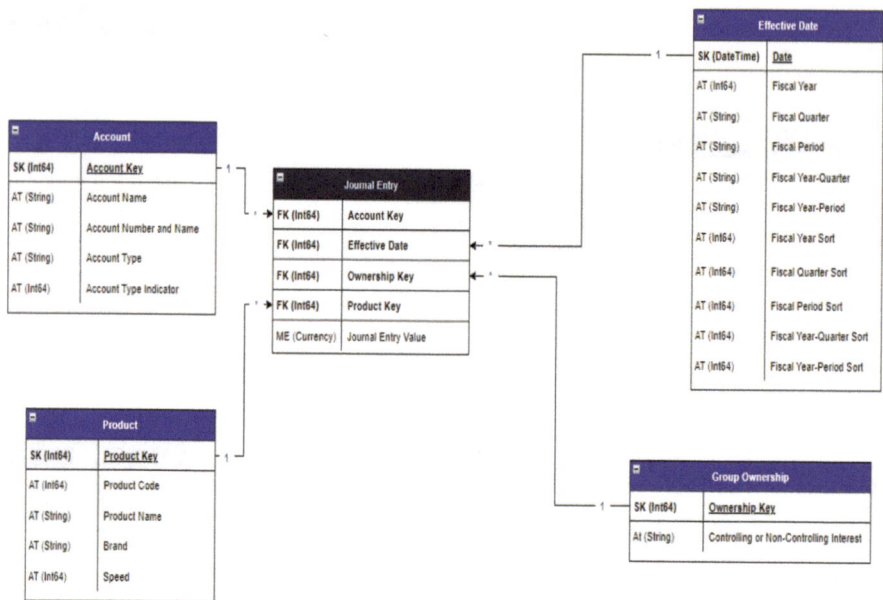

Figure 6-10. *StarSchema.co.uk Aggregation 4 by Effective Date, Account Key, Ownership Key, and Product Key*

CHAPTER 6 LOGICAL ACCOUNT BALANCE MODELS

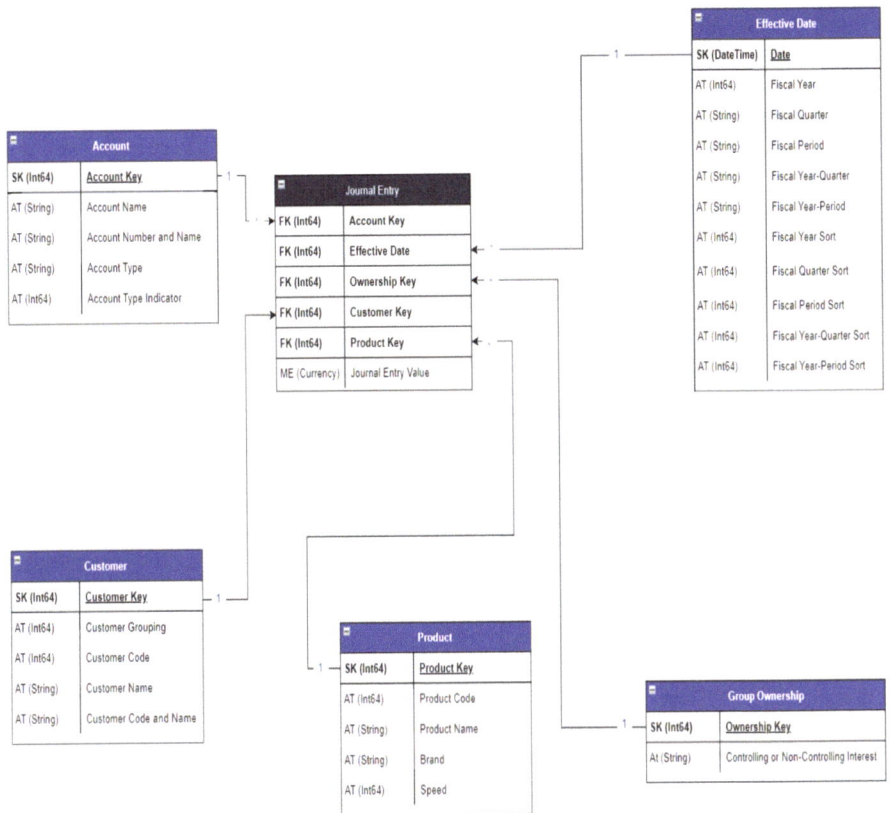

Figure 6-11. *StarSchema.co.uk Aggregation 5 by Effective Date, Account Key, Ownership Key, Customer Key, and Product Key*

CHAPTER 6   LOGICAL ACCOUNT BALANCE MODELS

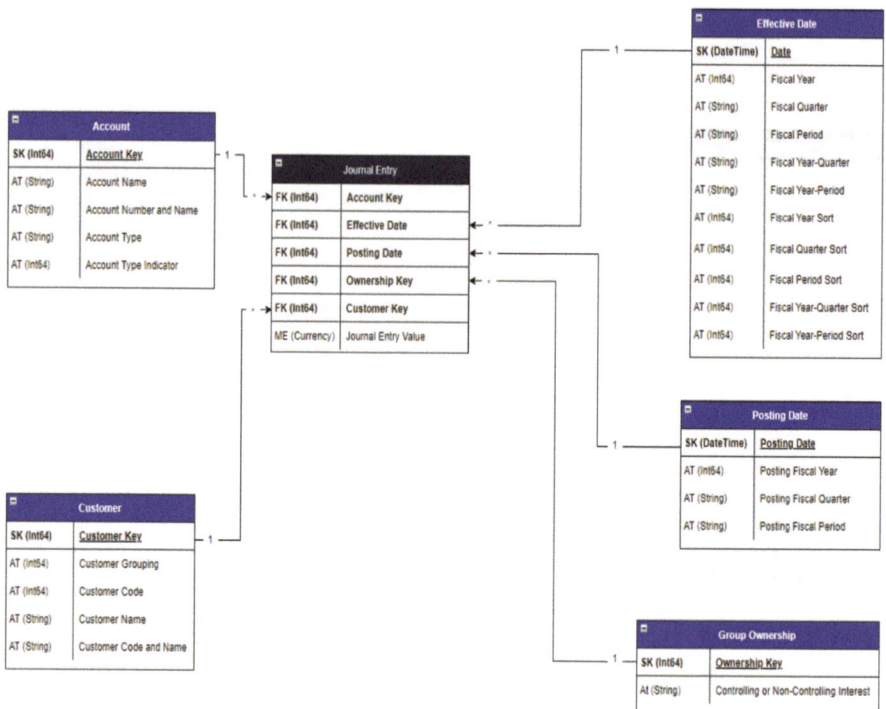

Figure 6-12. *StarSchema.co.uk Aggregation 6 by Effective Date, Account Key, Ownership Key, Posting Date, and Customer Key*

CHAPTER 6   LOGICAL ACCOUNT BALANCE MODELS

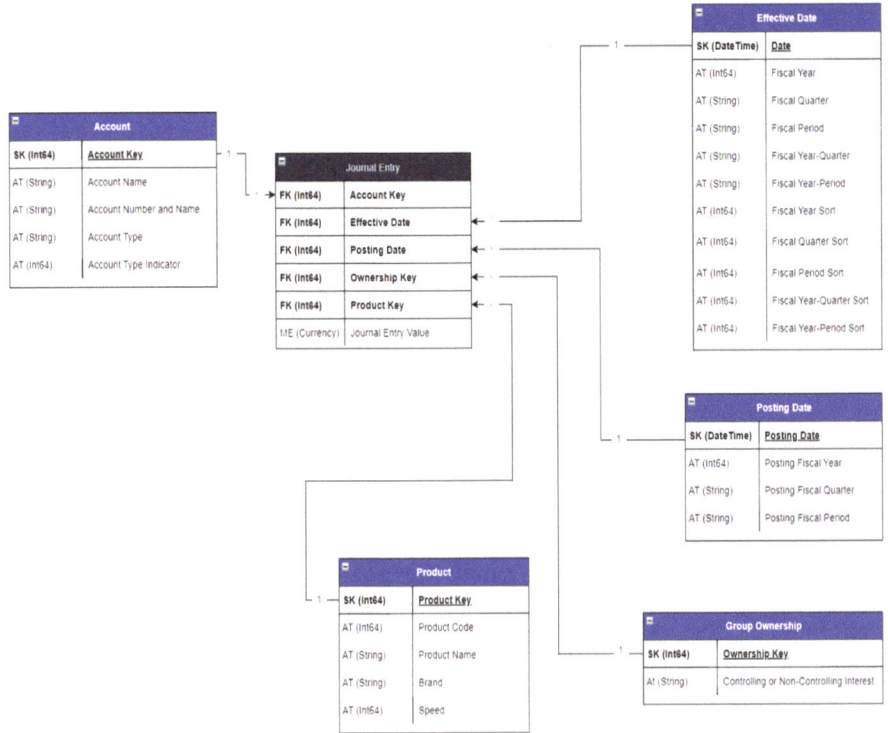

Figure 6-13. *StarSchema.co.uk Aggregation 7 by Effective Date, Account Key, Ownership Key, Posting Date, and Product Key*

CHAPTER 6   LOGICAL ACCOUNT BALANCE MODELS

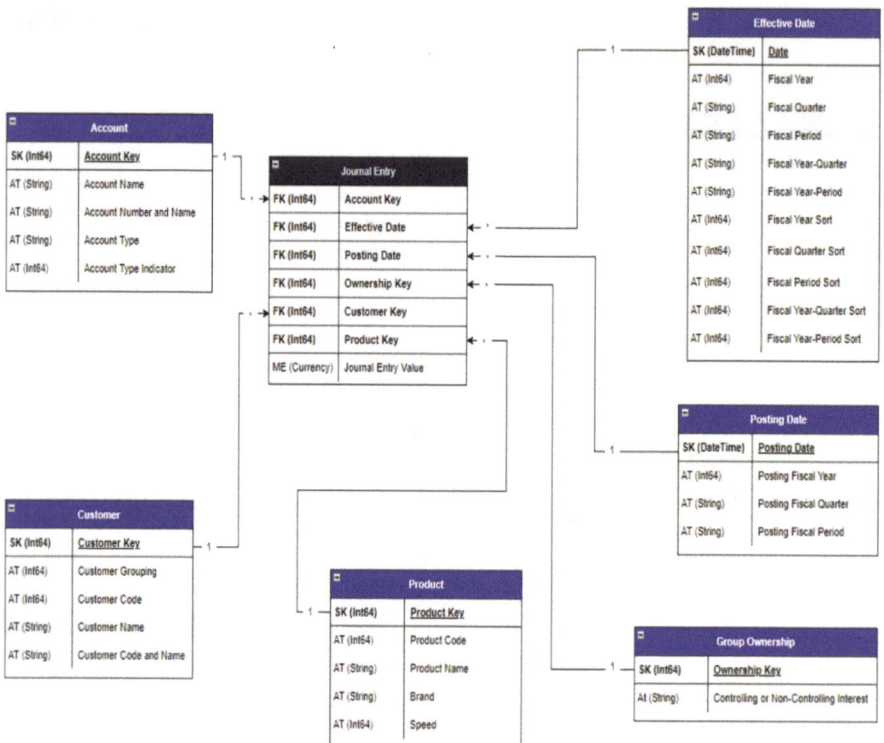

Figure 6-14. *StarSchema.co.uk Aggregation 8 by Effective Date, Account Key, Ownership Key, Posting Date, Customer Key, and Product Key*

Summary

- Logical models are used in technical discussions and as blueprints when creating physical semantic models in Power BI or Microsoft Fabric.

- Logical data models contain information about data types and field types.

CHAPTER 6 LOGICAL ACCOUNT BALANCE MODELS

- It is unknowable in advance how users will slice and dice the model; therefore, it is advisable to create aggregations for all eventualities.

- The trial balance logical model contains the minimum information required to calculate account balances; this forms the basis for Chapter 7.

- The example journal entry logical model contains a detailed solution representative of real-life scenarios; this forms the basis for Chapter 8.

CHAPTER 7

The Trial Balance Semantic Model

In the previous chapter, we learned about the trial balance logical model optimized for calculating *account balances*. We also learned, in previous chapters, that producing a trial balance is the precursory step in creating an income statement and, therefore, a model based on the trial balance is reusable.

In this chapter, we will create a trial balance semantic model based on the trial balance logical model from the previous chapter. In doing so, we will produce an identical semantic model for Tyrell Corp and Weyland Industries, except with different inputs. We will go through each of the semantic model stages covering Power Query, data modelling, and DAX. Finally, we will examine the outputs to understand how the semantic model can be used to reproduce income statements.

In this chapter, there are five sections:

1. Semantic Model Inputs
2. Power Query Transformations
3. Building the Data Model
4. DAX
5. Calculating Line-Items, Subtotals, and Subsets

CHAPTER 7   THE TRIAL BALANCE SEMANTIC MODEL

Semantic Model Inputs

In this chapter, we will follow along with the Tyrell Corp example, and thus the input tables into the model are

1. Tyrell Corp Accounts
2. Tyrell Corp Effective Date
3. Tyrell Corp Group Ownership
4. Tyrell Corp Trial Balance

If you are following along using the Weyland Industries example, replace Tyrell Corp with Weyland Industries, that is, Weyland Industries Accounts as opposed to Tyrell Corp Accounts. Regardless of the entity chosen – Tyrell Corp or Weyland Industries – the steps in the second (Power Query), third (data modelling), and fourth (DAX) sections are identical. However, the output will be different given the nature of the input-driven approach (see Chapter 3), that is, Tyrell Corp is using the accounts for Tyrell Corp as an input, whereas Weyland Industries is using the accounts for Weyland Industries as an input.

All these files can be found in the resources accompanying this book.

Power Query Transformations

This section covers the steps in transforming the data inputs into the tables present in the logical data model using Power Query in Power BI Desktop. These same transformations are required, regardless of whether Power BI Desktop or Microsoft Fabric is used.

CHAPTER 7   THE TRIAL BALANCE SEMANTIC MODEL

The Power Query transformations are covered in six stages:

- **Stage 1**: Create shared expressions
- **Stage 2**: Trial balance fact table
- **Stage 3**: Group Ownership dimension
- **Stage 4**: Account dimension
- **Stage 5**: Effective Date dimension
- **Stage 6**: Measure table

Each of these stages contains many individual steps.

Stage 1: Create Shared Expressions

Step 1: In the Power Query editor, select the **New Source** drop-down (**1**) and **Text/CSV** (**2**).

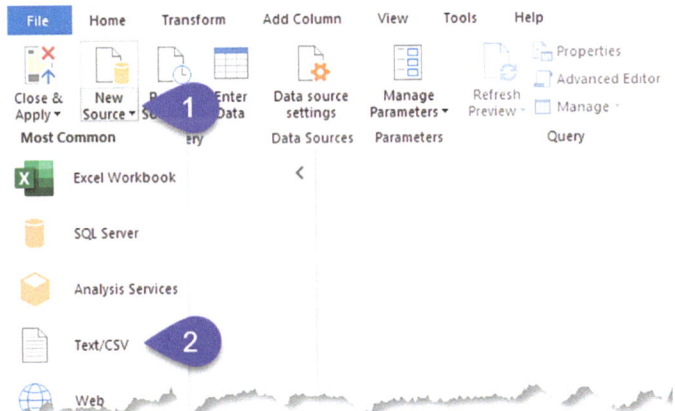

Figure 7-1. New data source

CHAPTER 7   THE TRIAL BALANCE SEMANTIC MODEL

Step 2: Select the file **Tyrell Corp Trial Balance (1)** and click **Open (2)**.

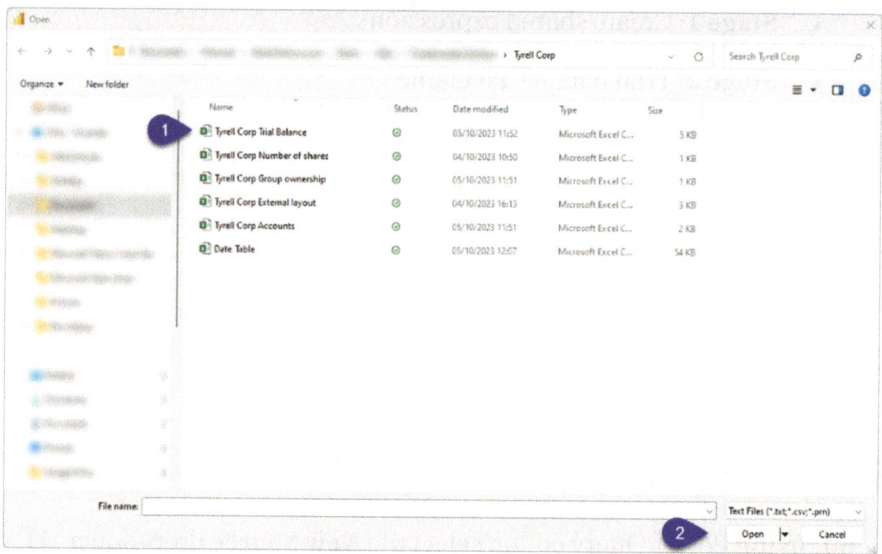

Figure 7-2. Tyrell Corp Trial Balance file

CHAPTER 7 THE TRIAL BALANCE SEMANTIC MODEL

Step 3: Click **OK (1)** to bring the table into the model.

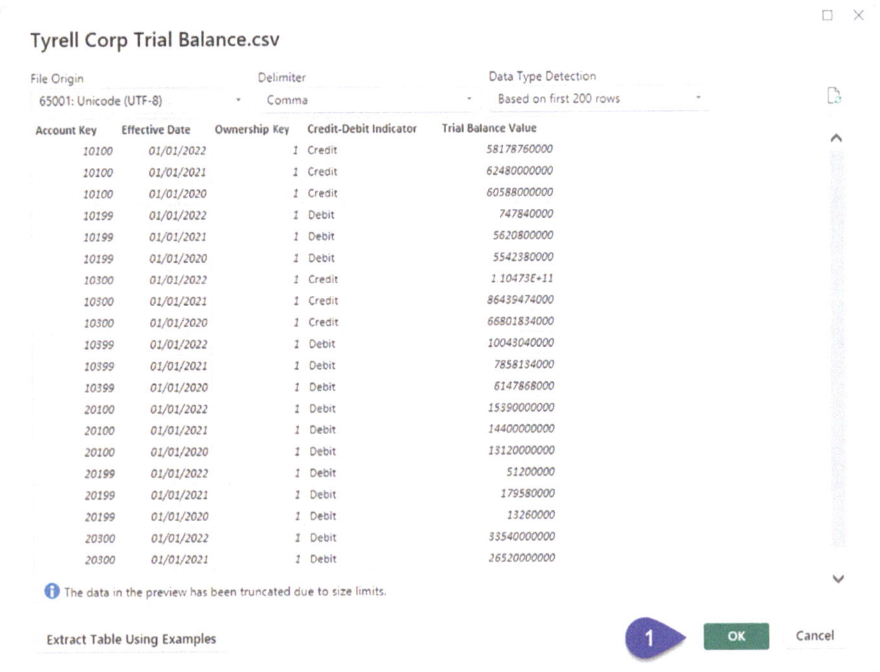

Tyrell Corp Trial Balance.csv

Account Key	Effective Date	Ownership Key	Credit-Debit Indicator	Trial Balance Value
10100	01/01/2022	1	Credit	58178760000
10100	01/01/2021	1	Credit	62480000000
10100	01/01/2020	1	Credit	60588000000
10199	01/01/2022	1	Debit	747840000
10199	01/01/2021	1	Debit	5620800000
10199	01/01/2020	1	Debit	5542380000
10300	01/01/2022	1	Credit	1.10473E+11
10300	01/01/2021	1	Credit	86439474000
10300	01/01/2020	1	Credit	66801834000
10399	01/01/2022	1	Debit	10043040000
10399	01/01/2021	1	Debit	7858134000
10399	01/01/2020	1	Debit	6147868000
20100	01/01/2022	1	Debit	15390000000
20100	01/01/2021	1	Debit	14400000000
20100	01/01/2020	1	Debit	13120000000
20199	01/01/2022	1	Debit	51200000
20199	01/01/2021	1	Debit	179580000
20199	01/01/2020	1	Debit	13260000
20300	01/01/2022	1	Debit	33540000000
20300	01/01/2021	1	Debit	26520000000

ⓘ The data in the preview has been truncated due to size limits.

Extract Table Using Examples   **(1)** **OK**   Cancel

Figure 7-3. *Tyrell Corp Trial Balance*

CHAPTER 7   THE TRIAL BALANCE SEMANTIC MODEL

Step 4: Check types as shown in Figure 7-4.

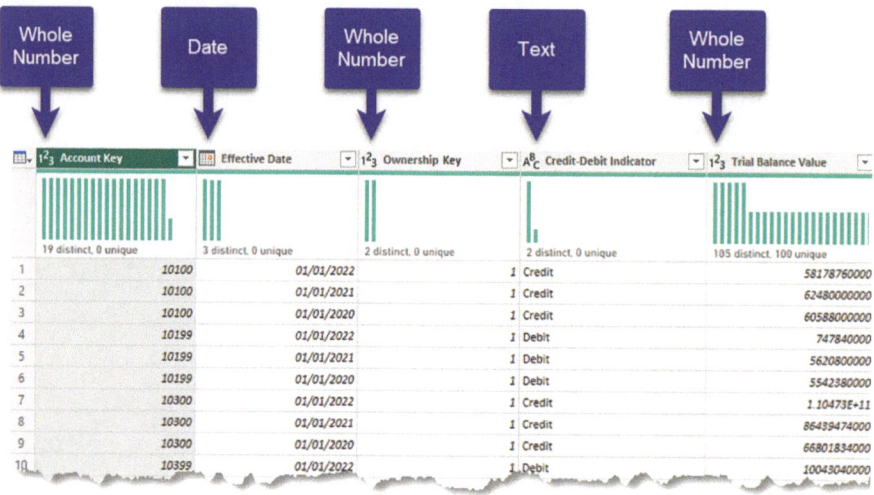

Figure 7-4. *Tyrell Corp Trial Balance data types*

Step 5: To update any data types, on the right click the column header **(1)**, select **Change Type (2)**, and select the **required data type (i.e., Whole Number) (3)**.

CHAPTER 7   THE TRIAL BALANCE SEMANTIC MODEL

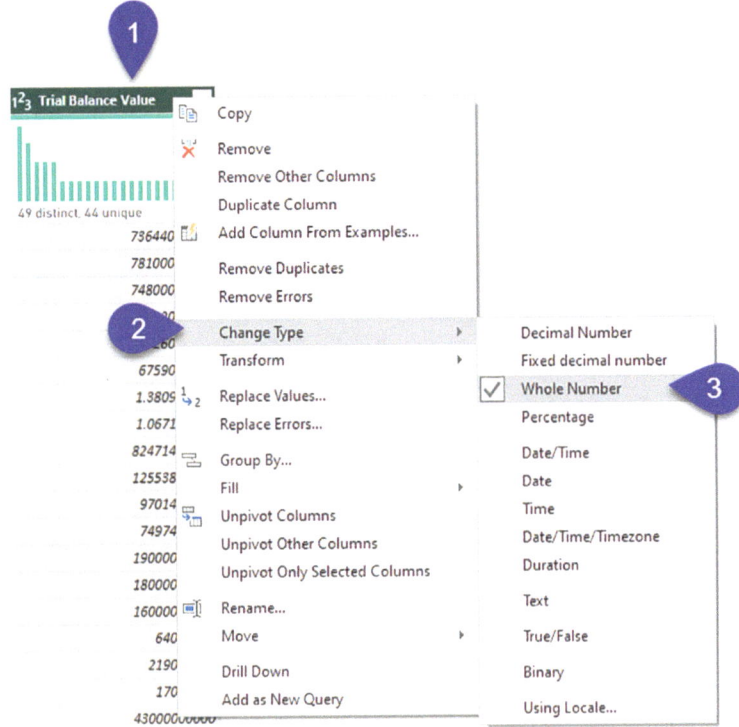

Figure 7-5. *Tyrell Corp Trial Balance change data types*

CHAPTER 7   THE TRIAL BALANCE SEMANTIC MODEL

Step 6: Repeat steps 1–4 for all files – **Tyrell Corp Group Ownership (1)**, **Tyrell Corp Accounts (2)**, and **Tyrell Corp Effective Date (3)**.

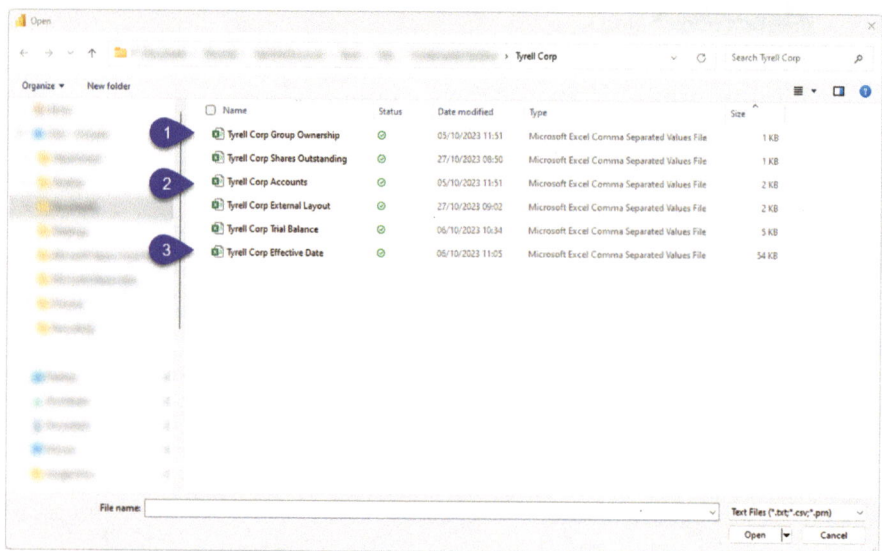

Figure 7-6.   Tyrell Corp other data files

Step 7: Check and update data types for the **Tyrell Corp Group Ownership**.

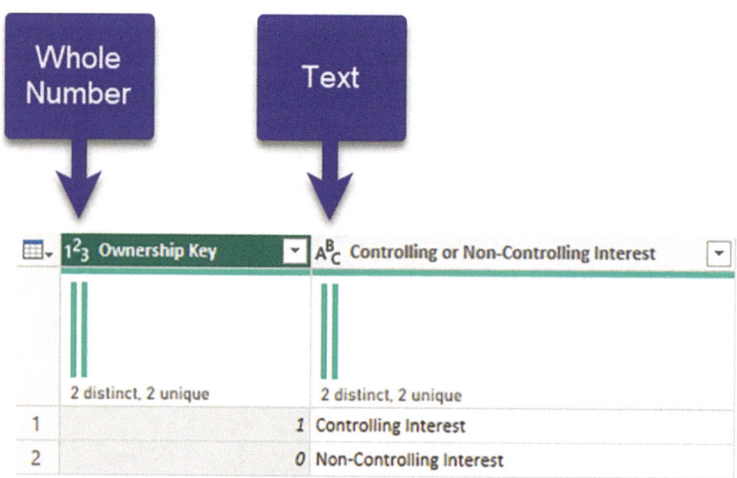

Figure 7-7.   Tyrell Corp Group Ownership data types

CHAPTER 7   THE TRIAL BALANCE SEMANTIC MODEL

Step 8: Check and update data types for the **Tyrell Corp Accounts**.

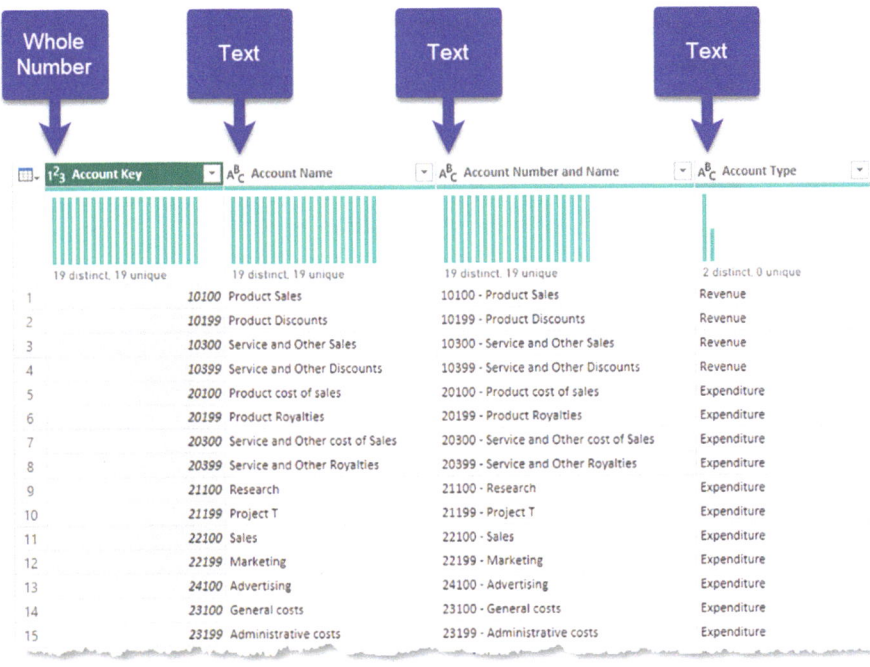

Figure 7-8. *Tyrell Corp Accounts data types*

Step 9: Check and update data types for **Tyrell Corp Effective Date**.

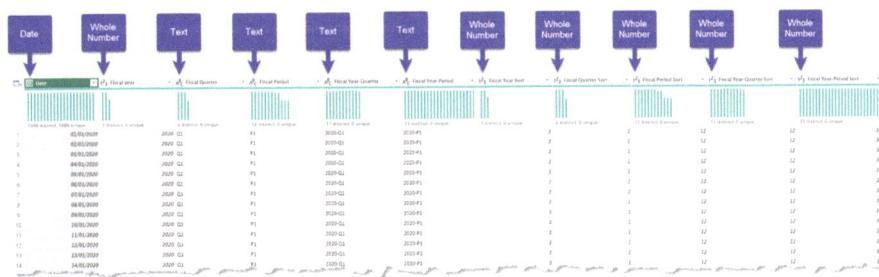

Figure 7-9. *Tyrell Corp Effective Date data types*

115

CHAPTER 7   THE TRIAL BALANCE SEMANTIC MODEL

Step 10: In the Queries pane, right-click **Tyrell Corp Trial Balance (1)** and click the selected **Enable load (2)** to disable the load (should no longer have tick to the left of *Enable load,* and *Tyrell Corp Trial Balance* should be in italics).

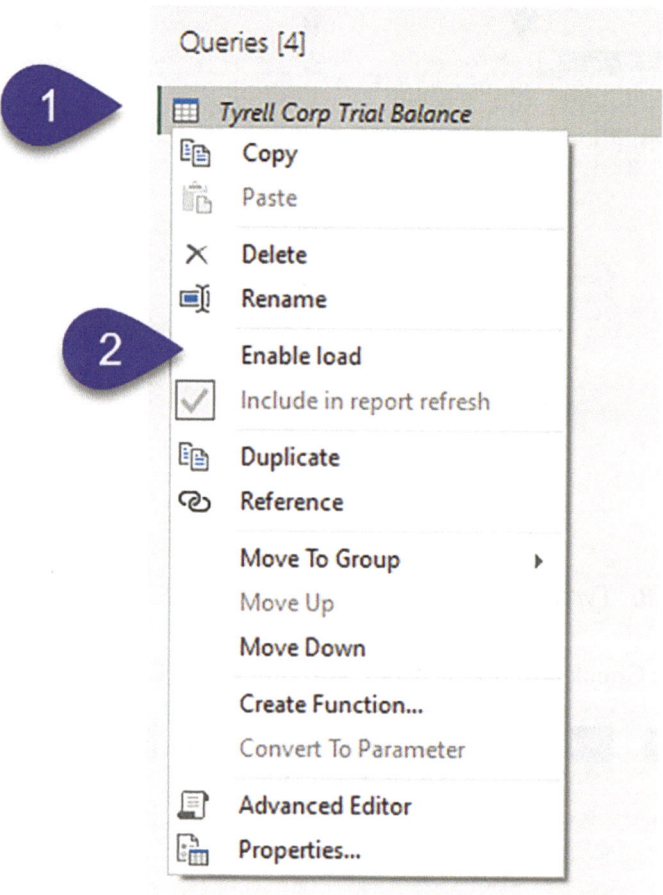

Figure 7-10. *Tyrell Corp Trial Balance disable load*

Step 11: Repeat step 10 for **Tyrell Corp Group Ownership (1)**, **Tyrell Corp Accounts (2)**, and **Tyrell Corp Effective Date (3)**.

Figure 7-11. *Tyrell Corp Group Ownership, Accounts, and Effective Date disable load*

Step 12: Select **Tyrell Corp Trial Balance (1)**, hold down shift and select **Tyrell Corp Effective Date (2)**, and right-click **Tyrell Corp Effective Date (2)** and select **Move To Group (3)** and select **New Group... (4)**.

Figure 7-12. *Tyrell Corp Trial Balance, Group Ownership, Accounts, and Effective Date move to group*

CHAPTER 7   THE TRIAL BALANCE SEMANTIC MODEL

Step 13: In the pop-up box under **Name (1)**, type *Shared Expressions* and select **OK (2)**.

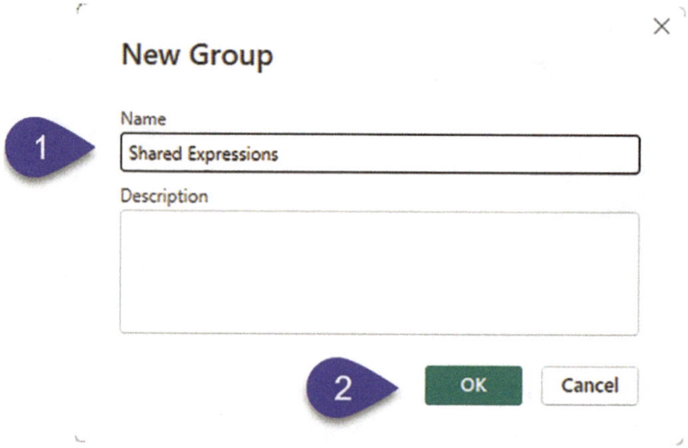

Figure 7-13. *Tyrell Corp New Group Shared Expressions*

Step 14: In the Queries pane all 4 data source should now be shown: **Tyrell Corp Trial Balance (1)**, **Tyrell Corp Group Ownership (2)**, **Tyrell Corp Accounts (3)**, and **Tyrell Corp Effective Date (4)**

Figure 7-14. *Tyrell Corp Shared Expressions Group*

CHAPTER 7   THE TRIAL BALANCE SEMANTIC MODEL

Stage 2: Trial Balance Fact Table

Step 1: In the Queries pane, right-click **Tyrell Corp Trial Balance (1)** and select **Reference (2)**.

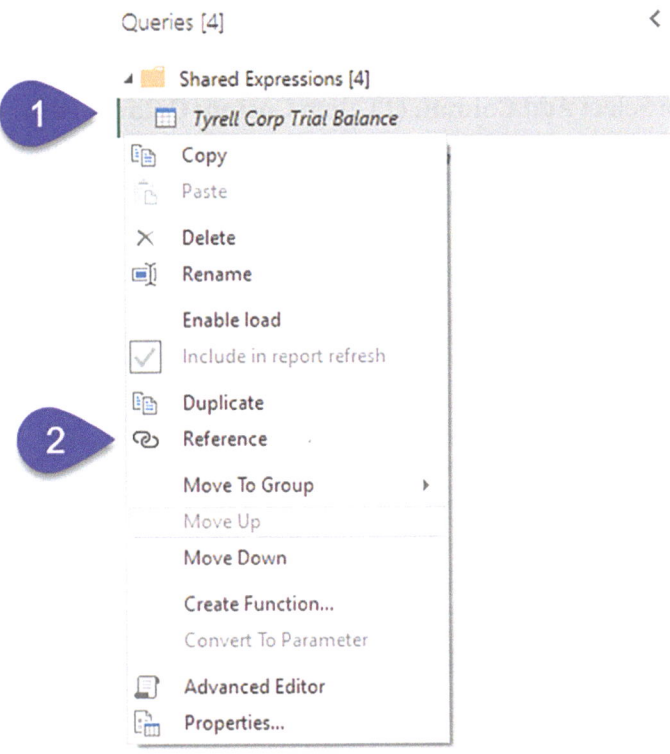

Figure 7-15. Tyrell Corp Trial Balance reference

Step 2: Select the referenced query **Tyrell Corp Trial Balance (2)** **(1)**, and in the query settings under **Name (2)**, type *Trial Balance* and press enter.

CHAPTER 7   THE TRIAL BALANCE SEMANTIC MODEL

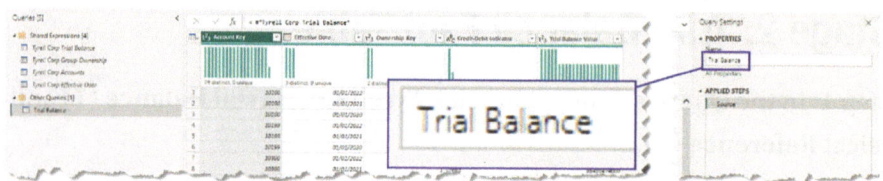

Figure 7-16. Trial Balance

Step 3: Select **Add Column (1)**, then **Custom Column (2)**, and under **New Column Name (3)**, type *Value*, and under **Custom column formula (4)**, type the formula shown, then click **OK (5)**.

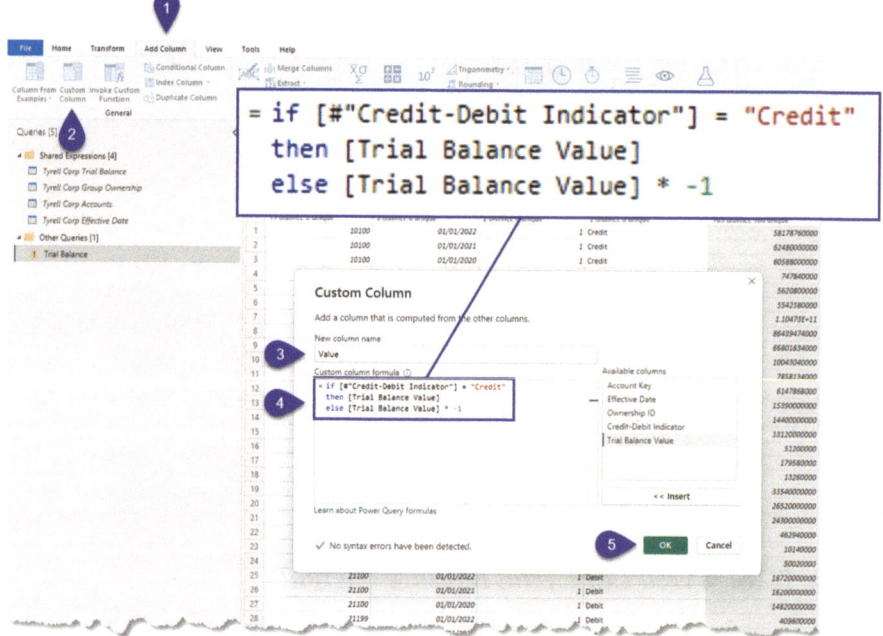

Figure 7-17. Trial Balance Value custom column

Step 4: Select **Credit-Debit Indicator (1)**, hold down *control*, then select **Trial Balance Value (2)**. Right-click *Trial Balance Value* and select **Remove Columns (1)**.

CHAPTER 7   THE TRIAL BALANCE SEMANTIC MODEL

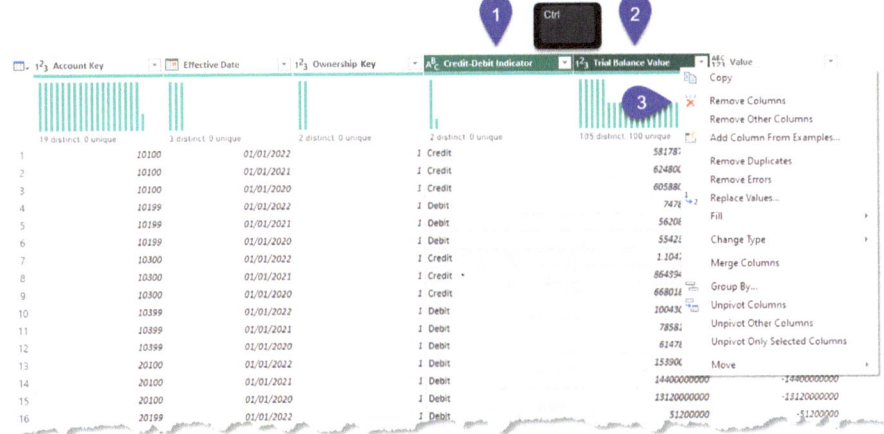

Figure 7-18. Trial Balance remove columns

Step 5: On the *value* column, select **ABC123 (1)**, then **Whole Number (2)**.

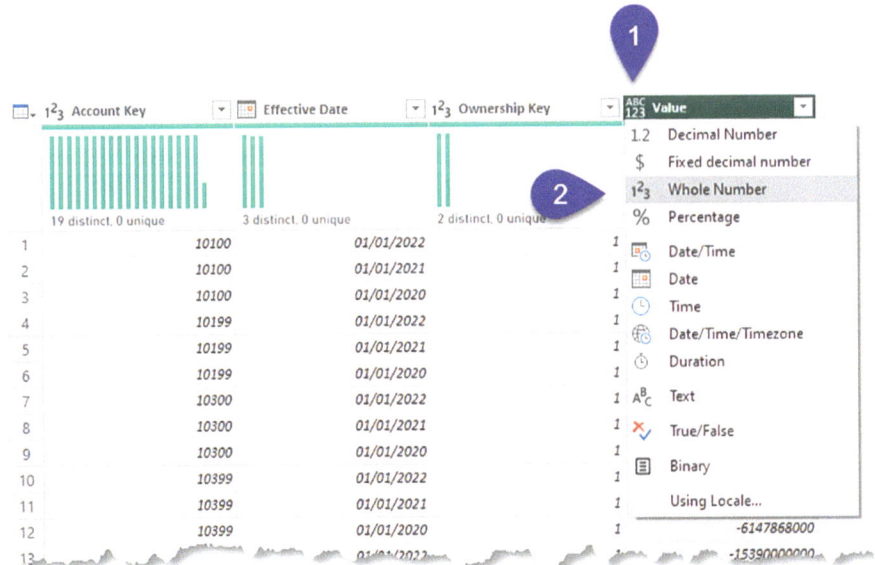

Figure 7-19. Trial Balance change data types

121

CHAPTER 7   THE TRIAL BALANCE SEMANTIC MODEL

Step 6: Right-click **Trial Balance (1)**, select **Move To Group (2)**, and select **New Group (3)**.

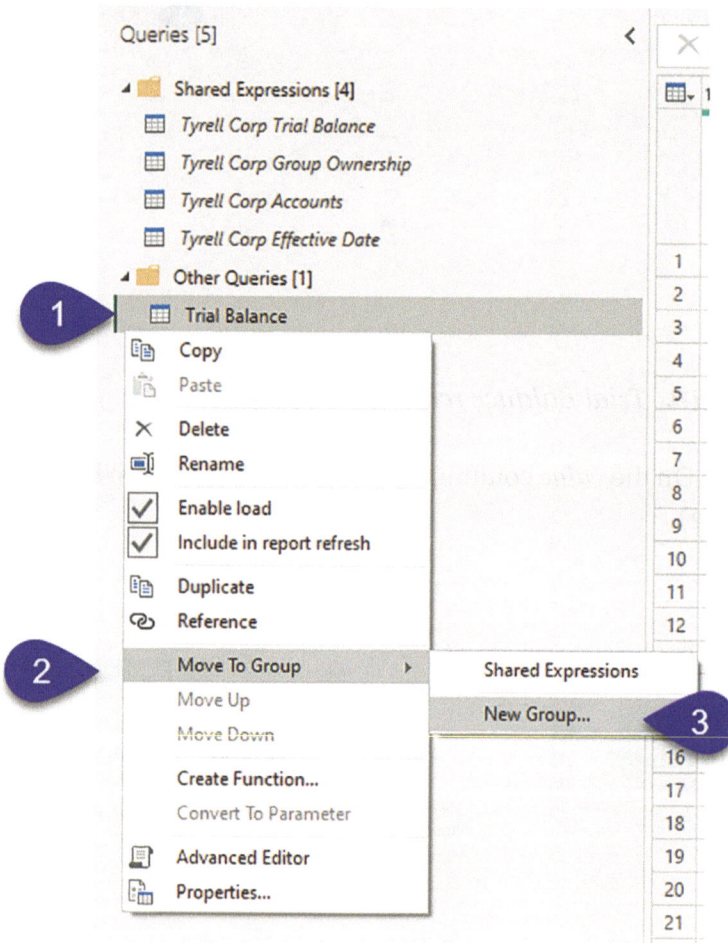

Figure 7-20. *Trial Balance new group*

CHAPTER 7   THE TRIAL BALANCE SEMANTIC MODEL

Step 7: In the pop-up box under **Name (1)**, type *Fact Tables* and select **OK (2)**.

Figure 7-21. Fact table group

Stage 3: Group Ownership Dimension

Step 1: In the Queries pane, right-click **Tyrell Corp Group Ownership (1)** and select **Reference (2)**.

123

CHAPTER 7   THE TRIAL BALANCE SEMANTIC MODEL

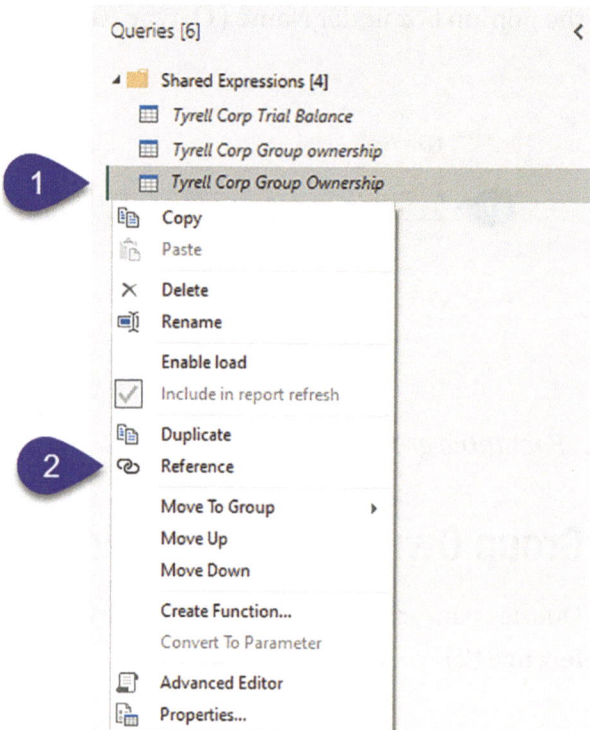

Figure 7-22. Reference Group Ownership

Step 2: Select the referenced query **Tyrell Corp Group Ownership (2) (1)**, and in the query settings under **Name (2)**, type *Group Ownership* and press enter.

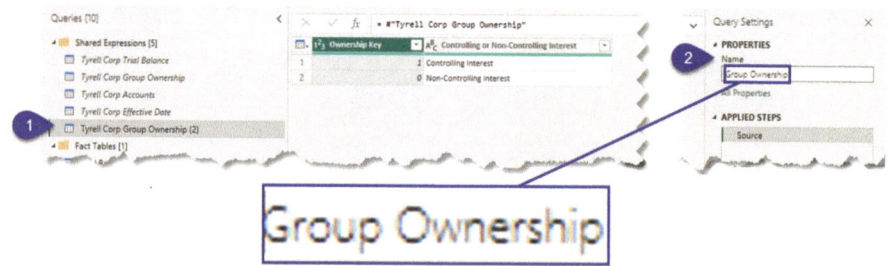

Figure 7-23. Rename to Group Ownership

124

CHAPTER 7 THE TRIAL BALANCE SEMANTIC MODEL

Step 3: Right-click **Group Ownership (1)**, select **Move To Group (2)**, and select **New Group (3)**.

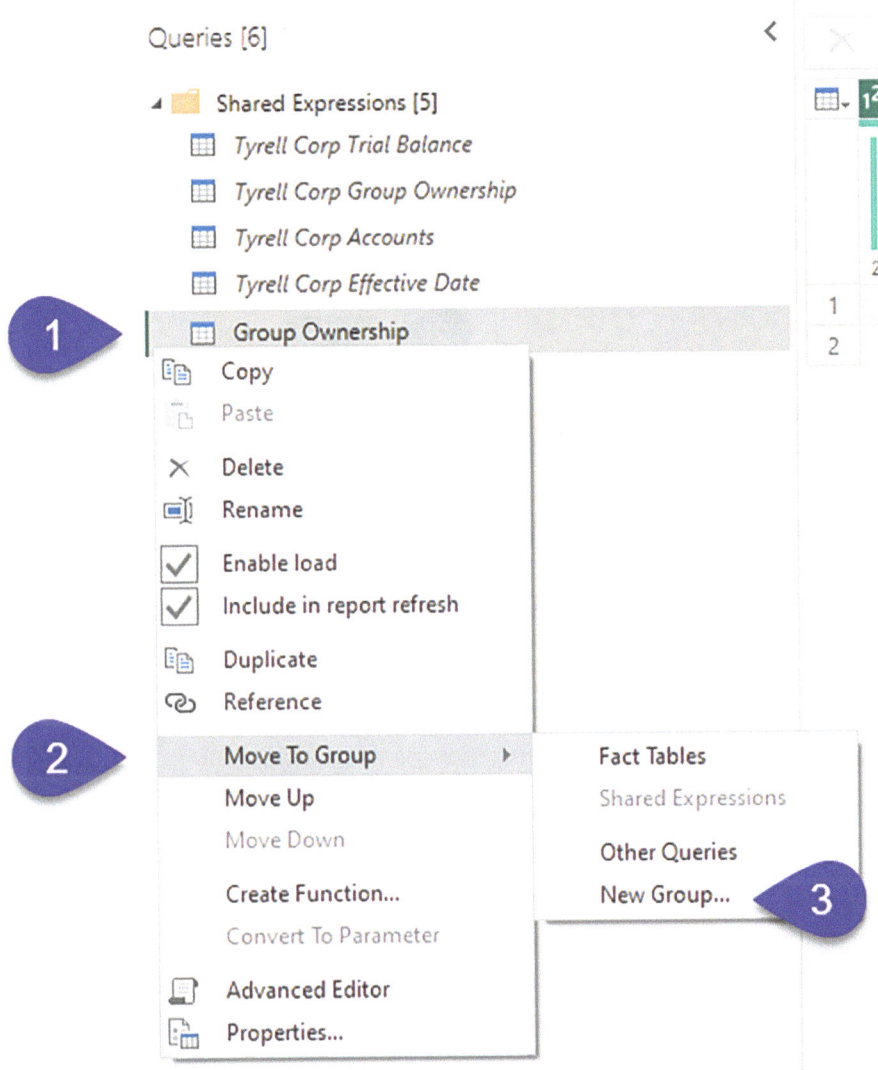

Figure 7-24. *Move Group Ownership to a new group*

125

CHAPTER 7   THE TRIAL BALANCE SEMANTIC MODEL

Step 4: In the pop-up box under **Name (1)**, type *Dimensions* and select **OK (2)**.

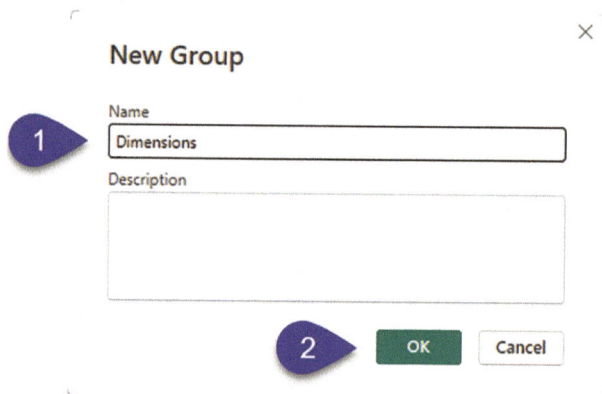

Figure 7-25. Dimensions group

Stage 4: Account Dimension

Step 1: In the Queries pane, right-click **Tyrell Corp Accounts (1)** and select **Reference (2)**.

CHAPTER 7   THE TRIAL BALANCE SEMANTIC MODEL

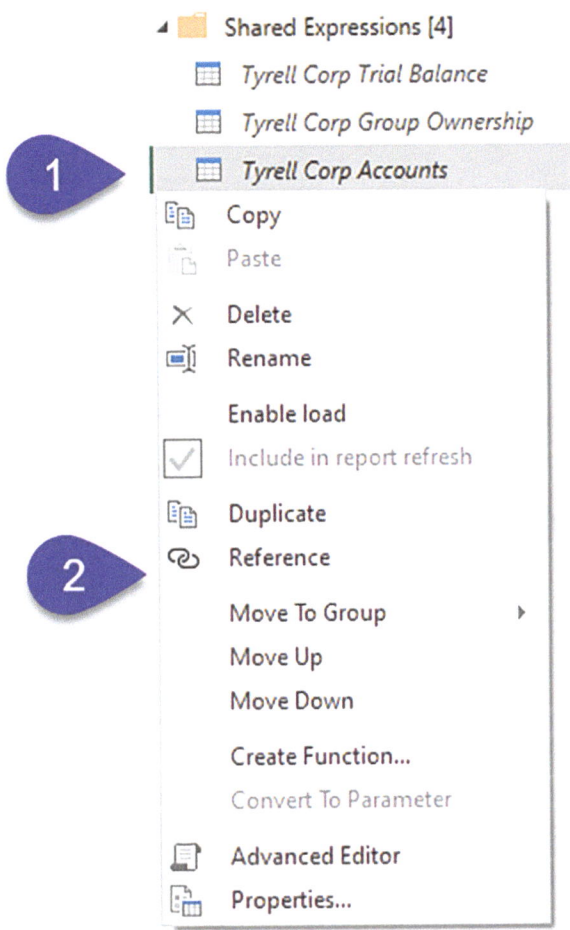

Figure 7-26. Reference Tyrell Corp Accounts

Step 2: Select the referenced query **Tyrell Corp Accounts (2) (1)**, and in the query settings under **Name (2)**, type **Account** and press enter.

CHAPTER 7   THE TRIAL BALANCE SEMANTIC MODEL

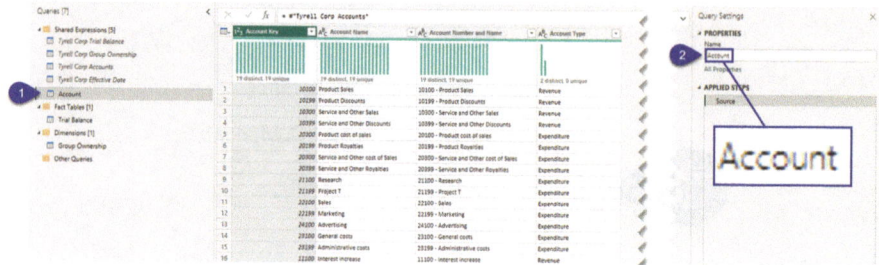

Figure 7-27. Rename Tyrell Corp Accounts

Step 3: Select **Add Column (1)**, then **Custom Column (2)**, and under **New Column Name (3)**, type *Account Type Indicator*, and under **Custom column formula (4)**, type the formula shown, then click **OK (5)**.

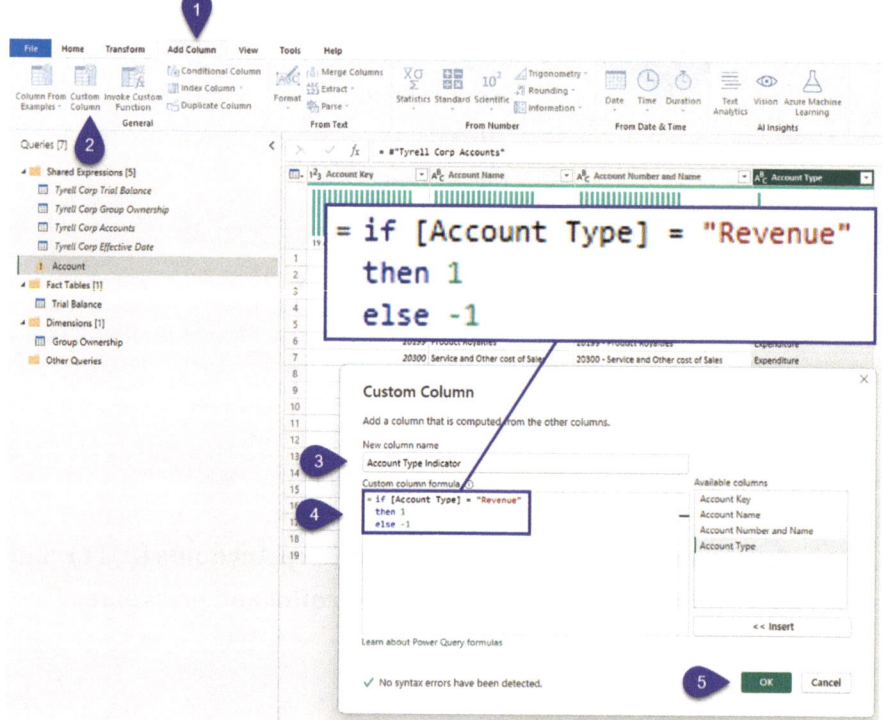

Figure 7-28. Account Type Indicator custom column

128

CHAPTER 7   THE TRIAL BALANCE SEMANTIC MODEL

Step 4: To update the data types, on the right click the **Account Type Indicator (1)**, select **Change Type (2)**, and select the **Whole Number (3)**.

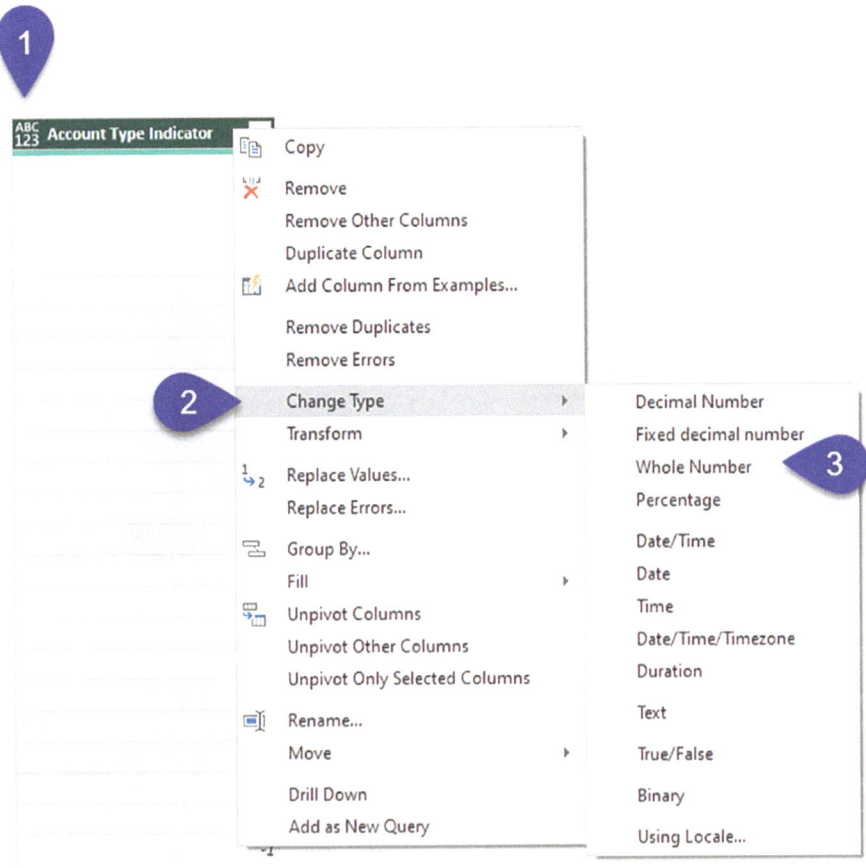

***Figure 7-29.** Change Account Type Indicator data type*

129

CHAPTER 7   THE TRIAL BALANCE SEMANTIC MODEL

Step 5: Right-click Account **(1)**, select **Move To Group (2)**, and select **Dimensions (3)**.

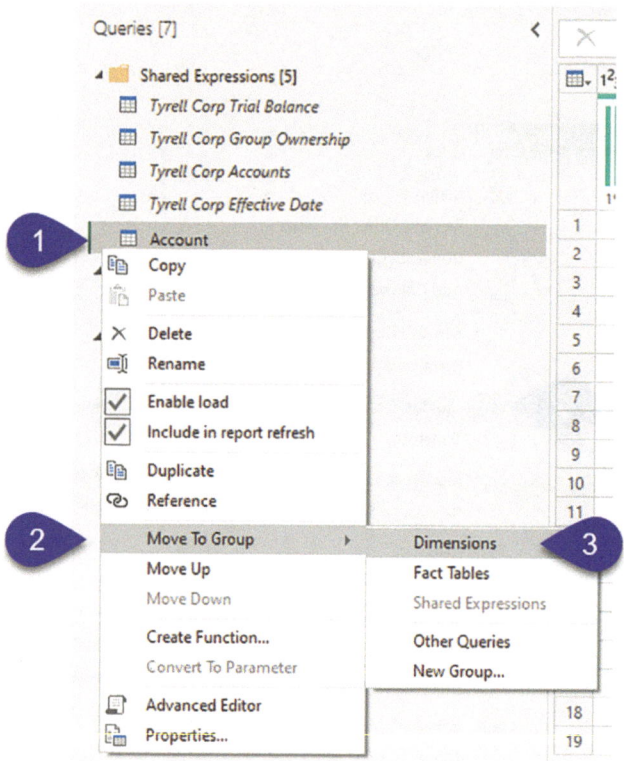

Figure 7-30. *Move account to dimension grouping*

Stage 5: Effective Date Dimension

Step 1: In the Queries pane, right-click **Tyrell Corp Effective Date (1)** and select **Reference (2)**.

CHAPTER 7   THE TRIAL BALANCE SEMANTIC MODEL

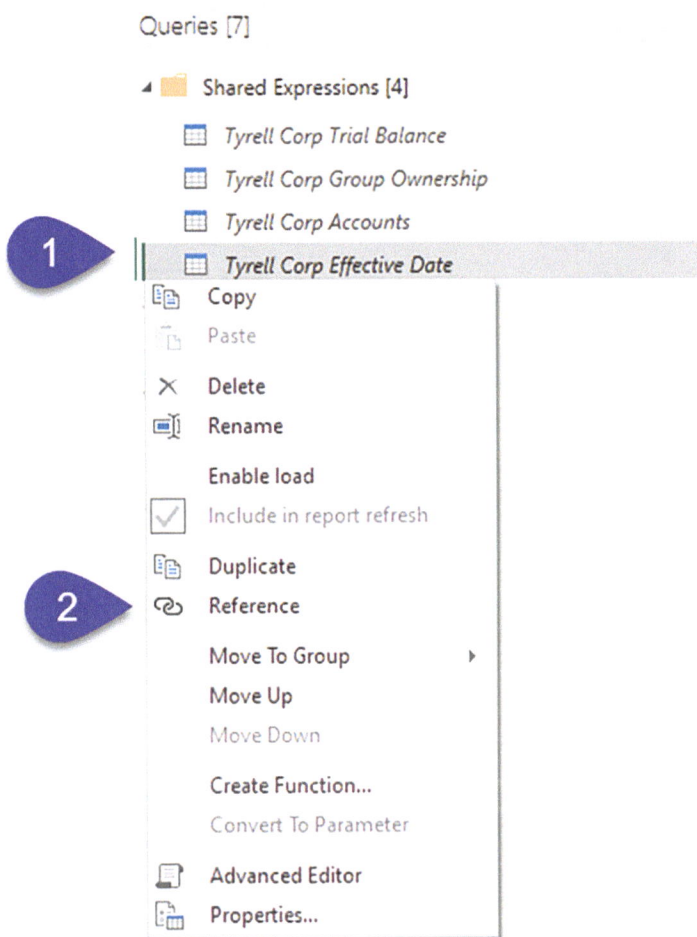

Figure 7-31. Reference effective date

CHAPTER 7   THE TRIAL BALANCE SEMANTIC MODEL

Step 2: Select the referenced query **Tyrell Corp Effective Date (2) (1)**, and in the query settings under **Name (2)**, type Effective *Date* and press enter.

Figure 7-32. Rename to effective date

Step 3: Right-click **Effective Date (1)**, select **Move To Group (2)**, and select **Dimensions (3)**.

CHAPTER 7   THE TRIAL BALANCE SEMANTIC MODEL

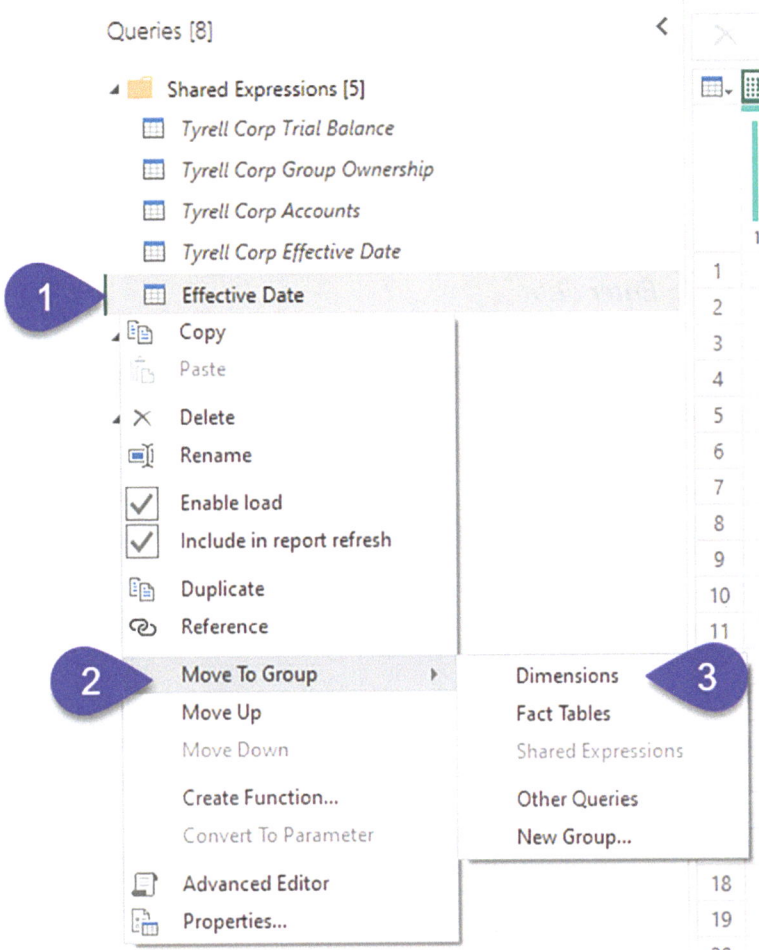

***Figure 7-33.** Move effective date to a dimension group*

Stage 6: Measure Table

Step 1: On the tab **Home (1)**, select **Enter Data (2)**.

CHAPTER 7   THE TRIAL BALANCE SEMANTIC MODEL

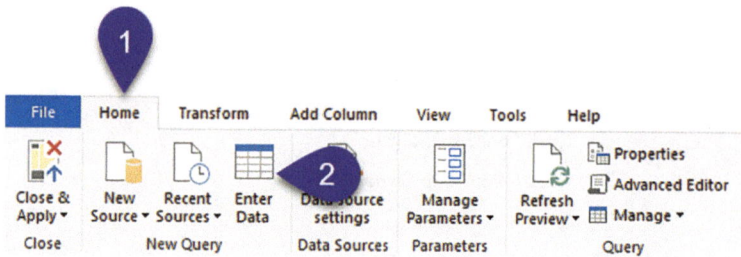

Figure 7-34. Enter data

Step 2: In the create table pop-up box, type the name **Measure (1)** select **OK (2)**.

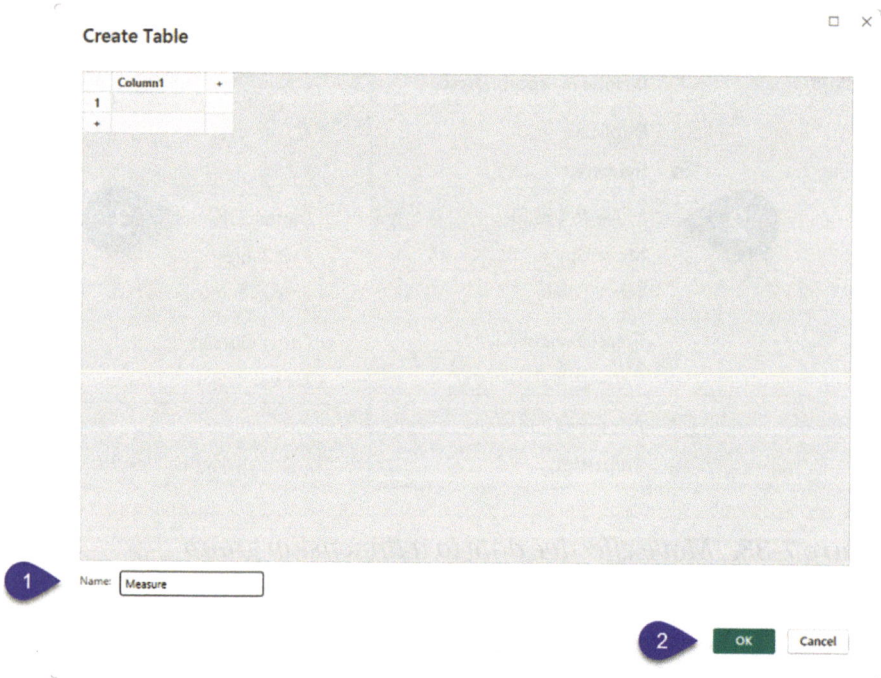

Figure 7-35. Measure table

134

CHAPTER 7   THE TRIAL BALANCE SEMANTIC MODEL

Step 3: Right-click **Measure (1)**, select **Move To Group (2)**, and select **New Group… (3)**.

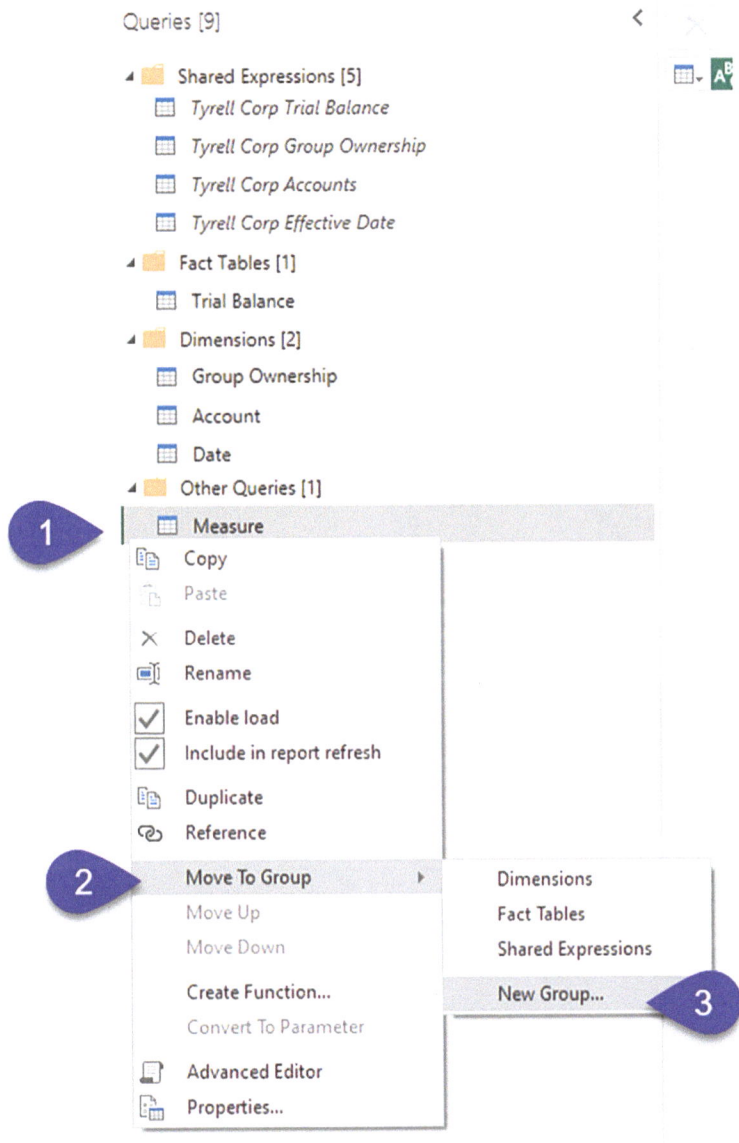

Figure 7-36. *Measure table new group*

135

CHAPTER 7   THE TRIAL BALANCE SEMANTIC MODEL

Step 4: In the pop-up box under **Name (1)**, type *Measure* and select **OK (2)**.

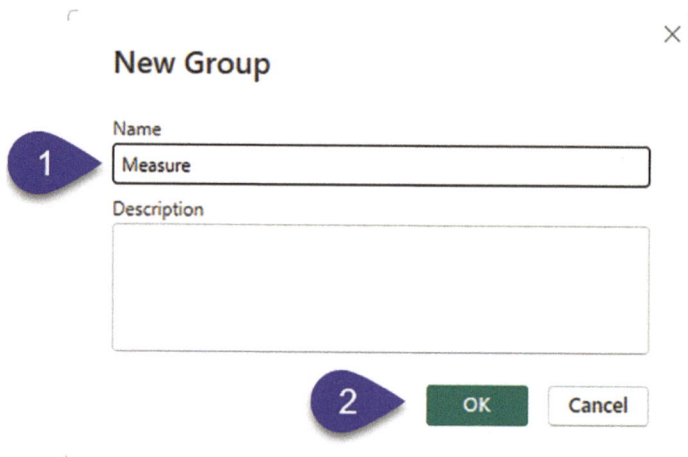

Figure 7-37. *New measure group*

Step 5: Navigate to the tab **Home (1)** and select **Close & Apply (2)**.

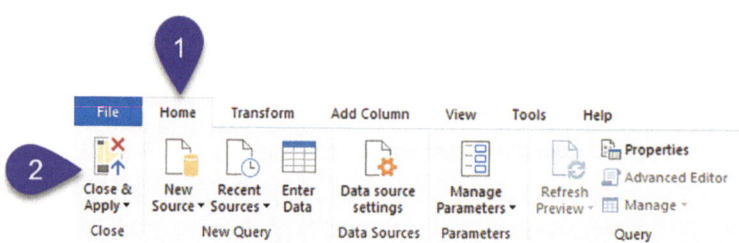

Figure 7-38. *Close and apply*

136

CHAPTER 7   THE TRIAL BALANCE SEMANTIC MODEL

Building the Data Model
Create Relationships

Step 1: Navigate to the **model view (1)**, arrange the tables as shown **(2)**, select the tab **Home (3)**, and select **Manage relationships (4)**.

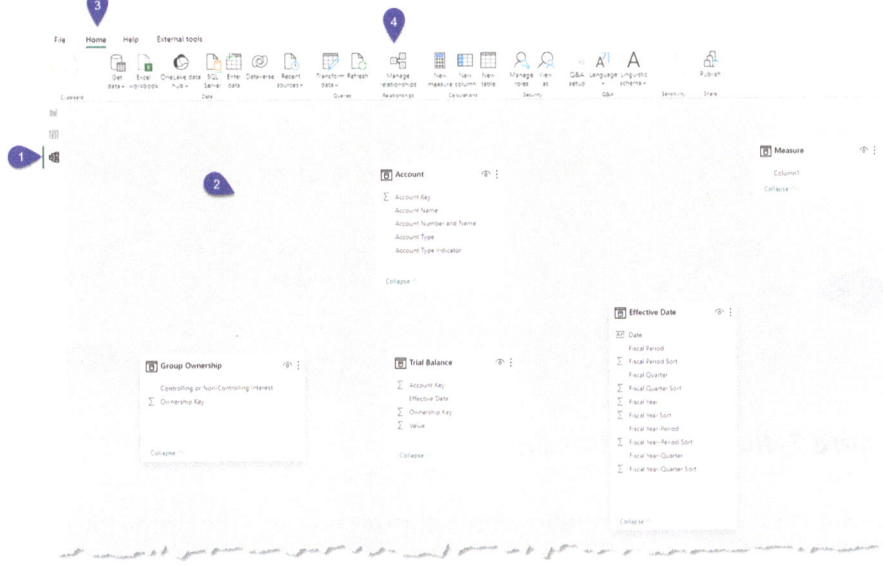

Figure 7-39. Model view no relationships

137

CHAPTER 7   THE TRIAL BALANCE SEMANTIC MODEL

Step 2: In the manage relationships pop-up box, select **New… (1)**.

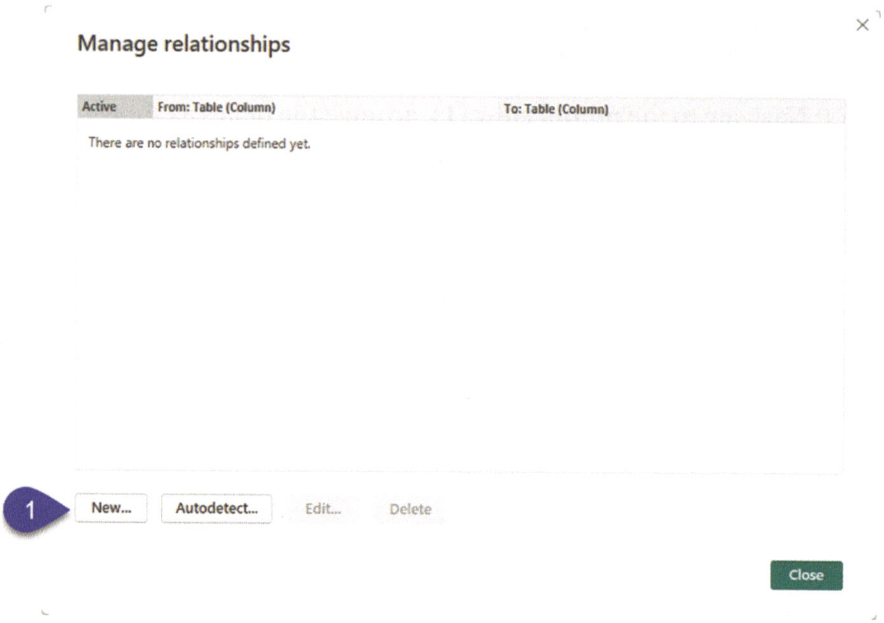

Figure 7-40. New relationship

Step 3: In the Create relationships pop-up box, use the drop-down to select the table **Account (1)**, select the column **Account Key (2)**, use the drop-down to select the table **Trial Balance (3)**, select the column **Account Key (4)**, select cardinality **One to Many (1:*) (5)**, tick **Make this relationship active** (should be done by default) **(6)**, select cross filter direction **Single (7)**, and select **OK (8)**.

CHAPTER 7   THE TRIAL BALANCE SEMANTIC MODEL

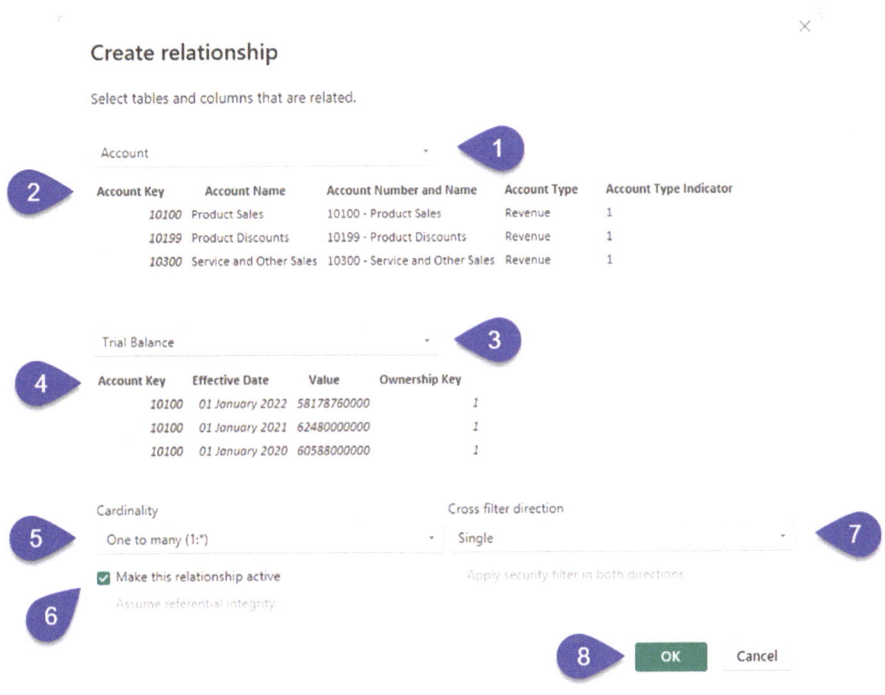

Figure 7-41. *Create relationship*

Step 4: The relationship is now created between **'Account'[Account Key] and 'Trial Balance'[Account Key] (1)**; repeat steps 2 and 3 creating relationships between **'Effective Date'[Date] and 'Trial Balance'[Effective Date] (2)** and between **'Group Ownership'[Ownership Key] and 'Trial Balance'[Ownership Key] (3)**.

CHAPTER 7 THE TRIAL BALANCE SEMANTIC MODEL

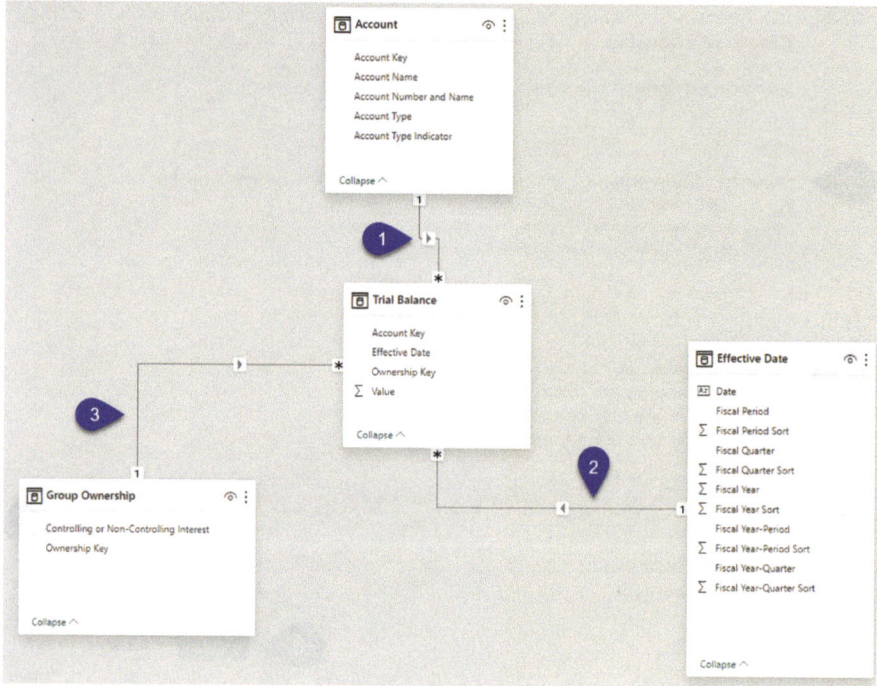

Figure 7-42. Model view with relationships

Mark As Date Table

Step 1: In the Data section, right-click **Effective Date (1)**, hover over **Mark as date table (2)**, and select **Mark as date table (3)**.

CHAPTER 7   THE TRIAL BALANCE SEMANTIC MODEL

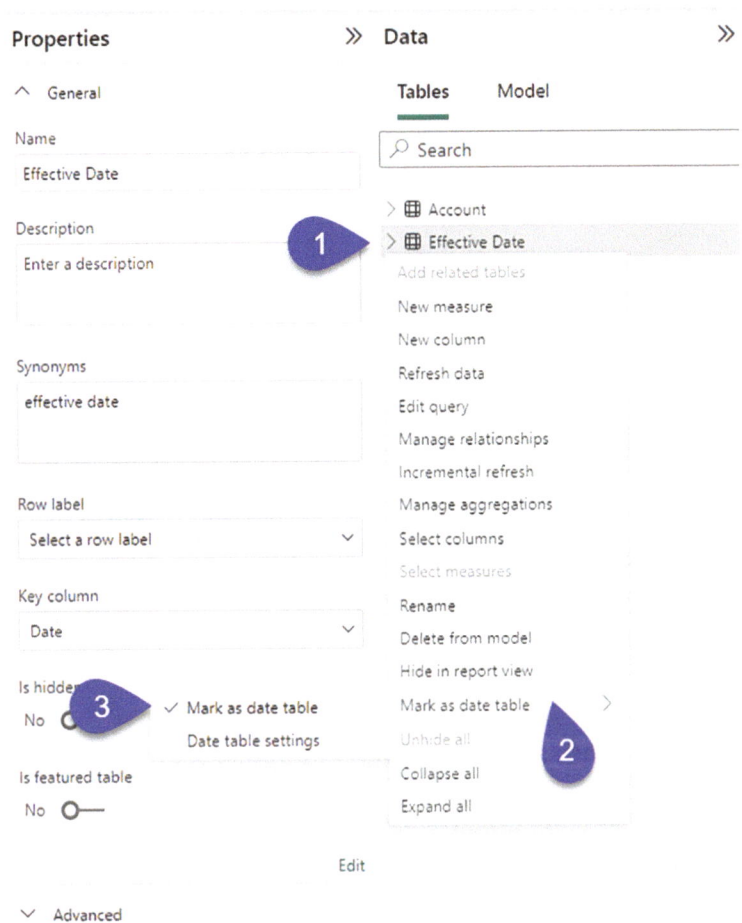

Figure 7-43. *Effective date mark as date table*

CHAPTER 7 THE TRIAL BALANCE SEMANTIC MODEL

Step 2: In the pop-up box, select **Date (1)** and click **OK (2)**.

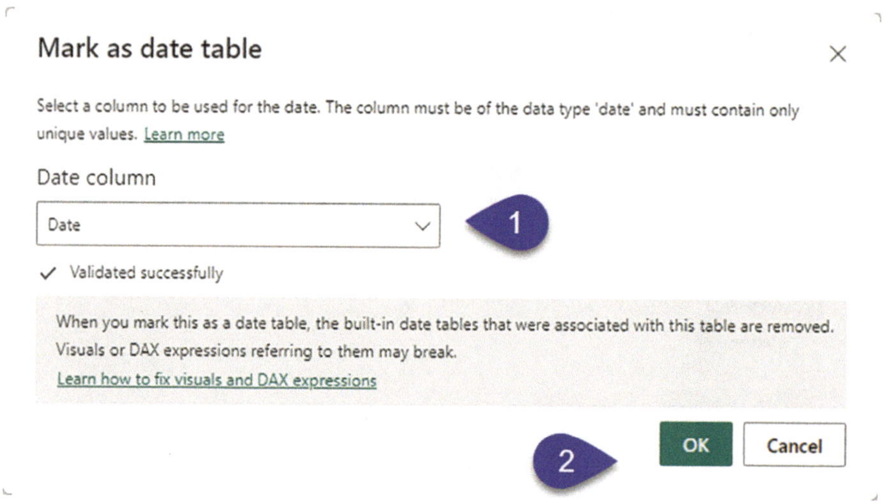

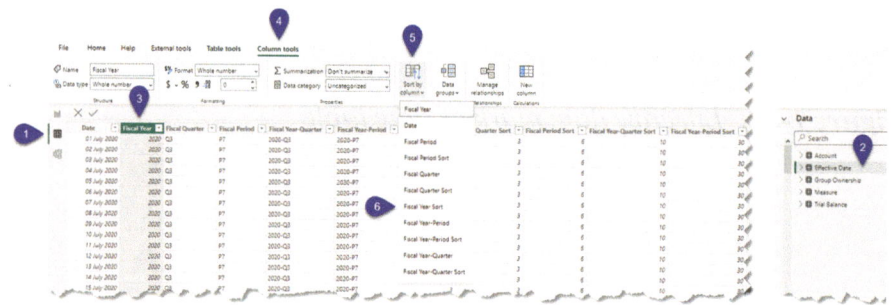

Figure 7-44. Mark date as date column

Dates Sort Order

Step 1: In the **Table View (1)**, select **Effective Date (2)**, select **Fiscal Year (3)**, select **Column tools (4)**, select **Sort by column (5)**, and select **Fiscal Year Sort (6)**.

Figure 7-45. Date sort order

Step 2: Repeat step 1 for **Fiscal Quarter (1)** by **Fiscal Quarter Sort (2)**, for **Fiscal Period (3)** by **Fiscal Period Sort (4)**, for **Fiscal Year-Quarter (5)** by **Fiscal Year-Quarter Sort (6)**, and for **Fiscal Year-Period (7)** by **Fiscal Year-Period Sort (8)**.

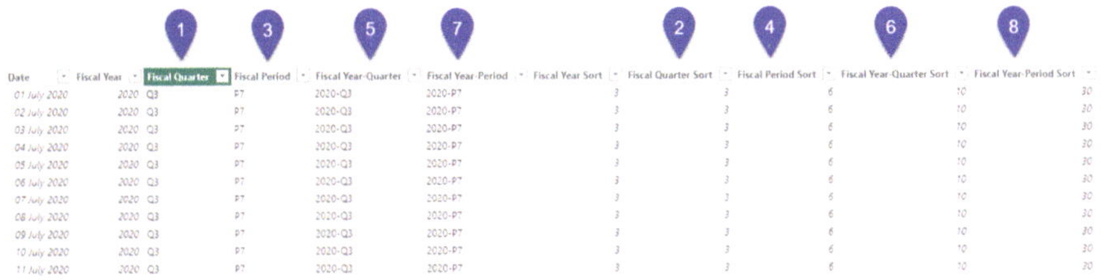

Date	Fiscal Year	Fiscal Quarter	Fiscal Period	Fiscal Year-Quarter	Fiscal Year-Period	Fiscal Year Sort	Fiscal Quarter Sort	Fiscal Period Sort	Fiscal Year-Quarter Sort	Fiscal Year-Period Sort
01 July 2020	2020	Q3	P7	2020-Q3	2020-P7	3	3	6	10	30
02 July 2020	2020	Q3	P7	2020-Q3	2020-P7	3	3	6	10	30
03 July 2020	2020	Q3	P7	2020-Q3	2020-P7	3	3	6	10	30
04 July 2020	2020	Q3	P7	2020-Q3	2020-P7	3	3	6	10	30
05 July 2020	2020	Q3	P7	2020-Q3	2020-P7	3	3	6	10	30
06 July 2020	2020	Q3	P7	2020-Q3	2020-P7	3	3	6	10	30
07 July 2020	2020	Q3	P7	2020-Q3	2020-P7	3	3	6	10	30
08 July 2020	2020	Q3	P7	2020-Q3	2020-P7	3	3	6	10	30
09 July 2020	2020	Q3	P7	2020-Q3	2020-P7	3	3	6	10	30
10 July 2020	2020	Q3	P7	2020-Q3	2020-P7	3	3	6	10	30
11 July 2020	2020	Q3	P7	2020-Q3	2020-P7	3	3	6	10	30

Figure 7-46. *Date sort all fields*

DAX

The DAX in this section produces the calculation for *net credit less debit* and *net debit less credit* as outlined in Chapter 5.

Calculating *net credit less debit* and *net debit less credit* is broken down into three steps:

- **Step 01: Sum**: Calculates the sum of the values in the trial balance fact table. The transformations made mean this calculation is effectively credit less debit.
- **Step 02: Account Type Indicator**: Calculates the max and min account type indicators.
- **Step 03: Line-items**: Calculates individual account balances

When producing the DAX, each calculation should be added to the measure table and placed in a folder named after the step to keep it organized (see Chapter 14).

CHAPTER 7 THE TRIAL BALANCE SEMANTIC MODEL

Step 01: Sum

As per Chapter 5, the measure for summing values in the trial balance fact table is

```
Actuals Sum= SUM( 'Trial Balance'[Value] )
```

Step 02: Account Type Indicator

As per Chapter 5, the measure for the maximum account type indicator is

```
Actuals Net Credit Less Debit Indicator=
    Max ( 'Account'[Account Type Indicator] )
```

As per Chapter 5, the measure for the minimum account type indicator is

```
Actuals Net Debit Less Credit Indicator=
    Min ( 'Account'[Account Type Indicator] )
```

Step 03: Line-items

For net credit less debit, the actual sum is multiplied by the net credit less debit indicator:

```
[Actuals Net Credit Less Debit]=
      [Actuals Sum] × [Actuals Net Credit Less Debit
      Indicator]
```

For net debit less credit, the actual sum is multiplied by the net debit less credit indicator:

```
[Actuals Net Debit Less Credit]=
      [Actuals Sum] × [Actuals Net Debit Less Credit Indicator]
```

CHAPTER 7   THE TRIAL BALANCE SEMANTIC MODEL

Calculating Line-Items, Subtotals, and Subsets

This semantic model can be used to calculate line-items, subtotals, and subsets. For instance, Figure 7-47 shows that the total value of accounts pertaining to gross margin from the model matches the gross margin on Tyrell Corps external income statement which is displayed in millions.

	2022	2021	2020	Account Number and Name	2022	2021	2020
Revenue:	$						
Product		63,968	62,475	62,665	10100 - Product Sales	64,806,720,000	68,728,000,000	68,816,000,000
Service and other		115,746	90,223	69,876	10199 - Product Discounts	-839,040,000	-6,253,140,000	-6,150,690,000
Total revenue		179,714	152,698	132,541	10300 - Service and Other Sales	127,044,456,000	99,245,322,000	76,698,402,000
Cost of revenue:					10399 - Service and Other Discounts	-11,298,420,000	-9,022,302,000	-6,822,634,000
Product		17,729	16,401	15,055	20100 - Product cost of sales	17,670,000,000	16,200,000,000	15,040,000,000
Service and other		37,490	30,272	27,057	20199 - Product Royalties	58,880,000	201,480,000	14,960,000
Total cost of revenue		55,219	46,673	42,112	20300 - Service and Other cost of Sales	36,980,000,000	30,260,000,000	27,000,000,000
Gross margin	①	124,495	106,025	90,429	20399 - Service and Other Royalties	509,820,000	11,570,000	57,340,000
Research and development		22,051	18,400	16,720	Total	② 124,495,016,000	106,024,830,000	90,428,778,000
Project T		451						
Sales and marketing		19,233	18,009	17,290				
General and administrative		5,360	4,701	4,750				
Operating income		77,852	64,915	51,869				
Other income, net		300	913	70				
Income before income taxes		78,152	65,828	51,739				
Provision for income taxes		9,680	9,003	7,990				
Net income		68,472	56,825	43,749				
Non-controlling interest		9,445	5,661	6,829				
Controlling interest	$	59,027	51,165	36,920				
Earnings per share:								
Basic		$10.10	$8.47	$6.22				
Diluted		$9.66	$8.62	$6.16				
Weighted average shares outstanding:								
Basic		5,847	6,038	5,936				
Diluted		6,107	5,934	5,993				

***Figure 7-47.** Power BI Matrix Tyrell Corp vs. external layout*

Calculations can also be combined with logic outside the model to recreate income statements in their entirety. For instance, Figure 7-48 shows how Excel is being used retrieving line-items from the semantic model using cube formulas and subtotals are created using sum formulas.

145

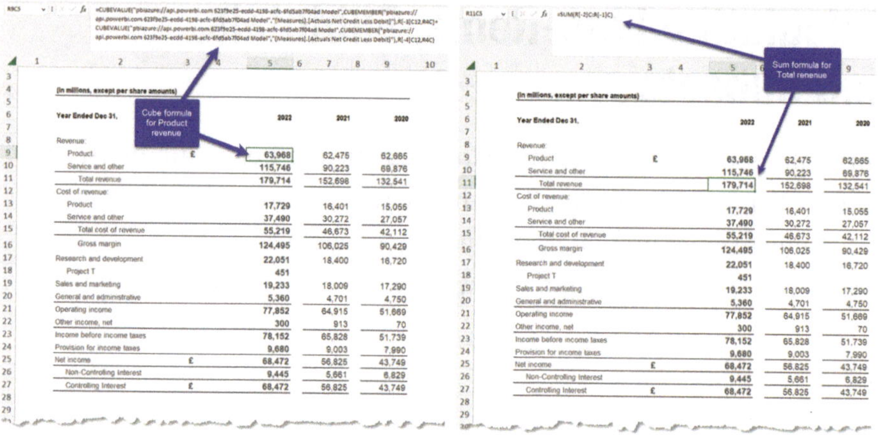

CHAPTER 7   THE TRIAL BALANCE SEMANTIC MODEL

Figure 7-48. *Tyrell Corp Excel cube formulas and regular formulas*

Summary

- An input-driven approach based on the trial balance can be used to reproduce the income statement.

- Part of the logic resides outside the semantic model, that is, adding line-items together in Excel to calculate subtotals.

- Given the approach is based on the trial balance, it is reusable across entities as demonstrated by an identical semantic model (except the inputs) for Tyrell Corp and Weyland Industries.

CHAPTER 8

A Journal Entry Semantic Model

In the previous chapter, we learned how to create a trial balance semantic model. This input-driven solution enables end users to reproduce income statements when logic in the semantic model is combined with additional logic outside the model.

In this chapter, we will create a journal entry semantic model based on the StarSchema.co.uk logical models in Chapter 6. In doing so, we will go through the Power BI stages covering Power Query, data modelling, and DAX.

In this chapter, there are four sections:

1. Semantic Model Inputs
2. Power Query Transformations
3. Building the Data Model
4. DAX

CHAPTER 8   A JOURNAL ENTRY SEMANTIC MODEL

Semantic Model Inputs

The input tables into the model are

1. StarSchema.co.uk Accounts
2. StarSchema.co.uk Effective Date
3. StarSchema.co.uk Posting Date
4. StarSchema.co.uk Group Ownership
5. StarSchema.co.uk Customer
6. StarSchema.co.uk Product
7. StarSchema.co.uk Journal Entry
8. StarSchema.co.uk Journal Entry Aggregation 1
9. StarSchema.co.uk Journal Entry Aggregation 2
10. StarSchema.co.uk Journal Entry Aggregation 3
11. StarSchema.co.uk Journal Entry Aggregation 4
12. StarSchema.co.uk Journal Entry Aggregation 5
13. StarSchema.co.uk Journal Entry Aggregation 6
14. StarSchema.co.uk Journal Entry Aggregation 7
15. StarSchema.co.uk Journal Entry Aggregation 8

Each of these 15 files can be found in the resources accompanying this book.

Power Query Transformations

This section covers using Power Query to transform data inputs into the tables required in the data model. The same transformations are required regardless of whether you are using Power BI Desktop or Microsoft Fabric.

The Power Query transformations are covered in nine stages:

- **Stage 1**: Create shared expressions
- **Stage 2**: Journal entry fact tables
- **Stage 3**: Group Ownership dimension
- **Stage 4**: Account dimension
- **Stage 5**: Effective Date dimension
- **Stage 6**: Customer dimension
- **Stage 7**: Product dimension
- **Stage 8**: Posting Date dimension
- **Stage 9**: Measure table

Each of these stages contains many individual steps.

Stage 1: Create Shared Expressions

Step 1: In the Power Query editor, select the **New Source** drop-down (**1**) and **Text/CSV** (**2**).

CHAPTER 8   A JOURNAL ENTRY SEMANTIC MODEL

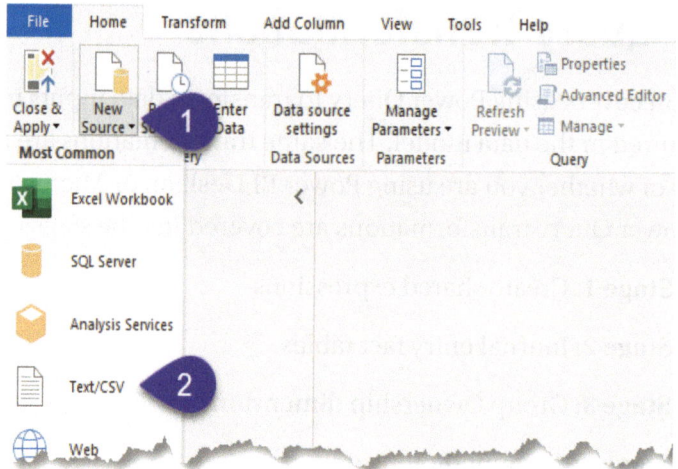

Figure 8-1. Import Text/CSV files

Step 2: Select the file **StarSchema.co.uk Journal Entry (1)** and click **Open (2)**.

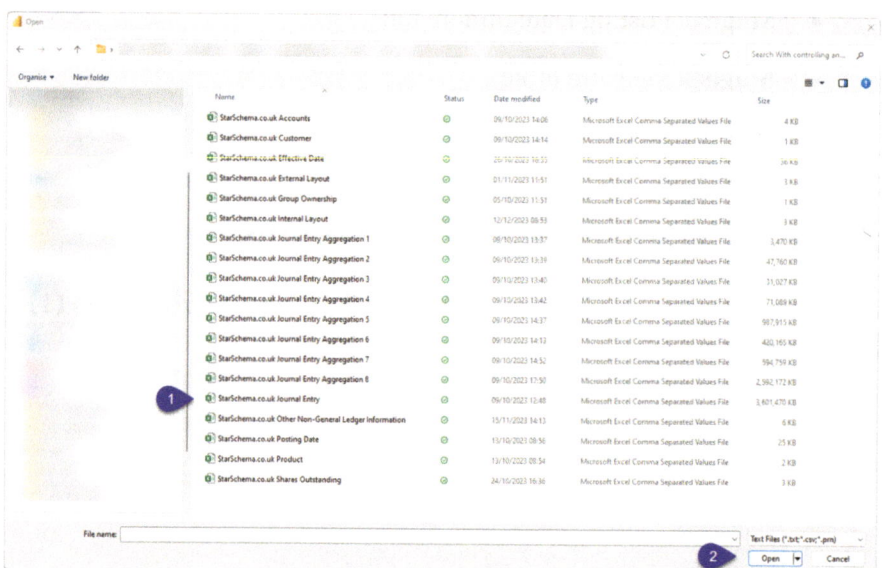

Figure 8-2. Import StarSchema.co.uk Journal Entry

CHAPTER 8   A JOURNAL ENTRY SEMANTIC MODEL

Step 3: Click **OK (1)** to bring the table into the model.

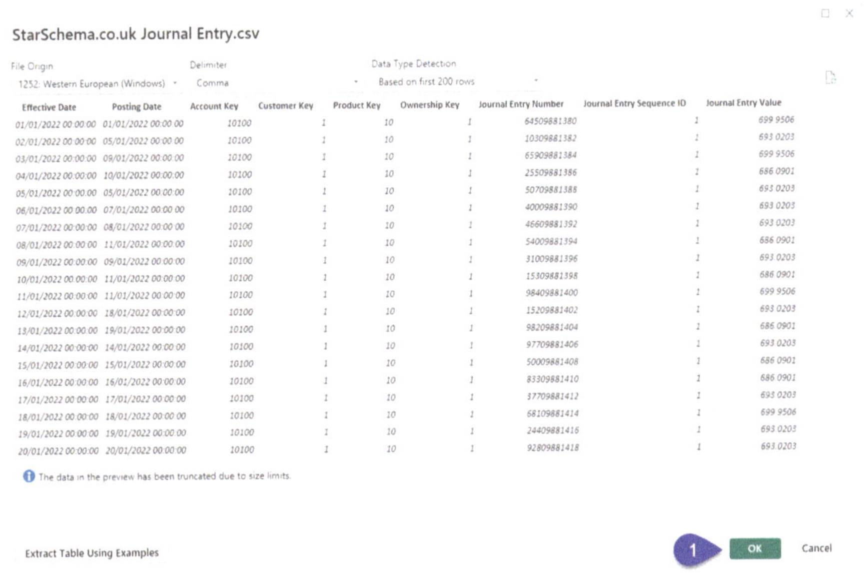

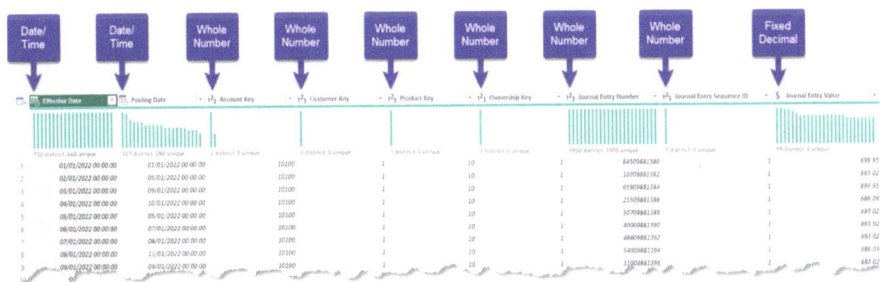

Figure 8-3. StarSchema.co.uk Journal Entry preview

Step 4: Check types as shown in Figure 8-4.

Figure 8-4. StarSchema co uk Journal Entry data types

Step 5: Repeat steps 1–4 for all StarSchema.co.uk files – **StarSchema.co.uk Accounts (1)**, **StarSchema.co.uk Customer (2)**, **StarSchema.co.uk Effective Date (3)**, **StarSchema.co.uk Group Ownership (4)**,

151

CHAPTER 8   A JOURNAL ENTRY SEMANTIC MODEL

StarSchema.co.uk Journal Entry Aggregation 1 (5), StarSchema.co.uk Journal Entry Aggregation 2 (6), StarSchema.co.uk Journal Entry Aggregation 3 (7), StarSchema.co.uk Journal Entry Aggregation 4 (8), StarSchema.co.uk Journal Entry Aggregation 5 (9), StarSchema.co.uk Journal Entry Aggregation 6 (10), StarSchema.co.uk Journal Entry Aggregation 7 (11), StarSchema.co.uk Journal Entry Aggregation 8 (12), StarSchema.co.uk Posting Date (13), StarSchema.co.uk Product (14).

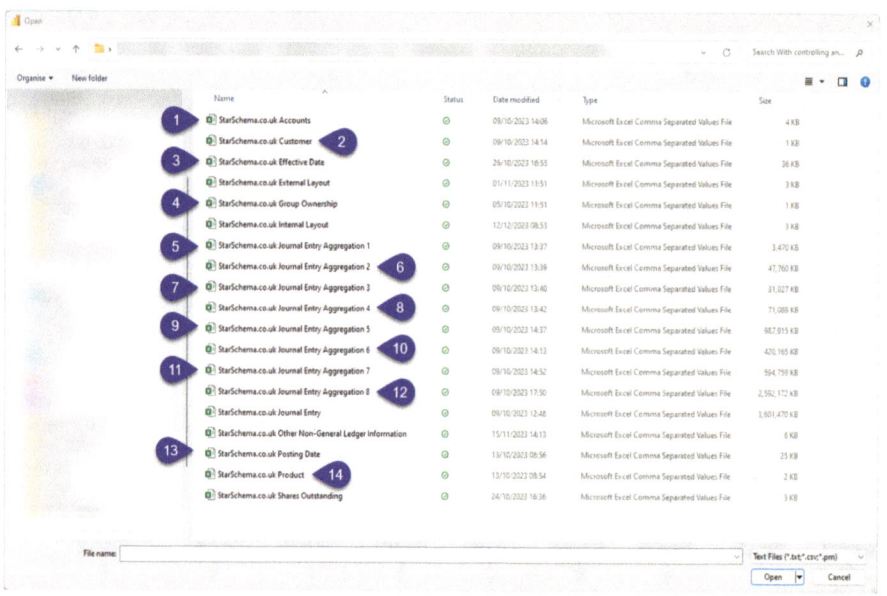

Figure 8-5.   StarSchema.co.uk CSV file import

Step 6: Check and update data types for **StarSchema co uk Journal Entry Aggregation 1**.

CHAPTER 8 A JOURNAL ENTRY SEMANTIC MODEL

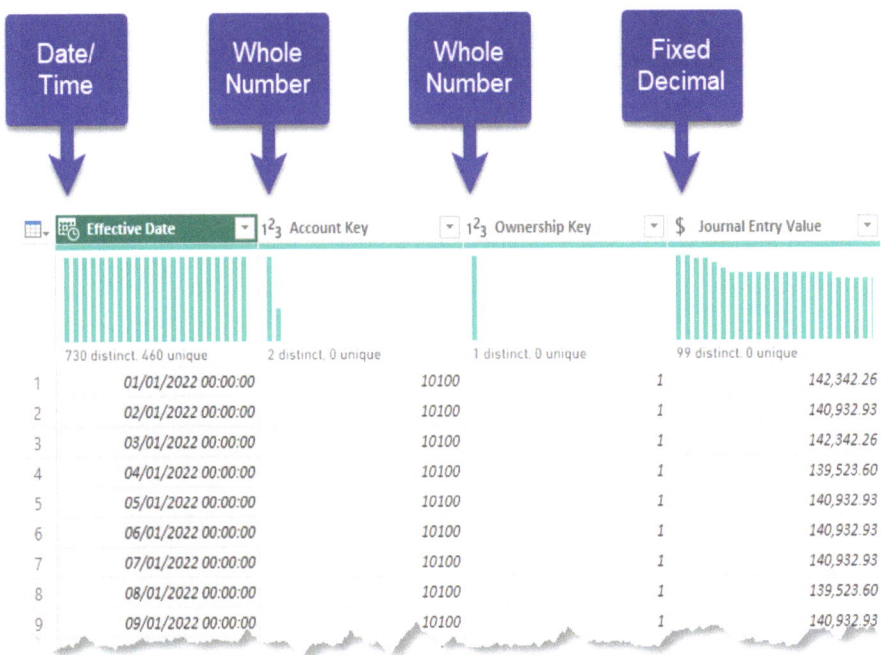

Figure 8-6. *StarSchema co uk Journal Entry Aggregation 1 data types*

Step 7: Check and update data types for **StarSchema co uk Journal Entry Aggregation 2**.

CHAPTER 8   A JOURNAL ENTRY SEMANTIC MODEL

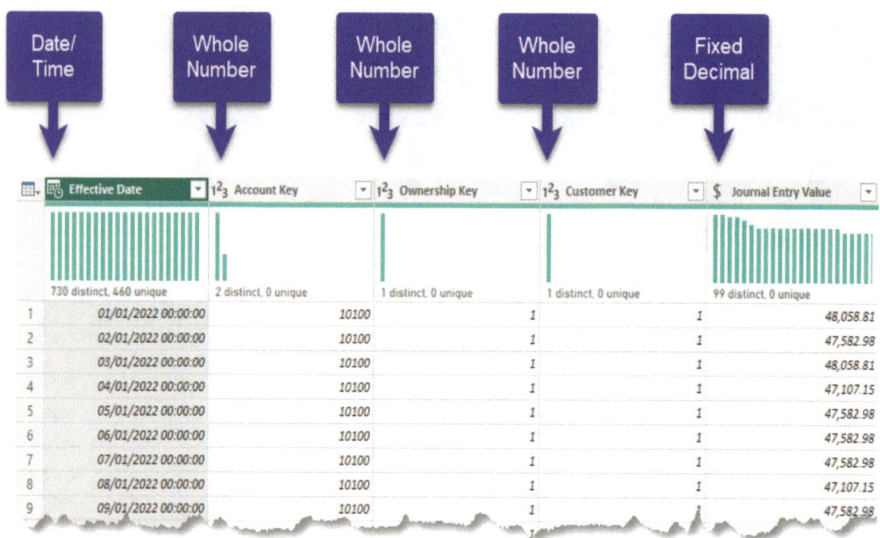

Figure 8-7.   StarSchema co uk Journal Entry Aggregation 2 data types

Step 8: Check and update data types for **StarSchema co uk Journal Entry Aggregation 3**.

Figure 8-8.   StarSchema co uk Journal Entry Aggregation 3 data types

CHAPTER 8   A JOURNAL ENTRY SEMANTIC MODEL

Step 9: Check and update data types for **StarSchema co uk Journal Entry Aggregation 4**.

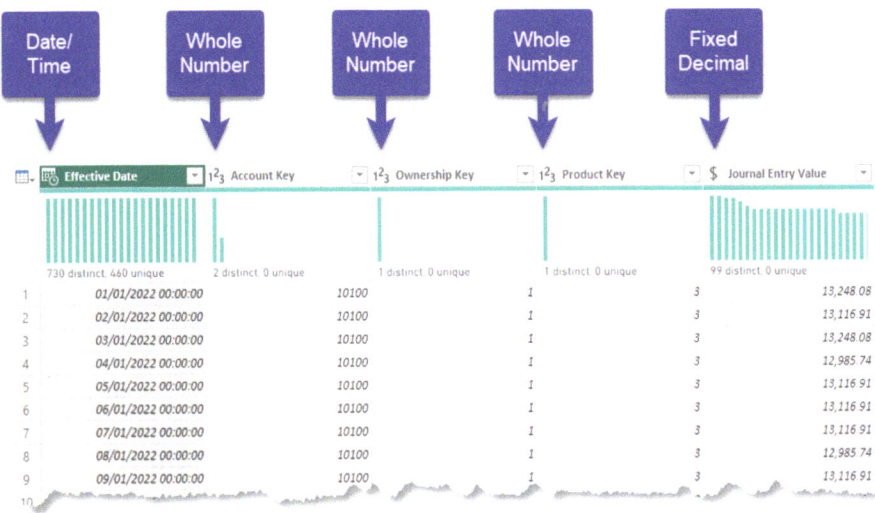

Figure 8-9. *StarSchema co uk Journal Entry Aggregation 4 data types*

Step 10: Check and update data types for **StarSchema co uk Journal Entry Aggregation 5**.

155

CHAPTER 8   A JOURNAL ENTRY SEMANTIC MODEL

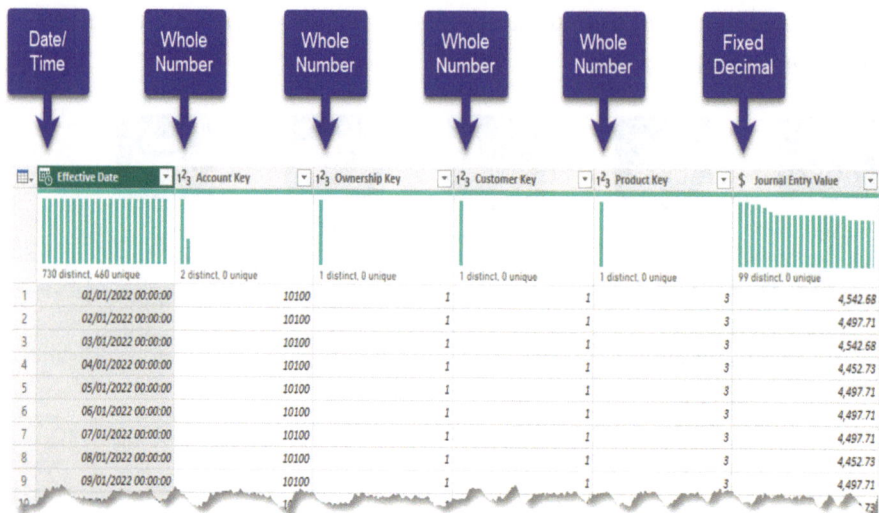

Figure 8-10.   StarSchema co uk Journal Entry Aggregation 5 data types

Step 11: Check and update data types for **StarSchema co uk Journal Entry Aggregation 6**.

CHAPTER 8   A JOURNAL ENTRY SEMANTIC MODEL

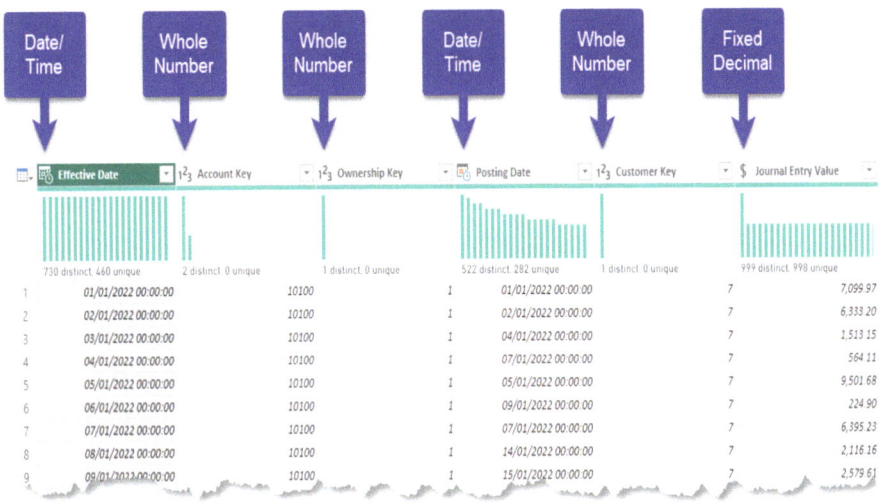

Figure 8-11. *StarSchema co uk Journal Entry Aggregation 6 data types*

Step 12: Check and update data types for **StarSchema co uk Journal Entry Aggregation 7**.

Figure 8-12. *StarSchema co uk Journal Entry Aggregation 7 data types*

Step 13: Check and update data types for **StarSchema co uk Journal Entry Aggregation 8**.

CHAPTER 8   A JOURNAL ENTRY SEMANTIC MODEL

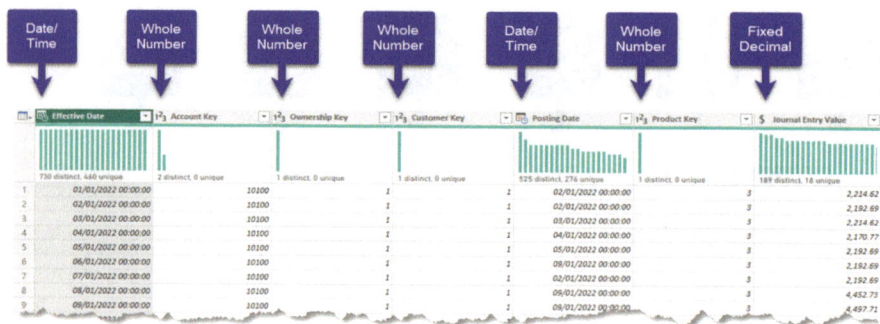

Figure 8-13. *StarSchema co uk Journal Entry Aggregation 8 data types*

Step 14: Check and update data types for **StarSchema co uk Accounts**.

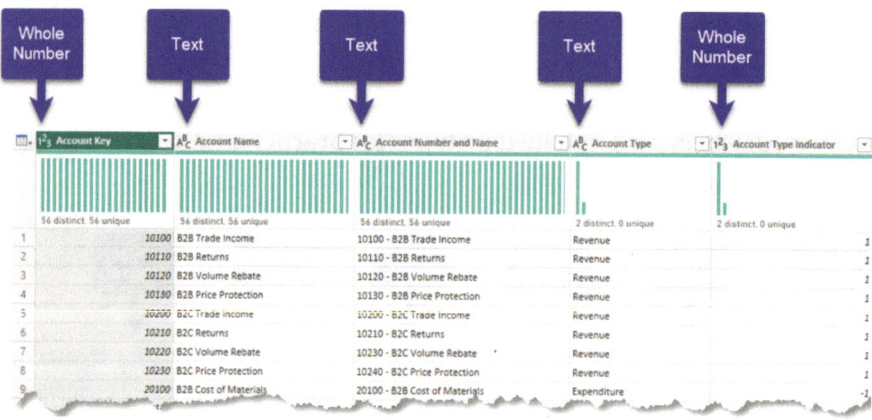

Figure 8-14. *StarSchema co uk Account data types*

Step 15: Check and update data types for **StarSchema co uk Customer**.

CHAPTER 8   A JOURNAL ENTRY SEMANTIC MODEL

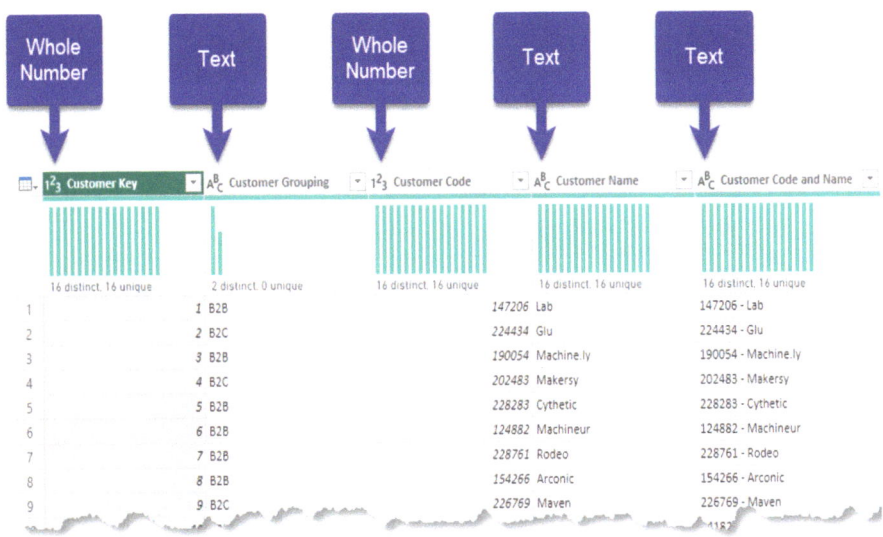

Figure 8-15. StarSchema co uk Customer data types

Step 16: Check and update data types for **StarSchema co uk Effective Date**.

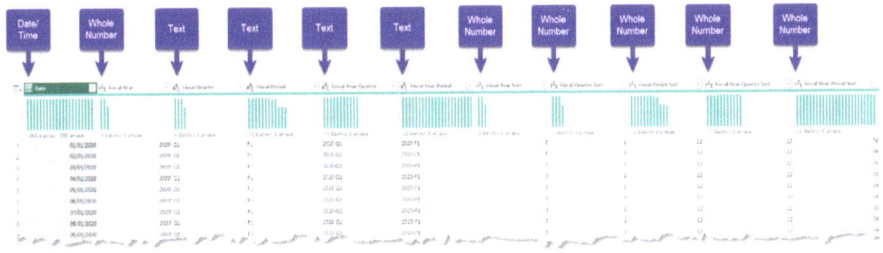

Figure 8-16. StarSchema co uk Effective Date data types

Step 17: Check and update data types for **StarSchema co uk Group Ownership**.

159

CHAPTER 8   A JOURNAL ENTRY SEMANTIC MODEL

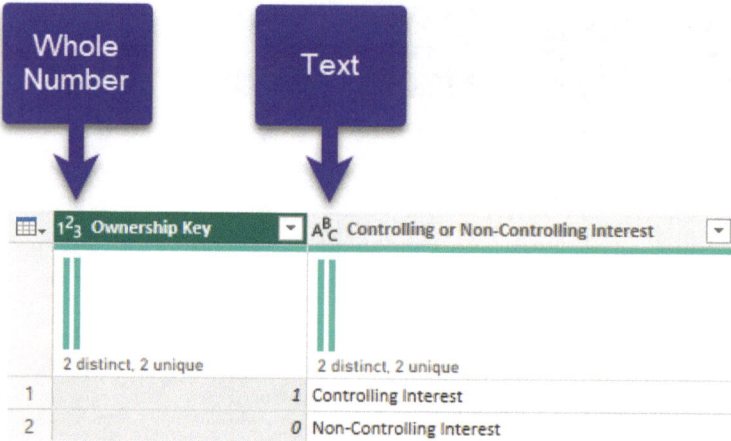

Figure 8-17. StarSchema co uk Group Ownership data types

Step 18: Check and update data types for **StarSchema co uk Posting Date**.

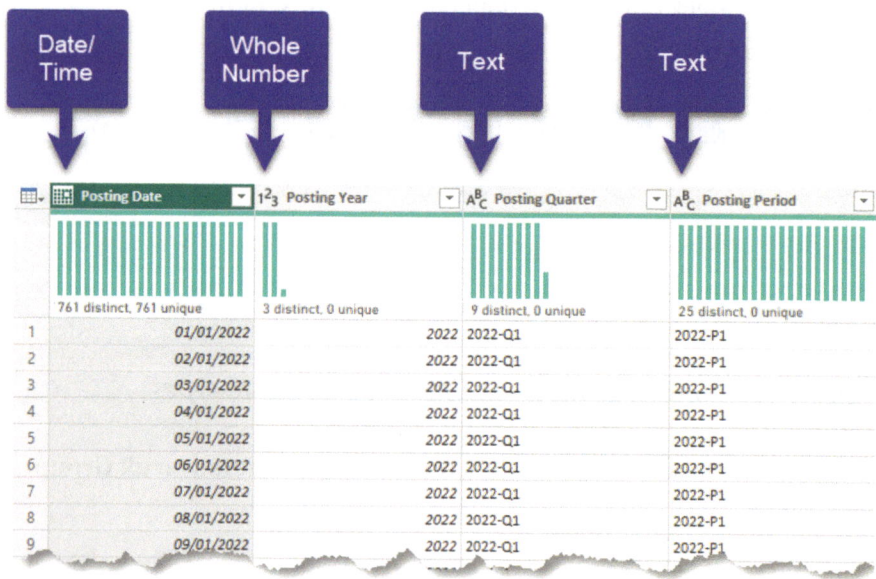

Figure 8-18. StarSchema co uk Posting Date data types

Step 19: Check and update data types for **StarSchema co uk Product**.

Figure 8-19. StarSchema co uk Product data types

Step 20: In the Queries pane, right-click **Star Schema.co.uk Journal Entry (1)** and click the selected **Enable load (2)** to disable the load (should no longer have tick to the left of *Enable load*, and *Star Schema Journal Entry* should be in italics).

CHAPTER 8   A JOURNAL ENTRY SEMANTIC MODEL

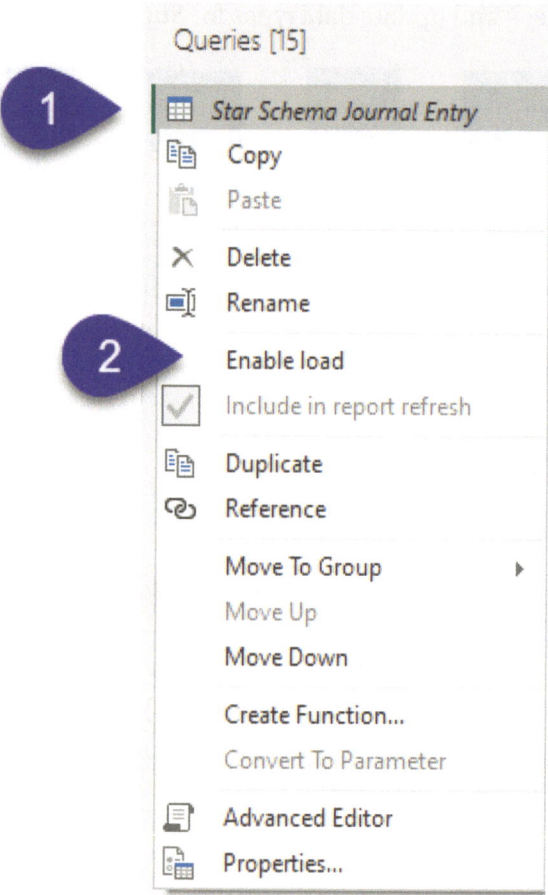

Figure 8-20. *StarSchema co uk Journal Entry Disable Load*

Step 21: Repeat step 20 for all StarSchema co uk files – **StarSchema co uk Journal Entry Aggregation 1 (1)**, **StarSchema co uk Journal Entry Aggregation 2 (2)**, **StarSchema co uk Journal Entry Aggregation 3 (3)**, **StarSchema co uk Journal Entry Aggregation 4 (4)**, **StarSchema co uk Journal Entry Aggregation 5 (5)**, **StarSchema co uk Journal Entry Aggregation 6 (6)**, **StarSchema co uk Journal Entry Aggregation 7 (7)**,

CHAPTER 8 A JOURNAL ENTRY SEMANTIC MODEL

StarSchema co uk Journal Entry Aggregation 8 (8), **StarSchema co uk Accounts (9)**, **StarSchema co uk Customer (10)**, **StarSchema co uk Effective Date (11)**, **StarSchema co uk Group Ownership (12)**, **StarSchema co uk Posting Date (13)**, **StarSchema co uk Product (14)**.

Figure 8-21. StarSchema.co.uk enable load

Step 22: Select **StarSchema co uk Journal Entry (1)**, hold down shift and select **Star Schema co uk Product (2)**, right-click **Star Schema co uk Product (2)**, select **Move to group (3)**, and select **New Group... (4)**.

163

CHAPTER 8　A JOURNAL ENTRY SEMANTIC MODEL

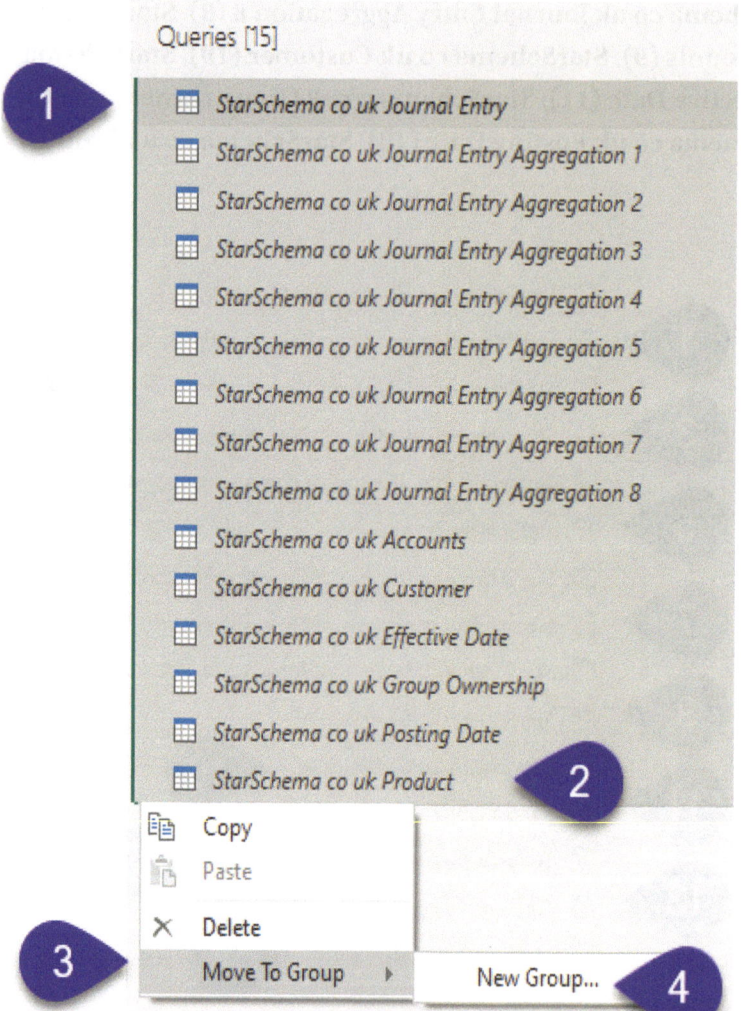

Figure 8-22. Move shared expression to a New Group

CHAPTER 8   A JOURNAL ENTRY SEMANTIC MODEL

Step 23: In the pop-up box under **Name (1)**, type *Shared Expressions* and select **OK (2)**.

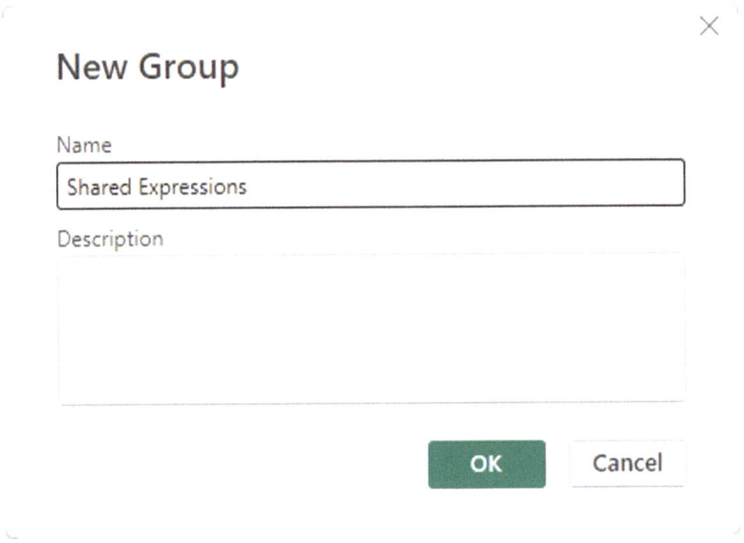

Figure 8-23. Create Shared Expressions group

Stage 2: Journal Entry Fact Tables

Step 1: In the Queries pane, right-click **Star Schema co uk Journal Entry (1)** and select **Reference (2)**.

165

CHAPTER 8   A JOURNAL ENTRY SEMANTIC MODEL

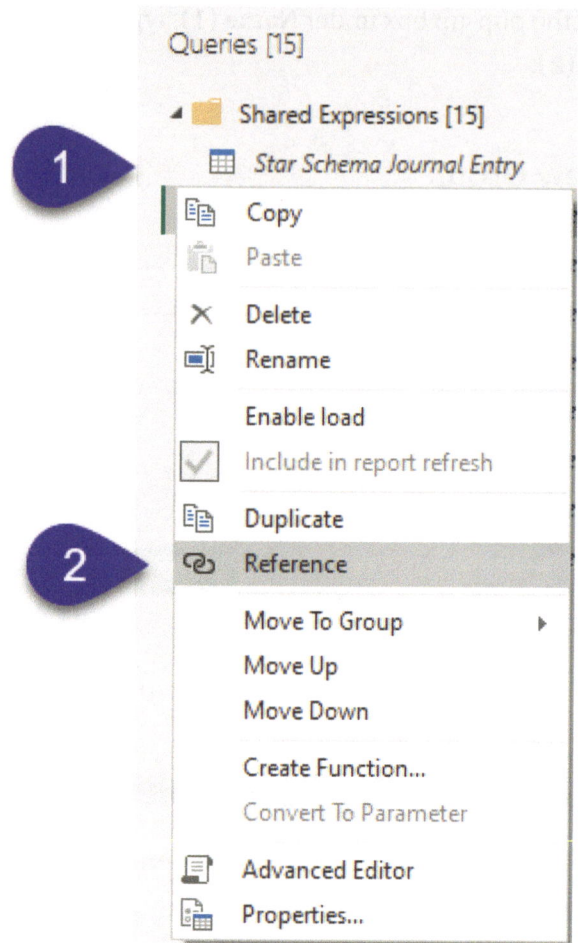

Figure 8-24. *StarSchema co uk Journal Entry reference*

CHAPTER 8 A JOURNAL ENTRY SEMANTIC MODEL

Step 2: Select the referenced query **Star Schema co uk Journal Entry (2) (1)**, and in the query settings under **Name (2)**, type *Journal Entry* and press enter.

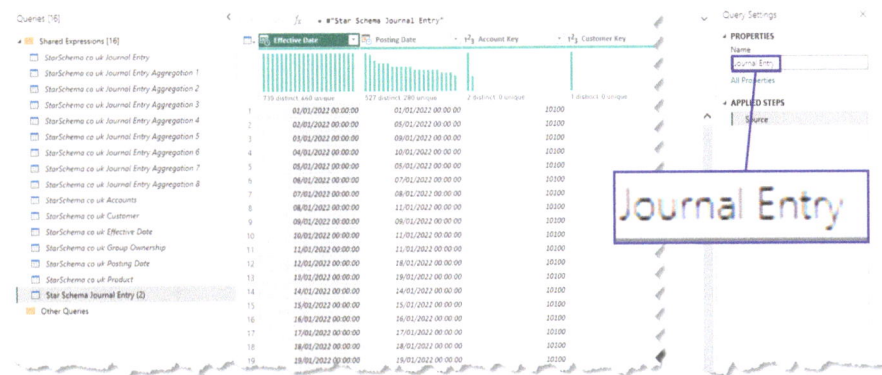

Figure 8-25. *Star Schema co uk Journal Entry (2) renamed to Journal Entry*

Step 3: Right-click **Journal Entry (1)**, select **Move To Group (2)**, and **New Group (3)**.

167

CHAPTER 8   A JOURNAL ENTRY SEMANTIC MODEL

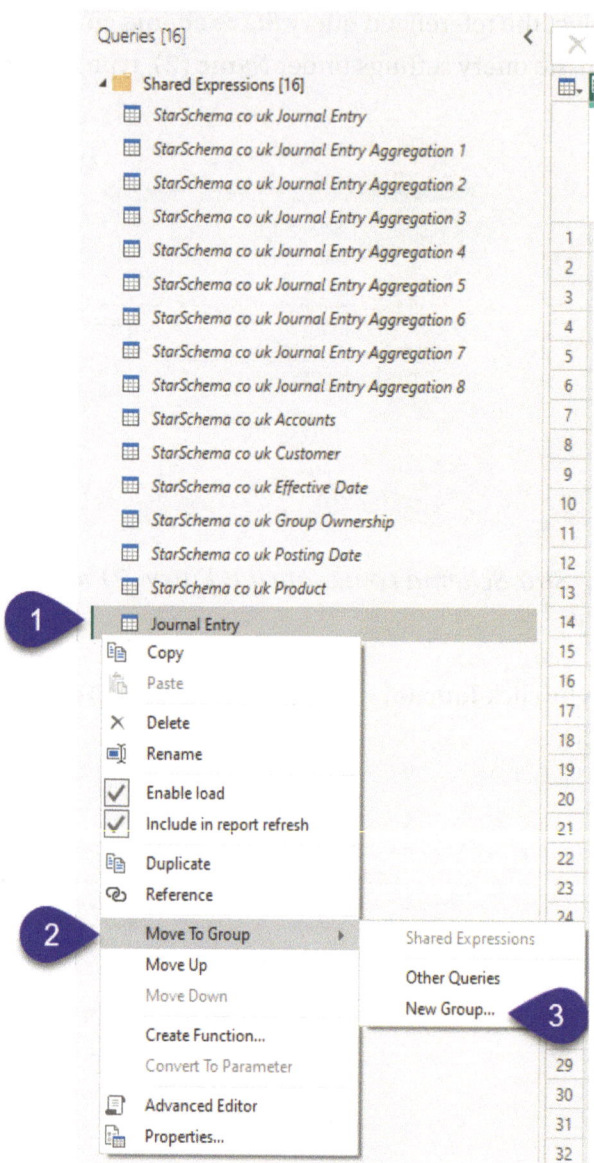

Figure 8-26. *Journal Entry move to new group*

CHAPTER 8   A JOURNAL ENTRY SEMANTIC MODEL

Step 4: In the pop-up box under **Name (1)**, type *Fact Tables* and select **OK (2)**.

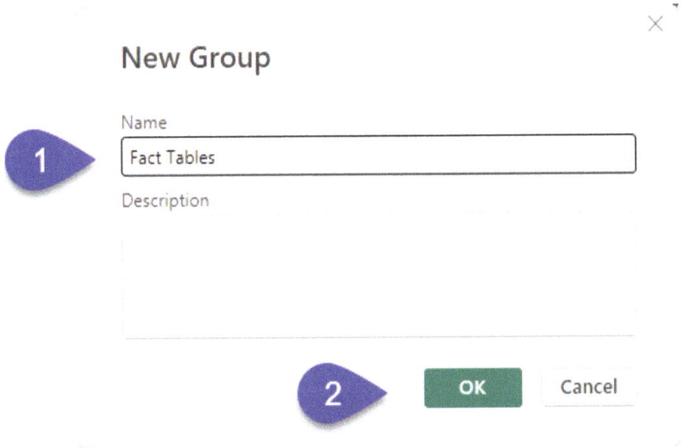

Figure 8-27. Create Fact Tables group

Step 5: Repeat steps 1 and 2 for *StarSchema co uk Journal Entry Aggregations 1–8*, renaming in step 2 with the prefix *StarSchema co uk* removed and the suffix *(2)* removed – that is, renaming StarSchema co uk Journal Entry Aggregation 1 (2) as *Journal Entry Aggregation 2* – then move to the Fact Tables group.

169

CHAPTER 8   A JOURNAL ENTRY SEMANTIC MODEL

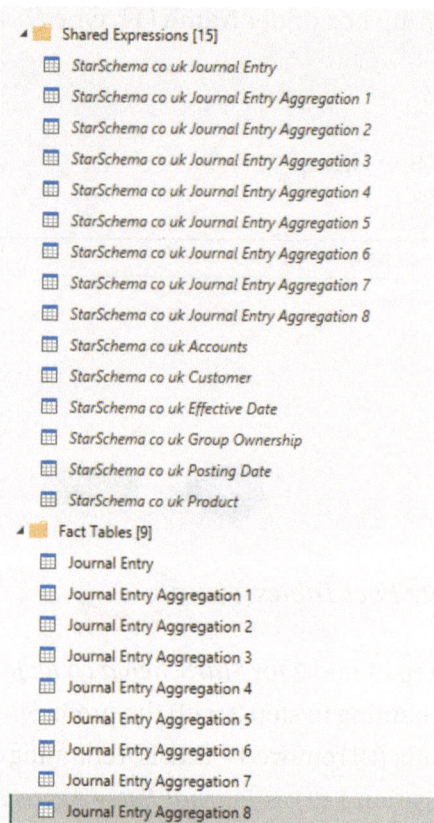

Figure 8-28. *StarSchema.co.uk reference, rename and move aggregations to the Fact Tables group*

CHAPTER 8　A JOURNAL ENTRY SEMANTIC MODEL

Stage 3: Group Ownership dimension

Step 1: In the Queries pane, right click on **Star Schema co uk Group Ownership (1)** and select **Reference (2)**

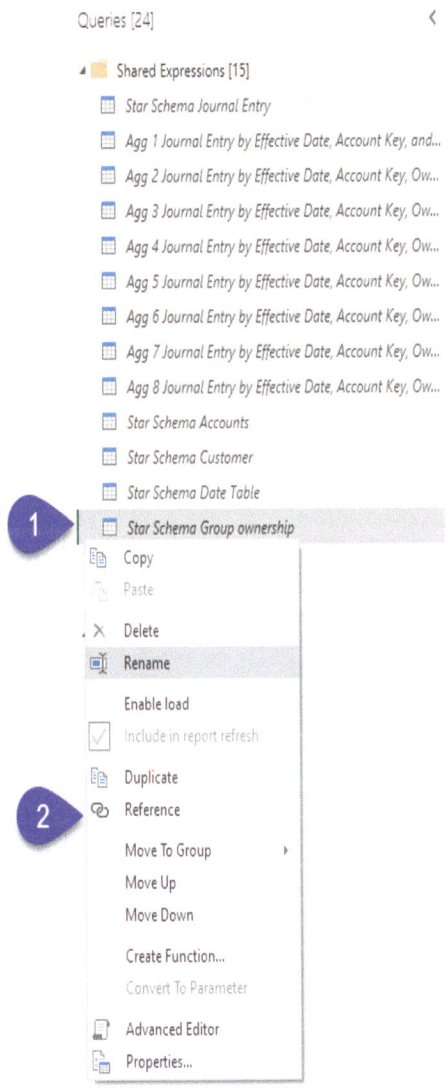

Figure 8-29. *StarSchema co uk Group Ownership reference*

171

CHAPTER 8   A JOURNAL ENTRY SEMANTIC MODEL

Step 2: Select the referenced query **Star Schema co uk Group Ownership (2) (1)**, and in the query settings under **Name (2)**, type **Group Ownership** and press enter.

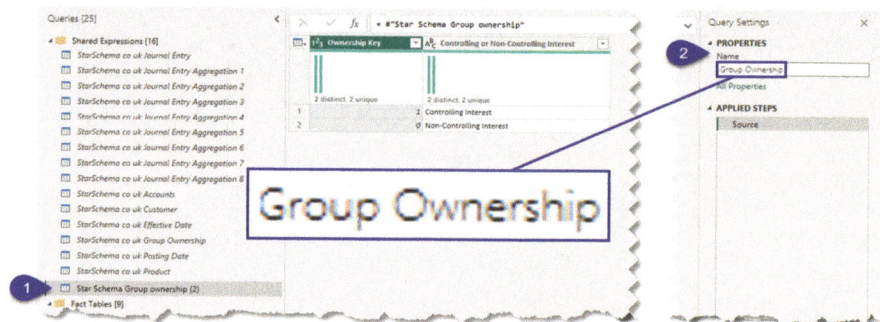

Figure 8-30. *StarSchema co uk Group Ownership (2) renamed to Group Ownership*

Step 3: Right-click Group Ownership **(1)**, select **Move To Group (2)**, and select **New Group... (3)**.

CHAPTER 8   A JOURNAL ENTRY SEMANTIC MODEL

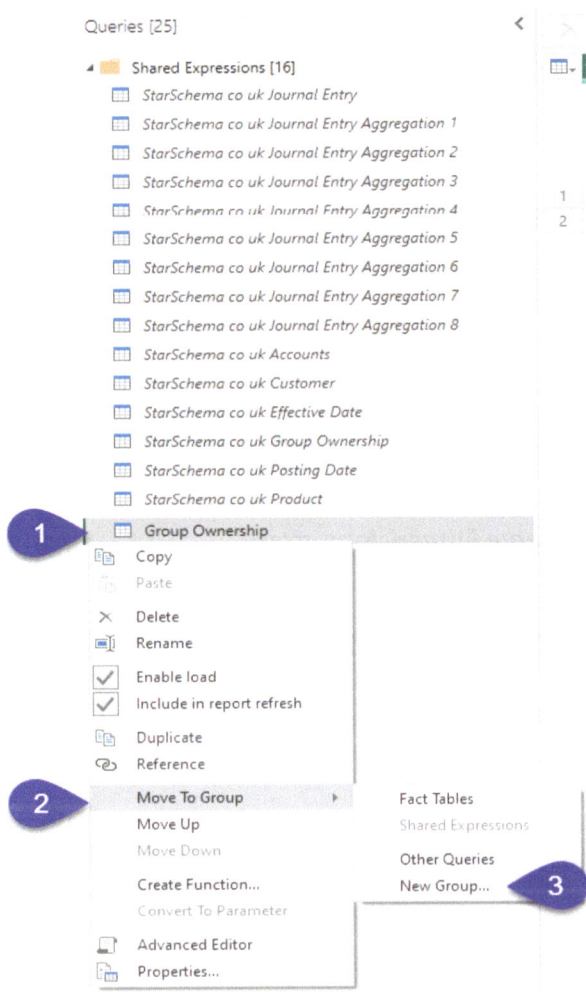

***Figure 8-31.** Group Ownership moved to a new group*

Step 4: In the pop-up box under **Name (1)**, type *Dimensions* and select **OK (2)**.

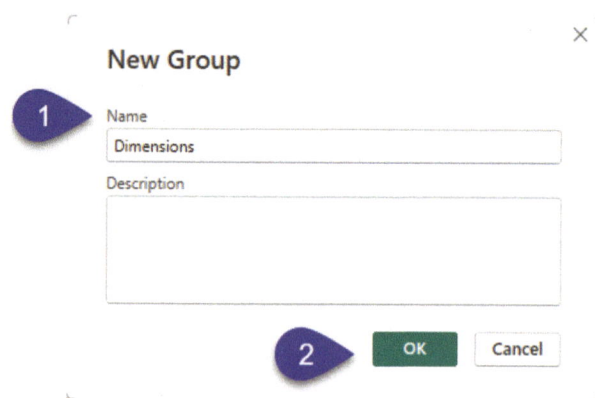

Figure 8-32. Create Dimensions group

Stage 4: Accounts Dimension

Step 1: In the Queries pane, right-click **Star Schema co uk Accounts (1)** and select **Reference (2)**.

CHAPTER 8   A JOURNAL ENTRY SEMANTIC MODEL

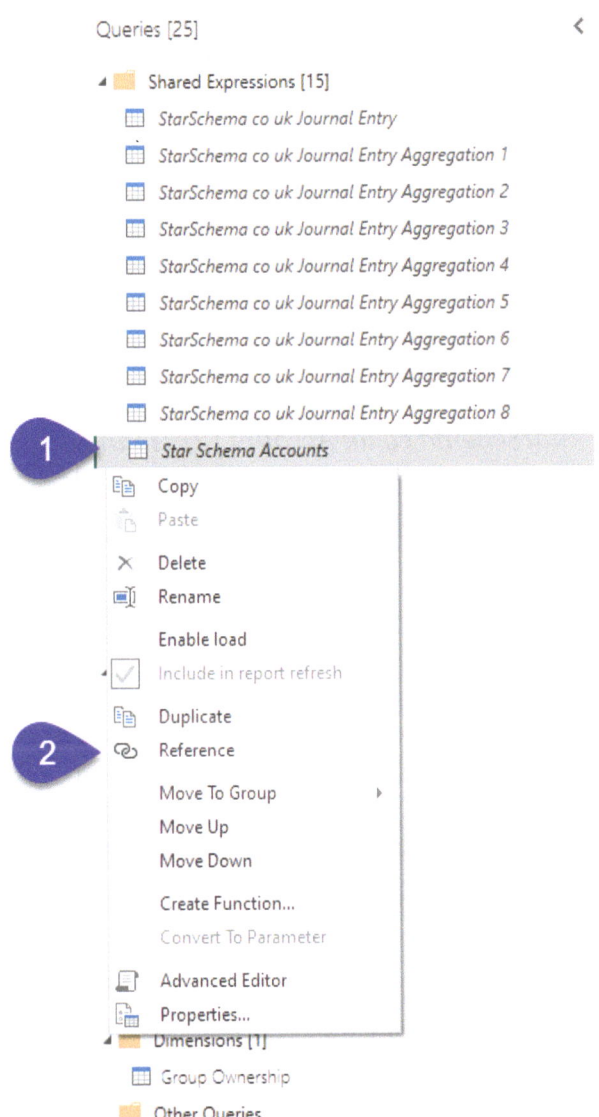

Figure 8-33. StarSchema co uk Accounts reference

175

CHAPTER 8   A JOURNAL ENTRY SEMANTIC MODEL

Step 2: Select the referenced query **Star Schema co uk Accounts (2) (1)**, and in the query settings under **Name (2)**, type **Account** and press enter.

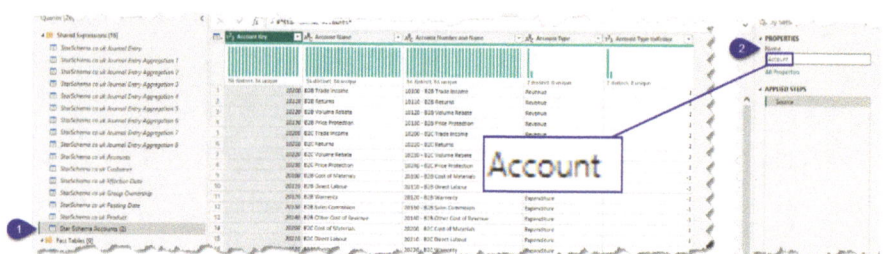

Figure 8-34. *StarSchema co uk Account (2) renamed to Account*

Step 3: Right-click **Account (1)**, select **Move To Group (2)**, and select **Dimensions (3)**.

CHAPTER 8   A JOURNAL ENTRY SEMANTIC MODEL

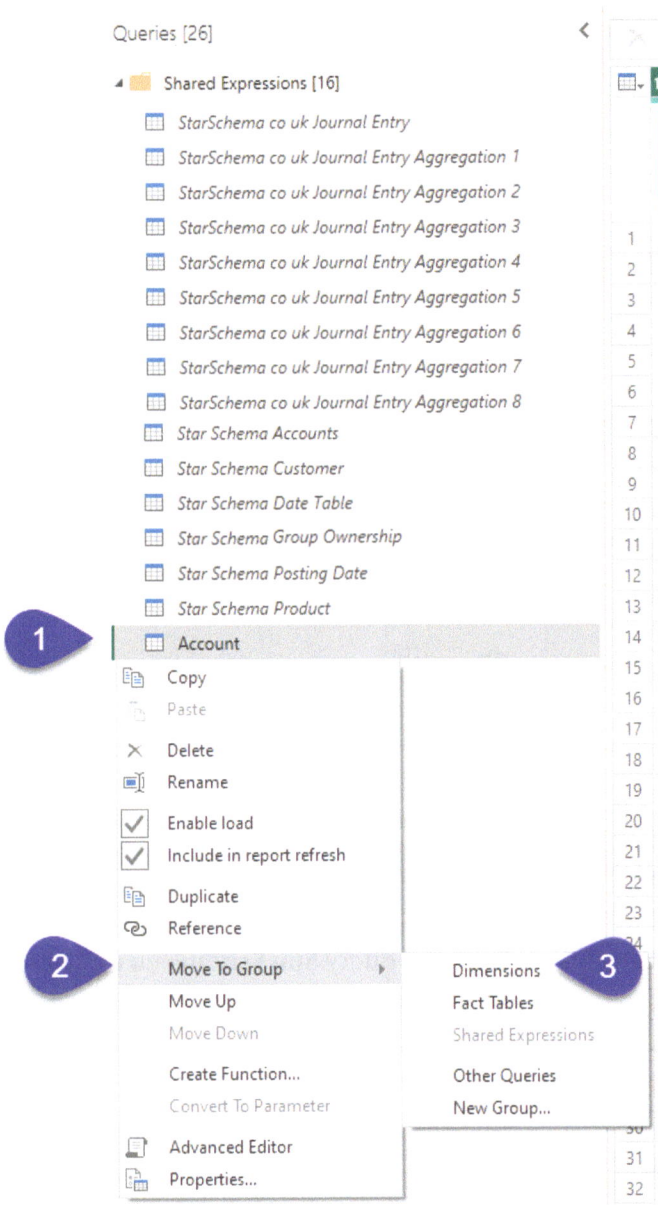

Figure 8-35. *Move Account to Dimensions*

CHAPTER 8   A JOURNAL ENTRY SEMANTIC MODEL

Stage 5: Effective Date Dimension

Step 1: In the Queries pane, right-click **Star Schema co uk Effective Date** **(1)** and select **Reference (2)**.

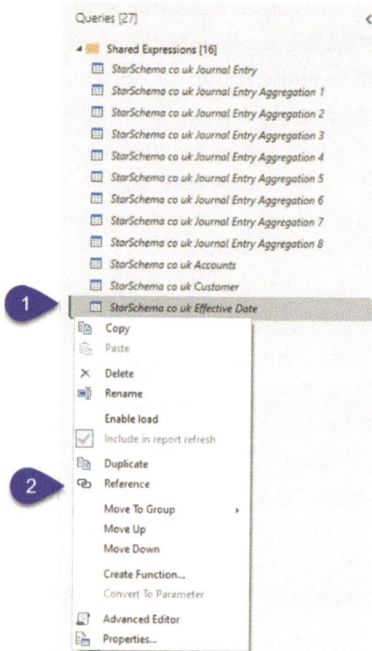

Figure 8-36. StarSchema co uk Effective Date reference

Step 2: Select the referenced query **StarSchema co uk Effective Date (2) (1)**, and in the query settings under **Name (2)**, type **Effective Date** and press enter.

CHAPTER 8 A JOURNAL ENTRY SEMANTIC MODEL

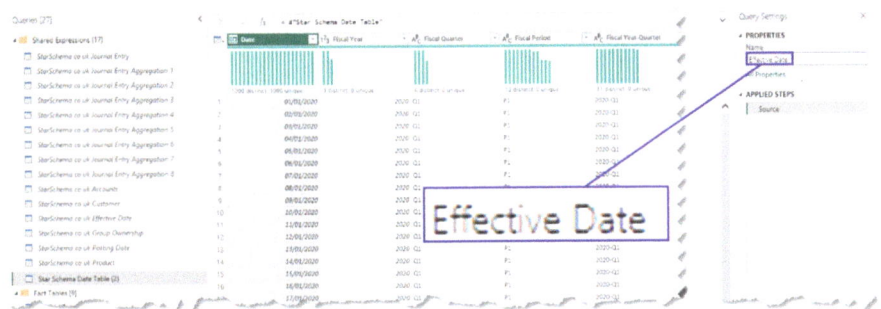

Figure 8-37. *StarSchema co uk Effective Date (2) renamed to Effective Date*

Step 3: Right-click **Effective Date (1)**, select **Move To Group (2)**, and select **Dimensions (3)**.

CHAPTER 8   A JOURNAL ENTRY SEMANTIC MODEL

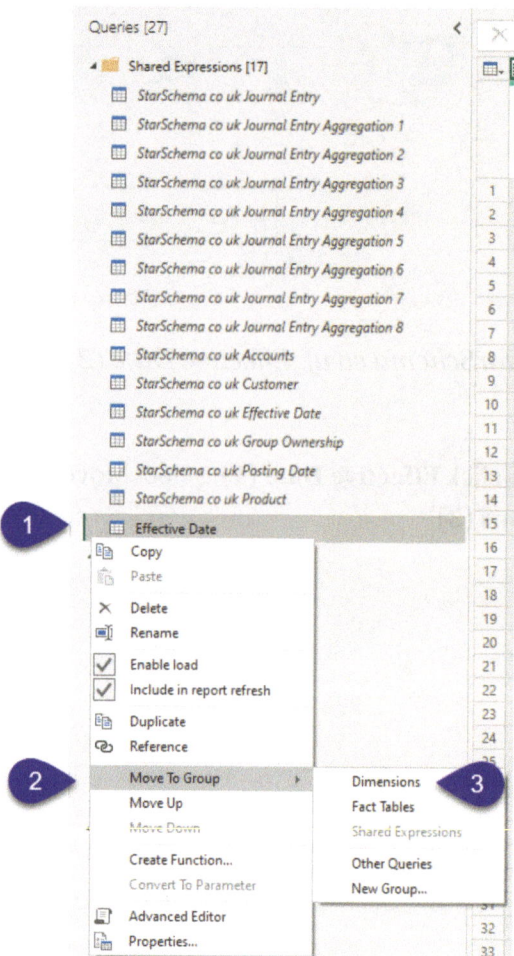

Figure 8-38. *Move Effective Date to Dimensions group*

Stage 6: Customer Dimension

Step 1: In the Queries pane, right-click **StarSchema co uk Customer (1)** and select **Reference (2)**.

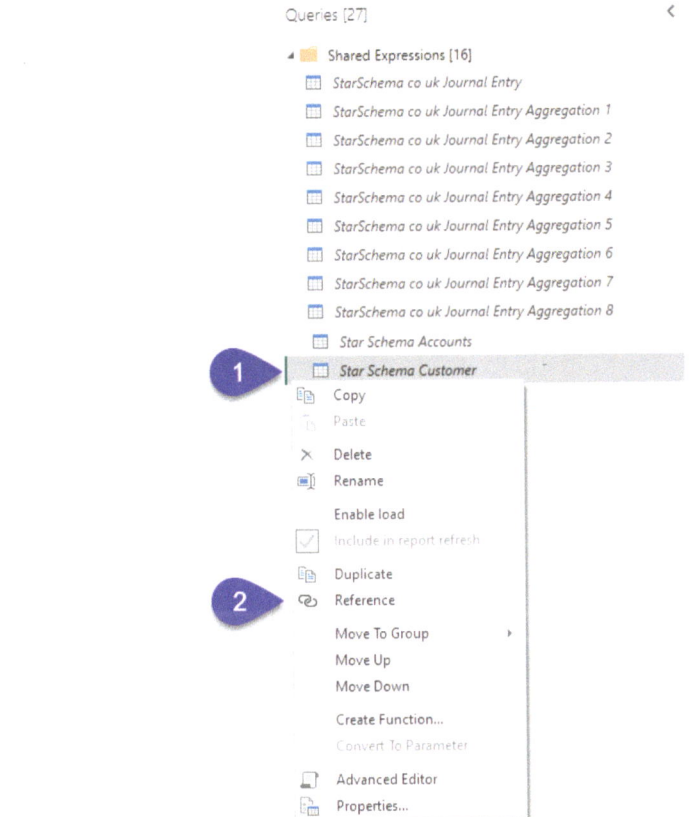

Figure 8-39. StarSchema co uk Customer reference

Step 2: Select the referenced query **StarSchema co uk Customer (2) (1)**, and in the query settings under **Name (2)**, type **Customer** and press enter.

CHAPTER 8   A JOURNAL ENTRY SEMANTIC MODEL

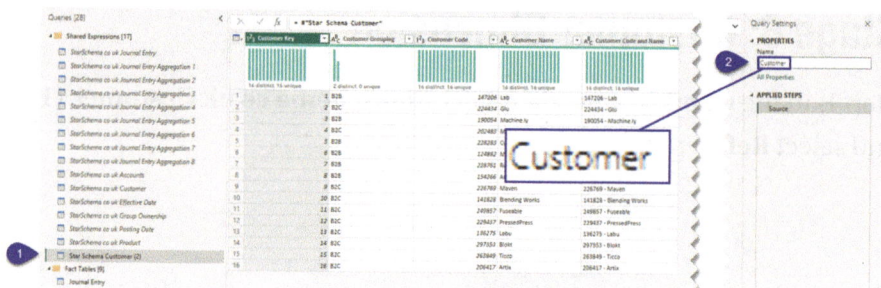

Figure 8-40. StarSchema co uk Customer (2) renamed to Customer

Step 3: Right-click **Customer (1)**, select **Move To Group (2)**, and select **Dimensions (3)**.

CHAPTER 8 A JOURNAL ENTRY SEMANTIC MODEL

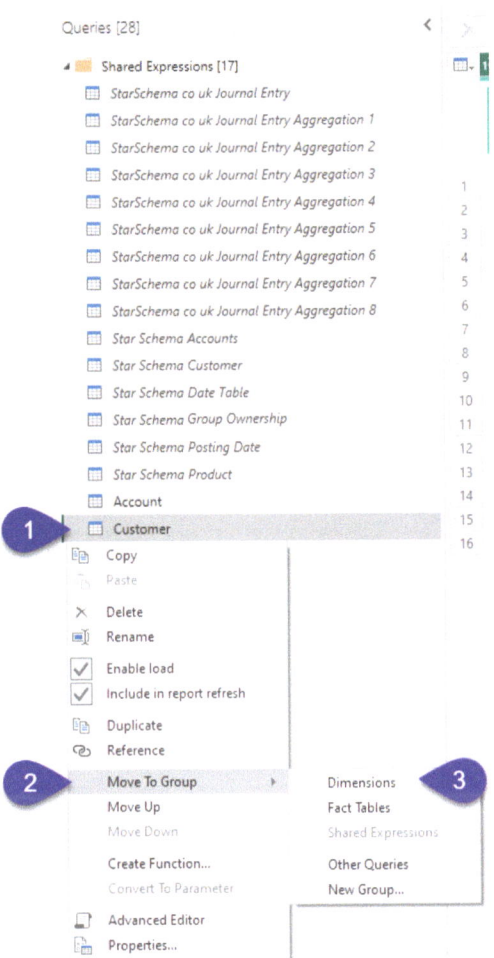

Figure 8-41. Move Customer to Dimensions

Chapter 8   A Journal Entry Semantic Model

Stage 7: Product Dimension

Step 1: In the Queries pane, right-click **StarSchema co uk Product (1)** and select **Reference (2)**.

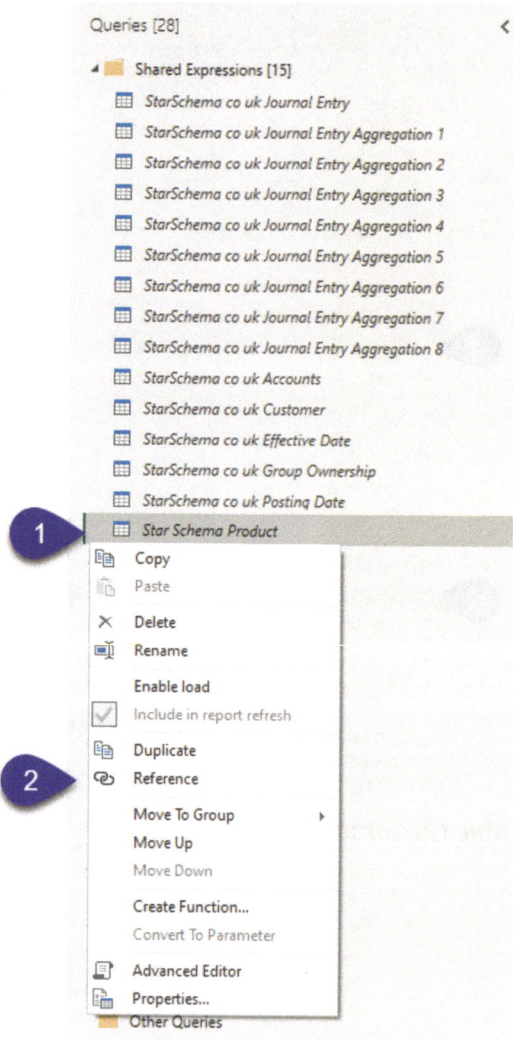

Figure 8-42. StarSchema co uk Product reference

CHAPTER 8   A JOURNAL ENTRY SEMANTIC MODEL

Step 2: Select the referenced query **StarSchema co uk Product (2) (1)**, and in the query settings under **Name (2)**, type **Product** and press enter.

Figure 8-43. StarSchema co uk Product (2) renamed to Product

Step 3: Right-click **Product (1)**, select **Move To Group (2)**, and select **Dimensions (3)**.

185

CHAPTER 8   A JOURNAL ENTRY SEMANTIC MODEL

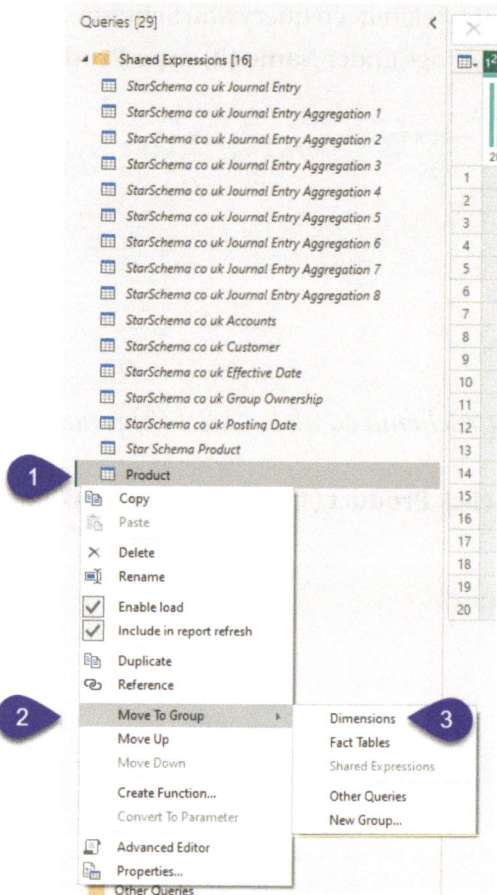

Figure 8-44.   Move Product to the Dimensions table

Stage 8: Posting Date Dimension

Step 1: In the Queries pane, right-click **StarSchema co uk Posting Date (1)** and select **Reference (2)**.

CHAPTER 8   A JOURNAL ENTRY SEMANTIC MODEL

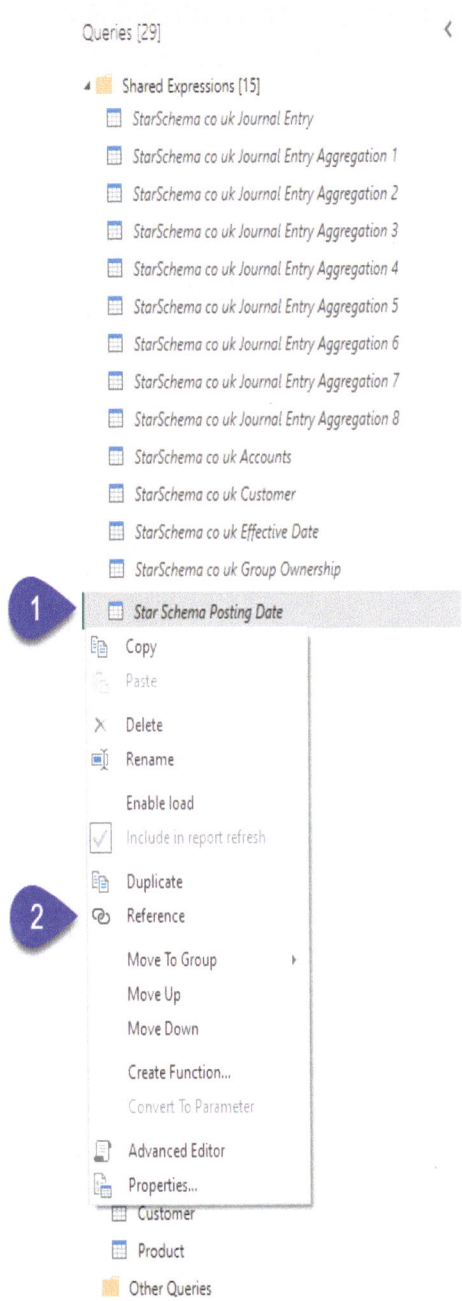

Figure 8-45. *StarSchema co uk reference Posting Date*

CHAPTER 8   A JOURNAL ENTRY SEMANTIC MODEL

Step 2: Select the referenced query **Star Schema Posting Date (2)** **(1)**, and in the query settings under **Name (2)**, type **Posting Date** and press enter.

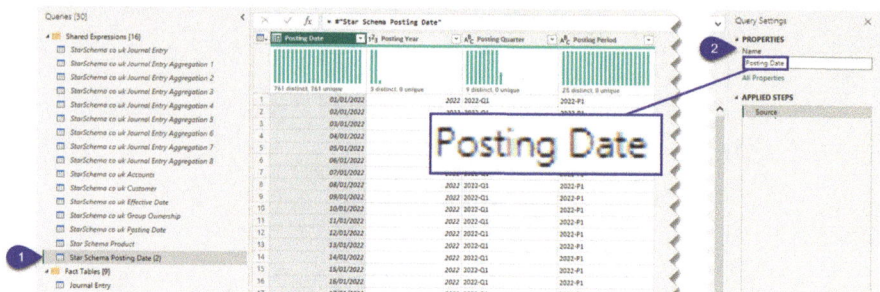

Figure 8-46. *StarSchema co uk Posting Date (2) renamed to Posting Date*

CHAPTER 8   A JOURNAL ENTRY SEMANTIC MODEL

Step 3: Right-click **Posting Date (1)**, select **Move To Group (2)**, and select **Dimensions (3)**.

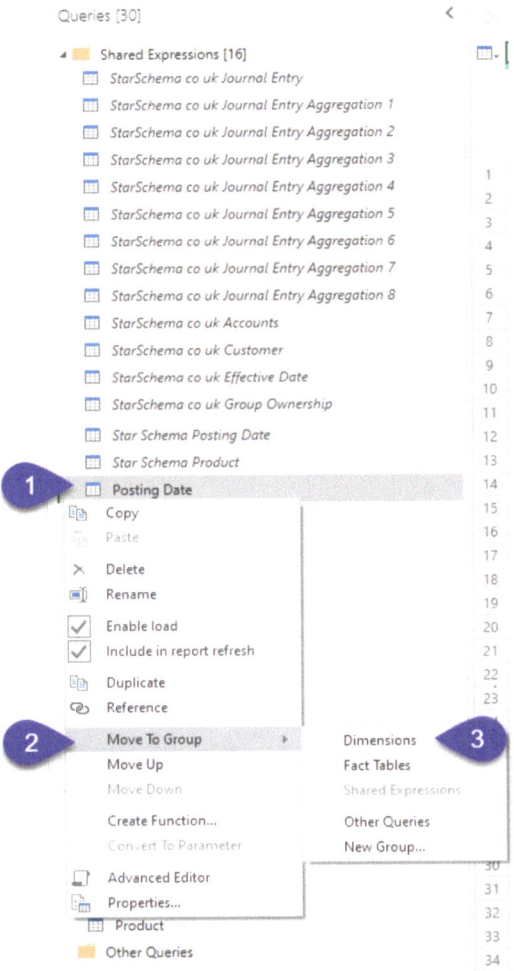

Figure 8-47. Move Posting Date to the Dimensions group

189

CHAPTER 8   A JOURNAL ENTRY SEMANTIC MODEL

Stage 9: Measure Table

Step 1: On the tab **home (1)**, select **Enter Data (2)**.

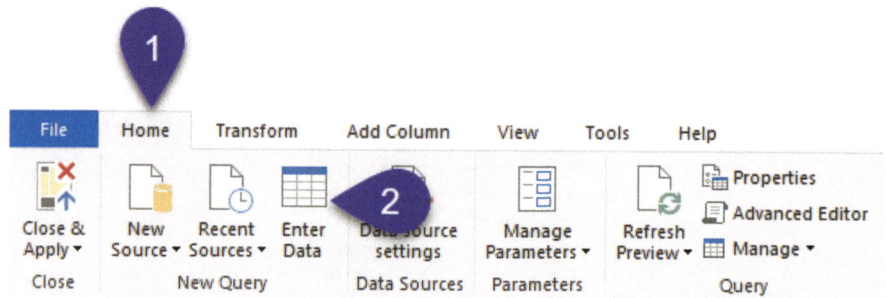

Figure 8-48.   Enter data

Step 2: In the Create table pop-up box, type the name **Measure (1)** and select **OK (2)**.

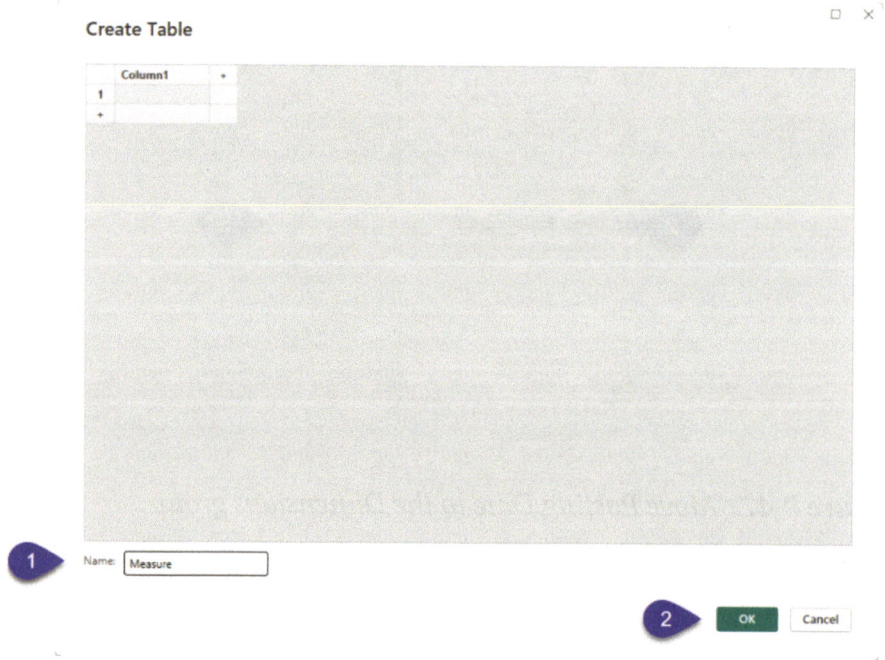

Figure 8-49.   Create a measure table

CHAPTER 8   A JOURNAL ENTRY SEMANTIC MODEL

Step 3: Right-click **Measure (1)**, select **Move To Group (2)**, and select **New Group… (3)**.

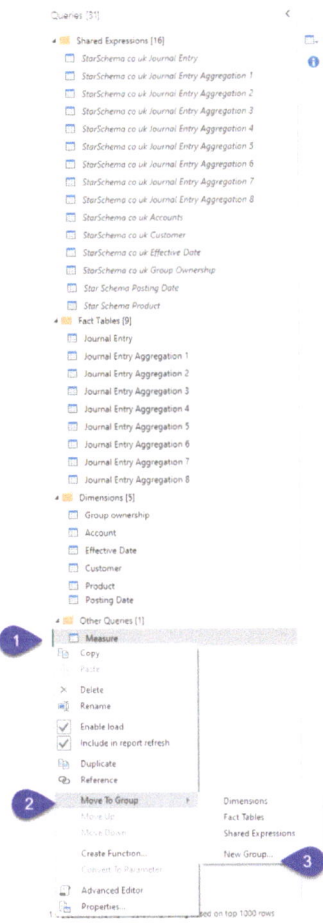

Figure 8-50. *Move Measure to a new group*

CHAPTER 8 A JOURNAL ENTRY SEMANTIC MODEL

Step 4: In the pop-up box under **Name (1)**, type *Measure*, and select **OK (2)**.

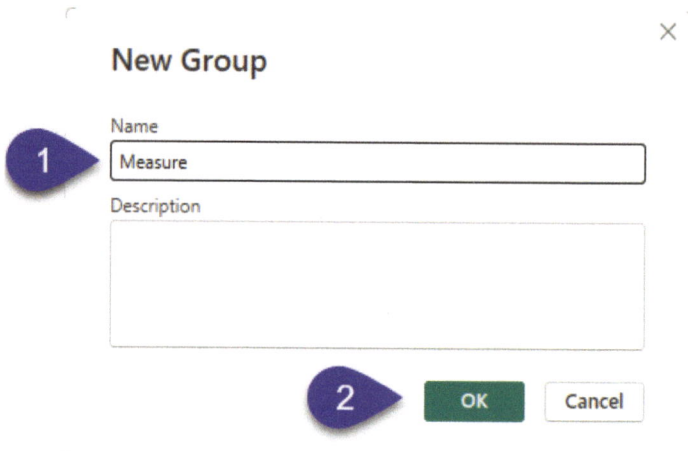

Figure 8-51. Create a new Measure group

Step 5: Navigate to the tab **Home (1)** and select **Close & Apply (2)**.

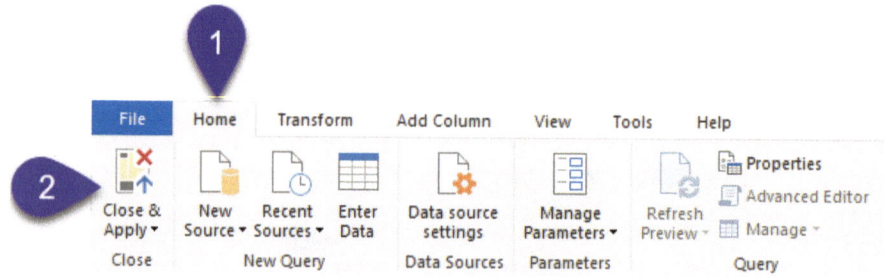

Figure 8-52. StarSchema.co.uk close and apply

Building the Data Model

Create Relationships

Create the relationships as per the StarSchema.co.uk logical data models in Chapter 6 (section "An Example Journal Entry Logical Model" and section "Journal Entry Aggregation Logical Models").

Mark As Date Table

As per the previous chapter (section "Mark As Date Table"), mark Effective Date as the date table.

Date Sort Order

As per the previous chapter (section "Date Sort Order"), sort date information.

DAX

This section produces the calculation for *net credit less debit* and *net debit less credit* as outlined in Chapter 5. The DAX is identical to Chapter 7, except the sum which – as per Chapter 6 – uses the appropriate aggregation.

Calculations for *net credit less debit* and *net debit less credit* are broken down into three steps:

- **Step 01: Sum**: Calculates the sum of the values in the appropriate fact table
- **Step 02: Account Type Indicator**: Calculates the max and min account type indicator
- **Step 03: Line-items**: Calculates *net credit less debit* and *net debit less credit* based on steps 01 and 02

CHAPTER 8   A JOURNAL ENTRY SEMANTIC MODEL

As with Chapter 7, when producing the DAX, each measure should be placed in a folder using the name of the step (i.e., Step 01: Sum) to keep it organized.

Step 01: Sum

The first step is to sum the values in the journal entry fact table. This is done in four parts:

- **Part 1**: Calculate the sum of journal entry values for each fact table.
- **Part 2**: Determine which dimensions are in scope.
- **Part 3**: Depending on which dimensions are in scope, calculate the sum of journal entry value in the appropriate fact table.
- **Part 4**: Return the result.

```
Actuals Sum =
// Part 1: Create a sum for each of the fact tables
VAR NonAgg = SUM( 'Journal Entry'[Journal Entry Value])
VAR agg1 = SUM( 'Journal Entry Aggregation 1'[Journal Entry Value])
VAR agg2 = SUM( 'Journal Entry Aggregation 2'[Journal Entry Value])
VAR agg3 = SUM( 'Journal Entry Aggregation 3'[Journal Entry Value])
VAR agg4 = SUM( 'Journal Entry Aggregation 4'[Journal Entry Value])
VAR agg5 = SUM( 'Journal Entry Aggregation 5'[Journal Entry Value])
VAR agg6 = SUM( 'Journal Entry Aggregation 6'[Journal Entry Value])
VAR agg7 = SUM( 'Journal Entry Aggregation 7'[Journal Entry Value])
VAR agg8 = SUM( 'Journal Entry Aggregation 8'[Journal Entry Value])

// Part 2: Determine which dimensions are in scope
VAR JournalEntryFactTableFiltered = ISFILTERED('Journal Entry')
VAR ProductNotFiltered = ISFILTERED('Product') = FALSE()
```

CHAPTER 8   A JOURNAL ENTRY SEMANTIC MODEL

```
VAR PostingDateNotFiltered = ISFILTERED('Posting
Date')  = FALSE()
VAR CustomerNotFiltered= ISFILTERED('Customer')   = FALSE()

// Part 3: Depending on which dimensions are in scope, use the
appropriate fact table sum

VAR result =
    SWITCH
        (
        TRUE(),
        JournalEntryFactTableFiltered , NonAgg,
        ProductNotFiltered && PostingDateNotFiltered
                && CustomerNotFiltered , agg1,
        ProductNotFiltered && PostingDateNotFiltered, agg2,
        ProductNotFiltered && CustomerNotFiltered , agg3,
        PostingDateNotFiltered && CustomerNotFiltered , agg4,
        PostingDateNotFiltered, agg5,
        ProductNotFiltered, agg6,
        CustomerNotFiltered , agg7,
        agg8
        )

// Stage 4: Return the result
RETURN result
```

With this approach, aggregation tables are manually selected. There are, however, alternative aggregation approaches available such as *manage aggregation* and *auto aggregation*. The manual aggregation approach has been outlined in the book because:

1. Aggregations should optimize query performance for all eventualities (see Chapter 6).

CHAPTER 8 A JOURNAL ENTRY SEMANTIC MODEL

2. Aggregations for the income statement do not require the more complex elements handled by the manage aggregation feature because the base calculation is always a sum of the journal entry values (see Chapter 6).

3. From a learning perspective, it is best to understand exactly how aggregations work – technology invariably changes, and thus it is important to understand the principles.

4. The manual approach works with Power BI import mode.

Step 02: Account Type Indicator

As per Chapter 5, the maximum account type indicator is used for net credits less debits:

```
Actuals Net Credit Less Debit Indicator=
    Max ( 'Account'[Account Type Indicator] )
```

As per Chapter 5, the minimum account type indicator is used for net debits less credits:

```
Actuals Net Debit Less Credit Indicator=
    Min ( 'Account'[Account Type Indicator] )
```

Step 03: Lineitems

As per Chapter 5, for net credit less debit, the actual sum is multiplied by the net credit less debit indicator:

```
[Actuals Net Credit Less Debit]=
    [Actuals Sum] × [Actuals Net Credit Less Debit Indicator]
```

As per Chapter 5, for net debit less credit, the actual sum is multiplied by the net debit less credit indicator:

```
[Actuals Net Debit Less Credit]=
    [Actuals Sum] × [Actuals Net Debit Less Credit Indicator]
```

Summary

- An extension of the trial balance model can be used to calculate net credit less debit and net debit less credit for journal entries.

- Using a journal entry semantic model, users can view account balances from a range of perspectives.

- A journal entry semantic model uses aggregations to ensure values are returned to end users from the most performant table.

PART III

Producing External Income Statement Semantic Models

The majority of what we have learned so far comes together in this part, in which we build semantic models containing the logic required to produce external income statements. This is a progression on the semantic models in the previous part which required additional logic outside the model – that is, Excel formulas or visual calculations – to produce income statements.

We first learn about the four subtotal and subset types: net credit less debit, net debit less credit, all credit less debit, and all debit less credit. The first two of these calculations were covered in the previous part; however, when we introduce the concept of lines on the income statement into the semantic model, two further options are required. We will then learn about extending the logical account balance models from Chapter 6 to include

1. **Layout dimension**: Contains the income statement presentation logic, such as which lines appear, the order in which they appear, which calculations are performed, and how each line is formatted.

PART III   PRODUCING EXTERNAL INCOME STATEMENT SEMANTIC MODELS

2. **Shares outstanding fact table**: An additional fact table is required to calculate weighted shares outstanding and earnings per share.

Finally, extensions are made to the trial balance semantic models (Chapter 7) and a journal entry semantic model (Chapter 8), resulting in semantic models which produce external income statements in their entirety.

This part comprises the following chapters:

- Chapter 9, "The Four Subtotal and Subset Types"
- Chapter 10, "External Reporting Logical Models"
- Chapter 11, "External Reporting Semantic Models"

CHAPTER 9

The Four Subtotal and Subset Types

In this chapter, we will learn about the four subtotal and subset types: net credit less debit, net debit less credit, all credit less debit, and all debit less credit. We will also learn why four options are required and work through examples for each calculation type.

In this chapter, there are three main sections:

1. The Four Subtotal and Subset Options
2. Why Four Options of Subtotal and Subset Are Required
3. Examples of the Four Subtotal and Subset Options

The Four Subtotal and Subset Options

As per challenge 16 (Chapter 3), end users start at the highest level (the entire income statement), then drill down into individual lines. For instance, drill down from line-item *product revenue* to the accounts which make up this line-item. The behavior when drilling from an income statement line containing accounts of one account type is straightforward, as both the income statement line and the accounts are treated in the same way; revenue lines and accounts are credit less debit, and expense lines and accounts are debit less credit. However, subtotal and subset lines can contain a mix of both revenue and expense accounts; for these income statement lines, there are four options:

1. **Net credit less debit (NCLD)**: The subtotal or subset line is credit less debit, and the accounts drilled into are based on their own account type.

2. **All credit less debit (ACLD)**: The subtotal or subset line is credit less debit, and the accounts drilled into are credit less debit.

3. **Net debit less credit (NDLC)**: The subtotal or subset line is debit less credit, and the accounts drilled into are based on their own account type.

4. **All debit less credit (ADLC)**: The subtotal or subset line is debit less credit, and the accounts drilled into are debit less credit.

These four options are summarized in Table 9-1.

Table 9-1. Summary of the four drill-down options for subtotals and subsets

Subtotal or Subset Calculation Type	Subtotal or Subset Line	Account Drill Down
Net credit less debit	Credit less debit	Based on account type
All credit less debit	Credit less debit	Credit less debit
Net debit less credit	Debit less credit	Based on account type
All debit less credit	Debit less credit	Debit less credit

CHAPTER 9 THE FOUR SUBTOTAL AND SUBSET TYPES

Why Four Options of Subtotal and Subset Are Required

Credit less debit and debit less credit calculations are both essential when producing income statements (Chapter 2). For both credit less debit and debit less credit subtotals and subsets, two further options are required as when these income statement lines are drilled into the accounts can be based on

- **Account type (the net calculations) which is typically preferred by accountants**: These calculations have the advantage that accounts always return the same value, that is, an expense account is always debit less credit

- **The subtotal or subset (all the calculations) which is typically preferred by non-accountants**: These calculations have the advantage that drilled into accounts always sum up to the subtotal or subset value, that is, the sum of drilled into accounts for net income matches the net income line.

When a semantic model has multiple layouts (Part 4), each layout is tailored to a specific audience, and the behavior of subtotals and subsets can be set accordingly.

Examples of the Four Subtotal and Subset Options

To further elaborate on the four options, the example in Table 9-2 shows subtotals of a single account type and the drill-down behavior to accounts.

CHAPTER 9   THE FOUR SUBTOTAL AND SUBSET TYPES

Table 9-2. Revenue and cost of sales subtotals

Subtotal	Drill Down to Account	Account Type	Credit	Debit	Account Balance	Calculation Type
Revenue		Revenue	100	5	95	Credit less debit
	Trade revenue	Revenue	100		100	Credit less debit
	Returns	Revenue		5	−5	Credit less debit
Cost of sales		Expense	7	50	43	Debit less credit
	Trade costs	Expense		50	50	Debit less credit
	Volume discounts	Expense	7		−7	Debit less credit

These subtotals follow both accounting rules and the typical mathematical behavior, that is, the cost of sales account balance (43) is both debit (50) less credit (7) and the sum of the account balances for *trade costs* (50) and *volume discounts* (-7). Subtotals are now created which mix these account types.

Subtotal Option 1: Net Credit Less Debit

Table 9-3 shows how for net credit less debit (NCLD)

- Accounts return the same value in any context, that is, the account balance of *trade costs* is always 50 (the same figure is shown in Tables 9-2 and 9-3).

CHAPTER 9 THE FOUR SUBTOTAL AND SUBSET TYPES

- The gross profit/(loss) subtotal of 52 is non-additive; the sum of the account balance for the drilled through accounts does not equal 52 (100 − 5 + 50 − 7 ≠ 52).

Table 9-3. Gross profit – subtotal net credit less debit

Line Drill Down to Account	Related Account Type(s)	Credit	Debit	Account Balance	Calculation Type
Gross profit/(loss)	Revenue + Expense	107	55	52	Credit less debit
Trade revenue	Revenue	100		100	Credit less debit
Returns	Revenue		5	−5	Credit less debit
Trade costs	Expense		50	50	Debit less credit
Volume discount	Expense	7		−7	Debit less credit

The formula for net credit less debit (as covered in Chapter 5) is

$$NCLD = \sum ('Trial\ Balance'[Value]) \times \max('Account'[Account\ Type\ Indicator])$$

The max of 'Account'[Account Type Indicator] is

- **1 for the gross profit/(loss) subtotal**: The indicator for revenue accounts is 1, which is higher than the −1 indicator for expense accounts.

- **1 for drilled into revenue accounts**: Only the indicator for revenue accounts is in scope.
- **−1 for drilled into expense accounts**: Only the indicator for expense accounts is in scope.

Thus, the 'Account'[Account Type Indicator] enables the debit less credit calculation which is used for drilled into expense accounts.

Subtotal Option 2: All Credit Less Debit

Table 9-4 shows how for all credit less debit (ACLD)

- Accounts return different values dependent on the context in which they are evaluated, that is, the account balance of *trade costs* is −50 when the user has drilled down from gross profit/(loss), but 50 when the user has drilled down from cost of sales (see Table 9-2).
- The gross profit/(loss) subtotal of 52 is additive; the sum of the account balance for the drilled through accounts equals 52 (100 − 5 − 50 + 7 = 52).

CHAPTER 9   THE FOUR SUBTOTAL AND SUBSET TYPES

Table 9-4. Gross profit – subtotal all credit less debit

Line	Drill Down to Account	Related Account Type(s)	Credit	Debit	Account Balance	Calculation Type
	Gross profit/(loss)	Revenue + Expense	107	55	52	Credit less debit
	Trade revenue	Revenue	100		100	Credit less debit
	Returns	Revenue		5	–5	Credit less debit
	Trade costs	Expense		50	–50	Credit less debit
	Volume discount	Expense	7		7	Credit less debit

As the values in the fact table are credit less debit (see Chapter 5), this column can be summed without the need for further enhancements:

$$ACLD = \sum('Trial\ Balance'[Value])$$

Subtotal Option 3: Net Debit Less Credit

Table 9-5 shows how for net debit less credit (NDLC)

- Accounts return the same value in any context, that is, the account balance of *trade revenue* is always 100 (the same figure is shown in Tables 9-2 and 9-5).

- The gross loss/(profit) subtotal of –52 is non-additive; the sum of the account balance for the drilled through accounts does not equal –52 (100 – 5 + 50 – 7 ≠ –52).

207

CHAPTER 9 THE FOUR SUBTOTAL AND SUBSET TYPES

Table 9-5. Gross loss – subtotal net debit less credit

Line Drill Down to Account	Related Account Type(s)	Credit	Debit	Account Balance	Calculation Type
Gross loss/(profit)	Revenue + Expense	107	55	−52	Debit less credit
Trade revenue	Revenue	100		100	Credit less debit
Returns	Revenue		5	−5	Credit less debit
Trade costs	Expense		50	50	Debit less credit
Volume discount	Expense	7		−7	Debit less credit

The formula for net debit less credit (as covered in Chapter 5) is

$$NDLC = \sum('Trial\ Balance'[Value]) \times \min('Account'[Account\ Type\ Indicator'])$$

The min of 'Account'[Account Type Indicator] is

- **−1 for the gross loss/(profit) subtotal**: The indicator for expense accounts is −1, which is lower than the 1 indicator for revenue accounts.

CHAPTER 9   THE FOUR SUBTOTAL AND SUBSET TYPES

- **1 for drilled into revenue accounts**: Only the indicator for revenue accounts is in scope.

- **-1 for drilled into expense accounts**: Only the indicator for expense accounts is in scope.

Thus, the 'Account' [Account Type Indicator] enables the credit less debit calculation for drilled into revenue accounts.

Subtotal Option 4: All Debit Less Credit

Table 9-6 shows how for all debit less credit (ADLC)

- Accounts return different values dependent on the context in which they are evaluated, that is, the account balance of *trade revenue* is –100 when the user has drilled down from gross loss/(profit) but 100 when the user has drilled down from revenue (see Table 9-2).

- The gross loss/(profit) subtotal of –52 is additive; the sum of the account balance for the drilled through accounts equals –52 (–100 + 5 + 50 – 7 = –52).

CHAPTER 9   THE FOUR SUBTOTAL AND SUBSET TYPES

Table 9-6. *Gross loss – all credit less debit*

Line Drill Down to Account	Related Account Type(s)	Credit	Debit	Account Balance	Calculation Type
Gross loss/(profit)	Revenue + Expense	107	55	−52	Debit less credit
Trade revenue	Revenue	100		−100	Debit less credit
Returns	Revenue		5	5	Debit less credit
Trade costs	Expense		50	50	Debit less credit
Volume discount	Expense	7		−7	Debit less credit

As the values in the fact table are credit less debit (see Chapter 5), this column can be summed, then multiplied by −1 to convert credit less debit to debit less credit:

$$ADLC = \sum('Trial\ Balance'[Value]) \times -1$$

Summary

- Subtotal and subset options where all accounts are of the same type are straightforward; the subtotal or subset and drilled into accounts follow the same credit less debit or debit less credit calculation.

CHAPTER 9 THE FOUR SUBTOTAL AND SUBSET TYPES

- Subtotals and subsets can, however, comprise both revenue and expense accounts, resulting in four potential options:

  - **Net credit less debit (NCLD)**: The subtotal or subset line is credit less debit, and the accounts drilled into are based on their own account type.

  - **All credit less debit (ACLD)**: The subtotal or subset line is credit less debit, and the accounts drilled into are credit less debit.

  - **Net debit less credit (NDLC)**: The subtotal or subset line is debit less credit, and the accounts drilled into are based on their own account type.

  - **All debit less credit (ADLC)**: The subtotal or subset line is debit less credit, and the accounts drilled into are debit less credit.

- Net calculations are preferred by accountants and follow the rules of double-entry bookkeeping.

- All calculations create subtotals which are the sum of their parts and are typically preferred by non-accountants.

CHAPTER 10

External Reporting Logical Models

In the previous chapter, we learned about the four subtotal and subset types. We also learned, in Chapter 6, how to create the trial balance logical model and a journal entry logical model; these logical models were used as blueprints for the semantic models in Chapters 7 and 8, respectively.

In this chapter, we will learn how to reproduce external income statements in their entirety by extending the logical account balance models from Chapter 6. To do so, we will firstly learn about the external layout table, which contains the external income statement presentation logic, what lines appear, in which order they appear, which calculations are performed, and how each line is formatted. We will then cover extending the Chapter 6 logical models, adding a 'Layout' snowflake dimension, which is derived from the external layout table, and the 'Shares Outstanding' snapshot fact table.

In this chapter, there are two main sections:

1. The External Layout Table
2. Extending the Trial Balance Logical Model and a Journal Entry Logical Model

CHAPTER 10   EXTERNAL REPORTING LOGICAL MODELS

The External Layout Table

External Layout Table Overview

The external layout table is an essential input into income statement models; this enables models to move from modelling account balances to modelling external income statements in their entirety. Table 10-1 contains a completed external layout table for Tyrell Corp:

CHAPTER 10 EXTERNAL REPORTING LOGICAL MODELS

Table 10-1. Tyrell Corp completed external layout table

Income Statement Key	Line Name	Calculation Type	1st From	1st To	2nd From	2nd To	Is Hidden	Format String Default
1	Revenue:	Blank					No	0;0-0-;;@
2	Product	Line item	10100	10200			No	#,##0,,,;(#,##0..);-
3	Service and other	Line item	10300	10400			No	#,##0,,,;(#,##0..);-
4	Total revenue	Subtotal NCLD	2	3			No	#,##0,,,;(#,##0..);-
5	Cost of revenue:	Blank					No	0;0-0-;;@
6	Product	Line item	20100	20200			No	#,##0,,,;(#,##0..);-
7	Service and other	Line item	20300	20400			No	#,##0,,,;(#,##0..);-
8	Total cost of revenue	Subtotal NCLD	6	7			No	#,##0,,,;(#,##0..);-
9	Gross Margin	Subtotal NCLD	2	7			No	#,##0,,,;(#,##0..);-
10	Research and development	Line item	21100	21200			No	#,##0,,,;(#,##0..);-
11	Project T	Subset NCLD	21120	21120			No	#,##0,,,;(#,##0..);-
12	Sales and marketing	Line item	22100	22200			No	#,##0,,,;(#,##0..);-
13	General and administrative	Line item	23100	23200	24100	24200	No	#,##0,,,;(#,##0..);-
14	Operating income	Subtotal NCLD	2	13			No	#,##0,,,;(#,##0..);-

(*continued*)

Table 10-1. (continued)

Income Statement Key	Line Name	Calculation Type	1st From	1st To	2nd From	2nd To	Is Hidden	Format String Default
15	Other income, net	Line item	11100	11200			No	#,##0,;(#,##0..);-
16	Income before taxes	Subtotal NCLD	2	15			No	#,##0,;;(#,##0..);-
17	Provision for taxes	Line item	30100	30200			No	#,##0,;;(#,##0..);-
18	Net income	Subtotal NCLD	2	17			No	#,##0,;;(#,##0..);-
19	Non-controlling	NCI					No	#,##0,;;(#,##0..);-
20	Controlling	CI					No	#,##0,;;(#,##0..);-
21		Blank					No	0;0-0;;@
22	Earnings per share:	Blank					No	0;0-0;;@
23	Basic	Divide	20	27			No	"$"0.00;("$"0.00);-
24	Diluted	Divide	20	28			No	"$"0.00;("$"0.00);-
25		Blank					No	0;0-0;;@
26	Weighted average shares:	Blank					No	0;0-0;;@
27	Basic	Basic shares					No	#,##0,;(#,##0..);-
28	Diluted	Diluted shares					No	#,##0,;(#,##0..);-

Line Name, Income Statement Key, and Is Hidden

The line name, income statement key, and is hidden columns determine

1. **The name of each line**: That is, the first line is called "Revenue:".

2. **What order lines appear in**: That is, "Revenue:" appears first (income statement key 1) and "Diluted" appears last (income statement key 28).

3. **If any lines are hidden**: That is, the first line "Revenue:" (income statement key 1) is not hidden.

Income Statement Line Calculations

The calculation types – 1st from, 1st to, 2nd from, and 2nd to – determine the calculation performed. For instance:

- Sales and marketing (income statement key 12) calculates account balances for those accounts between 22100 and 22200 and between 24100 and 24200.

- Net income (income statement key 18) is a subtotal net credit less debit (NCLD) of all line-items between income statement keys 2 and 17.

- Project T (income statement key 11) is a subset net credit less debit (NCLD) of account 21120.

- NCI and CI are specialist calculations which include all income statement accounts for the non-controlling and controlling interests, respectively.

- Basic earnings per share (income statement key 23) divides income statement key 20 by income statement key 27.
- Basic (income statement key 27) and diluted (income statement key 28) weighted average shares are specialist calculations summing weighted average shares from the 'Shares Outstanding' snapshot fact table.

Calculation Type Overview

Each of the calculation types is designed to overcome one or more of the calculation challenges outlined in Chapter 3. Table 10-2 provides an overview of the available calculation types and all the related challenges, except for bespoke calculations (challenge 7), which is covered separately in Chapter 12.

Table 10-2. *Summary of the calculation types*

Calculation Type	Comment	Related Calculation Challenge(s)
Line item	Summing accounts of a single account type	1 (line item)
Subtotal NCLD	Subtotal net credit less debit	2 (subtotal)
Subtotal ACLD	Subtotal all credit less debit	2 (subtotal)
Subtotal NDLC	Subtotal net debit less credit	2 (subtotal)
Subtotal ADLC	Subtotal all debit less credit	2 (subtotal)
Subset NCLD	Subtotal net credit less debit	3 (subset)
Subset ACLD	Subtotal all credit less debit	3 (subset)

(continued)

CHAPTER 10 EXTERNAL REPORTING LOGICAL MODELS

Table 10-2. (*continued*)

Calculation Type	Comment	Related Calculation Challenge(s)
Subset NCLD	Subtotal net debit less credit	3 (subset)
Subset ADLC	Subtotal all debit less credit	3 (subset)
CI	Controlling interest	4 (controlling and non-controlling interests)
NCI	Non-controlling interest	4 (controlling and non-controlling interests)
Basic shares	Sum basic shares	5 (weighted average shares)
Diluted shares	Sum diluted shares	5 (weighted average shares)
Divide	Dividing one line by another	6 (earnings per share) and 8 (percentage)
Blank	Spaces between lines	9 (blank lines)

Income Statement Line Formatting

Format string default determines the formatting for each line. For instance:

- Provision for taxes (income statement key 17) is returned in millions using brackets for negatives.

- Blank line (income statement key 21) is formatted to return blank when the result is zero.

- Basic earnings per share (income statement key 23) returns a currency to two decimal places with negatives in brackets.

CHAPTER 10   EXTERNAL REPORTING LOGICAL MODELS

Completing the External Layout Table

To complete the external layout table for any given entity, there are ten steps. Each of these ten steps is discussed as follows.

Step 1: Understand the External Income Statement

To complete the external layout table, it is first necessary to understand the chosen entity's external income statement. Figure 10-1 shows the Tyrell Corp external income statement, and Figure 10-2 shows this same income statement with annotations explaining each line.

		2022	2021	2020
Revenue:	$			
Product		63,968	62,475	62,665
Service and other		115,746	90,223	69,876
Total revenue		179,714	152,698	132,541
Cost of revenue:				
Product		17,729	16,401	15,055
Service and other		37,490	30,272	27,057
Total cost of revenue		55,219	46,673	42,112
Gross margin		124,495	106,025	90,429
Research and development		22,051	18,400	16,720
Project T		451		
Sales and marketing		19,233	18,009	17,290
General and administrative		5,360	4,701	4,750
Operating income		77,852	64,915	51,669
Other income, net		300	913	70
Income before income taxes		78,152	65,828	51,739
Provision for income taxes		9,680	9,003	7,990
Net income		68,472	56,825	43,749
Non-controlling interest		9,445	5,661	6,829
Controlling interest	$	59,027	51,165	36,920
Earnings per share:				
Basic		$10.10	$8.47	$6.22
Diluted		$9.66	$8.62	$6.16
Weighted average shares outstanding:				
Basic		5,847	6,038	5,936
Diluted		6,107	5,934	5,993

Figure 10-1. *Tyrell Corp external income statement*

CHAPTER 10   EXTERNAL REPORTING LOGICAL MODELS

#			2022	2021	2020
1	Revenue:	$			
2	Product Accounts 10100 to 10200		63,968	62,475	62,665
3	Service and other Accounts 10300 to 10400		115,746	90,223	69,876
4	Total revenue Line-items 2 to 3		179,714	152,698	132,541
5	Cost of revenue:				
6	Product Accounts 20100 to 20200		17,729	16,401	15,055
7	Service and other Accounts 20300 to 20400		37,490	30,272	27,057
8	Total cost of revenue Line-items 6 to 7		55,219	46,673	42,112
9	Gross margin Line-items 2 to 7		124,495	106,025	90,429
10	Research and development Accounts 21100 to 21200		22,051	18,400	16,720
11	Project T Accounts 21199 (subset of Research and development)		451		
12	Sales and marketing Accounts 22100 to 22200 and 24100 to 24200		19,233	18,009	17,290
13	General and administrative Accounts 23100 to 23200		5,360	4,701	4,750
14	Operating income Line-items 2 to 13		77,852	64,915	51,669
15	Other income, net Accounts 11100 to 11200		300	913	70
16	Income before income taxes Line-items 2 to 15		78,152	65,828	51,739
17	Provision for income taxes Accounts 30100 to 30200		9,680	9,003	7,990
18	Net income Line-items 2 to 17		68,472	56,825	43,749
19	Non-controlling interest		9,445	5,661	6,829
20	Controlling interest	$	59,027	51,165	36,920
21					
22	Earnings per share:				
23	Basic Line 20 divided by line 27		$10.10	$8.47	$6.22
24	Diluted Line 20 divided by line 28		$9.66	$8.62	$6.16
25					
26	Weighted average shares outstanding:				
27	Basic Number of shares		5,847	6,038	5,936
28	Diluted Number of shares after all conversions		6,107	5,934	5,993

Figure 10-2. Tyrell Corp external income statement annotated

By annotating the external income statement with the calculation logic and numbering each line, Figure 10-2 contains all the information needed to populate the external layout table.

Step 2: Add the Income Statement Keys

Step 2 involves adding income statement keys to the layout table; these sequential integers become primary keys in the 'Layout' snowflake dimension used for relating accounts to line-items, sorting each line, and for subtotal and divide calculations. In the Tyrell Corp example, the income statement keys range from 1 to 28 (Table 10-3).

CHAPTER 10 EXTERNAL REPORTING LOGICAL MODELS

Table 10-3. *Tyrell Corp external layout table income statement keys*

Income Statement Key
1
2
3
4
5
6
7
8
9
10
11
12
13
14
15
16
17
18
19
20

(*continued*)

CHAPTER 10 EXTERNAL REPORTING LOGICAL MODELS

Table 10-3. (*continued*)

Income Statement Key
21
22
23
24
25
28
27
28

Step 3: Add the Line Name

Step 3 involves placing line names against the associated income statement key. Table 10-4 shows the line names which appear on the income statement for Tyrell Corp.

Table 10-4. *Tyrell Corp external layout table with line names*

Income Statement Key	Line Name
1	Revenue:
2	Product
3	Service and other
4	Total revenue
5	Cost of revenue:
6	Product
7	Service and other

(*continued*)

CHAPTER 10 EXTERNAL REPORTING LOGICAL MODELS

Table 10-4. (*continued*)

Income Statement Key	Line Name
8	Total cost of revenue
9	Gross Margin
10	Research and development
11	Project T
12	Sales and marketing
13	General and administrative
14	Operating income
15	Other income, net
16	Income before taxes
17	Provision for taxes
18	Net income
19	Non-controlling
20	Controlling
21	
22	Earnings per share:
23	Basic
24	Diluted
25	
26	Weighted average shares:
27	Basic
28	Diluted

CHAPTER 10 EXTERNAL REPORTING LOGICAL MODELS

Certain line names are prefixed with spaces to achieve the required layout, that is, "   Project T". Other line names – such as *product* – appear twice: income statement keys 2 and 6. The requirement in these cases is to create unique line names, to maintain the sort order when querying the model using MDX. Therefore, in the case of duplicate line names, a space suffixes the second record. For instance:

- For income statement key 2, the line name "   Product" contains prefix spaces, but no suffix space, that is, "   Product"

- For income statement key 6, the line name "   Product " contains prefix spaces and a suffix space, that is, "   Product "

Step 4: Complete Line-Items

Step 4 involves adding all the line-items; these are the lines which are directly related to an account and consist of accounts of a single account type (calculation challenge 1). Each account should appear only once; otherwise, double counting occurs, and net income will be incorrect. Sometimes, the range of accounts is broken, as in the case of the sales and marketing (income statement key 12); this line-item sums those accounts between 22100 and 22200 and between 24100 and 24200. For each line-item:

- The calculation type should equal *Line item*.

- The from and to columns should represent the accounts from and to.

- If the line is to be hidden, the *is hidden* column should contain yes, else it should contain no.

CHAPTER 10   EXTERNAL REPORTING LOGICAL MODELS

- The format string default should display either
  - **Millions:** "#, ##0,,;(#, ##0,,);-"
  - **Thousands:** "#, ##0,;(#, ##0,);-"
  - **Absolute:** "#, ##0;(#, ##0);-"

Table 10-5 contains the layout table with the line-items completed for Tyrell Corp.

CHAPTER 10 ■ EXTERNAL REPORTING LOGICAL MODELS

Table 10-5. Tyrell Corp external layout table with line-items

Income Statement Key	Line Name	Calculation Type	1st From	1st To	2nd From	2nd To	Is Hidden	Format String Default
1	Revenue:							
2	Product	Line item	10100	10200			No	#,##0,,,;(#,##0..);-
3	Service and other	Line item	10300	10400			No	#,##0,,,;(#,##0..);-
4	Total revenue							
5	Cost of revenue:							
6	Product	Line item	20100	20200			No	#,##0,,,;(#,##0..);-
7	Service and other	Line item	20300	20400			No	#,##0,,,;(#,##0..);-
8	Total cost of revenue							
9	Gross Margin							
10	Research and development	Line item	21100	21200			No	#,##0,,,;(#,##0..);-
11	Project T							
12	Sales and marketing	Line item	22100	22200	24100	24200	No	#,##0,,,;(#,##0..);-
13	General and administrative	Line item	23100	23200			No	#,##0,,,;(#,##0..);-
14	Operating income							

(*continued*)

227

CHAPTER 10 EXTERNAL REPORTING LOGICAL MODELS

Table 10-5. (*continued*)

Income Statement Key	Line Name	Calculation Type	1st From	1st To	2nd From	2nd To	Is Hidden	Format String Default
15	Other income, net	Line item	11100	11200			No	#,##0,,;(#,##0,,);-
16	Income before taxes							
17	Provision for taxes	Line item	30100	30200			No	#,##0,,;(#,##0,,);-
18	Net income							
19	Non-controlling							
20	Controlling							
21								
22	Earnings per share:							
23	Basic							
24	Diluted							
25								
26	Weighted average shares:							
27	Basic							
28	Diluted							

228

CHAPTER 10 EXTERNAL REPORTING LOGICAL MODELS

Step 5: Complete Subtotals

Step 5 involves adding the subtotals (calculation challenge 2). For each subtotal:

- The calculation type should equal Subtotal NCLD, Subtotal ACLD, Subtotal NDLC, or Subtotal ADLC depending on the desired subtotal behavior (see Chapter 9).
- The from and to columns should represent the income statement key from and to.
- If the line is to be hidden, the *is hidden* column should contain yes, else it should contain no.
- The format string default should display either
  - **Millions**: "#, ##0,,;(#, ##0,,);-"
  - **Thousands**: "#, ##0,;(#, ##0,);-"
  - **Absolute**: "#, ##0;(#, ##0);-"

Table 10-6 contains the layout table with the subtotals completed for Tyrell Corp.

CHAPTER 10 EXTERNAL REPORTING LOGICAL MODELS

Table 10-6. Tyrell Corp external layout table with subtotals

Income Statement Key	Line Name	Calculation Type	1st From	1st To	2nd From	2nd To	Is Hidden	Format String Default
1	Revenue:							
2	Product	Line item	10100	10200			No	#,##0,,;(#,##0..);-
3	Service and other	Line item	10300	10400			No	#,##0,,;(#,##0..);-
4	Total revenue	**Subtotal NCLD**	**2**	**3**			**No**	**#,##0,,;(#,##0..);-**
5	Cost of revenue:							
6	Product	Line item	20100	20200			No	#,##0,,;(#,##0..);-
7	Service and other	Line item	20300	20400			No	#,##0,,;(#,##0..);-
8	Total cost of revenue	**Subtotal NCLD**	**6**	**7**			**No**	**#,##0,,;(#,##0..);-**
9	Gross Margin	**Subtotal NCLD**	**2**	**7**			**No**	**#,##0,,;(#,##0..);-**
10	Research and development	Line item	21100	21200			No	#,##0,,;(#,##0..);-
11	Project T							
12	Sales and marketing	Line item	22100	22200	24100	24200	No	#,##0,,;(#,##0..);-

CHAPTER 10 EXTERNAL REPORTING LOGICAL MODELS

#	Label	Type					Format
13	General and administrative	Line item	23100	23200			No	#,##0.,;(#,##0..);-
14	Operating income	**Subtotal NCLD**	**2**	**13**			**No**	**#,##0.,;(#,##0..);-**
15	Other income, net	Line item	11100	11200			No	#,##0.,;(#,##0..);-
16	Income before taxes	**Subtotal NCLD**	**2**	**15**			**No**	**#,##0.,;(#,##0..);-**
17	Provision for taxes	Line item	30100	30200			No	#,##0.,;(#,##0..);-
18	Net income	**Subtotal NCLD**	**2**	**17**			**No**	**#,##0.,;(#,##0..);-**
19	Non-controlling							
20	Controlling							
21								
22	Earnings per share:							
23	Basic							
24	Diluted							
25								
26	Weighted average shares:							
27	Basic							
28	Diluted							

CHAPTER 10　EXTERNAL REPORTING LOGICAL MODELS

Note for income statement keys 4 and 8, subtotal NCLD and subtotal NDLC will return identical results; this is because these subtotals consist of a single account type.

Step 6: Complete Subsets

Step 6 involves adding the subsets (calculation challenge 3). For each subset:

- The calculation type should equal *Subset NCLD*, *Subset ACLD*, *Subset NDLC*, or *Subset ADLC* depending on the desired subset behavior (see Chapter 9).

- The from and to columns should represent the account from and to.

- If the line is to be hidden, the *is hidden* column should contain yes, else it should contain no.

- The format string default should display either

  - **Millions**: "#, ##0,,;(#, ##0,,);-"
  - **Thousands**: "#, ##0,;(#, ##0,);-"
  - **Absolute**: "#, ##0;(#, ##0);-"

Table 10-7 contains the layout table with a single subset completed for Tyrell Corp, where Project T is a material component of research and development and therefore requires calling out separately.

CHAPTER 10 EXTERNAL REPORTING LOGICAL MODELS

Table 10-7. Tyrell Corp external layout table with subsets

Income Statement Key	Line Name	Calculation Type	1st From	1st To	2nd From	2nd To	Is Hidden	Format String Default
1	Revenue:							
2	Product	Line item	10100	10200			No	#,##0,,;(#,##0..);-
3	Service and other	Line item	10300	10400			No	#,##0,,;(#,##0..);-
4	Total revenue	Subtotal NCLD	2	3			No	#,##0,,;(#,##0..);-
5	Cost of revenue:							
6	Product	Line item	20100	20200			No	#,##0,,;(#,##0..);-
7	Service and other	Line item	20300	20400			No	#,##0,,;(#,##0..);-
8	Total cost of revenue	Subtotal NCLD	6	7			No	#,##0,,;(#,##0..);-
9	Gross Margin	Subtotal NCLD	2	7			No	#,##0,,;(#,##0..);-
10	Research and development	Line item	21100	21200			No	#,##0,,;(#,##0..);-
11	**Project T**	**Subset NCLD**	**21120**	**21120**			**No**	**#,##0,,;(#,##0..);-**
12	Sales and marketing	Line item	22100	22200	24100	24200	No	#,##0,,;(#,##0..);-
13	General and administrative	Line item	23100	23200			No	#,##0,,;(#,##0..);-
14	Operating income	Subtotal NCLD	2	13			No	#,##0,,;(#,##0..);-

(continued)

CHAPTER 10 EXTERNAL REPORTING LOGICAL MODELS

Table 10-7. (*continued*)

Income Statement Key	Line Name	Calculation Type	1st From	1st To	2nd From	2nd To	Is Hidden	Format String Default
15	Other income, net	Line item	11100	11200			No	#,##0,,;(#,##0..);-
16	Income before taxes	Subtotal NCLD 2	15				No	#,##0,,;(#,##0..);-
17	Provision for taxes	Line item	30100	30200			No	#,##0,,;(#,##0..);-
18	Net income	Subtotal NCLD 2	17				No	#,##0,,;(#,##0..);-
19	Non-controlling							
20	Controlling							
21								
22	Earnings per share:							
23	Basic							
24	Diluted							
25								
26	Weighted average shares:							
27	Basic							
28	Diluted							

Step 7: Complete Controlling and Non-controlling Interests

Step 7 involves adding the controlling and non-controlling interests (calculation challenge 4). For each controlling or non-controlling interest:

- The calculation type should equal *CI* for controlling interest and *NCI* for non-controlling interest.
- If the line is to be hidden, the *is hidden* column should contain yes, else it should contain no.
- The format string default should display either
  - **Millions**: "#, ##0,,;(#, ##0,,);-"
  - **Thousands**: "#, ##0,;(#, ##0,);-"
  - **Absolute**: "#, ##0;(#, ##0);-"

Table 10-8 contains the layout table with the controlling and non-controlling interests completed for Tyrell Corp.

CHAPTER 10 EXTERNAL REPORTING LOGICAL MODELS

Table 10-8. *Tyrell Corp external layout table with controlling and non-controlling interests*

Income Statement Key	Line Name	Calculation Type	1st From	1st To	2nd From	2nd To	Is Hidden	Format String Default
1	Revenue:							
2	Product	Line item	10100	10200			No	#,##0,,;(#,##0,,);-
3	Service and other	Line item	10300	10400			No	#,##0,,;(#,##0,,);-
4	Total revenue	Subtotal NCLD	2	3			No	#,##0,,;(#,##0,,);-
5	Cost of revenue:							
6	Product	Line item	20100	20200			No	#,##0,,;(#,##0,,);-
7	Service and other	Line item	20300	20400			No	#,##0,,;(#,##0,,);-
8	Total cost of revenue	Subtotal NCLD	6	7			No	#,##0,,;(#,##0,,);-
9	Gross Margin	Subtotal NCLD	2	7			No	#,##0,,;(#,##0,,);-
10	Research and development	Line item	21100	21200			No	#,##0,,;(#,##0,,);-
11	Project T	Subset NCLD	21120	21120			No	#,##0,,;(#,##0,,);-
12	Sales and marketing	Line item	22100	22200	24100	24200	No	#,##0,,;(#,##0,,);-

CHAPTER 10 EXTERNAL REPORTING LOGICAL MODELS

13	General and administrative	Line item	23100	23200			No	#,##0,,;(#,##0..);-
14	Operating income	Subtotal NCLD	2		13		No	#,##0,,;(#,##0..);-
15	Other income, net	Line item	11100	11200			No	#,##0,,;(#,##0..);-
16	Income before taxes	Subtotal NCLD	2		15		No	#,##0,,;(#,##0..);-
17	Provision for taxes	Line item	30100	30200			No	#,##0,,;(#,##0..);-
18	Net income	Subtotal NCLD	2		17		No	#,##0,,;(#,##0..);-
19	Non-controlling	**NCI**					**No**	**#,##0,,;(#,##0..);-**
20	Controlling	**CI**					**No**	**#,##0,,;(#,##0..);-**
21								
22	Earnings per share:							
23	Basic							
24	Diluted							
25								
26	Weighted average shares:							
27	Basic							
28	Diluted							

CHAPTER 10   EXTERNAL REPORTING LOGICAL MODELS

Step 8: Complete Weighted Average Shares

Step 8 involves adding the weighted average shares (calculation challenge 5). For each weighted average share line:

- The calculation type should equal *shares* with a prefix for the type of weighted average share calculation, that is, basic shares (income statement key 27) or diluted shares (income statement key 28).

- If the line is to be hidden, the *is hidden* column should contain yes, else it should contain no.

- The format string default should display either

    - **Millions**: "#, ##0,,;(#, ##0,,);-"

    - **Thousands**: "#, ##0,;(#, ##0,);-"

    - **Absolute**: "#, ##0;(#, ##0);-"

Table 10-9 contains the layout table with the basic and diluted shares completed for Tyrell Corp.

CHAPTER 10 EXTERNAL REPORTING LOGICAL MODELS

Table 10-9. Tyrell Corp external layout table with basic and diluted shares

Income Statement Key	Line Name	Calculation Type	1st From	1st To	2nd From	2nd To	Is Hidden	Format String Default
1	Revenue:							
2	Product	Line item	10100	10200			No	#,##0,,;(#,##0..);-
3	Service and other	Line item	10300	10400			No	#,##0,,;(#,##0..);-
4	Total revenue	Subtotal NCLD	2	3			No	#,##0,,;(#,##0..);-
5	Cost of revenue:							
6	Product	Line item	20100	20200			No	#,##0,,;(#,##0..);-
7	Service and other	Line item	20300	20400			No	#,##0,,;(#,##0..);-
8	Total cost of revenue	Subtotal NCLD	6	7			No	#,##0,,;(#,##0..);-
9	Gross Margin	Subtotal NCLD	2	7			No	#,##0,,;(#,##0..);-
10	Research and development	Line item	21100	21200			No	#,##0,,;(#,##0..);-
11	Project T	Subset NCLD	21120	21120			No	#,##0,,;(#,##0..);-
12	Sales and marketing	Line item	22100	22200	24100	24200	No	#,##0,,;(#,##0..);-
13	General and administrative	Line item	23100	23200			No	#,##0,,;(#,##0..);-
14	Operating income	Subtotal NCLD	2	13			No	#,##0,,;(#,##0..);-

(continued)

CHAPTER 10 EXTERNAL REPORTING LOGICAL MODELS

Table 10-9. (continued)

Income Statement Key	Line Name	Calculation Type	1st From	1st To	2nd From	2nd To	Is Hidden	Format String Default
15	Other income, net	Line item	11100	11200			No	#,##0,,;(#,##0..);-
16	Income before taxes	Subtotal NCLD	2	15			No	#,##0,,;(#,##0..);-
17	Provision for taxes	Line item	30100	30200			No	#,##0,,;(#,##0..);-
18	Net income	Subtotal NCLD	2	17			No	#,##0,,;(#,##0..);-
19	Non-controlling	NCI					No	#,##0,,;(#,##0..);-
20	Controlling	CI					No	#,##0,,;(#,##0..);-
21								
22	Earnings per share:							
23	Basic							
24	Diluted							
25								
26	Weighted average shares:							
27	Basic	Basic shares					No	#,##0,,;(#,##0..);-
28	Diluted	Diluted shares					No	#,##0,,;(#,##0..);-

CHAPTER 10   EXTERNAL REPORTING LOGICAL MODELS

Step 9: Complete Earnings per Share

Step 9 involves adding earnings per share (calculation challenge 6). For each earnings per share line:

- The calculation type should equal *Divide*.

- The from and to columns should represent the income statement key numerator and denominator, respectively. For instance, basic earnings per share is income statement key 20 divided by income statement key 27.

- If the line is to be hidden, the *is hidden* column should contain yes, else it should contain no.

- The format string default should display the appropriate currency and rounding. For instance, "$"0.00;("$"0.00);- which in dollars is to two decimal places.

Table 10-10 contains the layout table with the basic earnings per shares and diluted earnings shares completed for Tyrell Corp.

CHAPTER 10 EXTERNAL REPORTING LOGICAL MODELS

Table 10-10. *Tyrell Corp external layout table with basic and diluted earnings per share*

Income Statement Key	Line Name	Calculation Type	1st From	1st To	2nd From	2nd To	Is Hidden	Format String Default
1	Revenue:	Blank						0;0-0;;@
2	Product	Line item	10100	10200			No	#,##0.,;(#,##0..);-
3	Service and other	Line item	10300	10400			No	#,##0.,;(#,##0..);-
4	Total revenue	Subtotal NCLD	2	3			No	#,##0.,;(#,##0..);-
5	Cost of revenue:	Blank						0;0-0;;@
6	Product	Line item	20100	20200			No	#,##0.,;(#,##0..);-
7	Service and other	Line item	20300	20400			No	#,##0.,;(#,##0..);-
8	Total cost of revenue	Subtotal NCLD	6	7			No	#,##0.,;(#,##0..);-
9	Gross Margin	Subtotal NCLD	2	7			No	#,##0.,;(#,##0..);-
10	Research and development	Line item	21100	21200			No	#,##0.,;(#,##0..);-
11	Project T	Subset NCLD	21120	21120			No	#,##0.,;(#,##0..);-
12	Sales and marketing	Line item	22100	22200	24100	24200	No	#,##0.,;(#,##0..);-
13	General and administrative	Line item	23100	23200			No	#,##0.,;(#,##0..);-

CHAPTER 10 EXTERNAL REPORTING LOGICAL MODELS

14	Operating income	Subtotal NCLD	2	13	No	#,##0,;(#,##0..);-
15	Other income, net	Line item	11100	11200	No	#,##0,;(#,##0..);-
16	Income before taxes	Subtotal NCLD	2	15	No	#,##0,;(#,##0..);-
17	Provision for taxes	Line item	30100	30200	No	#,##0,;(#,##0..);-
18	Net income	Subtotal NCLD	2	7	No	#,##0,;(#,##0..);-
19	Non-controlling	NCI			No	#,##0,;(#,##0..);-
20	Controlling	CI			No	#,##0,;(#,##0..);-
21						
22	Earnings per share:					
23	**Basic**	**Divide**	**20**	**27**	**No**	**"$"0.00;("$"0.00);**
24	**Diluted**	**Divide**	**20**	**28**	**No**	**"$"0.00;("$"0.00);**
25						
26	Weighted average shares:					
27	Basic	Basic shares			No	#,##0,;(#,##0..);-
28	Diluted	Diluted shares			No	#,##0,;(#,##0..);-

243

CHAPTER 10   EXTERNAL REPORTING LOGICAL MODELS

Step 10: Complete Blanks

Step 10 involves adding the blank lines (calculation challenge 9). For each blank line:

- The calculation type should equal *blank*.
- If the line is to be hidden, the *is hidden* column should contain yes, else it should contain no.
- The format string default should convert zeros to blanks.

Table 10-11 contains the layout table with the blank lines completed for Tyrell Corp.

CHAPTER 10 EXTERNAL REPORTING LOGICAL MODELS

Table 10-11. Tyrell Corp external layout table with blank lines

Income Statement Key	Line Name	Calculation Type	1st From	1st To	2nd From	2nd To	Is Hidden	Format String Default
1	Revenue:	Blank					No	0;0-0;;@
2	Product	Line item	10100	10200			No	#,##0,,;(#,##0..);-
3	Service and other	Line item	10300	10400			No	#,##0,,;(#,##0..);-
4	Total revenue	Subtotal NCLD	2	3			No	#,##0,,;(#,##0..);-
5	Cost of revenue:	Blank					No	0;0-0;;@
6	Product	Line item	20100	20200			No	#,##0,,;(#,##0..);-
7	Service and other	Line item	20300	20400			No	#,##0,,;(#,##0..);-
8	Total cost of revenue	Subtotal NCLD	6	7			No	#,##0,,;(#,##0..);-
9	Gross Margin	Subtotal NCLD	2	7			No	#,##0,,;(#,##0..);-
10	Research and development	Line item	21100	21200			No	#,##0,,;(#,##0..);-
11	Project T	Subset NCLD	21120	21120			No	#,##0,,;(#,##0..);-
12	Sales and marketing	Line item	22100	22200	24100	24200	No	#,##0,,;(#,##0..);-
13	General and administrative	Line item	23100	23200			No	#,##0,,;(#,##0..);-

(*continued*)

CHAPTER 10 EXTERNAL REPORTING LOGICAL MODELS

Table 10-11. (continued)

Income Statement Key	Line Name	Calculation Type	1st From	1st To	2nd From	2nd To	Is Hidden	Format String Default
14	Operating income	Subtotal NCLD	2	13			No	#,##0,,,;(#,##0..);-
15	Other income, net	Line item	11100	11200			No	#,##0,,,;(#,##0..);-
16	Income before taxes	Subtotal NCLD	2	15			No	#,##0,,,;(#,##0..);-
17	Provision for taxes	Line item	30100	30200			No	#,##0,,,;(#,##0..);-
18	Net income	Subtotal NCLD	2	17			No	#,##0,,,;(#,##0..);-
19	Non-controlling	NCI					No	#,##0,,,;(#,##0..);-
20	Controlling	CI					No	#,##0,,,;(#,##0..);-
21		**Blank**					**No**	**0;0-0;;@**
22	Earnings per share:	**Blank**					**No**	**0;0-0;;@**
23	Basic	Divide	20	27			No	"$"0.00;("$"0.00);-
24	Diluted	Divide	20	28			No	"$"0.00;("$"0.00);-
25		**Blank**					**No**	**0;0-0;;@**
26	Weighted average shares:	**Blank**					**No**	**0;0-0;;@**
27	Basic	Basic shares					No	#,##0,,,;(#,##0..);-
28	Diluted	Diluted shares					No	#,##0,,,;(#,##0..);-

CHAPTER 10   EXTERNAL REPORTING LOGICAL MODELS

Extending the Trial Balance Logical Model and a Journal Entry Logical Model

To support external income statement reporting for Tyrell Corp, Weyland Industries, and StarSchema.co.uk, the logical models produced in Chapter 6 are required to be extended to include

1. 'Shares Outstanding' snapshot fact table: This contains the relevant weighted number of outstanding shares, that is, for Tyrell Corp, the basic and diluted weighted number of outstanding shares.

2. 'Effective Date'[Date] → 'Shares Outstanding'[Start of time period] relationship.

3. 'Layout' snowflake dimension: Derived from the external layout input table, this contains the logic surrounding how the external income statement is displayed.

4. 'Account'[Layout 1 Income Statement Key] foreign key: Derived from the external layout input table, this contains the logic surrounding how accounts are mapped to the external layout line-items.

5. 'Layout'[Income Statement Key] → 'Account'[Layout 1 Income Statement Key] relationship.

This section covers these five extensions, then applies these extensions to the logical models built in Chapter 6.

CHAPTER 10   EXTERNAL REPORTING LOGICAL MODELS

Extension 1: Adding the Shares Outstanding Fact Table

To calculate EPS, a 'Shares Outstanding' fact table is required in the model. This snapshot fact table related to the effective date table contains the

- **Start of time period**: A date reflecting the first day of the time period, that is, 1 January 2023
- **Time period**: The time period to which the weighted average share calculation relates, that is, Period 1 2023, Quarter 1 2023, or 2023
- **Calculation type**: The type of shares calculation, that is, basic or diluted
- **Weighted average shares outstanding**: The weighted average shares outstanding for the particular time period and calculation type

StarSchema.co.uk Example Shares Outstanding Table

As an example, the 2023 basic shares data for StarSchema.co.uk is shown in Table 10-12, where

- The start of time period contains the first date in the period. For instance, the start of time period is 1 Jan 2023 for time periods "2023," "2023-Q1," and "2023-P1."
- The time period contains the time period to which the basic shares value belongs. For instance, the time period "2023" refers to the weighted average number of shares outstanding in 2023, whereas the time period "2023-Q1" refers to the weighted average number of shares outstanding in quarter 1 of 2023.

CHAPTER 10 EXTERNAL REPORTING LOGICAL MODELS

- The calculation type contains the type of calculation, in this case, basic shares.
- The weighted average shares outstanding (millions) refers to the number of weighted average shares outstanding in millions. For instance, there were 5,496m weighted average shares outstanding in 2023.

Table 10-12. Shares outstanding for StarSchema.co.uk

Start of Time Period	Time Period	Calculation Type	Weighted Average Shares Outstanding (m)
1 Jan 2022	2023	Basic shares	5,496
1 Jan 2022	2023-Q1	Basic shares	5,468
1 Jan 2022	2023-P1	Basic shares	5,570
1 Feb 2022	2023-P2	Basic shares	5,372
1 Mar 2022	2023-P3	Basic shares	5,418
1 Apr 2022	2023-Q2	Basic shares	5,410
1 Apr 2022	2023-P4	Basic shares	5,408
1 May 2022	2023-P5	Basic shares	5,391

Extension 2: Creating the Relationship Between Effective Date and Shares Outstanding

To include the weighted average shares outstanding calculation for a selected date, an 'Effective Date' [Date] → 'Shares Outstanding'[Start of time period] relationship is required (Figure 10-3).

CHAPTER 10   EXTERNAL REPORTING LOGICAL MODELS

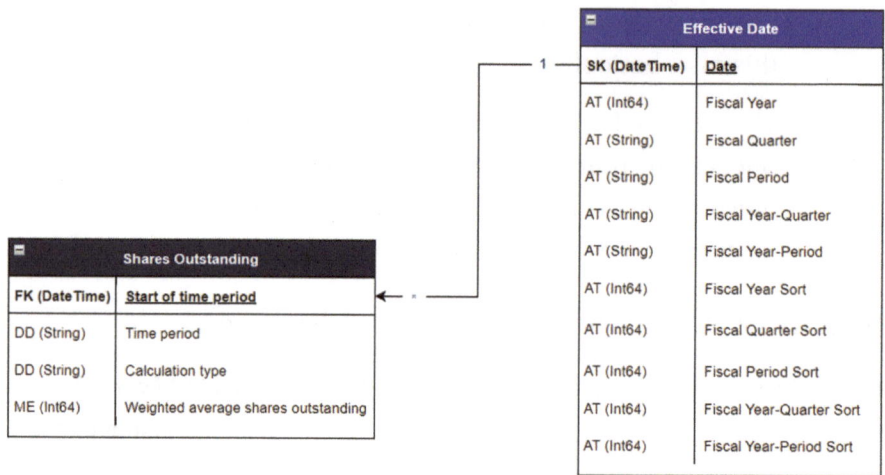

Figure 10-3. Shares outstanding logical model

Extension 3: Adding the Layout Snowflake Dimension

The 'Layout' snowflake dimension is derived from the layout table. The differences between the layout table and 'Layout' dimension exist so the model can efficiently perform the required calculations. The layout table is ingested by the model, and then, using Power Query (see Chapter 11), this is transformed to contain the fields in the dimension as per as per Figure 10-4.

CHAPTER 10 EXTERNAL REPORTING LOGICAL MODELS

Layout	
SK (Int64)	Income Statement Key
AT (String)	Line name
AT (String)	Calculation type
AT (Int64)	Show value
AT (Int64)	Subtotal from net credit less debit
AT (Int64)	Subtotal to net credit less debit
AT (Int64)	Subtotal from all credit less debit
AT (Int64)	Subtotal to all credit less debit
AT (Int64)	Subtotal from net debit less credit
AT (Int64)	Subtotal to net debit less credit
AT (Int64)	Subtotal from all debit less credit
AT (Int64)	Subtotal to all debit less credit
AT (Int64)	Subset from net credit less debit
AT (Int64)	Subset to net credit less debit
AT (Int64)	Subset from all credit less debit
AT (Int64)	Subset to all credit less debit
AT (Int64)	Subset from net debit less credit
AT (Int64)	Subset to net debit less credit
AT (Int64)	Subset from all debit less credit
AT (Int64)	Subset to all debit less credit
AT (Int64)	Numerator
AT (Int64)	Denominator
AT (String)	Format string default

Figure 10-4. Layout snowflake dimension

CHAPTER 10   EXTERNAL REPORTING LOGICAL MODELS

Extension 4: Adding a Foreign Key to the Account Dimension

Accounts are assigned to line-items in the 'Layout' snowflake dimension. To achieve this, the 'Account' table requires a foreign key containing the 'Account'[Layout 1 Income Statement Key] which is derived from the external layout table. For instance, in Table 10-13 'Account'[Account Key] 30100 is mapped to 'Account'[Layout 1 Income Statement Key] 2.

Table 10-13. Account table with mapping to layout 1

Account Key	Account Name	Account Type	Account Type Indicator	Layout 1 Income Statement Key
30100	Trade sales	Revenue	1	2
30101	Returns	Revenue	1	2
40100	Trade cost of sales	Expense	-1	4

Extension 5: Creating the Relationship Between Layout and Accounts

The layout logical model (Figure 10-5) contains the 'Layout'[Income Statement Key] → 'Account'[Layout 1 Income Statement Key] relationship, enabling lines from the external layout to be mapped to an account.

CHAPTER 10 EXTERNAL REPORTING LOGICAL MODELS

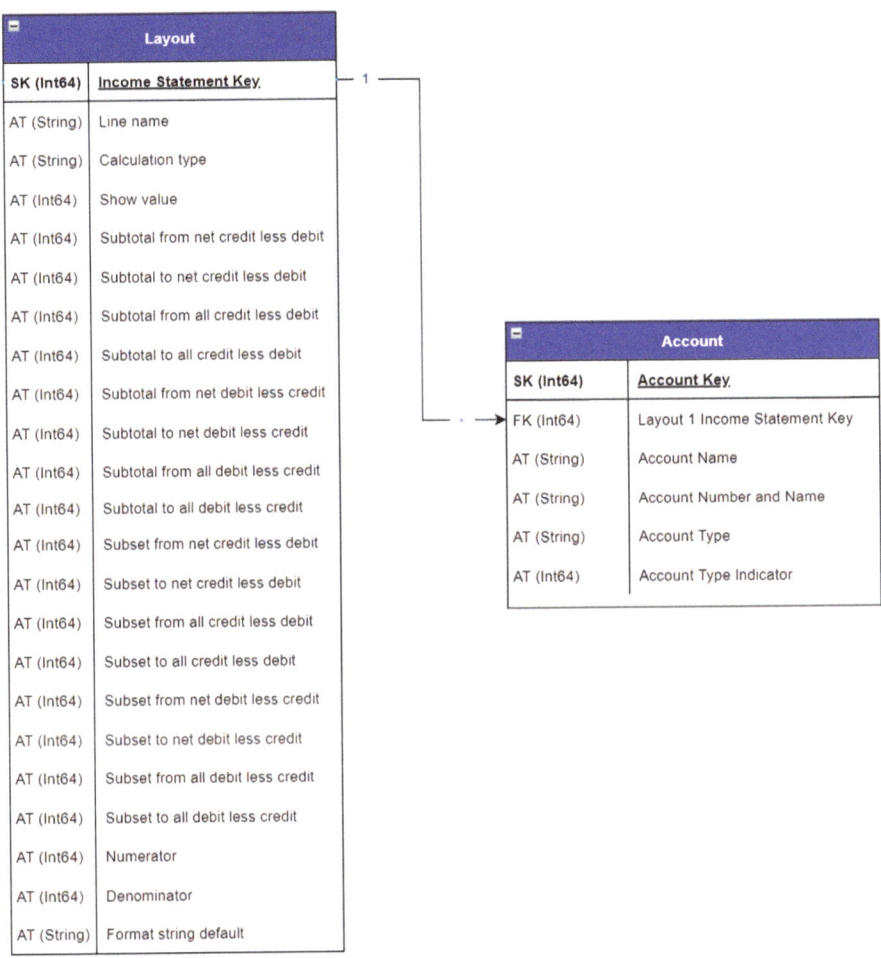

Figure 10-5. Layout to account relationship

253

CHAPTER 10   EXTERNAL REPORTING LOGICAL MODELS

External Reporting Logical Model

Trial Balance External Reporting Logical Model

Figure 10-6 shows the trial balance logical model (Chapter 6) with the five extensions required to support external income statements:

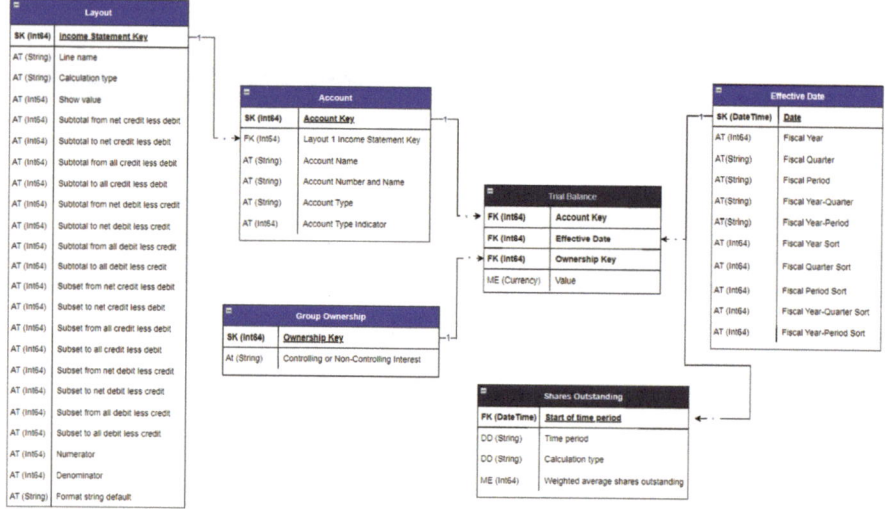

Figure 10-6. Trial balance external reporting logical model

A Journal Entry External Reporting Logical Model

Figure 10-7 shows a journal entry logical model for StarSchema.co.uk (Chapter 6) with the five extensions required to support external income statements.

CHAPTER 10 EXTERNAL REPORTING LOGICAL MODELS

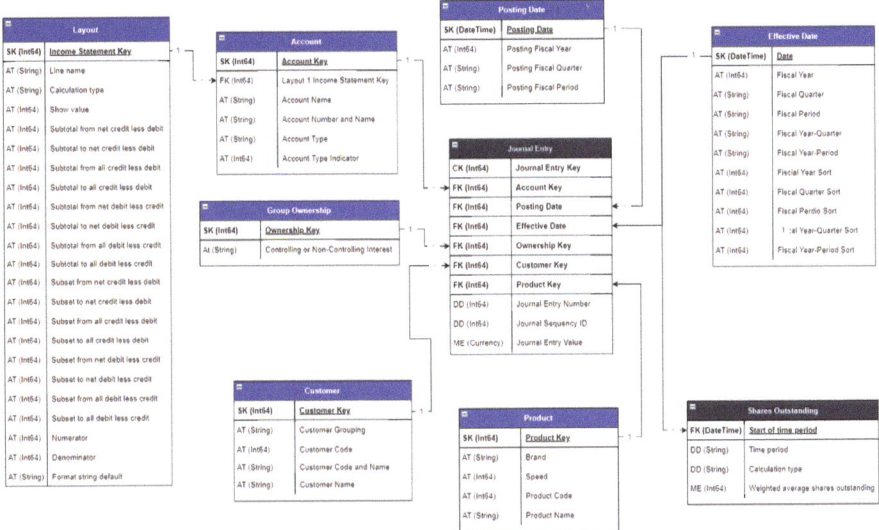

Figure 10-7. A journal entry external reporting logical model

Summary

- To calculate external income statements in their entirety, the logical account balance models from Chapter 6 require five extensions:

  - 'Shares Outstanding' snapshot fact table contains the relevant weighted number of outstanding shares, that is, for Tyrell Corp the basic and diluted weighted number of outstanding shares.

  - 'Effective Date'[Date] → 'Shares Outstanding'[Start of time period] relationship.

  - 'Layout' snowflake dimension contains the logic surrounding how the income statement is displayed.

255

CHAPTER 10 EXTERNAL REPORTING LOGICAL MODELS

- 'Account'[Layout 1 Income Statement Key] foreign key contains the logic surrounding how line-items are mapped to the 'Layout' snowflake dimension.

- 'Layout'[Income Statement Key] → 'Account'[Layout 1 Income Statement Key] relationship.

- The 'Layout' snowflake dimension and 'Account'[Layout 1 Income Statement Key] foreign key are both derived from a layout table which contains the income statement presentation logic.

CHAPTER 11

External Reporting Semantic Models

In the previous chapter, we learned about extensions to the trial balance logical model and a journal entry logical model. These extensions created the trial balance external reporting logical model and a journal entry external reporting logical model, both of which support the creation of income statements.

In this chapter, we will create trial balance external reporting semantic models and a journal entry external reporting semantic model. This involves extending the trial balance semantic models (Chapter 7) and a journal entry semantic model (Chapter 8), based on the external reporting logical models in Chapter 10. We will start with a base semantic model – either Tyrell Corp (Chapter 7), Weyland Industries (Chapter 7), or StarSchema.co.uk (Chapter 8) – then go through each semantic model stage covering Power Query, data modelling, DAX, and dynamic format strings.

In this chapter, there are five sections:

1. Semantic Model Inputs
2. Power Query Transformations
3. Building the Data Model
4. DAX Actuals Calculation
5. Dynamic Format Strings

CHAPTER 11   EXTERNAL REPORTING SEMANTIC MODELS

Semantic Model Inputs

This chapter builds upon the semantic models created in Chapters 7 and 8. The starting point is, therefore, either the Tyrell Corp or Weyland Industries trial balance semantic model (as created in Chapter 7) or the StarSchema.co.uk journal entry semantic model (as created in Chapter 8). You can either use the PBIX file you created in these chapters or download from the resources, either the Tyrell Corp Chapter 7 end, Weyland Industries Chapter 7 end, or StarSchema.co.uk Chapter 8 end.

Alongside the PBIX file, you will require the accompanying *External Layout* and *Shares Outstanding* inputs as described in the previous chapter; these can also be found in the resources. For instance, this chapter follows along using the StarSchema.co.uk files:

- StarSchema.co.uk External Layout
- StarSchema.co.uk Shares Outstanding

If you are following along using the Tyrell Corp or Weyland Industries example, replace StarSchema.co.uk with the relevant organization, that is, Tyrell Corp External Layout as opposed to StarSchema.co.uk External Layout. Regardless of the entity chosen – Tyrell Corp, Weyland Industries, or StarSchema.co.uk – the steps in the second (Power Query), third (data modelling), fourth (DAX actuals calculation), and fifth (dynamic format strings) sections are identical. However, the output will be different given the nature of the input-driven approach (see Chapter 3), that is, Tyrell Corp is using the external layout for Tyrell Corp as an input, whereas StarSchema.co.uk is using the external layout for StarSchema.co.uk as an input.

CHAPTER 11 EXTERNAL REPORTING SEMANTIC MODELS

Power Query Transformations

This section covers the additional data inputs and transformations. This is covered in four stages:

- **Stage 1**: Create shared expressions
- **Stage 2**: Shares outstanding fact table
- **Stage 3**: Layout dimension table
- **Stage 4**: Accounts dimension table

Each of these stages contains many individual steps.

Stage 1: Create Shared Expressions

Step 1: In the Power Query editor, select the **New Source** drop-down (**1**) and **Text/CSV** (**2**).

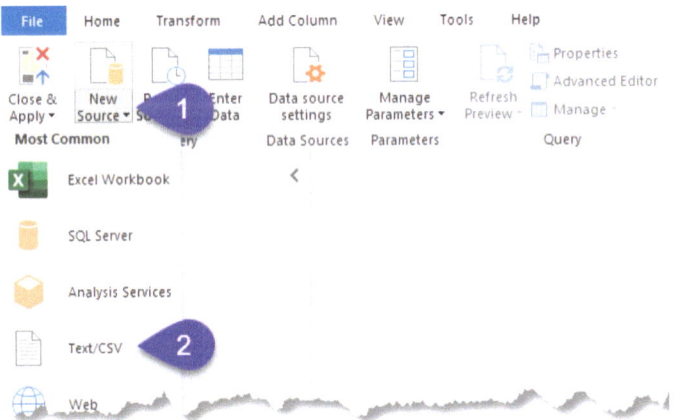

Figure 11-1. Ingest new source

Step 2: Select the file **StarSchema.co.uk Shares Outstanding** (**1**) and click **Open** (**2**).

259

CHAPTER 11   EXTERNAL REPORTING SEMANTIC MODELS

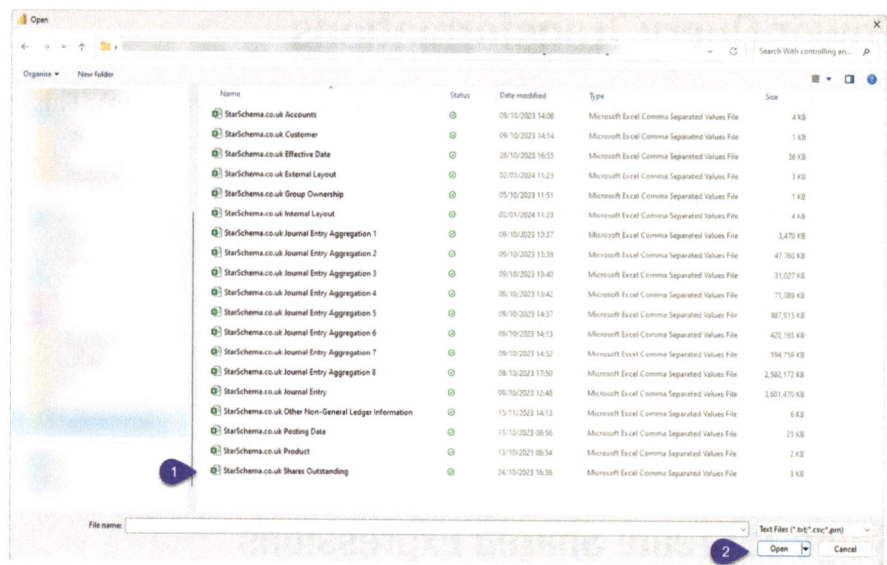

Figure 11-2. File explorer

Step 3: Click **OK (1)** to bring the table into the model.

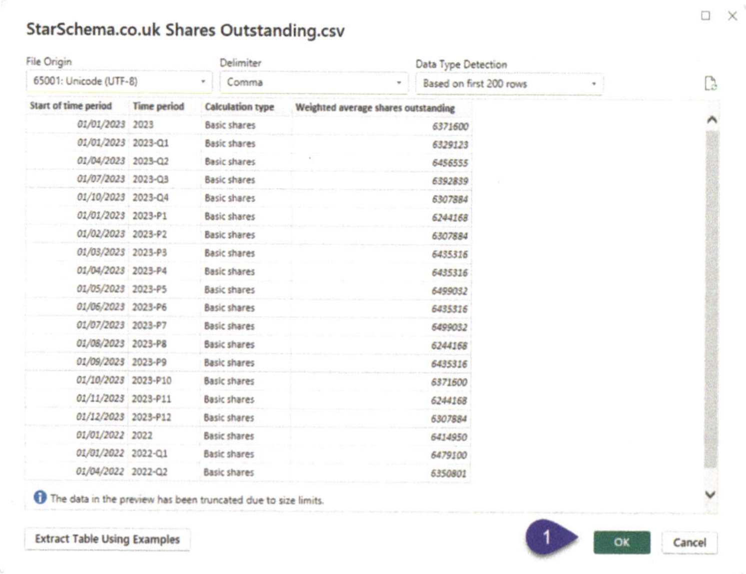

Figure 11-3. Ingest shares outstanding

CHAPTER 11   EXTERNAL REPORTING SEMANTIC MODELS

Step 4: Check types as shown in Figure 11-4.

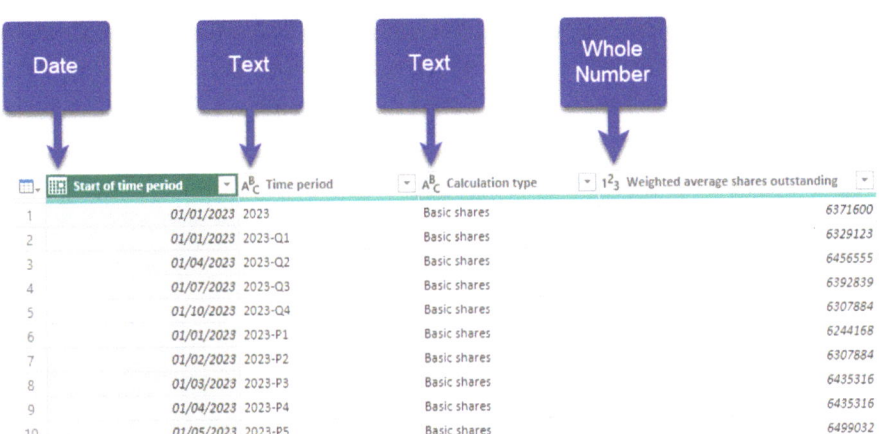

Figure 11-4. Shares outstanding data types

Step 5: Right-click **StarSchema co uk Shares Outstanding (1)** and select **Move To Group (2)** and select **Shared Expressions (3)**.

CHAPTER 11   EXTERNAL REPORTING SEMANTIC MODELS

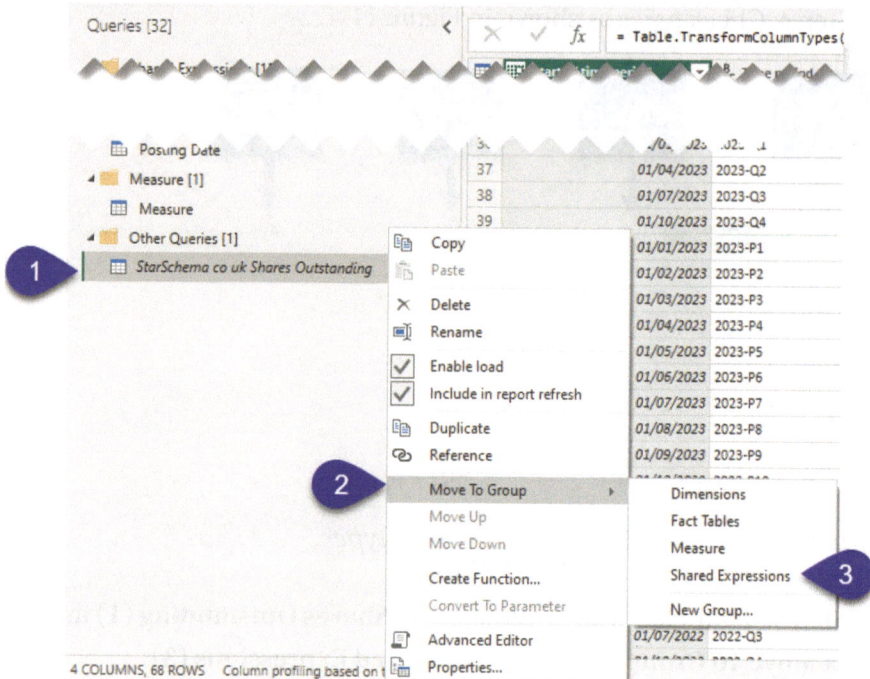

***Figure 11-5.** Shares outstanding move to shared expression group*

Step 6: In the Queries pane, right-click **StarSchema co uk Shares Outstanding (1)** and click the selected **Enable load (2)** to disable the load (should no longer have tick to the left of *Enable load,* and *Star Schema co uk Shares Outstanding* should be in italics).

CHAPTER 11   EXTERNAL REPORTING SEMANTIC MODELS

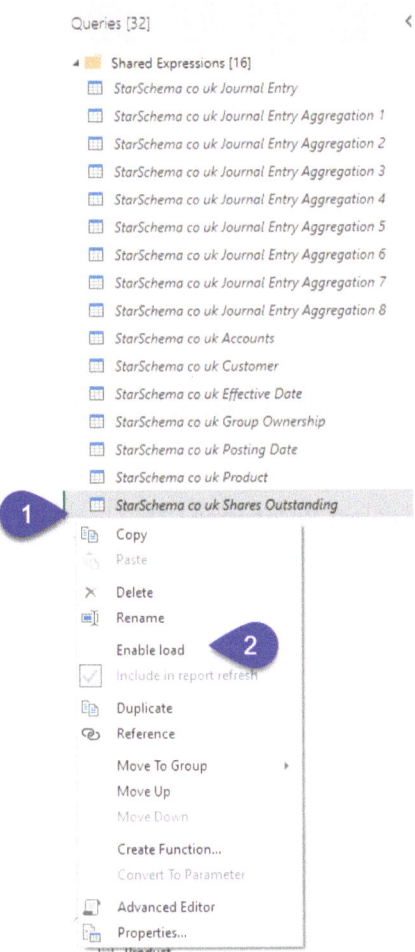

Figure 11-6. Shares outstanding disable load

Step 7: Repeat steps 1–6 for **StarSchema.co.uk External Layout**.

CHAPTER 11 EXTERNAL REPORTING SEMANTIC MODELS

Figure 11-7. External layout data types

Stage 2: Shares Outstanding Fact Table

Step 1: In the Queries pane, right-click **StarSchema co uk Shares Outstanding (1)** and select **Reference (2)**.

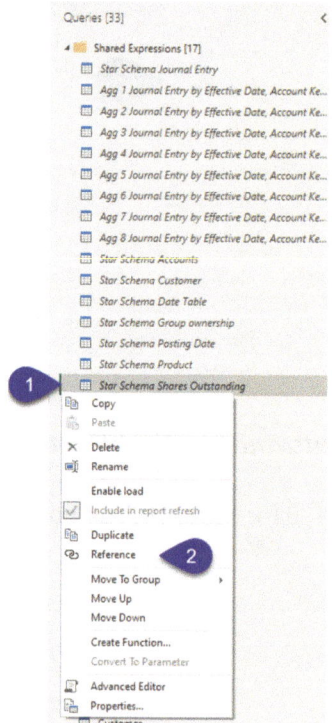

Figure 11-8. Shares outstanding reference

Step 2: Select the referenced query **StarSchema Shares Outstanding (2) (1)**, and in the query settings under **Name (2)**, type *Shares Outstanding* and press enter.

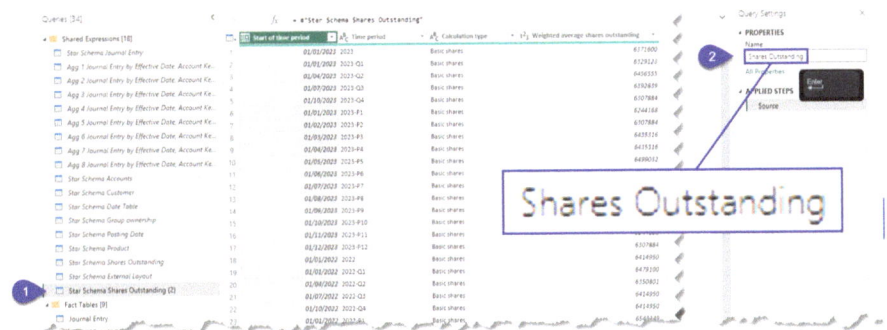

Figure 11-9. *Shares outstanding rename*

Step 3: Right-click **Shares Outstanding (1)**, select **Move To Group (2)**, and select **Fact Tables (3)**.

CHAPTER 11 EXTERNAL REPORTING SEMANTIC MODELS

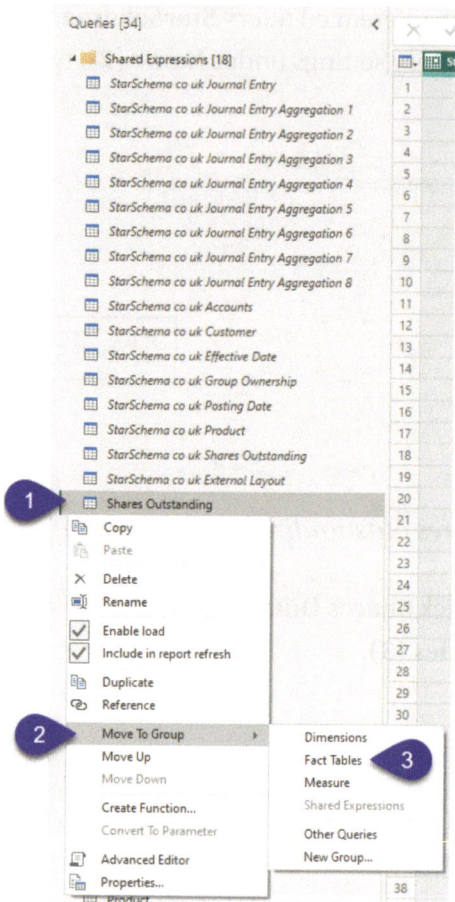

Figure 11-10. Shares outstanding move to fact table group

Stage 3: Layout Dimension Table

Producing the 'Layout' snowflake dimension from the layout table is broken down into six further stages:

1. Create the layout table

2. Add conditional logic to create subtotal columns

CHAPTER 11   EXTERNAL REPORTING SEMANTIC MODELS

3. Add conditional logic to create subset columns
4. Add conditional logic to create percentage columns
5. Add conditional logic to create Show Value columns
6. Remove unnecessary columns and change data types

Creating the Layout Table

Step 1: In the Queries pane, right-click **StarSchema co uk External Layout (1)** and select **Reference (2)**.

CHAPTER 11   EXTERNAL REPORTING SEMANTIC MODELS

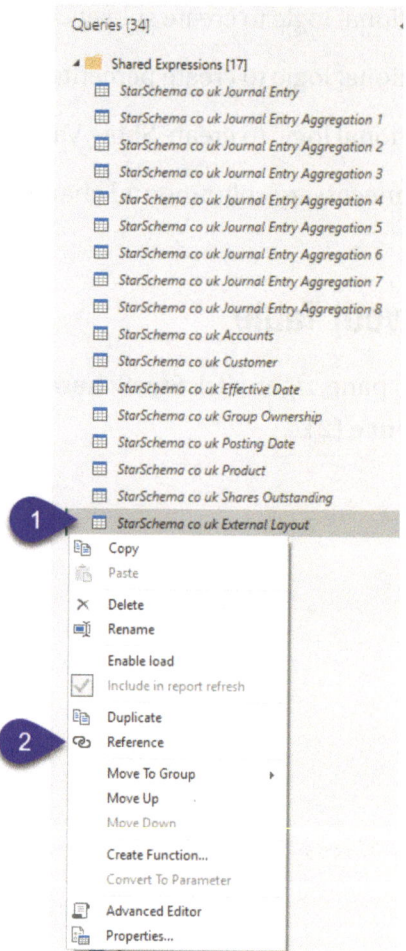

Figure 11-11. Reference external layout

Step 2: Select the referenced query **StarSchema co uk External Layout (2) (1)**, and in the query settings under **Name (2)**, type *Layout* and press enter.

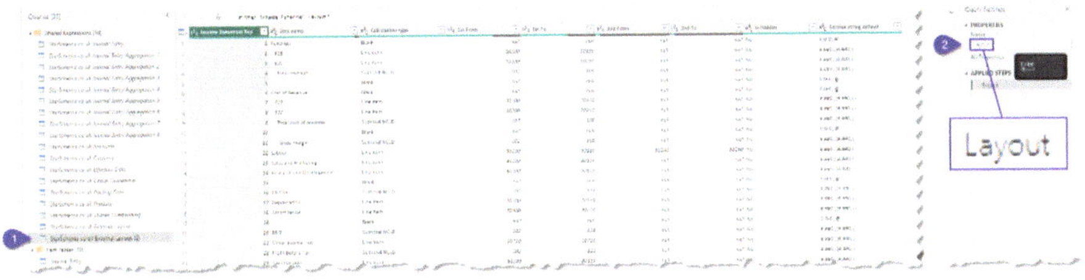

CHAPTER 11 EXTERNAL REPORTING SEMANTIC MODELS

Figure 11-12. Rename external layout

Step 3: Right-click **Layout (1)**, select **Move To Group (2)**, and **Dimensions (3)**.

269

CHAPTER 11   EXTERNAL REPORTING SEMANTIC MODELS

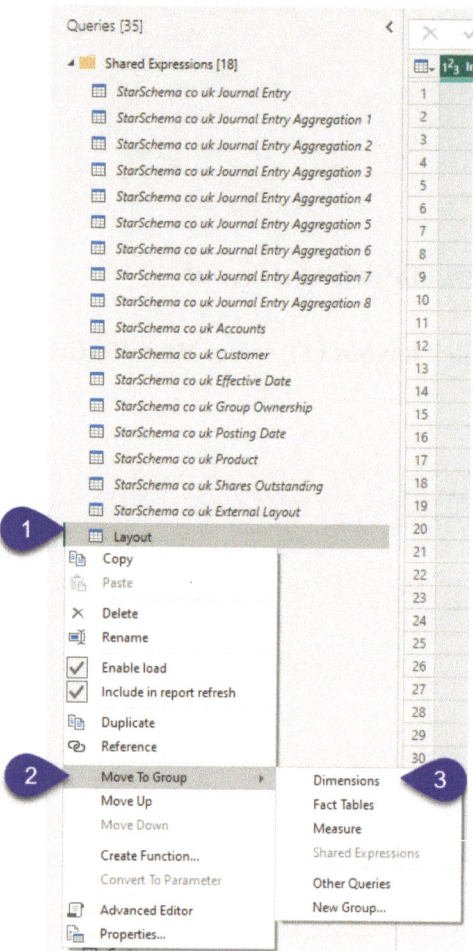

Figure 11-13. Move layout to the dimension group

Add Conditional Logic to Create Subtotal Columns

Step 1: In the Queries pane, select **Layout (1)**, select the tab **Add Column (2)**, and select **Conditional Column (3)**.

CHAPTER 11 EXTERNAL REPORTING SEMANTIC MODELS

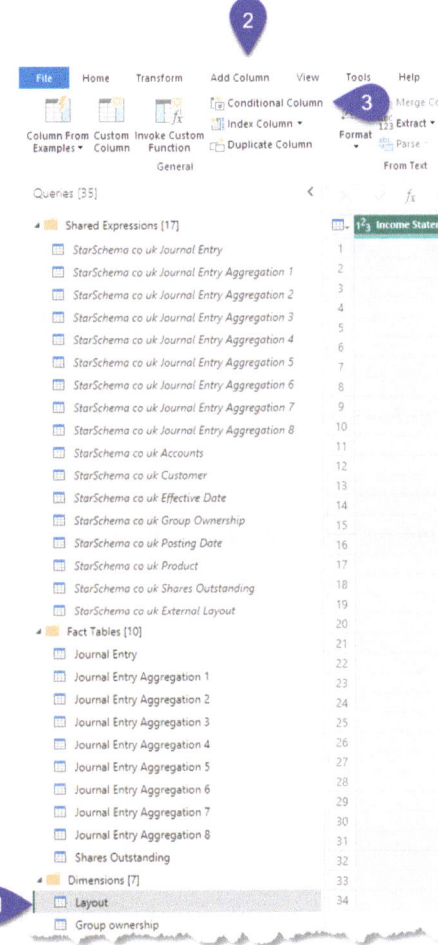

Figure 11-14. *Add conditional from column for subtotal from*

Step 2: In the Add Conditional Column box, type the name *Subtotal from* and the subtotal option, that is, **Subtotal from net credit less debit** (**1**); select the Column Name **Calculation type** (**2**); select the operator **equals** (**3**); type the name *Subtotal* and the subtotal option, that is, **Subtotal NCLD** (**4**); select the drop-down (**5**); select the option **Select a column** (**6**); select the column **1st From** (**7**); and click **OK** (**8**).

CHAPTER 11   EXTERNAL REPORTING SEMANTIC MODELS

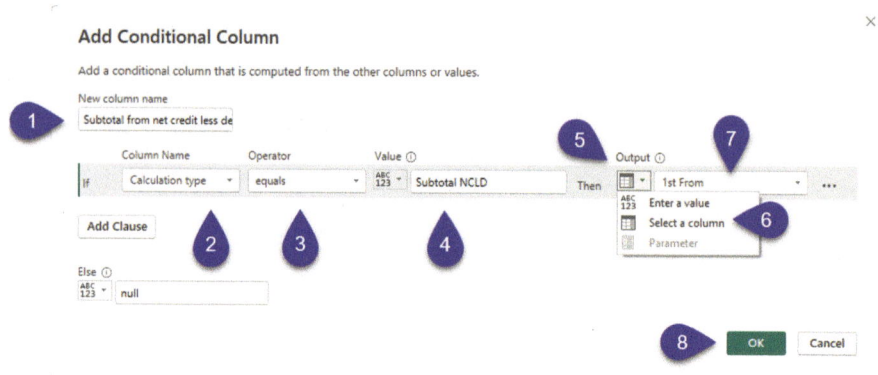

Figure 11-15.   Create subtotal from net credit less debit

Step 3: In the Queries pane, select **Layout (1)**, select the tab **Add Column (2)**, and select **Conditional Column (3)**.

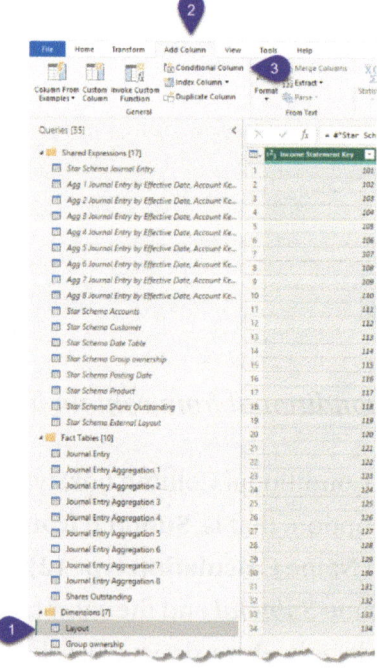

Figure 11-16.   Add conditional to column for subtotal to

272

Step 4: In the Add Conditional Column box, type the name *Subtotal to* and the subtotal option, that is, **Subtotal to net credit less debit (1)**; select the Column Name **Calculation type (2)**; select the operator **equals (3)**; type the name *Subtotal* and the subtotal option, that is, **Subtotal NCLD (4)**; select the drop-down **(5)**; select the option **Select a column (6)**; select the column **1st To (7)**; and click **OK (8)**.

Figure 11-17. Create subtotal to net credit less debit

Step 5: Repeat steps 1–4 for each subtotal option **NDLC**, **ACLD**, and **ADLC**.

Add Conditional Logic to Create Subset Columns

Step 1: In the Queries pane, select **Layout (1)**, select the tab **Add Column (2)**, and select **Conditional Column (3)**.

CHAPTER 11   EXTERNAL REPORTING SEMANTIC MODELS

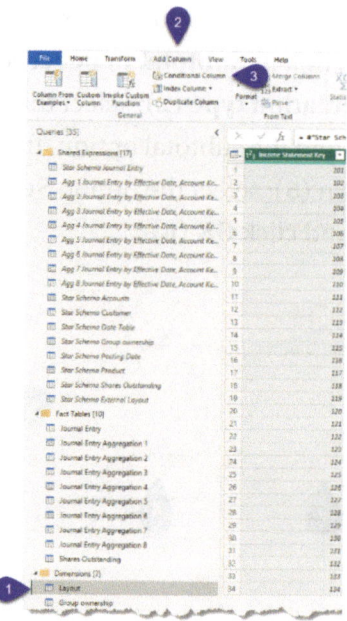

Figure 11-18. Add conditional to column for subset from

Step 2: In the Add Conditional Column box, type the name *Subset from* and the subset option, that is, **Subset from net credit less debit (1)**; select the Column Name **Calculation type (2)**; select the operator **equals (3)**; type the name *Subset* and the subset option, that is, **Subset NCLD (4)**; select the drop-down **(5)**; select the option **Select a column (6)**; select the column **1st From (7)**; and click **OK (8)**.

CHAPTER 11   EXTERNAL REPORTING SEMANTIC MODELS

Figure 11-19. Create subset from net credit less debit

Step 3: In the Queries pane, select **Layout (1)**, select the tab **Add Column (2)**, and select **Conditional Column (3)**.

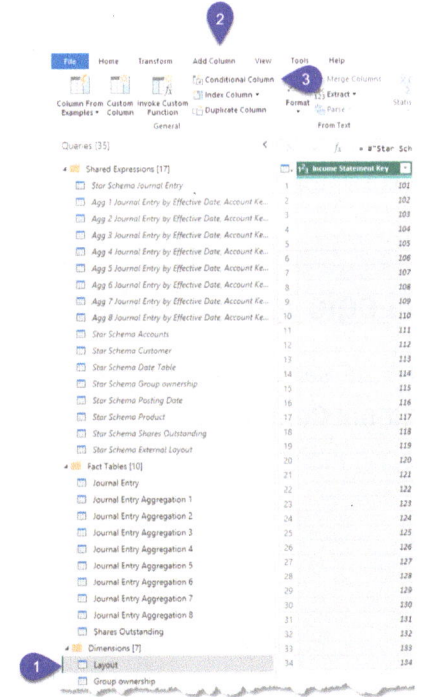

Figure 11-20. Add conditional to column for subset to

275

Step 4: In the Add Conditional Column box, type the name *Subset to* and the subset option, that is, **Subset to net credit less debit (1)**; select the Column Name **Calculation type (2)**; select the operator **equals (3)**; type the name *Subset* and the subset option, that is, **Subset NCLD (4)**; select the drop-down **(5)**; select the option **Select a column (6)**; select the column **1st To (7)**; and click **OK (8)**.

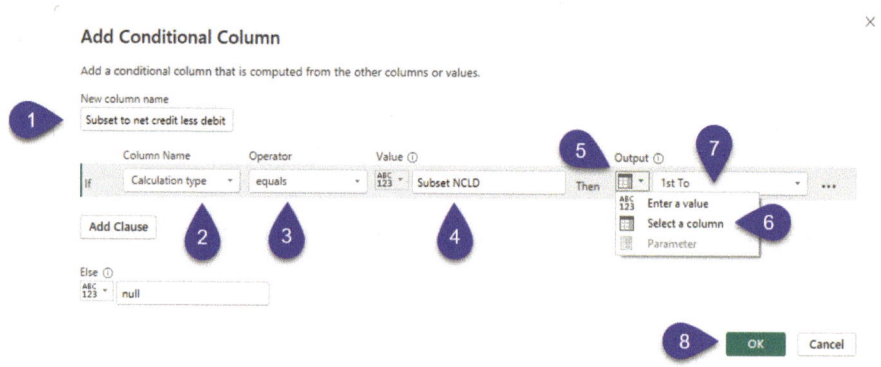

Figure 11-21. Create subset from net credit less debit to

Step 5: Repeat steps 1–4 for each subset option **NDLC**, **ACLD**, and **ADLC**.

Add Conditional Logic to Create Percentage Columns

Step 1: In the Queries pane, select **Layout (1)**, select the tab **Add Column (2)**, and select **Conditional Column (3)**.

CHAPTER 11   EXTERNAL REPORTING SEMANTIC MODELS

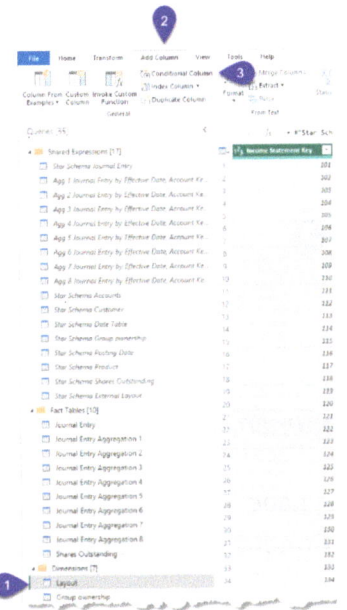

Figure 11-22. Add conditional to column for numerator

Step 2: In the Add Conditional Column box, type the name **Numerator** (**1**), select the Column Name **Calculation type** (**2**), select the operator **equals** (**3**), type the name **Divide** (**4**), select the drop-down (**5**), select the option **Select a column** (**6**), select the column **1st From** (**7**), and click **OK** (**8**).

277

CHAPTER 11 EXTERNAL REPORTING SEMANTIC MODELS

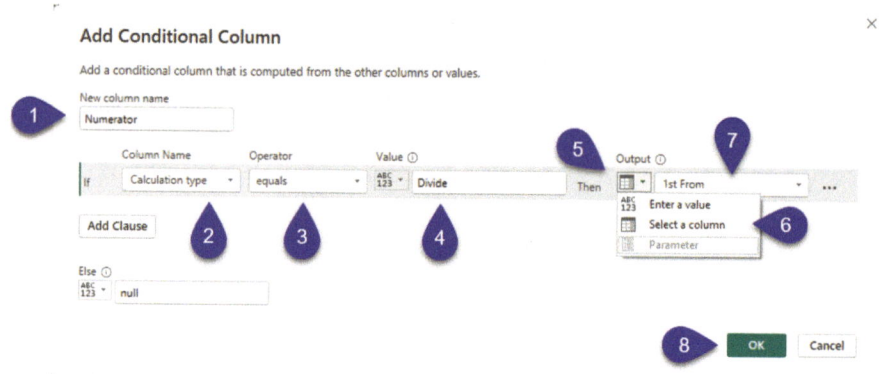

Figure 11-23. Create numerator 1st from

Step 3: In the Queries pane, select **Layout (1)**, select the tab **Add Column (2)**, and select **Conditional Column (3)**.

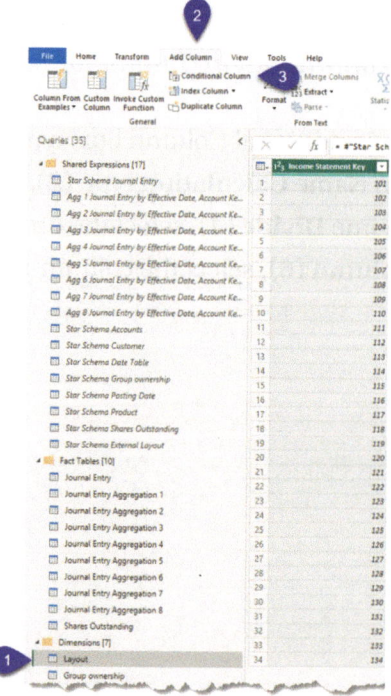

Figure 11-24. Add conditional to column for denominator

Step 4: In the Add Conditional Column box, type the name **Denominator (1)**, select the Column Name **Calculation type (2)**, select the operator **equals (3)**, type the name **Divide (4)**, select the drop-down **(5)**, select the option **Select a column (6)**, select the column **1st To (7)**, and click **OK (8)**.

Figure 11-25. Create denominator 1st

Add Conditional Logic to Create Show Value Columns

Step 1: In the Queries pane, select **Layout (1)**, select the tab **Add Column (2)**, and select **Conditional Column (3)**.

CHAPTER 11   EXTERNAL REPORTING SEMANTIC MODELS

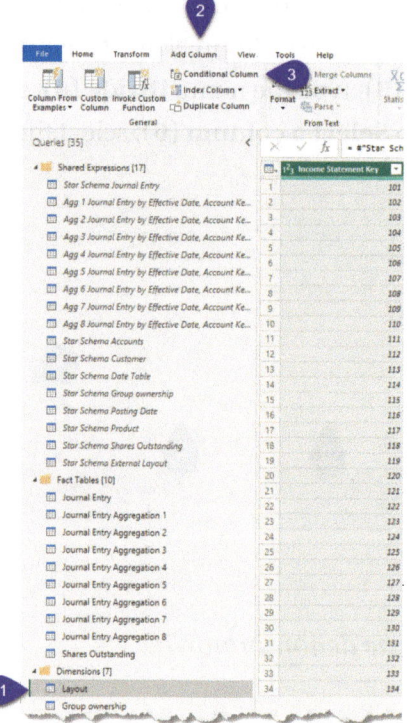

Figure 11-26. *Add conditional to column for show values*

Step 2: In the Add Conditional Column box, type the name **Show value** **(1)**, select the Column Name **Is Hidden (2)**, select the operator **does not equal (3)**, type the name **Yes (4)**, type the value 1 **(5)**, and click **OK (6)**.

CHAPTER 11 EXTERNAL REPORTING SEMANTIC MODELS

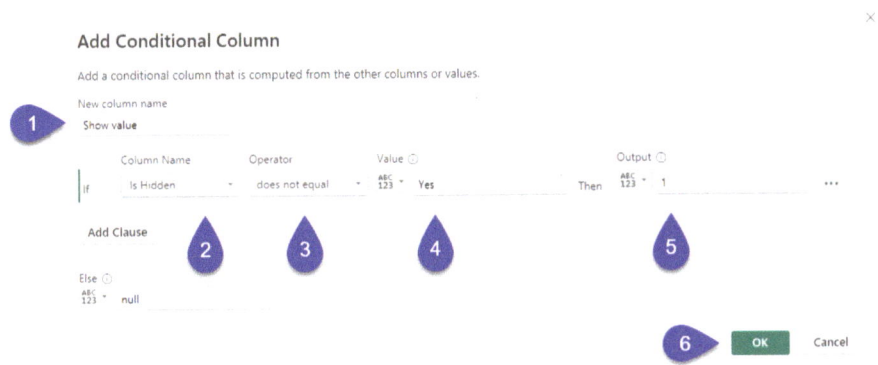

Figure 11-27. *Create show values from Is Hidden*

Remove Unnecessary Columns and Change Data Types

Step 1: Select **1st From (1)**, hold **shift** and select **Is Hidden (2)**, then right-click and select **Remove Columns (3)**.

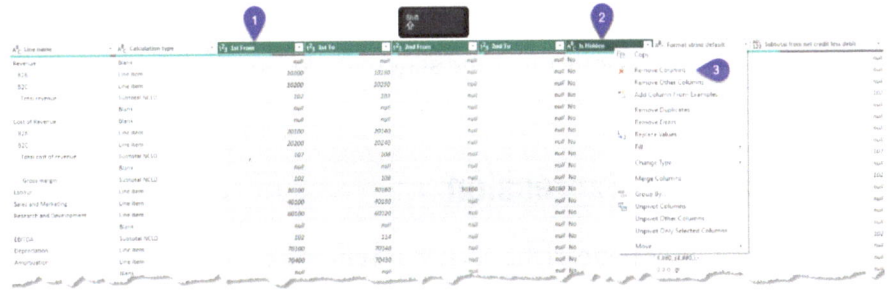

Figure 11-28. *Remove columns*

Step 2: Select **Subtotal from net credit less debit (1)**, hold **shift** and select **Show value (2)**, then right-click and select **Change Type (3)** and **Whole Number (4)**.

281

CHAPTER 11   EXTERNAL REPORTING SEMANTIC MODELS

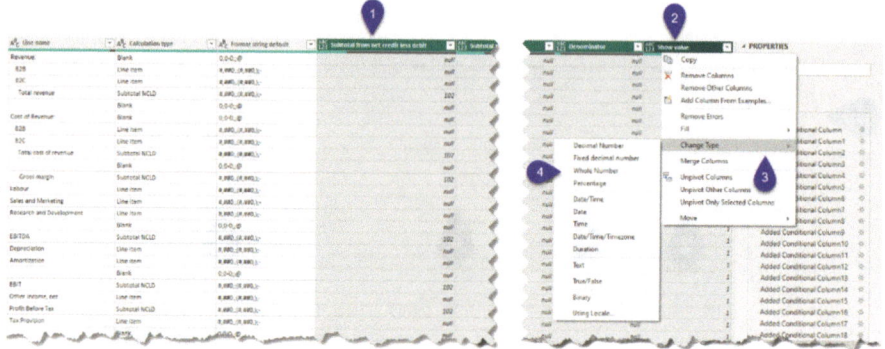

Figure 11-29. Change data type for conditional columns

Stage 4: Account Dimension Table

Adding the layout 1 income statement key to the account dimension table is broken down into two stages:

1. Creating the layout 1 shared expression

2. Adding the layout 1 income statement key to the account table

Layout 1 Shared Expression

Step 1: In the Queries pane, right-click **StarSchema co uk External Layout (1)** and select **Reference (2)**.

CHAPTER 11   EXTERNAL REPORTING SEMANTIC MODELS

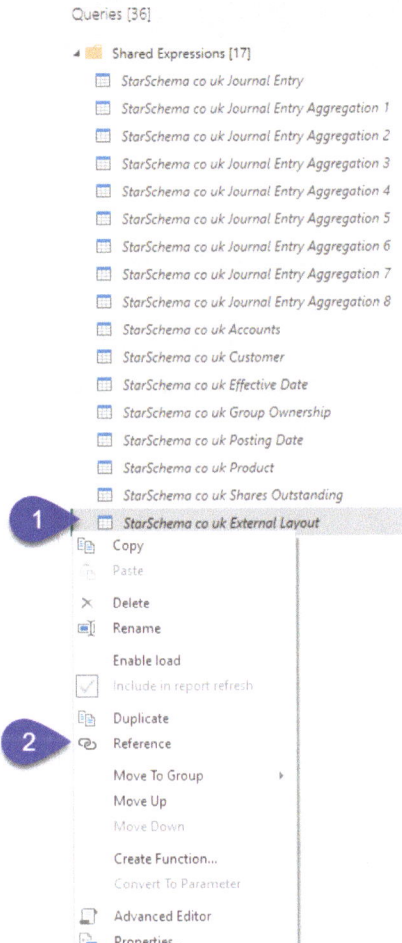

Figure 11-30.   Reference external layout

Step 2: Select the referenced query **StarSchema co uk External Layout** **(2) (1)**, and in the query settings under **Name (2)**, type *Layout 1 Shared Expression* and press *enter*.

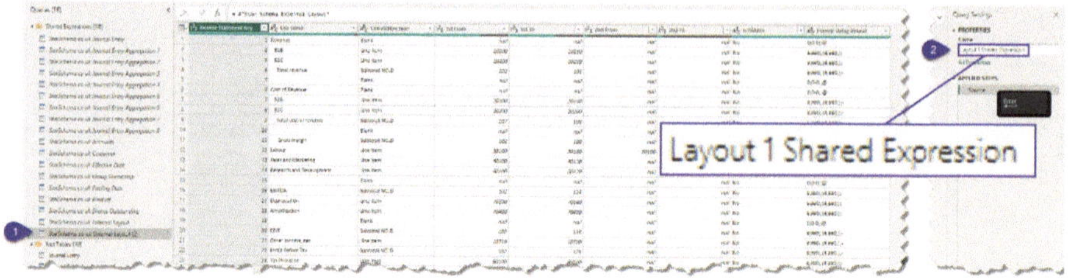

CHAPTER 11   EXTERNAL REPORTING SEMANTIC MODELS

Figure 11-31. Rename to Layout 1 Shared Expression

Step 3: In the Queries pane, right-click **Layout 1 Shared Expression (1)** and click the selected **Enable load (2)** to disable the load (should no longer have tick to the left of *Enable load*, and *Layout 1 Shared Expression* should be in italics).

CHAPTER 11   EXTERNAL REPORTING SEMANTIC MODELS

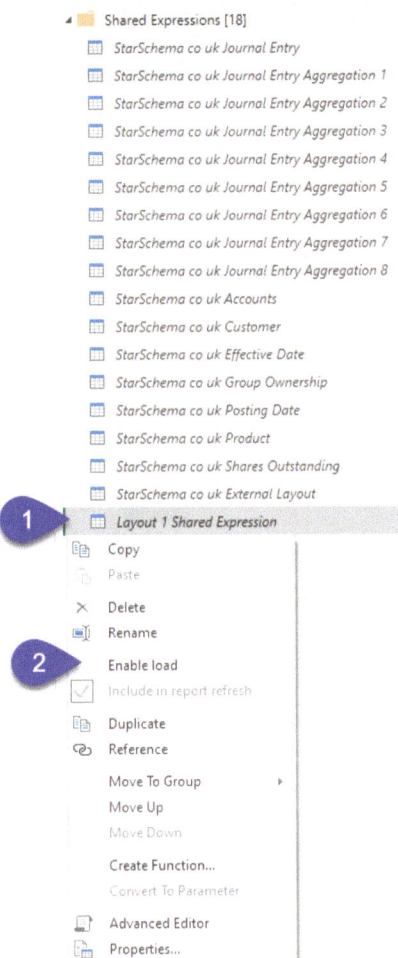

Figure 11-32. *Disable load for Layout 1 Shared Expression*

Step 4: Left-click **Calculation type (1)** and select **Line item (2)** and select **OK (3)**.

285

CHAPTER 11   EXTERNAL REPORTING SEMANTIC MODELS

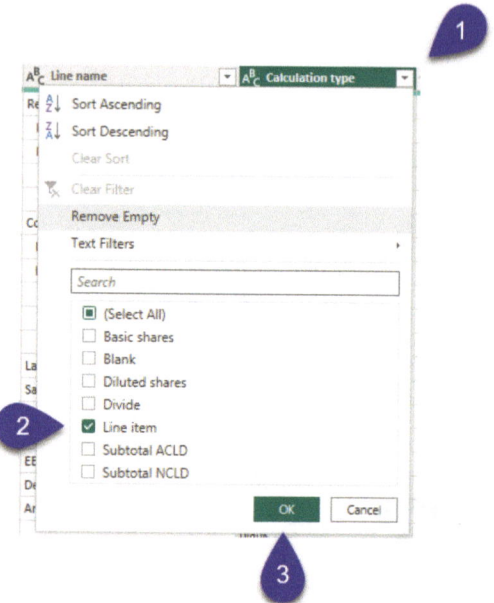

Figure 11-33.   Select line item

Step 5: Select the tab **Add Column (1)** and select **Custom Column (2)**.

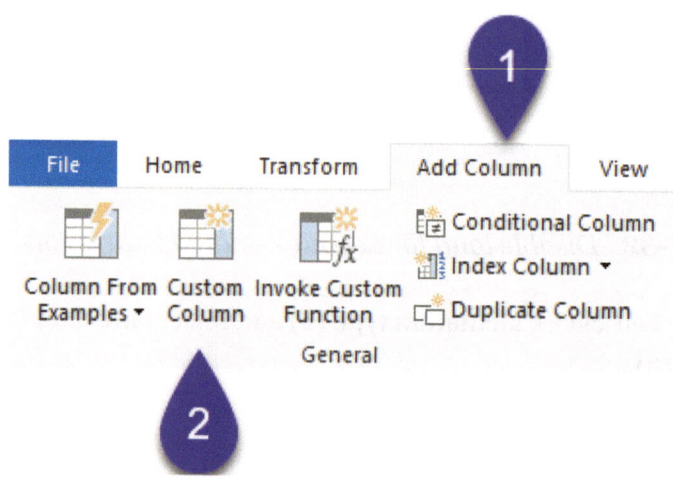

Figure 11-34.   Create custom column

CHAPTER 11 EXTERNAL REPORTING SEMANTIC MODELS

Step 6: In the Add Custom Column box, type the name **First range (1)**, type in the **Custom Column Formula (2)**:

Text.Combine(List.Transform({[1st From]..[1st To]},Text.From),";")

then click **OK (3)**.

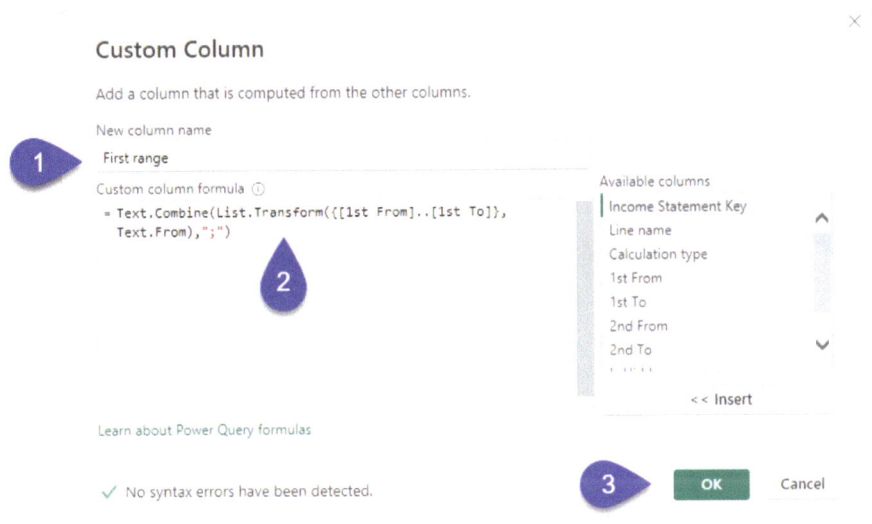

Figure 11-35. Custom column first range

Step 7: Select the tab **Add Column (1)** and select **Custom Column (2)**.

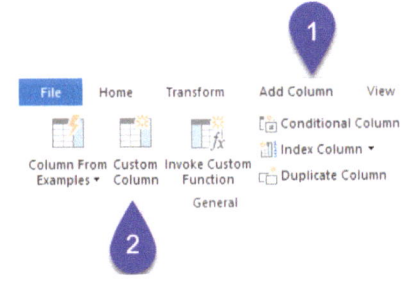

Figure 11-36. Create custom column for second range

CHAPTER 11   EXTERNAL REPORTING SEMANTIC MODELS

Step 8: In the Add Custom Column box, type the name **Second range (1)**, type in the **Custom Column Formula (3)**:

```
if [#"2nd From"] is null then null else
";"&
Text.Combine(List.Transform({[#"2nd From"]..[#"2nd To"]},
Text.From),";")
```

then click **OK (3)**.

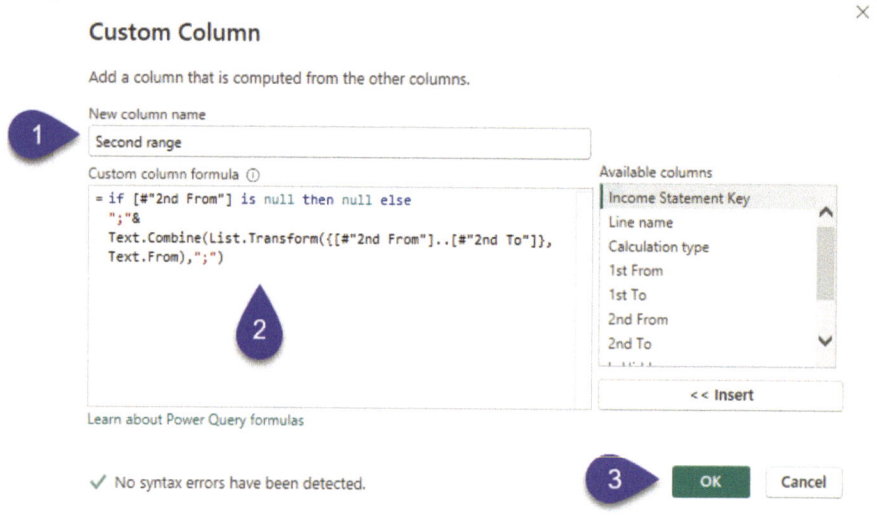

Figure 11-37. *Custom column second range*

Step 9: Select **First range (1)**, hold down control and select **Second range (2)**, then right-click and select **Merge Columns (3)**.

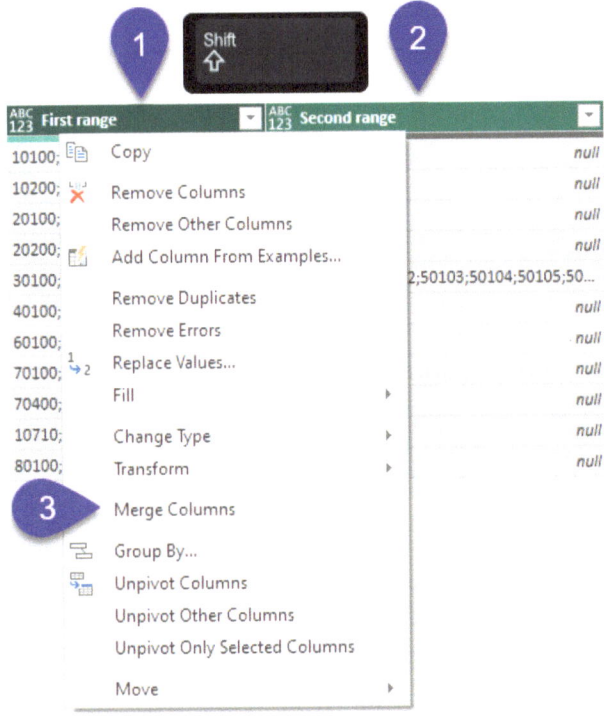

Figure 11-38. Merge first and second ranges

Step 10: Type **Account Key (1)** and select **OK (2)**.

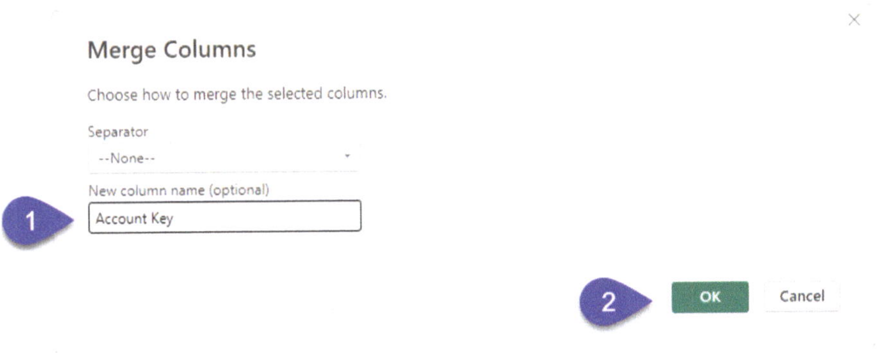

Figure 11-39. Create account key

CHAPTER 11   EXTERNAL REPORTING SEMANTIC MODELS

Step 11: Select **Income Statement Key (1)**, hold control and select **Account Key (2)**, then right-click and select **Remove Other Columns (3)**.

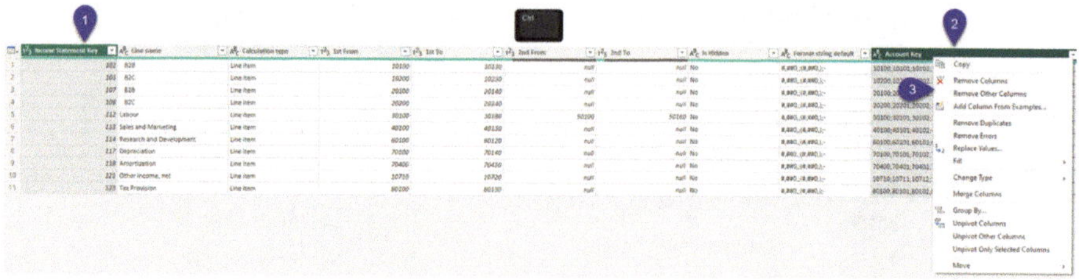

Figure 11-40. Remove other columns from layout 1 shared expression

Step 12: Right-click **Account Key (1)**, select **Split Column (2)**, and select **By Delimiter... (3)**.

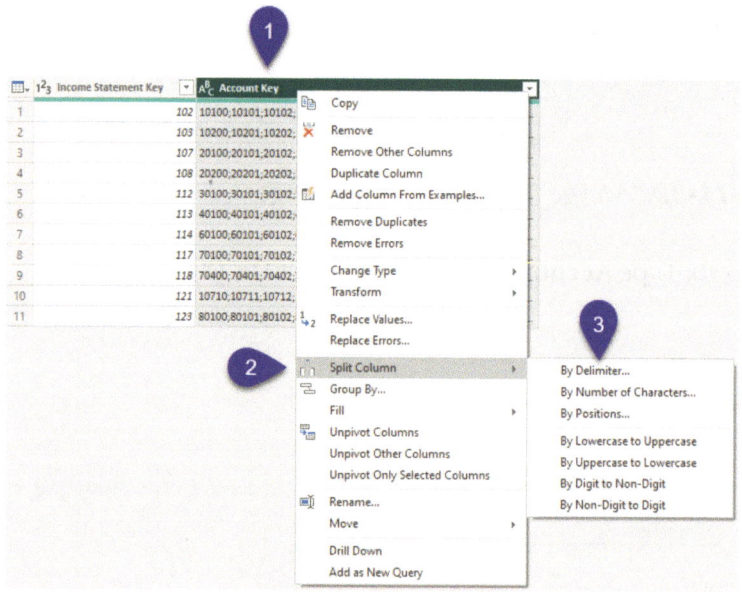

Figure 11-41. Select split column by delimiter

CHAPTER 11   EXTERNAL REPORTING SEMANTIC MODELS

Step 13: Select delimiter **Semicolon (1)**, select split at **Each occurrence of the delimiter (2)**, expand **Advanced options (3)**, select split into **Rows (4)**, select quote character **None (5)**, and click **OK (6)**.

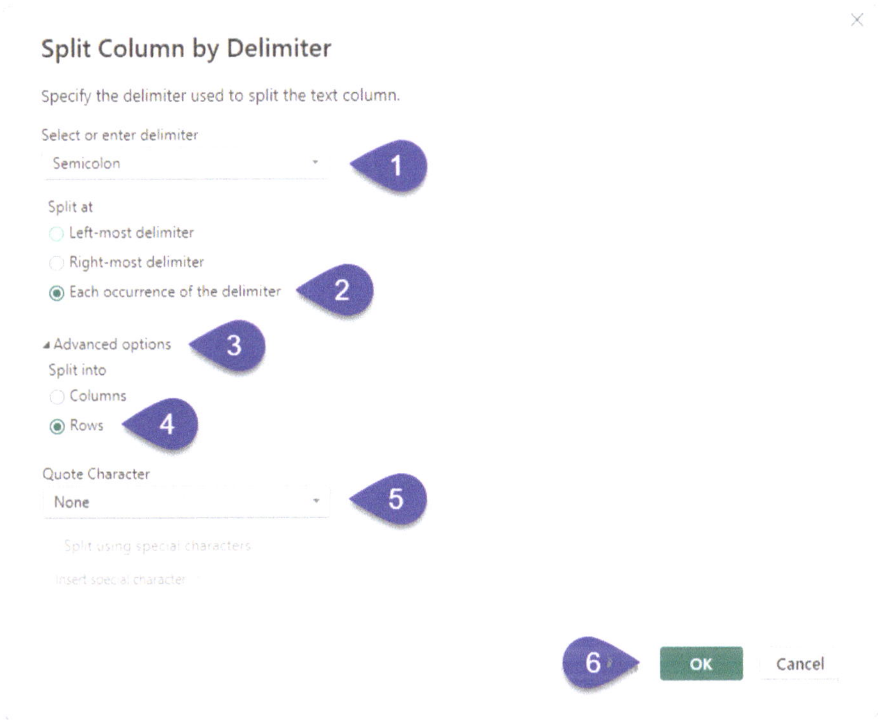

Figure 11-42. Split column by delimiter

Adding the Layout 1 Income Statement Key to the Account Table

Step 1: Select **Account (1)**, select the tab **Home (2)**, and select **Merge Queries (3)**.

CHAPTER 11   EXTERNAL REPORTING SEMANTIC MODELS

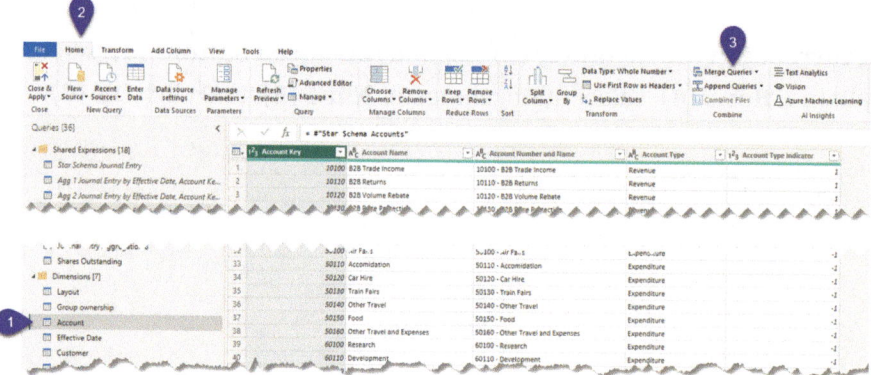

Figure 11-43. Select merge queries

Step 2: In the merge with the table **Account (1)**, select the column **Account Key (2)** in the drop-down, select the table **Layout 1 Shared Expression (3)**, select the column **Account Key (4)**, check the join kind is **Left Outer (5)**, and click **OK (6)**.

CHAPTER 11   EXTERNAL REPORTING SEMANTIC MODELS

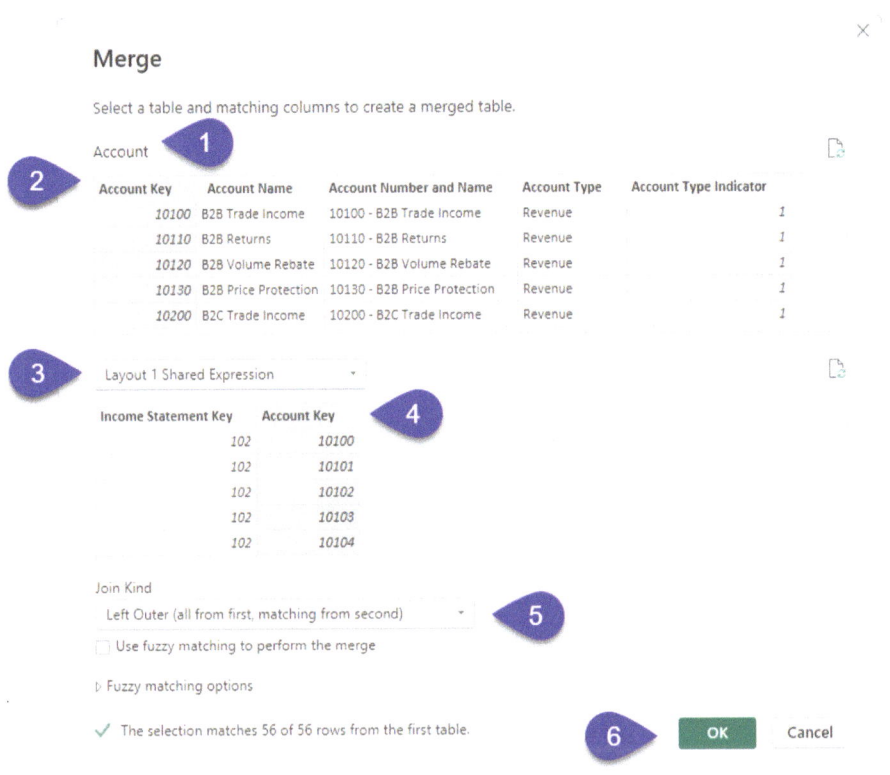

Figure 11-44. *Merge account with layout 1 shared expression*

Step 3: Click expand on the column **Layout 1 Shared Expression (1)**, select **Expand (2)**, select the column **Income Statement Key (3)**, deselect **Use original column name as prefix (4)**, and click **OK (5)**.

CHAPTER 11   EXTERNAL REPORTING SEMANTIC MODELS

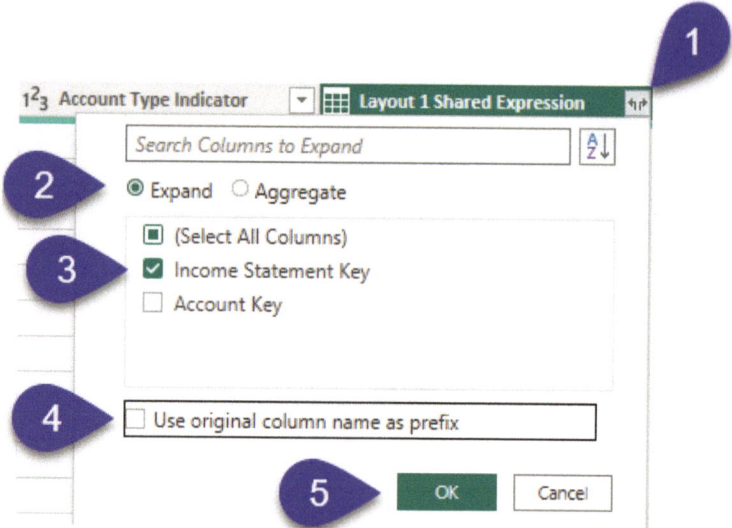

Figure 11-45. Expand layout 1 shared expression

Step 4: Select the tab **View (1)**, check **Formula Bar (2)**, select **Income Statement Key (3)**, preface the final text in the formula bar so the text reads **Layout 1 Income Statement Key (4)**, and press Enter.

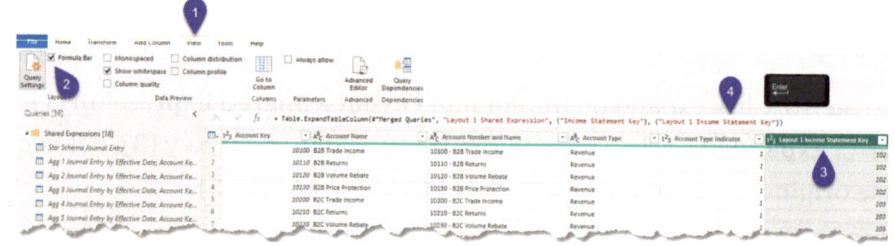

Figure 11-46. Rename to Layout 1 Income Statement Key

Step 5: Navigate to the tab **Home (1)** and select **Close & Apply (2)**.

CHAPTER 11 EXTERNAL REPORTING SEMANTIC MODELS

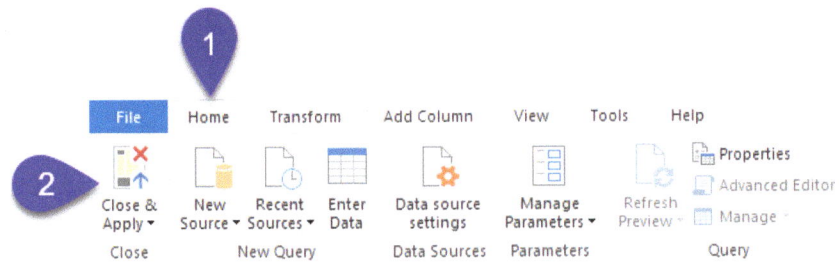

Figure 11-47. Close and apply

Building the Data Model
Creating Relationships

Step 1: Create a relationship between 'Layout'[Income Statement Key] and 'Account'[Layout 1 Income Statement Key].

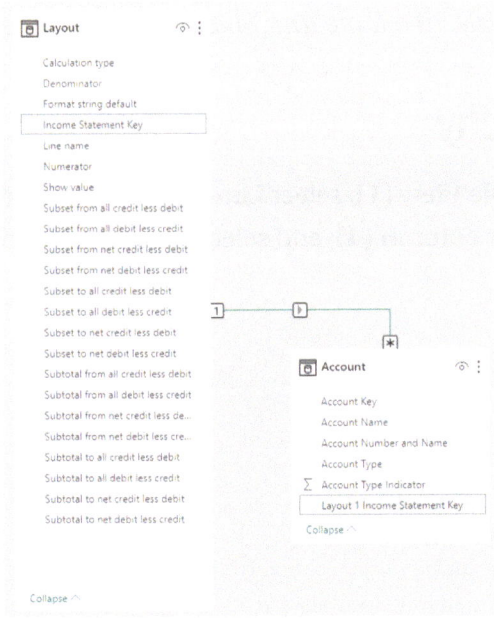

Figure 11-48. Relationship between Layout and Account

295

CHAPTER 11 EXTERNAL REPORTING SEMANTIC MODELS

Step 2: Create a relationship between 'Effective Date'[Date] and 'Shares Outstanding'[Start of time period].

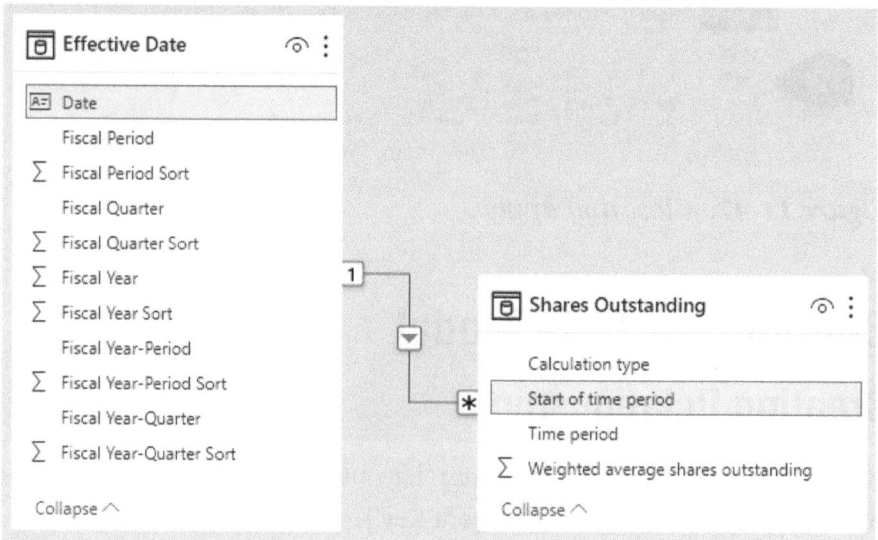

Figure 11-49. Effective Date and Shares Outstanding

Sort Hierarchy

Step 1: In the **Table View (1)**, select **Line name (2)**, select **Column tools (3)**, select **Sort by column (4)**, and select **Income Statement Key (5)**.

CHAPTER 11   EXTERNAL REPORTING SEMANTIC MODELS

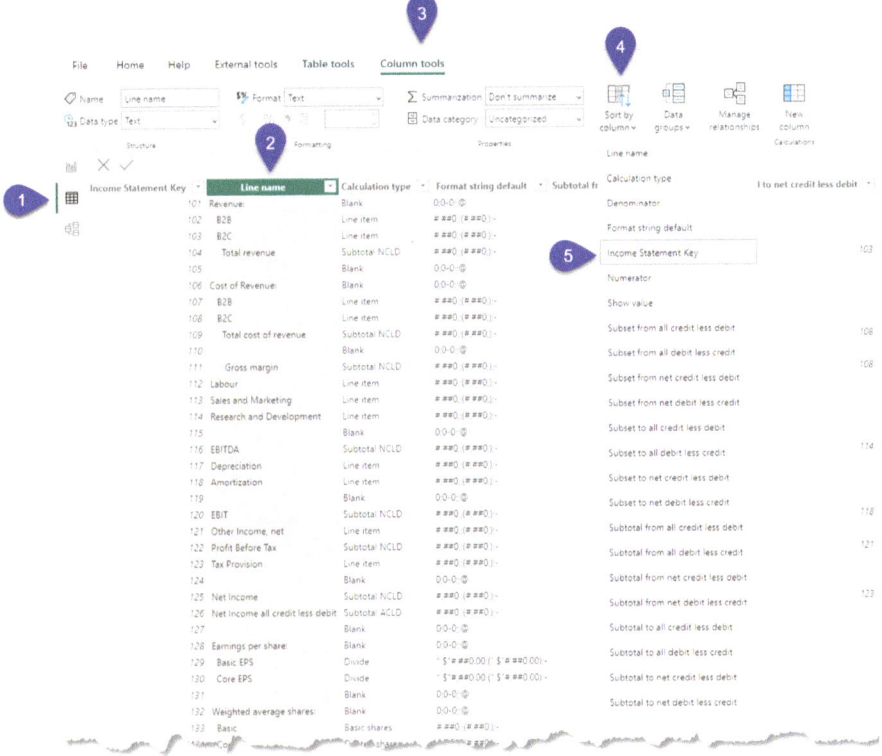

Figure 11-50. Layout table sort order

DAX Actuals Calculation

In Chapters 7 and 8, the first three steps of the actuals calculation were created:

- **Step 01: Sum**: Calculated the sum of values (credit less debit) in the trial balance (Tyrell Corp and Weyland Industries) or the relevant journal entry (StarSchema.co.uk) fact table

- **Step 02: Account Type Indicator**: Calculated the max and min account type indicator

- **Step 03: Line items**: Calculated account balances

CHAPTER 11   EXTERNAL REPORTING SEMANTIC MODELS

When the measure [Actuals net credit less debit] from Step 03 is evaluated in context of 'Layout' [Line item] and 'Effective date' [Year], values for each year are returned for the line-items on the income statement (Figure 11-51).

StarSchema.co.uk

Line name	2023	2022
Revenue:		
B2B	90,459,744.68	78,556,289.04
B2C	72,478,189.37	63,036,184.15
Total revenue		
Cost of Revenue:		
B2B	36,933,317.85	31,990,349.09
B2C	29,532,303.06	25,553,565.30
Total cost of revenue		
Gross margin		
Labour	18,392,118.44	15,352,566.82
Sales and Marketing	14,855,752.34	12,293,633.80
Research and Development	5,552,088.42	4,762,456.75
EBITDA		
Depreciation	20,949,355.14	18,358,624.98
Amortization	9,411,347.78	7,992,893.31
EBIT		
Other Income, net	307,790.16	251,406.79
Profit Before Tax		
Tax Provision	5,890,905.39	5,145,445.47
Net Income		
Net income attributable to non-controlling interests		
Net income attributable to controlling interests		
Earnings per share:		
Basic EPS		
Core EPS		
Weighted average shares:		
Basic		
Core		

Figure 11-51. *Star Schema.co.uk line-items by year with blank values shown*

To complete the income statement, nine more steps are required:

- **Step 04: Subtotals**: Calculations for each of the four subtotal types
- **Step 05: Subsets**: Calculations for each of the four subset types
- **Step 06: Controlling and non-controlling interests**: Calculations for controlling and non-controlling interests
- **Step 07: Weighted number of shares**: Calculations for the weighted number of shares outstanding
- **Step 08: Bespoke calculations**: Placeholder for future bespoke calculations (see Part 4)
- **Step 09: Divide**: Dividing one line on the income statement by another
- **Step 10: Add blank rows**: Spaces for presentation
- **Step 11: Show values**: Choosing which lines to display
- **Step 12: Combined calculation**: Combining all elements together

As with the measures created in the first three steps, DAX calculations should be placed in a folder named after the step to keep them organized.

Step 04: Subtotals

As per Chapter 9, there are four potential subtotal options:

1. Net credit less debit (NCLD)
2. Net debit less credit (NDLC)
3. All credit less debit (ACLD)
4. All debit less credit (ADLC)

Each subtotal requires a near-identical DAX and is broken down into three parts:

- **Part 1**: A calculated table variable.
  - Removes any filter context from the 'Layout' dimension, making all line-items in scope for the subtotal.
  - Reapplies filter context to the 'Layout' dimension, selecting only those line-items used in the subtotal; this is based on the subtotal from and to columns created using Power Query, that is, 'Layout'[*Subtotal from net credit less debit*] and 'Layout'[*Subtotal to net credit less debit*].
- **Part 2**: The appropriate actual is calculated based on the type of subtotal (as explained in Chapter 9) and the filter context from part 1.
- **Part 3**: Returns the result from part 2.

A fifth DAX calculation then brings together the four subtotals into one measure.

Subtotal Net Credit Less Debit

```
Actuals Subtotal Net Credit Less Debit =
// Part 1
VAR NCLD_filter_context_calculated_table =
    CALCULATETABLE(
        'Layout',
        REMOVEFILTERS( 'Layout' ),
        'Layout'[Income Statement Key]
```

```
                >= MIN(
                    'Layout'[Subtotal from net credit less debit]
                ),
            'Layout'[Income Statement Key]
                <= MIN(
                    'Layout'[Subtotal to net credit less debit]
                )
        )
// Part 2
VAR result =
    CALCULATE(
        [Actuals Net Credit Less Debit],
        NCLD_filter_context_calculated_table
    )
// Part 3

RETURN
    result
```

Subtotal Net Debit Less Credit

```
Actuals Subtotal Net Debit Less Credit =

// Part 1
VAR NDLC_filter_context_calculated_table =
    CALCULATETABLE(
        'Layout',
        REMOVEFILTERS( 'Layout' ),
        'Layout'[Income Statement Key]
            >= MIN(
                'Layout'[Subtotal from net debit less credit]
            ),
```

```
            'Layout'[Income Statement Key]
                <= MIN(
                    'Layout'[Subtotal to net debit less credit]
                )
        )
// Part 2
VAR result =
    CALCULATE(
        [Actuals Net Debit Less Credit],
        NDLC_filter_context_calculated_table
    )

// Part 3

RETURN
    result
```

Subtotal All Credit Less Debit

```
Actuals Subtotal All Credit Less Debit =
// Part 1
VAR ACLD_filter_context_calculated_table =
    CALCULATETABLE(
        'Layout',
        REMOVEFILTERS( 'Layout' ),
        'Layout'[Income Statement Key]
            >= MIN(
                'Layout'[Subtotal from all credit less debit]
            ),
        'Layout'[Income Statement Key]
            <= MIN(
                'Layout'[Subtotal to all credit less debit]
```

```
            )
        )
// Part 2
VAR result =
    CALCULATE(
        [Actuals Sum],
        ACLD_filter_context_calculated_table
    )
// Part 3

RETURN
    result
```

Subtotal All Debit Less Credit

```
Actuals Subtotal All Debit Less Credit =
// Part 1
VAR ADLC_filter_context_calculated_table =
    CALCULATETABLE(
        'Layout',
        REMOVEFILTERS( 'Layout' ),
        'Layout'[Income Statement Key]
            >= MIN(
                'Layout'[Subtotal from all debit less credit]
            ),
        'Layout'[Income Statement Key]
            <= MIN(
                'Layout'[Subtotal to all debit less credit]
            )
    )
```

```
// Part 2
VAR result =
    CALCULATE(
        [Actuals Sum] × -1,
        ADLC_filter_context_calculated_table
    )
// Part 3

RETURN
    result
```

Actuals Subtotal

To bring the four calculations together in a single measure, COALESCE is used; this returns the first measure, unless it is blank, in which case it moves to the next measure:

```
Actuals Subtotal =
COALESCE(
    [Actuals Subtotal Net Credit Less Debit],
    [Actuals Subtotal Net Debit Less Credit],
    [Actuals Subtotal All Credit Less Debit],
    [Actuals Subtotal All Debit Less Credit]
)
```

Step 05: Subset

As with subtotals, there are four potential options, each of which requires near-identical DAX and is broken down into three parts:

- **Part 1**: A calculated table variable.
  - Removes any filter context from the 'Layout' dimension, making all accounts in scope for the subset.
  - Applies filter context to the 'Account' dimension, selecting only those accounts used in the subset; this is based on the subset from and to columns created using Power Query, that is, 'Layout'[*Subset from net credit less debit*] and 'Layout'[*Subset to net credit less debit*].
- **Part 2**: The appropriate actual is calculated based on the type of subset (as explained in Chapter 9) and the filter context from part 1.
- **Part 3**: Returns the result from part 2.

A fifth DAX calculation then brings together the four subsets into one measure.

Subset Net Credit Less Debit

```
Actuals Subset Net Credit Less Debit =

// Part 1
VAR NCLD_filter_context_calculated_table =
    CALCULATETABLE(
        'Account',
        REMOVEFILTERS( 'Layout' ),
        'Account'[Account Key]
            >= MIN(
                'Layout'[Subset from net credit less debit]
            ),
         'Account'[Account Key]
            <= MIN(
```

```
                'Layout'[Subset to net credit less debit]
            )
    )
// Part 2
VAR result =
    CALCULATE(
        [Actuals Net Credit Less Debit],
        NCLD_filter_context_calculated_table
    )
// Part 3

RETURN
    result
```

Subset Net Debit Less Credit

```
Actuals Subset Net Debit Less Credit =
// Part 1
VAR NDLC_filter_context_calculated_table =
    CALCULATETABLE(
        'Account',
        REMOVEFILTERS( 'Layout' ),
        'Account'[Account Key]
            >= MIN(
                'Layout'[Subset from net debit less credit]
            ),
         'Account'[Account Key]
            <= MIN(
                'Layout'[Subset to net debit less credit]
            )
    )
```

```
// Part 2
VAR result =
    CALCULATE(
        [Actuals Net Debit Less Credit],
        NDLC_filter_context_calculated_table
    )
// Part 3
RETURN
    result
```

Subset All Credit Less Debit

```
Actuals Subset All Credit Less Debit =
// Part 1
VAR ACLD_filter_context_calculated_table =
        CALCULATETABLE(
          'Account',
          REMOVEFILTERS( 'Layout' ),
          'Account'[Account Key]
             >= MIN(
                 'Layout'[Subset from all credit less debit]
             ),
           'Account'[Account Key]
             <= MIN(
                 'Layout'[Subset to all credit less debit]
             )
        )
// Part 2
VAR result =
    CALCULATE(
```

CHAPTER 11   EXTERNAL REPORTING SEMANTIC MODELS

```
        [Actuals Sum],
        ACLD_filter_context_calculated_table
    )

// Part 3

RETURN
    result
```

Subset All Debit Less Credit

```
Actuals Subset All Debit Less Credit =

// Part 1
VAR ADLC_filter_context_calculated_table =
    CALCULATETABLE(
        'Account',
        REMOVEFILTERS( 'Layout' ),
        'Account'[Account Key]
            >= MIN(
                'Layout'[Subset from all debit less credit]
            ),
        'Account'[Account Key]
            <= MIN(
                'Layout'[Subset to all debit less credit]
            )
    )

// Part 2
VAR result =
    CALCULATE(
        [Actuals Sum] × -1,
        ADLC_filter_context_calculated_table
    )
```

```
// Part 3
RETURN
    result
```

Actuals Subset

As with subtotals, the four subset calculations are brought together in a single measure using COALESCE:

```
Actuals Subset =
COALESCE(
    [Actuals Subset Net Credit Less Debit],
    [Actuals Subset Net Debit Less Credit],
    [Actuals Subset All Credit Less Debit],
    [Actuals Subset All Debit Less Credit]
)
```

Step 06: Controlling and Non-controlling Interests

For controlling and non-controlling interests, all income statement accounts are in scope. The DAX for controlling and non-controlling interests is broken down into six parts:

- **Part 1**: Determines the calculation type
- **Part 2**: Removes the filter context from the 'Layout' dimension
- **Part 3**: Calculates actuals for controlling interest, based on the filter context from part 2 and where 'Group Ownership'[Ownership key] = 1 (controlling interest)

CHAPTER 11   EXTERNAL REPORTING SEMANTIC MODELS

- **Part 4**: Calculates actuals for non-controlling interest, based on the filter context from part 2 and where 'Group Ownership'[Ownership key] = 0 (non-controlling interest)

- **Part 5**: When part 1 equals "CI," returns part 3, and when part 1 equals "NCI," returns part 4

- **Part 6**: Returns the result from part 5

```
[Actuals Controlling and Non-Controlling Interest]=
// Part 1
VAR Calculation_type =
    SELECTEDVALUE(
        'Layout'[Calculation type]
    )
// Part 2
VAR Remove_context =
    CALCULATETABLE(
        'Layout',
        REMOVEFILTERS( 'Layout' )
    )
// Part 3
VAR CI =
    calculate(
        [Actuals Net Credit Less Debit],
        Remove_context,
        'Group ownership'[Ownership Key] = 1
    )
// Part 4
VAR NCI =
```

```
    calculate(
        [Actuals Net Credit Less Debit],
        Remove_context,
        'Group ownership'[Ownership Key] = 0
        )
// Part 5
VAR result =
    SWITCH(
        TRUE( ),
        Calculation_type = "CI", CI,
        Calculation_type = "NCI", NCI
        )
// Part 6
RETURN
    Result
```

Step 07: Weighted Number of Shares

The weighted number of shares calculation uses the 'Shares Outstanding' snapshot fact table. This snapshot fact table behaves differently from the 'Journal Entry' transactional fact table (used for StarSchema.co.uk) and 'Trial Balance' transactional fact table (used for Tyrell Corp and Weyland Industries). This is because snapshot fact tables are non-additive, whereas transactional fact tables are additive:

- **Additive behavior**: Values *can* be summed over time, that is, the values for gross profit in the 'Journal Entry' transactional fact table for P1-2023, P2-2023, and P3-2023 *can* be summed to equal the gross profit for Q1-2023.

- **Non-additive behavior**: Values *cannot* be summed over time, that is, the values for the basic number of weighted shares outstanding in the 'Shares Outstanding' snapshot fact table for P1-2023, P2-2023, and P3-2023 *cannot* be summed to equal the basic number of outstanding shares for Q1-2023.

Consequently, each row in the 'Shares Outstanding' snapshot fact table is valid for the specified date range, that is, P1-2023, Q1-2023, or 2023. Each row is also only valid for the specified calculation type, and the 'Shares Outstanding'[Calculation Type] must match the 'Layout'[Calculation Type], that is, the 'Shares Outstanding'[Calculation Type] and 'Layout'[Calculation Type] must both equal *Basic shares*.

Unlike the 'Trial Balance' and 'Journal Entry' transactional fact tables, the 'Shares Outstanding' snapshot fact table contains no relationship to the 'Account' dimension. As such, when users evaluate the weighted numbers of shares by account, no value should be shown; there is no business logic which links the weighted number of shares to a given account.

The DAX for weighted number of shares is broken down into six parts:

- **Part 1**: Returns null if the 'Account' dimension or 'Effective Date'[Date] is filtered, else returns 1.
- **Part 2**: Determines the calculation type in the 'Layout' dimension.
- **Part 3**: Determines the time period in scope, either the
  - 'Effective date' [Fiscal Year-Period]
  - 'Effective date' [Fiscal Year-Quarter]
  - 'Effective date' [Fiscal Year] converted to a string for consistent data types

CHAPTER 11   EXTERNAL REPORTING SEMANTIC MODELS

- **Part 4**: A calculated table variable for the 'Shares Outstanding' fact table where

  - 'Shares Outstanding'[Calculation Type] equals part 2

  - 'Shares Outstanding'[Time Period] equals part 3

- **Part 5**: The 'Shares Outstanding'[Weighted average shares outstanding] is calculated based on the filter context from part 4 and multiplied by part 1 to return null if the accounts table or an individual date is filtered.

- **Part 6**: Returns the result from part 5.

```
Number of Shares =
// Part 1
var Isaccountordatefiltered =
 if(
    or(
      ISFILTERED('Account'),
      ISFILTERED('Effective Date'[Date])
      ),
    blank()
 ,1)
// Part 2
VAR SelectedCalcualtionType = SELECTEDVALUE(
Layout[Calculation type] )

// Part 3
VAR SelectedTimePeriod =
```

CHAPTER 11   EXTERNAL REPORTING SEMANTIC MODELS

```
            SELECTEDVALUE(
            'Effective Date'[Fiscal Year-Period],
                SELECTEDVALUE(
                'Effective Date'[Fiscal Year-Quarter],
                    CONVERT (
                        SELECTEDVALUE( 'Effective Date'[Fiscal
                        Year] ),
                        STRING
                        )
                )
            )
// Part 4
VAR CalculateTableNumberofShares =
        CALCULATETABLE(
          'Shares Outstanding',
            'Shares Outstanding'[Calculation type]
            =SelectedCalcualtionType,
            'Shares Outstanding'[Time period] = SelectedTimePeriod
        )
// Part 5
VAR result =
        CALCULATE(
            SUM( 'Shares Outstanding'[Weighted average shares
            outstanding] ),
                CalculateTableNumberofShares
            )
        × Isaccountordatefiltered
// Part 6
    RETURN
        result
```

Step 08: Bespoke Calculations

As per Chapter 3, bespoke information is frequently included alongside the income statement, that is, the number of people employed by the entity. In this chapter, a placeholder is added returning a blank calculation; this is expanded upon in Chapter 13 with numerous examples.

```
Actuals Bespoke  = BLANK()
```

Step 09: Divide

A frequent requirement is to divide one line on the income statement by another. For instance:

- **Basic earnings per share (EPS)**: This is calculated by dividing net income (or the controlling interest in group reporting scenarios) by the basic number of shares.

- **Percentages**: Such as gross profit percentage, which is calculated by dividing gross profit by revenue.

Either side of the division (the numerator and denominator) can be any of the line types covered: line-items (step 03 covered in Chapters 7 and 8), subtotal (step 04), subset (step 05), controlling or non-controlling interests (step 06), weighted number of shares (step 07), or bespoke calculations (step 08).

For the denominator only, any filter context based on the 'Account' dimension should be ignored, else the divide returns nonsensical numbers when drilling to the account level. For instance, Table 11-1 shows the gross profit percentage, where gross profit (accounts 10100 – Trade revenue, 10101 – Returns, 20100 – Trade costs, and 20101 – Volume discount) is divided by revenue (accounts 10100 – Trade revenue and 10101 – Returns).

CHAPTER 11   EXTERNAL REPORTING SEMANTIC MODELS

Table 11-1. *Gross profit percentage including account context for the denominator*

Line Drill Down to Account	Numerator (10100, 10101, 20100, and 20101)	Denominator (10100 and 10101)	Divide
Gross profit, %	45	90	50%
10100 – Trade revenue	100	100	100%
10101 – Returns	(10)	(10)	100%
20100 – Trade costs	(50)	Null	Infinity
20101 – Volume discount	5	Null	Infinity

At a gross profit percentage level, the calculation returns the correct result. However, at the account level, this only returns values of 100% or infinity because of the 'Account' context. Table 11-2 shows how with the account context excluded from the denominator, the individual account divisions sum up to the gross profit percentage.

Table 11-2. Gross profit percentage excluding account context for the denominator

Line Drill Down to Account	Numerator (10100, 10101, 20100, and 20101)	Denominator (10100 and 10101)	Divide
Gross profit, %	45	90	50%
10100 – Trade revenue	100	90	111 %
10101 – Returns	(10)	90	(11)%
20100 – Trade costs	(50)	90	(56)%
20101 – Volume discount	5	90	6%

The DAX for the numerator and denominator calculation is broken down into three parts:

- **Part 1**: A calculated table variable for the 'Layout' dimension which

  - Removes any filter context from the 'Layout' dimension, making all lines in scope for the numerator or denominator.

  - Reapplies a filter context to the 'Layout' dimension, selecting only those lines used in either the numerator or denominator; this is based on the 'Layout'[*Numerator*] or 'Layout'[*Denominator*] columns created using Power Query.

- **Part 2**: The numerator and denominator calculate steps 03–08 based on the filter context from part 1 and – for the denominator only – remove the filter context from the 'Account' dimension.

- **Part 3**: Returns the result from part 2.

A third DAX calculation then divides the numerator by the denominator.

Actuals Divide Numerator

```
Actuals Divide Numerator =
// Part 1
VAR calculationfincialstatementstablednumerator =
    CALCULATETABLE
            (
            Layout,
            REMOVEFILTERS( Layout ),
            Layout[Income Statement Key] =
            MAX( Layout[Numerator] )
            )
// Part 2
VAR result =
    CALCULATE(
        [Actuals Net Credit Less Debit] +
        [Actuals Subtotal] +
        [Actuals Subset] +
        [Actuals Controlling and Non-Controlling Interest] +
        [Number of Shares] +
        [Actuals Bespoke],
            calculationfincialstatementstablednumerator    )
```

```
// Returns the result
RETURN
    result
```

Actuals Divide Denominator

```
Actuals Divide Denominator =
// Part 1
VAR calculationfincialstatementstabledenominator=
    CALCULATETABLE
            (
            Layout,
            REMOVEFILTERS( Layout ),
            Layout[Income Statement Key] = MAX( Layout
            [Denominator] )
            )
// Part 2
VAR result =
    CALCULATE(
        [Actuals Net Credit Less Debit] +
        [Actuals Subtotal] +
        [Actuals Subset] +
        [Actuals Controlling and Non-Controlling Interest] +
        [Number of Shares] +
        [Actuals Bespoke],
            Calculationfincialstatementstabledenominator,
            REMOVEFILTERS(Account)
        )
RETURN
    result
```

CHAPTER 11   EXTERNAL REPORTING SEMANTIC MODELS

Actuals Divide

```
Actuals Divide =
DIVIDE(
    [Actuals Divide Numerator],
    [Actuals Divide Denominator]
)
```

Step 10: Add Blank Rows

A blank row calculation is required to generate spaces between income statement lines. This calculation returns a value 0 for these lines, and the format string ensures these show as blank. To ensure users cannot drill down from blank lines to accounts, if the accounts table is in scope, blanks are not shown.

The DAX for the blank calculation is broken down into four parts:

- **Part 1**: Returns TRUE if the 'Accounts' dimension is in scope
- **Part 2**: Returns TRUE if the calculation type in the 'Layout' dimension equals "Blank"
- **Part 3**: Returns 0 when the calculation type equals "Blank" (part 2) and the 'Account' dimension is not in scope (part 1)
- **Part 4**: Returns the result from part 3

```
Actuals Blank =
//Part 1
VAR accountinscope =
    ISFILTERED( 'Account' )
```

```
//Part 2
VAR selectedcalculationtype =
    SELECTEDVALUE(
        'Layout'[Calculation type]
    ) = "Blank"
//Part 3
VAR blankrows =
    SWITCH(
        TRUE( ),
        accountinscope, BLANK( ),
        selectedcalculationtype, 0
    )
RETURN
    blankrows
```

Step 11: Show Values

Step 11 takes the minimum of 'Layout'[Show value]. For each income statement line, this returns either a 1 (for lines that should be visible) or null (for lines that should be hidden):

```
Actuals Show Value =

MIN( 'Layout'[Show Value] )
```

Step 12: Combined Calculation

Step 12 combines steps 03–10 and multiplies the result by step 11. This returns the visible line-items, subtotals, subsets, controlling interests, non-controlling interests, bespoke calculations, number of shares, divisions of one line by another, and any blank rows:

CHAPTER 11   EXTERNAL REPORTING SEMANTIC MODELS

```
Actuals =

COALESCE(
    [Actuals Net Credit Less Debit],
    [Actuals Subtotal],
    [Actuals Subset],
    [Actuals Controlling and Non-Controlling Interest],
    [Actuals Bespoke],
    [Number of Shares],
    [Actuals Divide],
    [Actuals Blank]
)
    × [Actuals Show Value]
```

Dynamic Format Strings

For the formatting of each line to be based on the 'Layout'[Format String Default], in the data view select the calculation **Actuals (1)**, select format option **Dynamic (2)**, click **Edit (3)**, and in the **formula bar (4)**, type

```
//Part 1
var selectedformatstring =
        SELECTEDVALUE( 'Layout'[Format String Default] )

//Part 2
var inscope = hasonevalue( 'Layout'[Format String Default] )

//Part 3
var result = if(inscope, selectedformatstring,
"#,##0,;(#,##0,);-")

//Part 4
return
    result
```

CHAPTER 11   EXTERNAL REPORTING SEMANTIC MODELS

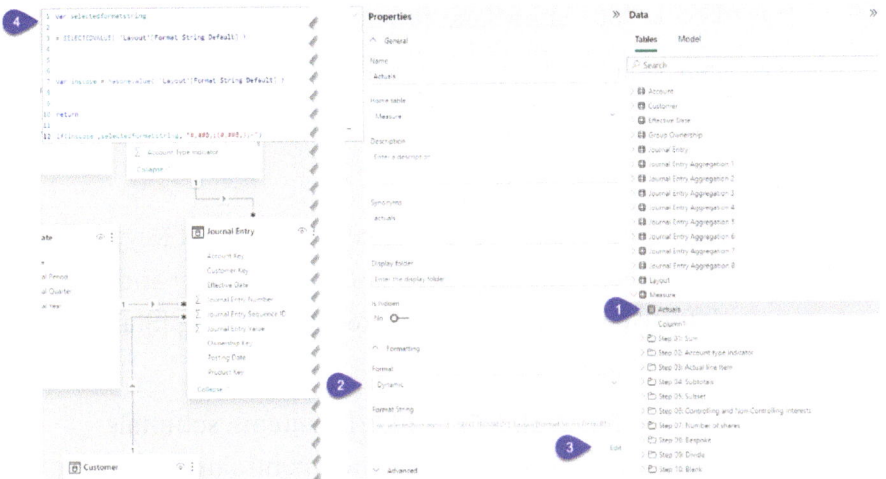

Figure 11-52. *StarSchema.co.uk dynamic format strings*

In this formula:

- **Part 1**: Selects the format string in the 'Layout' dimension

- **Part 2**: Checks only one format string is in scope

- **Part 3**: Returns the format string from part 1 if part 2 is true, else returns a number in thousands with no decimal places

- **Part 4**: Returns the result from part 3

Summary

- To meet external reporting requirements, the trial balance semantic models (Chapter 7) and a journal entry semantic model (Chapter 8) were extended to include

- The 'Layout' snowflake dimension
- The 'Shares Outstanding' snapshot fact table
- The foreign key 'Account'[Layout 1 Income Statement Key]
- The relationships 'Layout'[Income Statement Key] → 'Account'[Layout 1 Income Statement Key] and 'Effective Date'[Date] → 'Shares Outstanding'[Start of time period]
- DAX for calculating the visible line-items, subtotals, subsets, controlling interests, non-controlling interests, bespoke calculations, number of shares, divisions of one line by another, any blank rows, and combining these together in a single measure which excludes hidden rows
- Dynamic format strings to ensure each income statement line is formatted based on the value in the 'Layout'[Format string default]
- The reusability of this solution is highlighted as we have generated three different income statement semantic models using identical model extensions, DAX, and dynamic format strings.

PART IV

Producing Internal Income Statement Semantic Models

Producing a single layout for the income statement which mirrors external reporting provides many advantages. Namely, this income statement – unlike static reports – can be sliced and diced as well as drilled into. However, to fully realize the benefits outlined in Chapter 4, the semantic model must also support multiple layouts tailored to the appropriate audience; these additional layouts can contain non-statutory information contextualizing general ledger information, such as percentages and data from other sources. The nature of bespoke information means that we cannot cover every possible permutation in this book; instead, we focus on general techniques and cover common examples including data related to human resources and the sales pipeline.

We will first learn about extending the external reporting logical models from Chapter 10 to include

1. **Additional layouts**: Contain the income statement presentation logic for internal reports such as which lines appear, the order in which they appear, which calculations are performed, and how each line is formatted.

2. **The 'Other Non-General Ledger Information' snapshot fact table**: An additional fact table is required to calculate other non-general ledger information such as the number of full-time equivalent (FTE) employees.

We then extend the external reporting semantic models (Chapter 11), resulting in semantic models which support multiple layouts and produce internal income statements in their entirety.

In this part, we will also cover various considerations from a security and self-service perspective; these are the things to consider before making the semantic model available to end users. Finally, we review the sixteen challenges outlined in Chapter 3, covering how these have been simultaneously overcome with the approach outlined in this book.

This part comprises the following chapters:

- Chapter 12, "Internal Reporting Logical Models"
- Chapter 13, "Internal Reporting Semantic Models"
- Chapter 14, "Security and Self-Service Considerations"
- Chapter 15, "Review of the 16 Challenges"

CHAPTER 12

Internal Reporting Logical Models

In this chapter, we will learn how to reproduce internal income statements by extending the external reporting logical models from Chapter 10. Internal requirements (unlike external requirements) are not bound by accounting standards; entities can, and do, create a wide range of internal reporting. Given the range of requirements is unique to each entity, these internal logical models focus on general techniques.

In building internal reporting logical models, we will firstly learn about the internal layout table, which contains the internal income statement presentation logic: what lines appear, in which order they appear, which calculations are performed, and how each line is formatted. This includes additional elements to the external layout table, such as percentages (i.e., gross profit, %), and information from other departments, such as human resources and marketing. We will then cover extending the Chapter 10 logical models, adding an additional internal layout to the 'Layout' snowflake dimension, which is derived from the internal layout table, and the 'Other Non-General Ledger Information' snapshot fact table.

In this chapter, there are two sections:

1. The Internal Layout Table
2. Extending the External Reporting Logical Models

CHAPTER 12   INTERNAL REPORTING LOGICAL MODELS

The Internal Layout Table
Internal Layout Table Overview

The internal layout table is an essential input into internal income statement models. Table 12-1 contains a completed internal layout table for StarSchema.co.uk, the column names of which are identical to the external layout table.

CHAPTER 12 INTERNAL REPORTING LOGICAL MODELS

Table 12-1. StarSchema.co.uk internal layout table

Income Statement Key	Line Name	Calculation Type	1st From	1st To	2nd From	2nd To	Is Hidden	Format String Default
101	Revenue:	Blank					No	0;-0-0;;@
102	B2B	Line item	10100	10130			No	#,##0.;(#,##0.);-
103	B2C	Line item	10200	10230			No	#,##0.;(#,##0.);-
104	Total revenue	Subtotal NCLD	102	103			No	#,##0.;(#,##0.);-
105		Blank					No	0;-0-0;;@
106	Cost of Revenue:	Blank					No	0;-0-0;;@
107	B2B	Line item	20100	20140			No	#,##0.;(#,##0.);-
108	B2C	Line item	20200	20240			No	#,##0.;(#,##0.);-
109	Total cost of revenue	Subtotal NCLD	107	108			No	#,##0.;(#,##0.);-
110	Gross margin	Subtotal NCLD	102	108			No	#,##0.;(#,##0.);-

(*continued*)

329

Table 12-1. (continued)

Income Statement Key	Line Name	Calculation Type	1st From	1st To	2nd From	2nd To	Is Hidden	Format String Default
111	Gross margin, %	Divide	110	104			No	#,##0.0%;(#,##0.0%);-
112		Blank					No	0;0-0;;@
113	Labour	Line item	30100	30180	50100	50160	No	#,##0,;(#,##0,);-
114	Sales and Marketing	Line item	40100	40130			No	#,##0,;(#,##0,);-
115	Research and Development	Line item	60100	60120			No	#,##0,;(#,##0,);-
116		Blank					No	0;0-0;;@
117	EBITDA	Subtotal NCLD	102	115			No	#,##0,;(#,##0,);-
118	EBITDA, %	Divide	117	104			No	#,##0.0%;(#,##0.0%);-
119	Depreciation	Line item	70100	70140			No	#,##0,;(#,##0,);-
120	Amortization	Line item	70400	70430			No	#,##0,;(#,##0,);-
121		Blank					No	0;0-0;;@
122	EBIT	Subtotal NCLD	102	120			No	#,##0,;(#,##0,);-

CHAPTER 12 INTERNAL REPORTING LOGICAL MODELS

123	EBIT,%	Divide	122	104	No	#,##0.0%;(#,##0.0%);-
124	Other Income, net	Line item	10710	10720	No	#,##0,;(#,##0,);-
125		Blank			No	0;0-0;;@
126	Profit Before Tax	Subtotal NCLD	102	124	No	#,##0,;(#,##0,);-
127	Tax Provision	Line item	80100	80130	No	#,##0,;(#,##0,);-
128		Blank			No	0;0-0;;@
129	Net Income	Subtotal NCLD	102	127	No	#,##0,;(#,##0,);-
130	Net Income, %	Divide	129	104	No	#,##0.0%;(#,##0.0%);-
131	Net income attributable to non-controlling interests	NCI			No	#,##0,;(#,##0,);-
132	Net income attributable to controlling interests	CI			No	#,##0,;(#,##0,);-

(continued)

331

Table 12-1. (continued)

Income Statement Key	Line Name	Calculation Type	1st From	1st To	2nd From	2nd To	Is Hidden	Format String Default
133		Blank					No	0;0-0;;@
134	Earnings per share:	Blank					No	0;0-0;;@
135	Basic EPS	Divide	132	139			No	"$"#,##0.00;("$"#,##0.00);-
136	Core EPS	Divide	132	140			No	"$"#,##0.00;("$"#,##0.00);-
137		Blank					No	0;0-0;;@
138	Weighted average shares:	Blank					No	0;0-0;;@
139	Basic	Basic shares					No	#,##0;;(#,##0,);-
140	Core	Diluted shares					No	#,##0;;(#,##0,);-
141		Blank					No	0;0-0;;@
142	Research	Subset NCLD	60100	60100			Yes	#,##0;;(#,##0,);-

143	Research, % of R&D	Divide	142	115	No	#,##0.00%;(#,##0.00%);-
144	FTEs	FTE			No	#,##0,;(#,##0,);-
145	Number FTEs Departing	FTE Attrition			Yes	#,##0,;(#,##0,);-
146	Employee Attrition rate	Divide	145	144	No	#,##0.00%;(#,##0.00%);-
147		Blank			No	0;0-0;;@
148	All sales leads >= 75% probability	Sales 75			No	#,##0,;(#,##0,);-
149	All sales leads >= 50% probability	Sales 50			No	#,##0,;(#,##0,);-

CHAPTER 12   INTERNAL REPORTING LOGICAL MODELS

Completing the Internal Layout Table

To complete the internal layout table for any given entity, there are 12 steps. Each of these 12 steps is discussed as follows.

Step 1: Understand the Internal Income Statement

To complete the internal layout table, it is first necessary to understand the chosen entity's internal income statement. Figure 12-1 shows the StarSchema.co.uk internal income statement, and Figure 12-2 shows this same income statement with annotations explaining each line.

	2023	2022
Revenue: $		
B2B	90,460	78,556
B2C	72,478	63,036
Total revenue	162,938	141,592
Cost of Revenue:		
B2B	36,933	31,990
B2C	29,532	25,554
Total cost of revenue	66,466	57,544
Gross margin	96,472	84,049
Gross margin, %	59.2%	59.4%
Labour	18,392	15,353
Sales and Marketing	14,856	12,294
Research and Development	5,552	4,762
EBITDA	57,672	51,640
EBITDA, %	35.4%	36.5%
Depreciation	20,949	18,359
Amortization	9,411	7,993
EBIT	27,312	25,288
EBIT,%	16.8%	17.9%
Other Income, net	308	251
Profit Before Tax	27,619	25,540
Tax Provision	5,891	5,145
Net Income	21,729	20,394
Net Income, %	13.3%	14.4%
Net income attributable to non-controlling interests	4,780	4,487
Net income attributable to controlling interests $	16,948	15,908
Earnings per share:		
Basic EPS	$2.66	$2.48
Core EPS	$2.64	$2.45
Weighted average shares:		
Basic	6,372	6,415
Core	6,420	6,488
Research, % of R&D	37.55%	36.45%
FTEs	2,652	2,172
Employee Attrition rate	6.20%	7.34%
All sales leads >= 75% probability	32,157	26,047
All sales leads >= 50% probability	60,673	48,538

Figure 12-1. StarSchema.co.uk internal income statement

CHAPTER 12 INTERNAL REPORTING LOGICAL MODELS

#				2023	2022
1	Revenue:		$		
2	B2B	Accounts 10100 to 10130		90,460	78,556
3	B2C	Accounts 10200 to 10230		72,478	63,036
4	Total revenue	Line-items 2 to 3		162,938	141,592
5					
6	Cost of Revenue:				
7	B2B	Accounts 20100 to 20140		36,933	31,990
8	B2C	Accounts 20200 to 20240		29,532	25,554
9	Total cost of revenue	Line-items 7 to 8		66,466	57,544
10	Gross margin	Line-items 2 to 8		96,472	84,049
11	Gross margin, %	Line 10 divided by line 4		59.2%	59.4%
12					
13	Labour	Accounts 30100 to 30180		18,392	15,353
14	Sales and Marketing	Accounts 40100 to 40130		14,856	12,294
15	Research and Development	Accounts 60100 to 60120		5,552	4,762
16					
17	EBITDA	Line-items 2 to 15		57,672	51,640
18	EBITDA, %	Line 17 divided by line 4		35.4%	36.5%
19	Depreciation	Accounts 70100 to 70140		20,949	18,359
20	Amortization	Accounts 70400 to 70430		9,411	7,993
21					
22	EBIT	Line-items 2 to 20		27,312	25,288
23	EBIT, %	Line 22 divided by line 4		16.8%	17.9%
24	Other Income, net	Accounts 10710 to 10720		308	251
25					
26	Profit Before Tax	Line-items 2 to 24		27,619	25,540
27	Tax Provision	Accounts 80100 to 80130		5,891	5,145
28					
29	Net Income	Line-items 2 to 27		21,729	20,394
30	Net Income, %	Line 29 divided by line 4		13.3%	14.4%
31	Net income attributable to non-controlling interests			4,780	4,487
32	Net income attributable to controlling interests		$	16,948	15,908
33					
34	Earnings per share:				
35	Basic EPS	Line 32 divided by line 39		$2.66	$2.48
36	Core EPS	Line 32 divided by line 40		$2.64	$2.45
37					
38	Weighted average shares:				
39	Basic	Number of shares		6,372	6,415
40	Core	Number of shares after all conversions		6,420	6,488
41					
42	Research account 60100 (hidden)				
43	Research, % of R&D	Line 42 divided by line 15		37.55%	36.45%
44	FTEs	Number of employees from HR system		2,652	2,172
45	Number of employees leaving from HR system (hidden)				
46	Employee Attrition rate	Line 45 divided by line 44		6.20%	7.34%
50					
48	All sales leads >= 75% probability	Sales leads from CRM system		32,157	26,047
49	All sales leads >= 50% probability	Sales leads from CRM system		60,673	48,538

Figure 12-2. StarSchema.co.uk internal income statement annotated

By annotating the internal income statement with the calculation logic and numbering each line, Figure 12-2 contains all the information needed to populate the internal layout table.

Step 2: Add the Income Statement Keys

In all additional layout tables, the income statement keys are combined with those used in the previous layout tables. As these sequential integers become primary keys in the 'Layout' dimension, it is essential these are

CHAPTER 12 INTERNAL REPORTING LOGICAL MODELS

unique (see Chapter 5 on primary keys). In the StarSchema.co.uk example, the number 100 is added to each income statement line in Figure 12-2 to create a range from 101 to 149 (Table 12-2).

Table 12-2. StarSchema.co.uk internal layout table income statement keys

Income Statement Key
101
102
103
104
105
106
107
108
109
110
111
112
113

(continued)

Table 12-2. (*continued*)

Income Statement Key

114

115

116

117

118

119

120

121

122

123

124

125

126

127

128

129

(*continued*)

Table 12-2. (*continued*)

Income Statement Key
130
131
132
133
134
135
136
137
138
139
140
141
142
143
144
145

(*continued*)

CHAPTER 12　INTERNAL REPORTING LOGICAL MODELS

Table 12-2. (*continued*)

Income Statement Key
146
147
148
149

Step 3: Add the Line Name

Step 3 involves placing line names against the associated income statement key. Table 12-3 shows the line names which appear on the internal income statement for StarSchema.co.uk.

Table 12-3. StarSchema.co.uk internal layout table with line names

Income Statement Key	Line Name
101	Revenue:
102	B2B
103	B2C
104	Total revenue
105	
106	Cost of Revenue:
107	B2B

(*continued*)

Table 12-3. (*continued*)

Income Statement Key	Line Name
108	B2C
109	Total cost of revenue
110	Gross margin
111	Gross margin, %
112	
113	Labour
114	Sales and Marketing
115	Research and Development
116	
117	EBITDA
118	EBITDA, %
119	Depreciation
120	Amortization
121	
122	EBIT
123	EBIT,%
124	Other Income, net
125	
126	Profit Before Tax
127	Tax Provision
128	
129	Net Income

(*continued*)

Table 12-3. (*continued*)

Income Statement Key	Line Name
130	Net Income, %
131	Net income attributable to non-controlling interests
132	Net income attributable to controlling interests
133	
134	Earnings per share:
135	Basic EPS
136	Core EPS
137	
138	Weighted average shares:
139	Basic
140	Core
141	
142	Research
143	Research, % of R&D
144	FTEs
145	Number FTEs Departing
146	Employee Attrition rate
147	
148	All sales leads >= 75% probability
149	All sales leads >= 50% probability

As with the income statement keys, the requirement is to create unique line names to maintain the sort order when querying the model using MDX. Therefore, in the case of duplicate line names, spaces suffix records to ensure uniqueness. For instance, for income statement key 101, the line name is "Revenue: " with a suffix space to differentiate from "Revenue:" on the external layout.

Steps 4–10: Line-Items to Blanks

Steps 4-10 are identical to the external layout table (Chapter 10). Table 12-4 contains the StarSchema.co.uk internal layout table completed with line-items, subtotals, subsets, controlling interests (CI), non-controlling interests (NCI), basic shares, core shares, blanks, and divisions for basic and core EPS.

CHAPTER 12 INTERNAL REPORTING LOGICAL MODELS

Table 12-4. StarSchema.co.uk internal layout table with steps 4–10 completed

Income Statement Key	Line Name	Calculation Type	1st From	1st To	2nd From	2nd To	Is Hidden	Format String Default
101	Revenue:	Blank					No	0;0-0;;@
102	B2B	Line item	10100	10130			No	#,##0.;(#,##0,);-
103	B2C	Line item	10200	10230			No	#,##0.;(#,##0,);-
104	Total revenue	Subtotal NCLD	102	103			No	#,##0.;(#,##0,);-
105		Blank					No	0;0-0;;@
106	Cost of Revenue:	Blank					No	0;0-0;;@
107	B2B	Line item	20100	20140			No	#,##0.;(#,##0,);-
108	B2C	Line item	20200	20240			No	#,##0.;(#,##0,);-
109	Total cost of revenue	Subtotal NCLD	107	108			No	#,##0.;(#,##0,);-
110	Gross margin	Subtotal NCLD	102	108			No	#,##0.;(#,##0,);-

(continued)

CHAPTER 12 INTERNAL REPORTING LOGICAL MODELS

Table 12-4. (continued)

Income Statement Key	Line Name	Calculation Type	1st From	1st To	2nd From	2nd To	Is Hidden	Format String Default
111								
112	Gross margin, %	Blank					No	0;0-0;;@
113	Labour	Line item	30100	30180	50100	50160	No	#,##0,;(#,##0,);-
114	Sales and Marketing	Line item	40100	40130			No	#,##0,;(#,##0,);-
115	Research and Development	Line item	60100	60120			No	#,##0,;(#,##0,);-
116		Blank					No	0;0-0;;@
117	EBITDA	Subtotal NCLD	102	115			No	#,##0,;(#,##0,);-
118	EBITDA, %							
119	Depreciation	Line item	70100	70140			No	#,##0,;(#,##0,);-
120	Amortization	Line item	70400	70430			No	#,##0,;(#,##0,);-
121		Blank					No	0;0-0;;@

CHAPTER 12 INTERNAL REPORTING LOGICAL MODELS

122	EBIT	Subtotal NCLD	102	120	No	#,##0,;(#,##0,);-
123	EBIT,%					
124	Other Income, net	Line item	10710	10720	No	#,##0,;(#,##0,);-
125		Blank			No	0;0-0;;@
126	Profit Before Tax	Subtotal NCLD	102	124	No	#,##0,;(#,##0,);-
127	Tax Provision	Line item	80100	80130	No	#,##0,;(#,##0,);-
128		Blank			No	0;0-0;;@
129	Net Income	Subtotal NCLD	102	127	No	#,##0,;(#,##0,);-
130	Net Income, %					

(continued)

CHAPTER 12 INTERNAL REPORTING LOGICAL MODELS

Table 12-4. (*continued*)

Income Statement Key	Line Name	Calculation Type	1st From	1st To	2nd From	2nd To	Is Hidden	Format String Default
131	Net income attributable to non-controlling interests	NCI					No	#,##0;;(#,##0,);-
132	Net income attributable to controlling interests	CI					No	#,##0;;(#,##0,);-
133		Blank					No	0;0-0;;@
134	Earnings per share:	Blank					No	0;0-0;;@
135	Basic EPS	Divide	132	139			No	"$"#,##0.00;("$"#,##0.00);-
136	Core EPS	Divide	132	140			No	"$"#,##0.00;("$"#,##0.00);-
137		Blank					No	0;0-0;;@
138	Weighted average shares:	Blank					No	0;0-0;;@

CHAPTER 12 INTERNAL REPORTING LOGICAL MODELS

139	Basic	Basic shares		No	#,##0,;(#,##0,);-
140	Core	Diluted shares		No	#,##0,;(#,##0,);-
141		Blank		No	0;0-0;;@
142	Research	Subset NCLD	60100 60100	Yes	#,##0,;(#,##0,);-
143	Research, % of R&D				
144	FTEs				
145	Number FTEs Departing				
146	Employee Attrition rate				
147		Blank		No	0;0-0;;@
148	All sales leads >= 75% probability				
149	All sales leads >= 50% probability				

347

CHAPTER 12 INTERNAL REPORTING LOGICAL MODELS

Step 11: Complete Percentages

Step 11 involves adding percentages (calculation challenge 8). For each percentage line:

- The calculation type should equal *Divide*.

- The from and to columns should represent the income statement key numerator and denominator, respectively. For instance, gross margin, % is income statement key 110 divided by income statement key 104.

- If the line is to be hidden, the *is hidden* column should contain yes, else it should contain no.

- The format string default should display the appropriate format string, for instance, #,##0.0%;(#,##0.0%);- which is a percentage to one decimal place.

Table 12-5 contains the layout table with the percentages completed for the StarSchema.co.uk internal layout.

Table 12-5. *StarSchema.co.uk internal layout table with percentages completed*

Income Statement Key	Line Name	Calculation Type	1st From	1st To	2nd From	2nd To	Is Hidden	Format String Default
101	Revenue:	Blank					No	0;0-0;;@
102	B2B	Line item	10100	10130			No	#,##0.;(#,##0.);-
103	B2C	Line item	10200	10230			No	#,##0.;(#,##0.);-
104	Total revenue	Subtotal NCLD	102	103			No	#,##0.;(#,##0.);-
105		Blank					No	0;0-0;;@
106	Cost of Revenue:	Blank					No	0;0-0;;@
107	B2B	Line item	20100	20140			No	#,##0.;(#,##0.);-
108	B2C	Line item	20200	20240			No	#,##0.;(#,##0.);-
109	Total cost of revenue	Subtotal NCLD	107	108			No	#,##0.;(#,##0.);-
110	Gross margin	Subtotal NCLD	102	108			No	#,##0.;(#,##0.);-

(*continued*)

CHAPTER 12 INTERNAL REPORTING LOGICAL MODELS

Table 12-5. (*continued*)

Income Statement Key	Line Name	Calculation Type	1st From	1st To	2nd From	2nd To	Is Hidden	Format String Default
111	Gross margin, %	Divide	110	104			No	#,##0.0%;(#,##0.0%);-
112		Blank					No	0;0-0;;@
113	Labour	Line item	30100	30180	50100	50160	No	#,##0,;(#,##0,);-
114	Sales and Marketing	Line item	40100	40130			No	#,##0,;(#,##0,);-
115	Research and Development	Line item	60100	60120			No	#,##0,;(#,##0,);-
116		Blank					No	0;0-0;;@
117	EBITDA	Subtotal NCLD	102	115			No	#,##0,;(#,##0,);-
118	EBITDA, %	**Divide**	**117**	**104**			**No**	**#,##0.0%;(#,##0.0%);-**
119	Depreciation	Line item	70100	70140			No	#,##0,;(#,##0,);-
120	Amortization	Line item	70400	70430			No	#,##0,;(#,##0,);-
121		Blank					No	0;0-0;;@
122	EBIT	Subtotal NCLD	102	120			No	#,##0,;(#,##0,);-

350

123	EBIT,%	**Divide**	**122**	**104**	**No**	**#,##0.0%;(#,##0.0%);-**
124	Other Income, net	Line item	10710	10720	No	#,##0,;(#,##0,);-
125		Blank			No	0;0-0-;;@
126	Profit Before Tax	Subtotal NCLD	102	124	No	#,##0,;(#,##0,);-
127	Tax Provision	Line item	80100	80130	No	#,##0,;(#,##0,);-
128		Blank			No	0;0-0-;;@
129	Net Income	Subtotal NCLD	102	127	No	#,##0,;(#,##0,);-
130	Net Income, %	**Divide**	**129**	**104**	**No**	**#,##0.0%;(#,##0.0%);-**
131	Net income attributable to non-controlling interests	NCI			No	#,##0,;(#,##0,);-
132	Net income attributable to controlling interests	CI			No	#,##0,;(#,##0,);-

(*continued*)

CHAPTER 12 INTERNAL REPORTING LOGICAL MODELS

Table 12-5. (continued)

Income Statement Key	Line Name	Calculation Type	1st From	1st To	2nd From	2nd To	Is Hidden	Format String Default
133		Blank					No	0;0-0;;@
134	Earnings per share:	Blank					No	0;0-0;;@
135	Basic EPS	Divide	132	139			No	"$"#,##0.00;("$"#,##0.00);-
136	Core EPS	Divide	132	140			No	"$"#,##0.00;("$"#,##0.00);-
137		Blank					No	0;0-0;;@
138	Weighted average shares:	Blank					No	0;0-0;;@
139	Basic	Basic shares					No	#,##0.;(#,##0.);-
140	Core	Diluted shares					No	#,##0.;(#,##0.);-
141		Blank					No	0;0-0;;@
142	Research	Subset NCLD	60100	60100			Yes	#,##0.;(#,##0.);-

CHAPTER 12 INTERNAL REPORTING LOGICAL MODELS

143	Research, % of R&D	**Divide**	**142**	**115**	**No**	**#,##0.00%;(#,##0.00%);-**
144	FTEs	FTE			No	#,##0.;(#,##0,);-
145	Number FTEs Departing	FTE Attrition			Yes	#,##0.;(#,##0,);-
146	Employee Attrition rate	**Divide**	**145**	**144**	**No**	**#,##0.00%;(#,##0.00%);-**
147		Blank			No	0;0-0;;@
148	All sales leads >= 75% probability	Sales 75			No	#,##0,;(#,##0,);-
149	All sales leads >= 50% probability	Sales 50			No	#,##0,;(#,##0,);-

353

Step 12: Bespoke Calculations

Step 12 involves adding bespoke calculations (calculation challenge 7). Each bespoke calculation requires its own calculation type which will match the calculation type in the 'Other Non-General Ledger Information' snapshot fact table. In the StarSchema.co.uk example, the bespoke calculation types are

- **FTE**: The number of full-time equivalent (FTE) employees; the total hours worked by all employees divided by the employers' number of working hours in a week (i.e., 37.5 hours)
- **FTE Attrition**: The number of employees leaving the organization
- **Sales 75**: Future sales leads with a 75% probability of closing
- **Sales 50**: Future sales leads with a 50% probability of closing

These four metrics are common as FTE, FTE Attrition, Sales 75, and Sales 50 are key indicators for future profitability. For instance, a shrinking pipeline and increasing employee attrition could both indicate that profitability is likely to decline.

For each bespoke calculation line:

- The calculation type on the layout table should equal the bespoke calculation type on the 'Other Non-General Ledger' table, that is, FTE.
- If the line is to be hidden, the *is hidden* column should contain yes, else it should contain no.
- The format string default should display the appropriate format string.

Table 12-6 contains the layout table with the bespoke calculations completed for StarSchema.co.uk.

CHAPTER 12 INTERNAL REPORTING LOGICAL MODELS

Table 12-6. StarSchema.co.uk internal layout table with bespoke calculations completed

Income Statement Key	Line Name	Calculation Type	1st From	1st To	2nd From	2nd To	Is Hidden	Format String Default
101	Revenue:	Blank					No	0;0-0;;@
102	B2B	Line item	10100	10130			No	#,##0;;(#,##0);-
103	B2C	Line item	10200	10230			No	#,##0;;(#,##0);-
104	Total revenue	Subtotal NCLD	102	103			No	#,##0;;(#,##0);-
105		Blank					No	0;0-0;;@
106	Cost of Revenue:	Blank					No	0;0-0;;@
107	B2B	Line item	20100	20140			No	#,##0;;(#,##0);-
108	B2C	Line item	20200	20240			No	#,##0;;(#,##0);-
109	Total cost of revenue	Subtotal NCLD	107	108			No	#,##0;;(#,##0);-
110	Gross margin	Subtotal NCLD	102	108			No	#,##0;;(#,##0);-

(*continued*)

CHAPTER 12 INTERNAL REPORTING LOGICAL MODELS

Table 12-6. (continued)

Income Statement Key	Line Name	Calculation Type	1st From	1st To	2nd From	2nd To	Is Hidden	Format String Default
111	Gross margin, %	Divide	110	104			No	#,##0.0%;(#,##0.0%);-
112		Blank					No	0;0-0;;@
113	Labour	Line item	30100	30180	50100	50160	No	#,##0,;(#,##0,);-
114	Sales and Marketing	Line item	40100	40130			No	#,##0,;(#,##0,);-
115	Research and Development	Line item	60100	60120			No	#,##0,;(#,##0,);-
116		Blank					No	0;0-0;;@
117	EBITDA	Subtotal NCLD	102	115			No	#,##0,;(#,##0,);-
118	EBITDA, %	Divide	117	104			No	#,##0.0%;(#,##0.0%);-
119	Depreciation	Line item	70100	70140			No	#,##0,;(#,##0,);-
120	Amortization	Line item	70400	70430			No	#,##0,;(#,##0,);-
121		Blank					No	0;0-0;;@

CHAPTER 12 INTERNAL REPORTING LOGICAL MODELS

122	EBIT	Subtotal NCLD	102	120		No	#,##0,;(#,##0,);-
123	EBIT,%	Divide	122	104		No	#,##0.0%;(#,##0.0%);-
124	Other Income, net	Line item	10710	10720		No	#,##0,;(#,##0,);-
125		Blank				No	0;0-0;;@
126	Profit Before Tax	Subtotal NCLD	102	124		No	#,##0,;(#,##0,);-
127	Tax Provision	Line item	80100	80130		No	#,##0,;(#,##0,);-
128		Blank				No	0;0-0;;@
129	Net Income	Subtotal NCLD	102	127		No	#,##0,;(#,##0,);-
130	Net Income, %	Divide	129	104		No	#,##0.0%;(#,##0.0%);-
131	Net income attributable to non-controlling interests	NCI				No	#,##0,;(#,##0,);-
132	Net income attributable to controlling interests	CI				No	#,##0,;(#,##0,);-

(*continued*)

CHAPTER 12   INTERNAL REPORTING LOGICAL MODELS

Table 12-6. (*continued*)

Income Statement Key	Line Name	Calculation Type	1st From	1st To	2nd From	2nd To	Is Hidden	Format String Default
133		Blank					No	0;0-0;;@
134	Earnings per share:	Blank					No	0;0-0;;@
135	Basic EPS	Divide	132	139			No	" $"#,##0.00;(" $"#,##0.00);-
136	Core EPS	Divide	132	140			No	" $"#,##0.00;(" $"#,##0.00);-
137		Blank					No	0;0-0;;@
138	Weighted average shares:	Blank					No	0;0-0;;@
139	Basic	Basic shares					No	#,##0.;(#,##0.);-
140	Core	Diluted shares					No	#,##0.;(#,##0.);-
141		Blank					No	0;0-0;;@
142	Research	Subset NCLD	60100	60100			Yes	#,##0.;(#,##0.);-

CHAPTER 12 INTERNAL REPORTING LOGICAL MODELS

#	Name	Operation			Flag	Format
143	Research, % of R&D	Divide	142	115	No	#,##0.00%;(#,##0.00%);-
144	**FTEs**	**FTE**			**No**	**#,##0,;(#,##0,);-**
145	Number FTEs Departing	**FTE Attrition**			**Yes**	**#,##0,;(#,##0,);-**
146	Employee Attrition rate	Divide	145	144	No	#,##0.00%;(#,##0.00%);-
147		Blank			No	0;0-0;;@
148	All sales leads >= 75% probability	**Sales 75**			**No**	**#,##0,;(#,##0,);-**
149	All sales leads >= 50% probability	**Sales 50**			**No**	**#,##0,;(#,##0,);-**

CHAPTER 12   INTERNAL REPORTING LOGICAL MODELS

Extending the External Reporting Logical Models

To support internal income statement reporting for Tyrell Corp, Weyland Industries, and StarSchema.co.uk, the logical models produced in Chapter 10 are required to be extended to include

1. 'Other Non-General Ledger Information' snapshot fact table: This contains the relevant non-general information required to be displayed on the income statement, that is, for StarSchema.co.uk the FTE, FTE Attrition, Sales 75, and Sales 50.

2. 'Effective Date'[Date] → 'Other Non-General Ledger Information'[Start of time period] relationship.

3. 'Account'[Layout 2 Income Statement Key] foreign key: Derived from the internal layout input table, this contains the logic surrounding how accounts are mapped to the internal layout line-items.

4. 'Layout'[Income Statement Key] → 'Account' [Layout 2 Income Statement Key] inactive relationship.

5. 'Layout'[Layout version] attribute: This contains the layout version name, so end users can select the appropriate layout, that is, internal.

This section covers these five extensions and then applies these extensions to the logical models built in Chapter 10.

Extension 1: Adding the Other Non-general Ledger Information Snapshot Fact Table

To include bespoke calculations, an additional 'Other Non-General Ledger Information' fact table is required in the model. This snapshot fact table contains the following fields:

- **Start of time period**: A date reflecting the first day of the time period, that is, 1 January 2023.
- **Time period**: The time period to which the calculation relates, that is, Period 1 2023, Quarter 1 2023, or 2023.
- **Calculation type**: The type of bespoke calculation matching the calculation type in the layout table, that is, FTE.
- **Value**: The value for the calculation type and time period.

This structure is the same as the 'Shares Outstanding' fact table, except the measure field is *value* as opposed to *number of shares*. Consequently, the table works in a comparable way to 'Shares Outstanding'.

StarSchema.co.uk Example Other Non-general Ledger Information Table

As an example, the 2023 FTE data for StarSchema.co.uk is shown in Table 12-7 where

- The start of time period contains the first date in the period. For instance, the start of time period is 1 Jan 2023 for time periods "2023," "2023-Q1," and "2023-P1."
- The time period contains the time period to which the FTE value belongs. For instance, the time period "2023"

refers to the average number of FTEs in 2023, whereas the time period "2023-Q1" refers to the average number of FTEs in quarter 1 of 2023.

- The calculation type contains the type of calculation, in this case FTE, which matches income statement line 144.

- The value (thousands) refers to the average number of FTEs in thousands. For instance, there were 2,652k FTEs in 2023.

Table 12-7. Other non-general ledger information – 2023 FTE

Time Period	Start of Time Period	Calculation Type	Value (Thousands)
2023	1 Jan 2023	FTE	2,652k
2023-Q1	1 Jan 2023	FTE	2,387k
2023-Q2	1 Apr 2023	FTE	2,493k
2023-Q3	1 Jul 2023	FTE	2,572k
2023-Q4	1 Oct 2023	FTE	2,652k
2023-P1	1 Jan 2023	FTE	2,334k
2023-P2	1 Feb 2023	FTE	2,360k
2023-P3	1 Mar 2023	FTE	2,387k
2023-P4	1 Apr 2023	FTE	2,413k
2023-P5	1 May 2023	FTE	2,440k
2023-P6	1 Jun 2023	FTE	2,466k
2023-P7	1 Jul 2023	FTE	2,493k

(*continued*)

CHAPTER 12　INTERNAL REPORTING LOGICAL MODELS

Table 12-7. (*continued*)

Time Period	Start of Time Period	Calculation Type	Value (Thousands)
2023-P8	1 Aug 2023	FTE	2,519k
2023-P9	1 Sep 2023	FTE	2,546k
2023-P10	1 Oct 2023	FTE	2,572k
2023-P11	1 Nov 2023	FTE	2,599k
2023-P12	1 Dec 2023	FTE	2,652k

Extension 2: Creating the Relationship Between Effective Date and Other Non-general Ledger Information

To include the other non-general ledger calculations for a selected date, the 'Effective Date' [Date] → 'Other Non-General Ledger Information'[Start of time period] relationship is required (Figure 12-3).

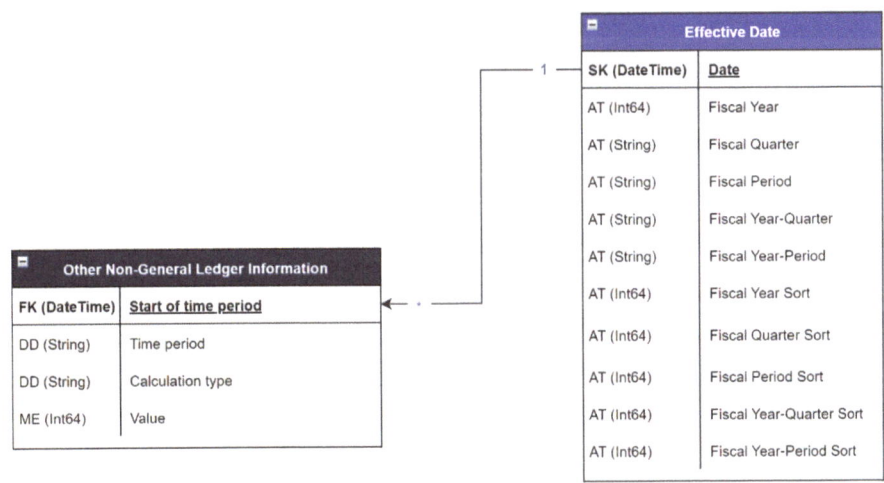

Figure 12-3. *Other non-general ledger information logical model*

CHAPTER 12   INTERNAL REPORTING LOGICAL MODELS

Extension 3: Adding an Additional Foreign Key to the Account Dimension

By introducing a secondary internal layout, accounts can be assigned to either a line-item from the external layout or the internal layout. To achieve this, the 'Account' dimension requires a secondary foreign key containing the 'Account'[Layout 2 Income Statement Key] which is derived from the internal layout table. For instance, in Table 12-8 'Account'[Account Key] 30100 is mapped to 'Account'[Layout 1 Income Statement Key] 2 and 'Account'[Layout 2 Income Statement Key] 102.

Table 12-8. *Account table with mapping to layout 1 and layout 2*

Account Key	Account Name	Account Type	Account Type Indicator	Layout 1 Income Statement Key	Layout 2 Income Statement Key
30100	Trade sales	Revenue	1	2	102
30101	Returns	Revenue	1	2	102
40100	Trade cost of sales	Expense	-1	4	104

If expanding beyond two layouts, each new layout requires an additional foreign key in the 'Account' dimension, that is, 'Account'[Layout 3 Income Statement Key] and 'Account'[Layout 4 Income Statement Key].

Extension 4: Creating the Inactive Relationship Between Layout and Account

The logical model (Figure 12-4) contains the 'Layout' [Income Statement Key] → 'Account'[Layout 2 Income Statement Key] inactive relationship, enabling lines from the internal layout to be mapped to accounts.

CHAPTER 12 INTERNAL REPORTING LOGICAL MODELS

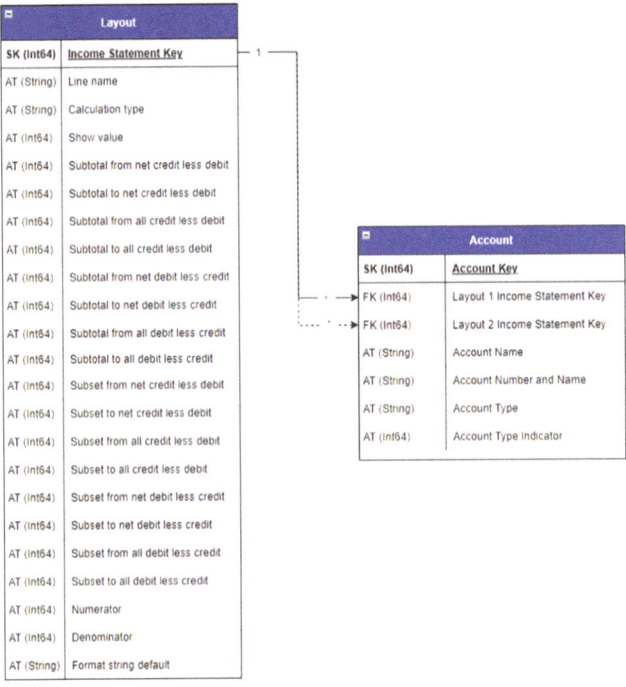

Figure 12-4. Layout and account dimension logical model with inactive relationship

Extension 5: Adding the Layout Version Attribute

The attribute 'Layout'[Layout version] is required so end users can choose to view a given income statement layout (Figure 12-5).

365

CHAPTER 12 INTERNAL REPORTING LOGICAL MODELS

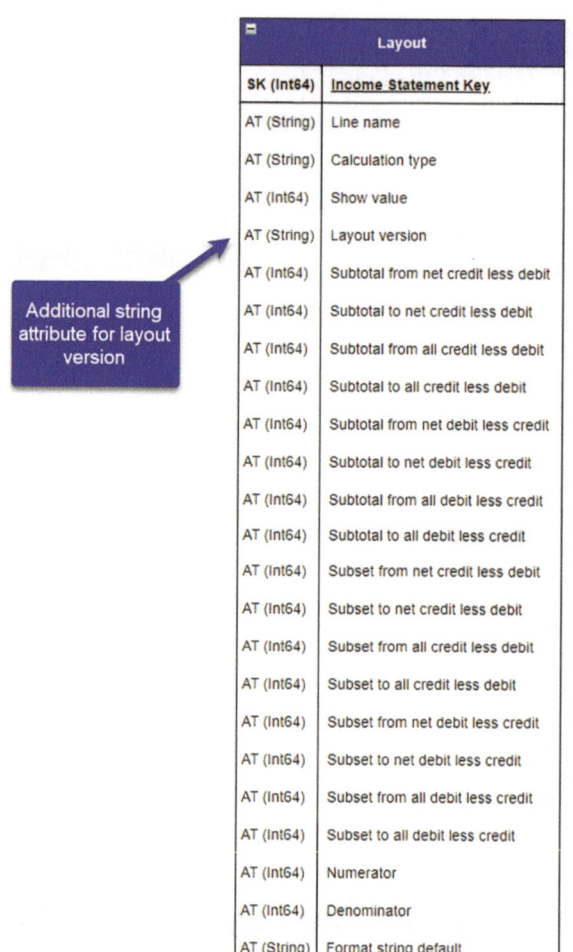

Figure 12-5. *Layout with layout version added*

In the StarSchema.co.uk example, end users can choose 'Layout'[Layout version]:

- **External (Layout 1)**: The calculation follows the 'Layout'[Income Statement Key] → 'Account'[Layout 1 Income Statement Key] *active* relationship; 'Account'[Layout 1 Income Statement Key] contains the mapping of accounts to the external layout.

- **Internal (Layout 2)**: The calculation follows the 'Layout'[Income Statement Key] → 'Account'[Layout 2 Income Statement Key] *inactive* relationship; 'Account'[Layout 2 Income Statement Key] contains the mapping of accounts to the internal layout.

Each layout version can be named appropriately. For instance, a third layout version for executives could be named "Executive."

Internal Reporting Logical Model

Trial Balance Internal Reporting Logical Model

Figure 12-6 shows the internal reporting logical model (Chapter 10) with the five extensions required to support a second layout and bespoke calculations.

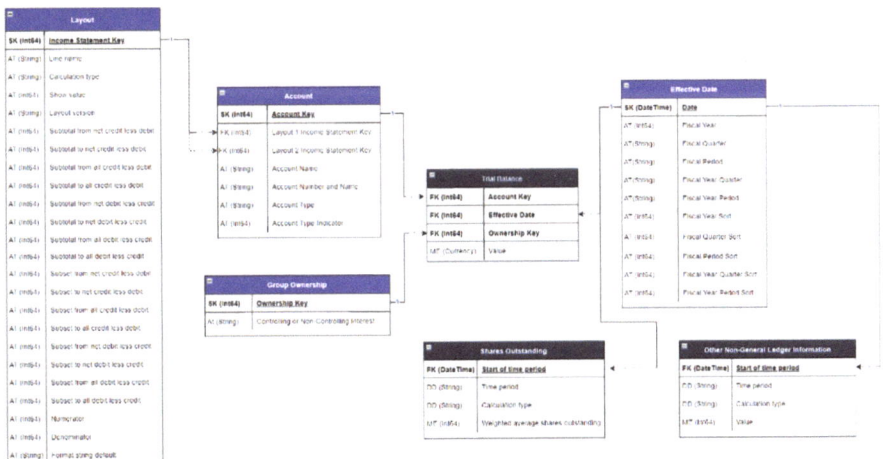

Figure 12-6. Trial balance internal reporting model

CHAPTER 12   INTERNAL REPORTING LOGICAL MODELS

A Journal Entry Internal Reporting Logical Model

Figure 12-7 shows a journal entry internal reporting logical model for StarSchema.co.uk (Chapter 10) with the five extensions required to support a second layout and bespoke calculations.

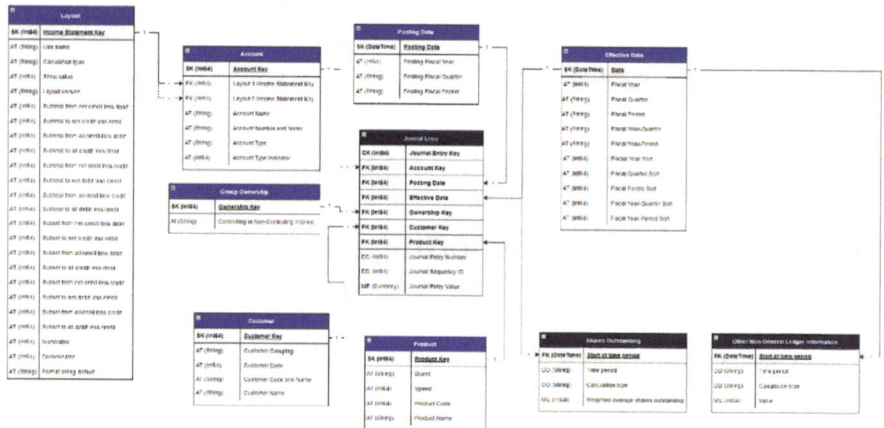

Figure 12-7. A journal entry internal reporting model

Summary

- To calculate internal income statements in their entirety, the external reporting logical models from Chapter 10 require five extensions:

  - 'Other Non-General Ledger Information' snapshot fact table contains the relevant bespoke calculation information, that is, for StarSchema.co.uk the FTE, FTE Attrition, Sales 75, and Sales 50.

  - 'Effective Date'[Date] → 'Other Non-General Ledger Information'[Start of time period] relationship.

CHAPTER 12   INTERNAL REPORTING LOGICAL MODELS

- 'Account'[Layout 2 Income Statement Key] foreign key contains the logic surrounding how line-items are mapped to the second layout.

- 'Layout'[Income Statement Key] → 'Account'[Layout 2 Income Statement Key] inactive relationship.

- 'Layout'[Layout version] attribute so end users can select the appropriate layout.

- The internal layout input table completion process is like the external layout input table (Chapter 10) with the addition of using divide to calculate percentages and bespoke calculations.

CHAPTER 13

Internal Reporting Semantic Models

In the previous chapter, we learned about extensions to the trial balance external reporting logical model and a journal entry external reporting logical model. These extensions created the trial balance internal reporting logical model and a journal entry internal reporting logical model, models with multiple income statement layouts that include percentages and other non-general ledger information.

In this chapter, we will create trial balance internal reporting semantic models and a journal entry internal reporting semantic model. This involves extending the trial balance external reporting semantic models and a journal entry external reporting semantic model from Chapter 11, based on the internal reporting logical models in Chapter 12. We will start with any of the three semantic models from Chapter 11 – either Tyrell Corp, Weyland Industries, or StarSchema.co.uk – then go through each semantic model stage covering Power Query, data modelling, and DAX.

In this chapter, there are four sections:

1. Semantic Model Inputs
2. Power Query Transformations
3. Building the Data Model
4. DAX Actuals Calculations

CHAPTER 13   INTERNAL REPORTING SEMANTIC MODELS

Semantic Model Inputs

This chapter builds upon the semantic models created in Chapter 11. The starting point is, therefore, either the Tyrell Corp external reporting semantic model, Weyland Industries external reporting semantic model, or the StarSchema.co.uk external reporting semantic model. You can either use the PBIX file you created in Chapter 11 or download from the resources: the Tyrell Corp Chapter 11 end, Weyland Industries Chapter 11 end, or StarSchema.co.uk Chapter 11 end.

Alongside the PBIX file, you will require the accompanying *Internal Layout* and *Other Non-General Ledger Information* inputs as described in the previous chapter; these can also be found in the resources. For instance, this chapter follows along using the StarSchema.co.uk files:

- StarSchema.co.uk Internal Layout
- StarSchema.co.uk Other Non-General Ledger Information

If you are following along using the Tyrell Corp or Weyland Industries example, replace StarSchema.co.uk with the relevant organization, that is, Tyrell Corp Internal Layout as opposed to StarSchema.co.uk Internal Layout. Regardless of the entity chosen – Tyrell Corp, Weyland Industries, or StarSchema.co.uk – the steps in parts two (Power Query), three (data modelling), and four (DAX) are identical. However, the output will be different given the nature of the input-driven approach (see Chapter 3), that is, Tyrell Corp is using the internal layout for Tyrell Corp as an input, whereas StarSchema.co.uk is using the internal layout for StarSchema.co.uk as an input.

CHAPTER 13   INTERNAL REPORTING SEMANTIC MODELS

Power Query Transformations

This section covers the steps in transforming the data inputs into the tables required for the data model using Power Query in Power BI Desktop. The same transformations are required, regardless of whether you are using Power BI Desktop or Microsoft Fabric. This is covered in four stages:

1. Create shared expressions
2. Other non-general ledger information
3. Layout dimension table
4. Accounts dimension table

Stage 1: Create Shared Expressions

Step 1: In the Power Query editor, select the **New Source** drop-down (**1**) and **Text/CSV** (**2**).

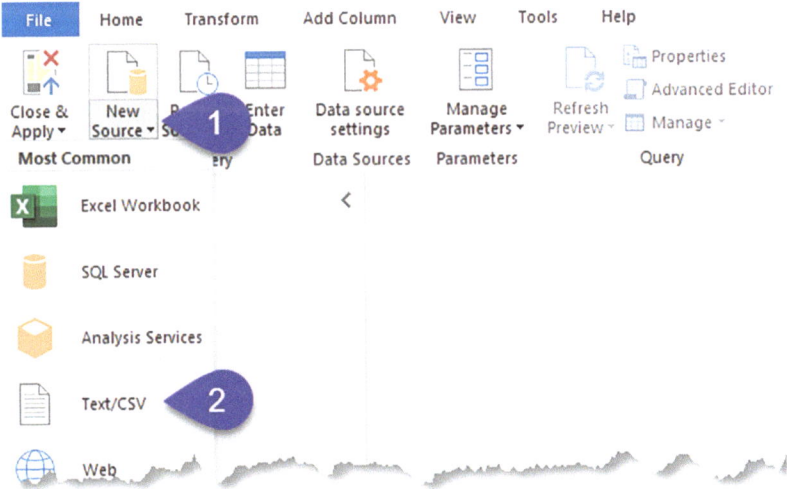

Figure 13-1. Ingest new data

CHAPTER 13   INTERNAL REPORTING SEMANTIC MODELS

Step 2: Select the file **StarSchema.co.uk Internal Layout (1)** and click **Open (2)**.

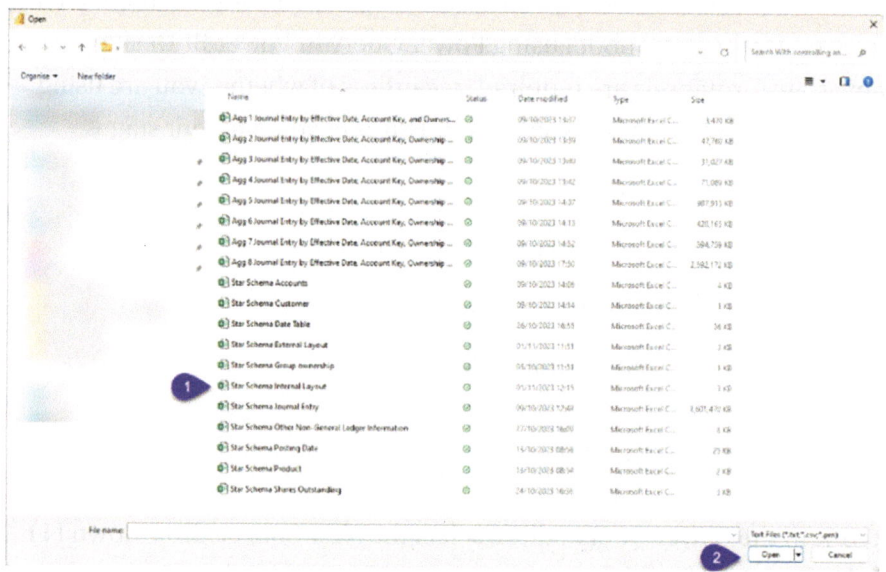

Figure 13-2.   StarSchema.co.uk internal layout file explorer

Step 3: Click **OK (1)** to bring the table into the model.

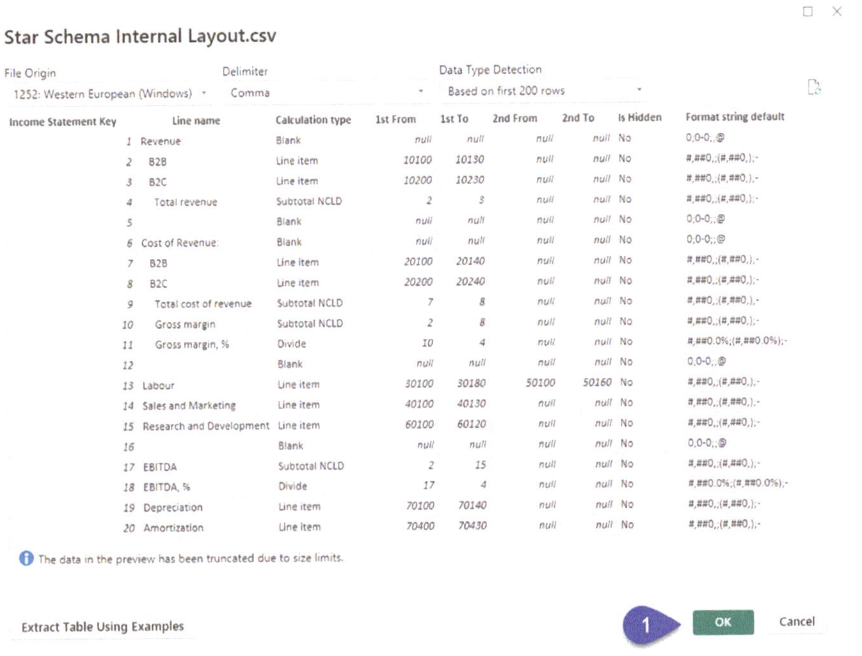

CHAPTER 13   INTERNAL REPORTING SEMANTIC MODELS

Figure 13-3. Ingest StarSchema.co.uk internal layout

Step 4: Check types as shown in Figure 13-4.

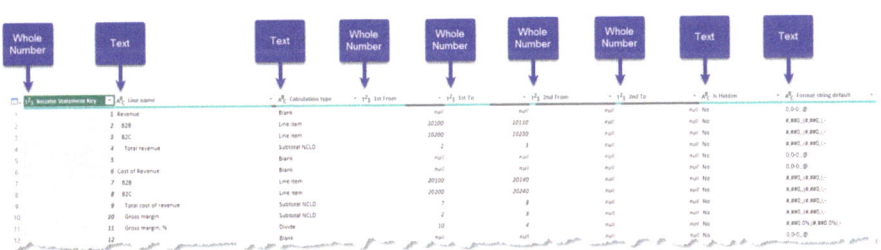

Figure 13-4. StarSchema.co.uk internal layout data types

Step 5: Right-click **StarSchema co uk Internal Layout (1)** and select **Move To Group (2)** and select **Shared Expressions (3)**.

375

CHAPTER 13   INTERNAL REPORTING SEMANTIC MODELS

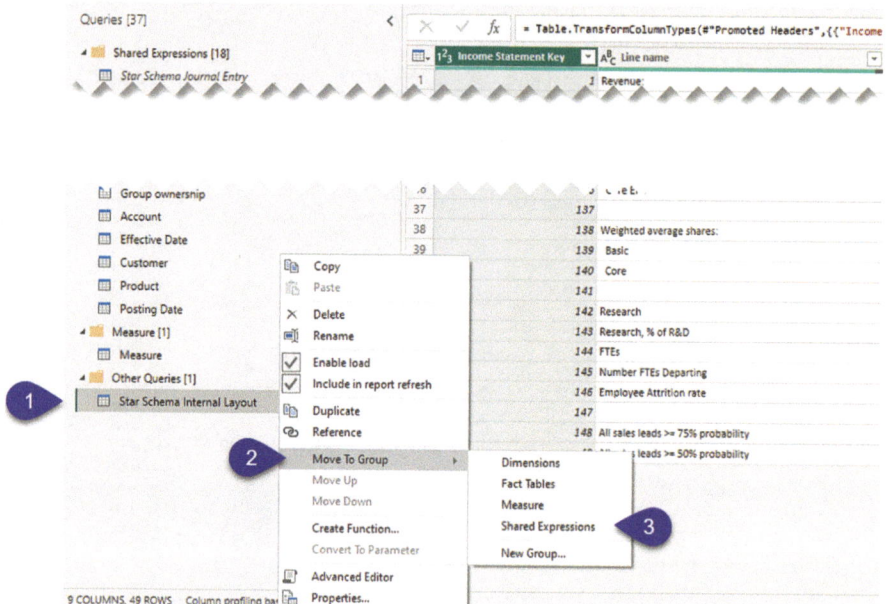

Figure 13-5. *StarSchema.co.uk internal layout move to shared expression*

Step 6: In the Queries pane, right-click **StarSchema co uk Internal Layout (1)** and click the selected **Enable load (2)** to disable the load (should no longer have tick to the left of Enable load, and Star Schema Journal Entry should be in italics).

CHAPTER 13 INTERNAL REPORTING SEMANTIC MODELS

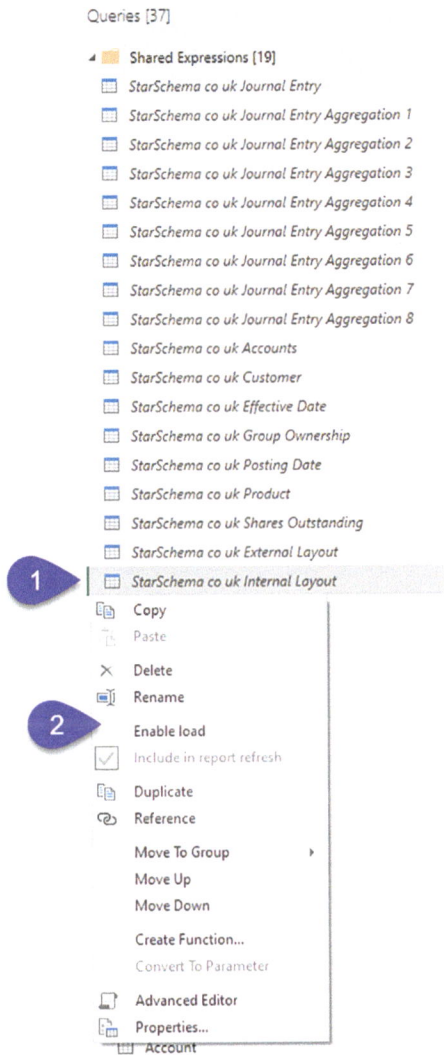

Figure 13-6. *StarSchema.co.uk internal layout disable load*

Step 7: Repeat steps 1–6 for **StarSchema.co.uk Other Non-general Ledger information**.

377

CHAPTER 13   INTERNAL REPORTING SEMANTIC MODELS

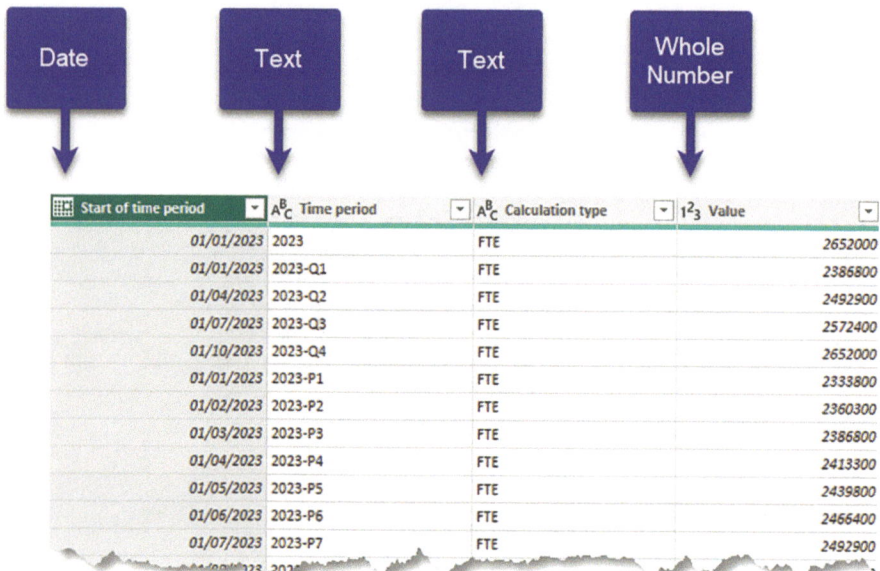

Figure 13-7. StarSchema.co.uk other non-general ledger information data types

Stage 2: Other Non-general Ledger Information

Step 1: In the Queries pane, right-click **StarSchema co uk Other Non-General Ledger Information (1)** and select **Reference (2)**.

CHAPTER 13 INTERNAL REPORTING SEMANTIC MODELS

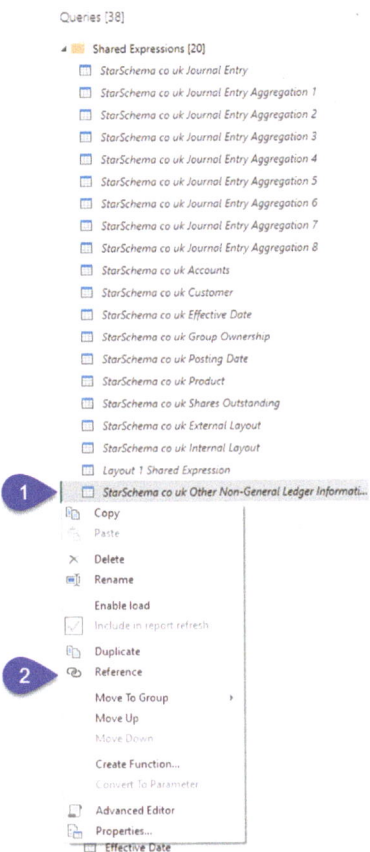

Figure 13-8. StarSchema.co.uk other non-general ledger information reference

Step 2: Select the referenced query **StarSchema co uk Other Non-General Ledger Information (2) (1)**, and in the query settings under **Name (2)**, type *Other Non-General Ledger Information* and press enter.

379

CHAPTER 13 INTERNAL REPORTING SEMANTIC MODELS

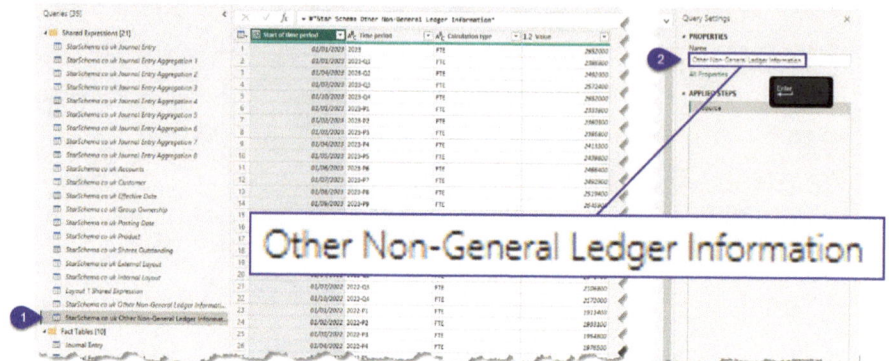

Figure 13-9. *StarSchema.co.uk other non-general ledger information rename*

Step 3: Right-click **Other Non-General Ledger Information (1)**, select **Move To Group (2)**, and select **Fact Tables (3)**.

CHAPTER 13   INTERNAL REPORTING SEMANTIC MODELS

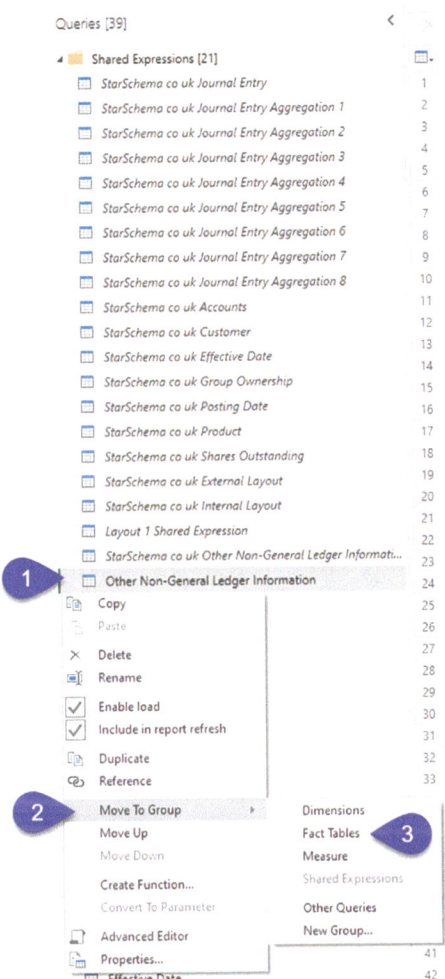

Figure 13-10.   StarSchema.co.uk other non-general ledger information move to fact table group

Stage 3: Layout Dimension

Step 1: In the Queries pane, select **StarSchema co uk External Layout (1)**, select the tab **Add Column (2)**, and select **Custom Column (3)**.

CHAPTER 13 INTERNAL REPORTING SEMANTIC MODELS

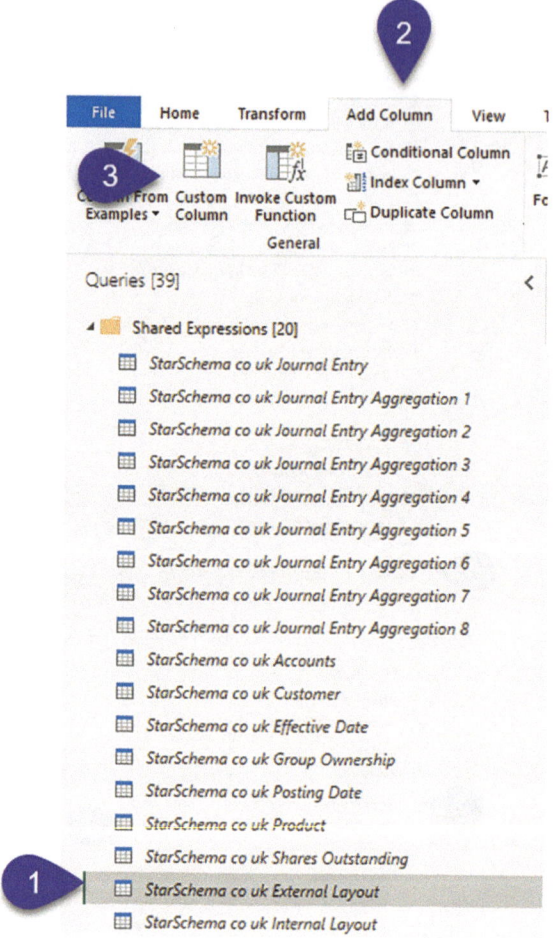

Figure 13-11. StarSchema.co.uk external layout custom column

Step 2: In the Custom Column box, type the new column name **Layout Version (1)** and custom column formula **"External" (2)** and select **OK (3)**.

CHAPTER 13 INTERNAL REPORTING SEMANTIC MODELS

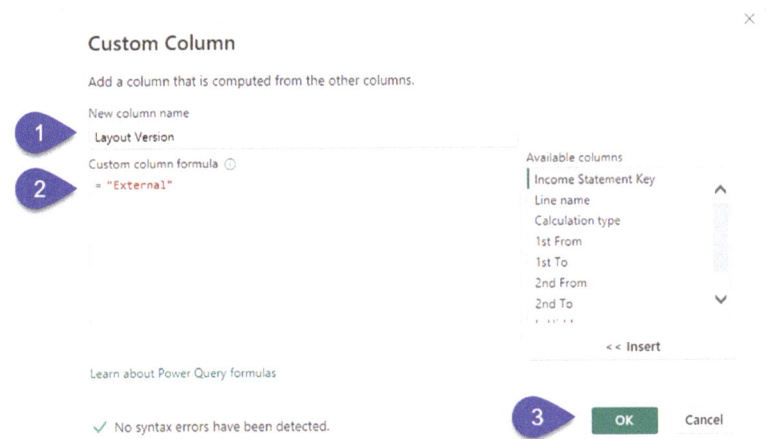

Figure 13-12. StarSchema.co.uk layout version external

Step 3: In the Queries pane, select **StarSchema co uk Internal Layout (1)**, select the tab **Add Column (2)**, and select **Custom Column (3)**.

CHAPTER 13 INTERNAL REPORTING SEMANTIC MODELS

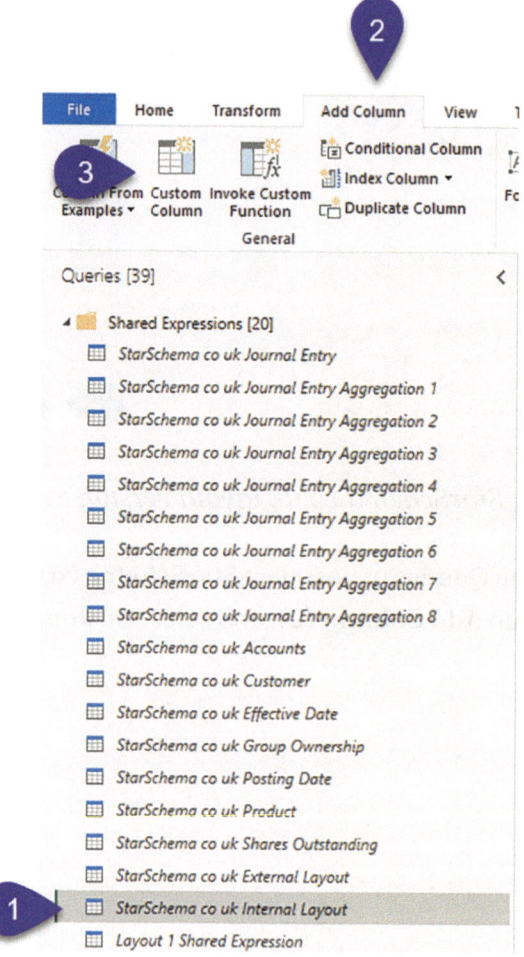

Figure 13-13. StarSchema.co.uk internal layout custom column

Step 4: In the Custom Column box, type the new column name **Layout Version (1)** and custom column formula **"Internal" (2)** and select **OK (3)**.

CHAPTER 13 INTERNAL REPORTING SEMANTIC MODELS

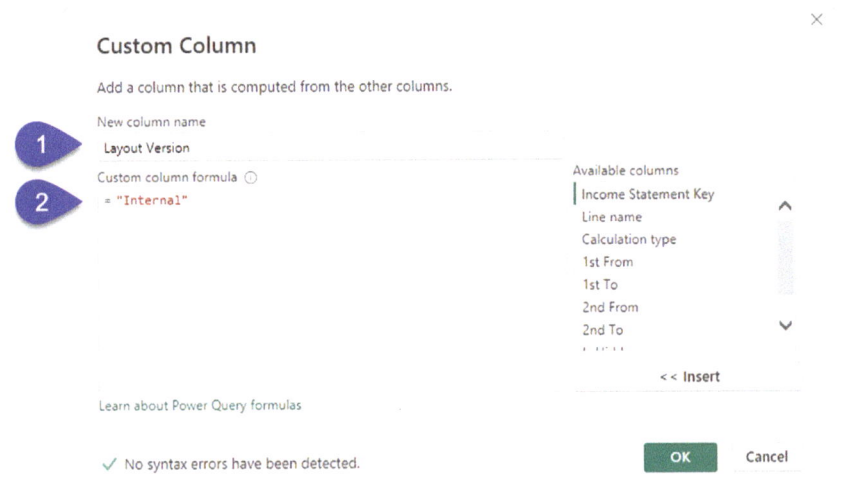

Figure 13-14. StarSchema.co.uk layout version internal

Step 5: In the Queries pane, select **StarSchema co uk Internal Layout (1)**, select the tab **Home (2)**, select **Append Queries (3)**, and select **Append Queries as New (4)**.

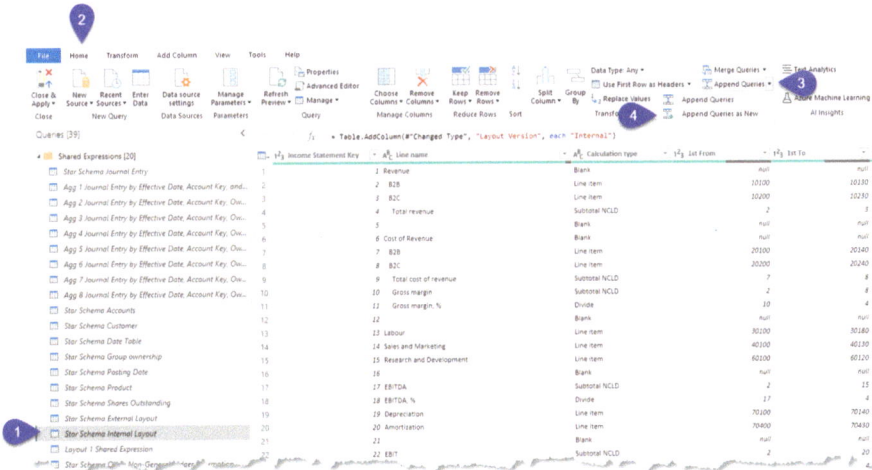

Figure 13-15. StarSchema.co.uk append layout as new

385

CHAPTER 13 INTERNAL REPORTING SEMANTIC MODELS

Step 6: In the Append box, select the first table **StarSchema co uk Internal Layout (1)**, select the second table **StarSchema co uk External Layout (2)**, and select **OK (3)**.

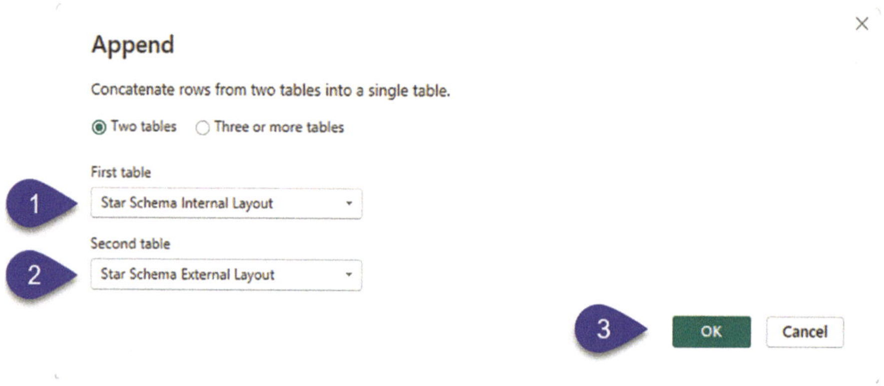

Figure 13-16. StarSchema.co.uk append layout as new

Step 7: Select the referenced query **Append1 (1)**, and in the query settings under **Name (2)**, type *Combined Layout* and press enter.

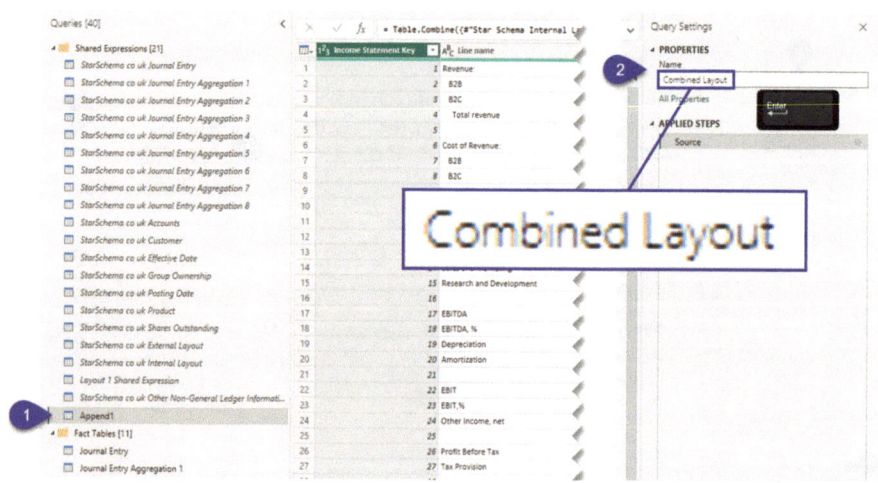

Figure 13-17. StarSchema.co.uk append1 rename

Step 8: Select Layout Version **ABC123 (1)** and select **Text (2)**.

CHAPTER 13   INTERNAL REPORTING SEMANTIC MODELS

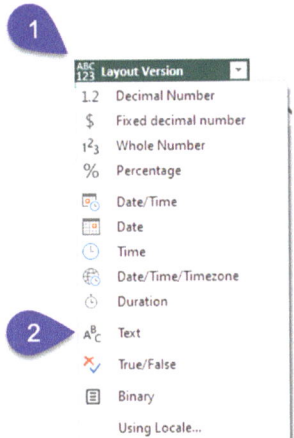

Figure 13-18. StarSchema.co.uk layout version change data type

Step 9: In the Queries pane, right-click **Combined Layout (1)** and click the selected **Enable load (2)** to disable the load (should no longer have tick to the left of Enable load, and StarSchema co uk Journal Entry should be in italics).

CHAPTER 13   INTERNAL REPORTING SEMANTIC MODELS

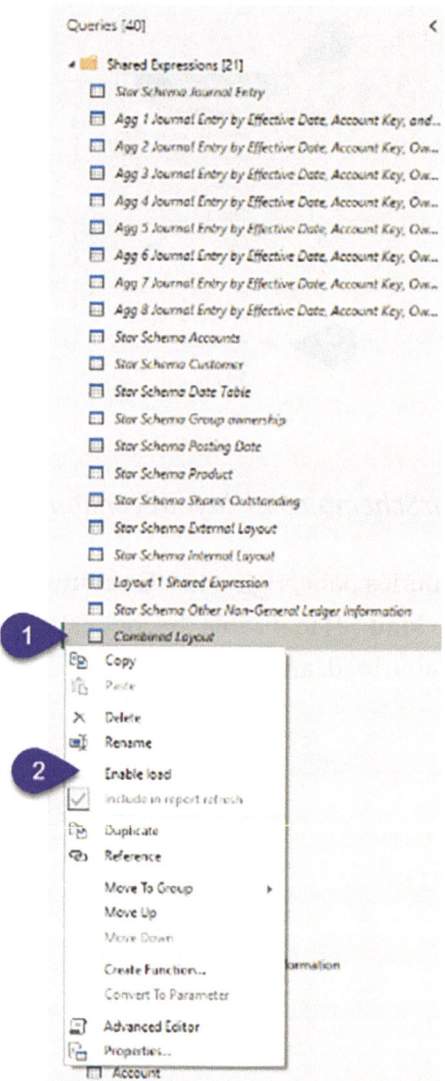

Figure 13-19. *StarSchema.co.uk combined layout disable load*

Step 10: In the Queries pane, select **Layout (1)**, select **Source (2)**, and update the formula to **Combined Layout (3)**.

CHAPTER 13 INTERNAL REPORTING SEMANTIC MODELS

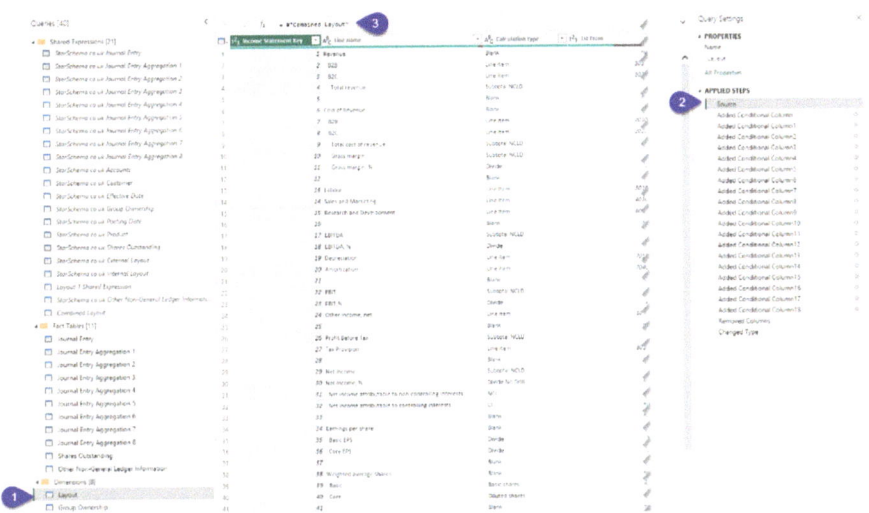

Figure 13-20. StarSchema.co.uk layout update source

Stage 4: Accounts Dimension Table

Step 1: In the Queries pane, right-click **Layout 1 Shared Expression (1)** and select **Duplicate (2)**.

CHAPTER 13   INTERNAL REPORTING SEMANTIC MODELS

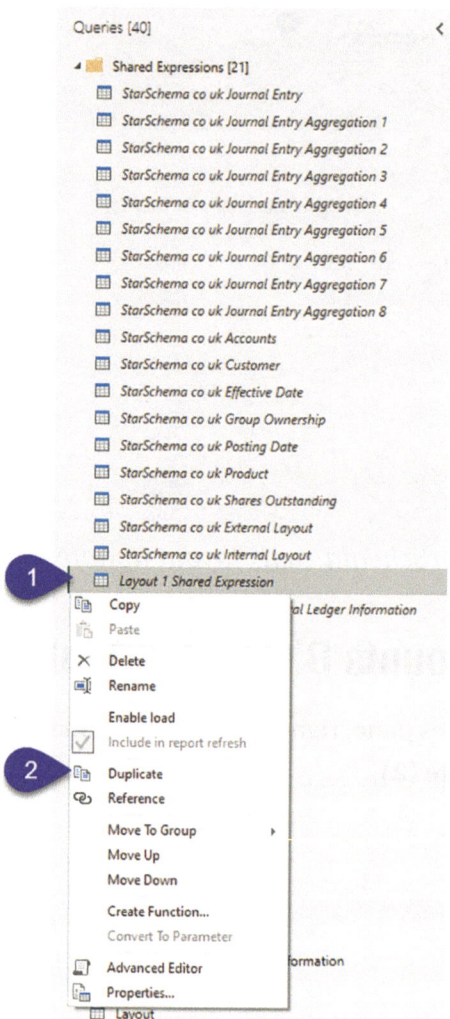

Figure 13-21. StarSchema.co.uk duplicate layout 1 shared expression

Step 2: Select the referenced query **Layout 1 Shared Expression (2) (1)**, and in the query settings under **Name (2)**, type *Layout 2 Shared Expression* and press enter.

CHAPTER 13 INTERNAL REPORTING SEMANTIC MODELS

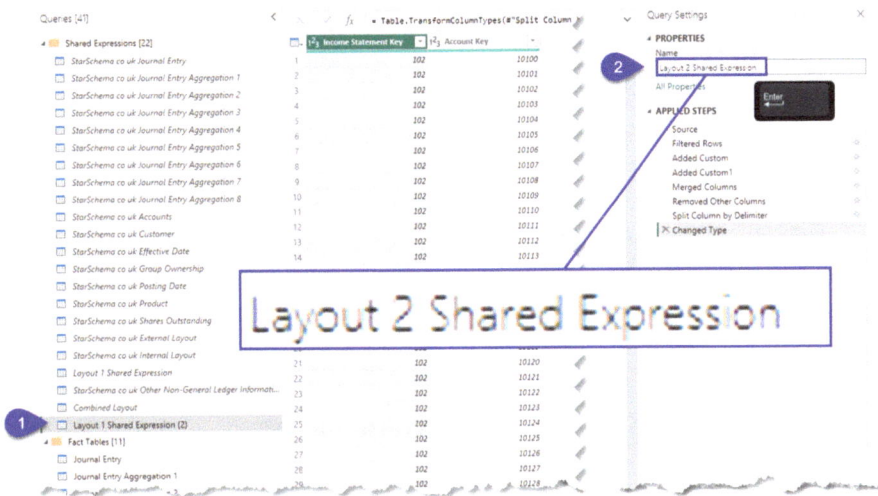

Figure 13-22. StarSchema.co.uk rename layout 2 shared expression

Step 3: In the Queries pane, select **Layout 2 Shared Expression (1)**, select **Source (2)**, and update the formula to **StarSchema co uk Internal Layout (3)**.

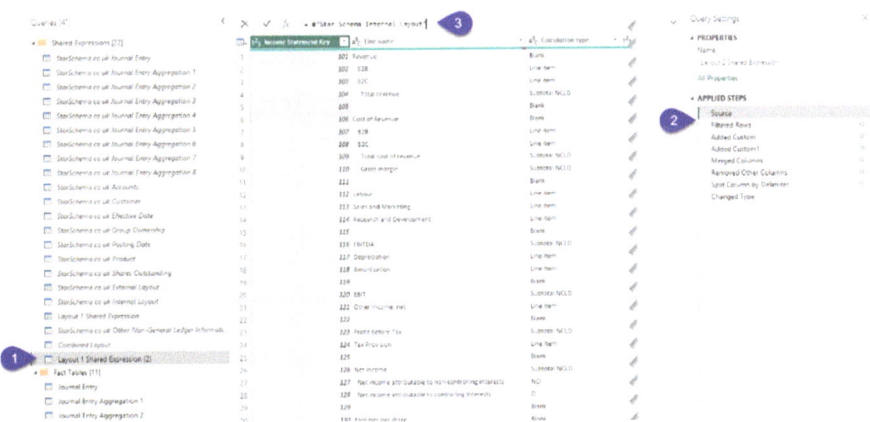

Figure 13-23. StarSchema.co.uk layout 2 shared expression update source

391

CHAPTER 13   INTERNAL REPORTING SEMANTIC MODELS

Step 4: In the Queries pane, select **Account (1)**, select tab **Home (2)**, and select **Merge Queries (3)**.

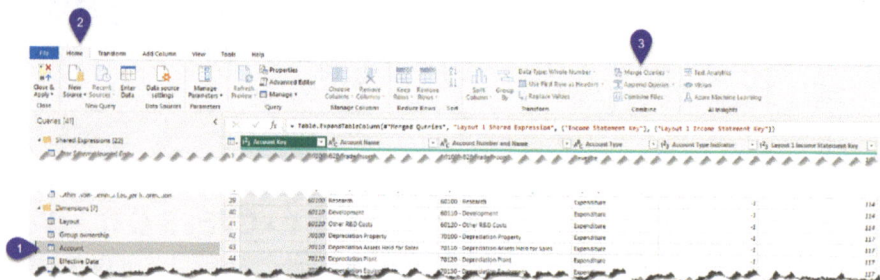

Figure 13-24.   StarSchema.co.uk account merge

Step 5: In the merge with the table **Account (1)**, select the column **Account Key (2)** in the drop-down, select the table **Layout 2 Shared Expression (3)**, select the column **Account Key (4)**, check the join kind is **left outer (5)**, and click **OK (6)**.

CHAPTER 13 INTERNAL REPORTING SEMANTIC MODELS

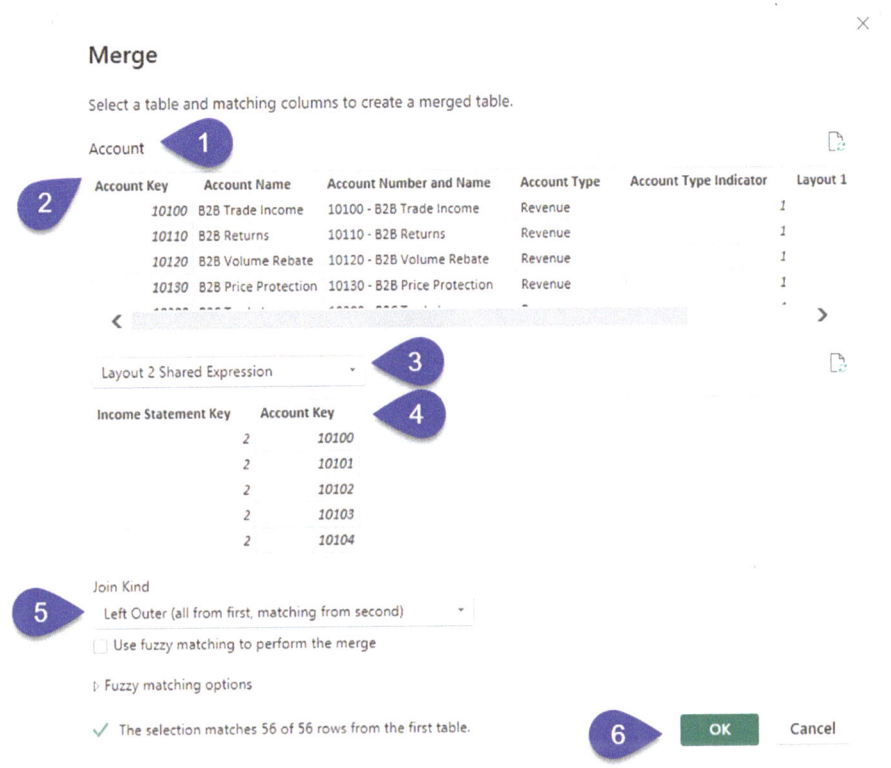

Figure 13-25. StarSchema.co.uk merge account and Layout 2 shared expression

Step 6: Click expand on the column **Layout 2 Shared Expression (1)**, select **Expand (2)**, select the column **Income Statement Key (3)**, deselect **Use original column name as prefix (4)**, and click **OK (5)**.

393

CHAPTER 13   INTERNAL REPORTING SEMANTIC MODELS

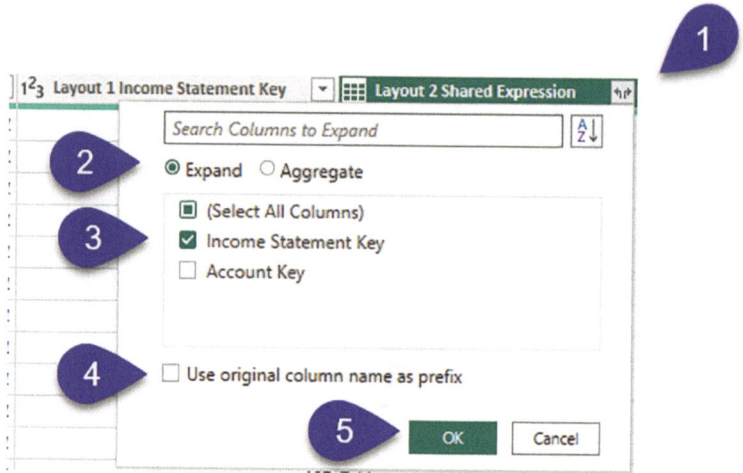

Figure 13-26. StarSchema.co.uk expand income statement key

Step 7: Update the final text in the formula bar so the text reads **Layout 2 Income Statement Key (1)** and press Enter.

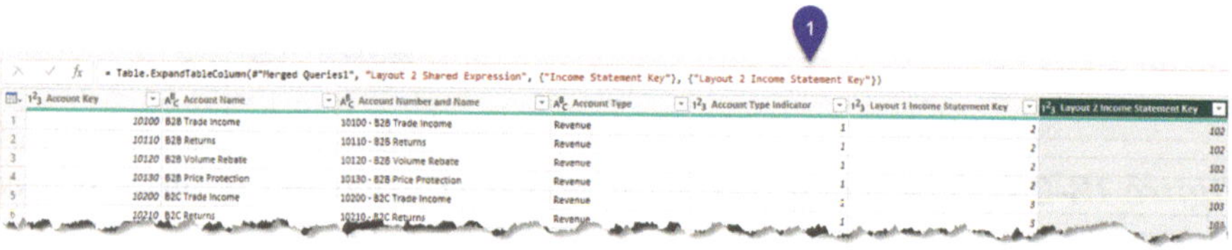

Figure 13-27. StarSchema.co.uk rename income statement key

Step 8: Navigate to the tab **Home (1)** and select **Close & Apply (2)**.

CHAPTER 13 INTERNAL REPORTING SEMANTIC MODELS

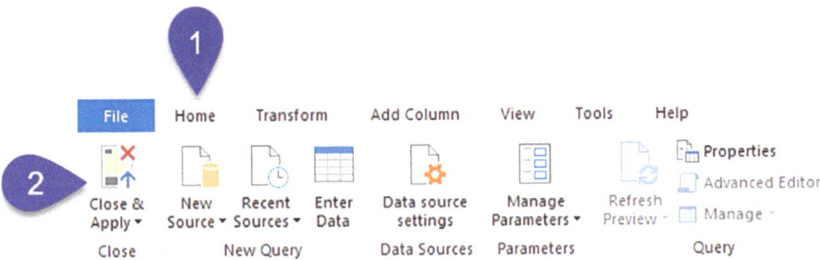

Figure 13-28. *Close and apply*

Building the Data Model
Creating Relationships

Step 1: Create an inactive relationship between 'Layout'[Income Statement Key] and 'Account'[Layout 2 Income Statement Key'].

CHAPTER 13 INTERNAL REPORTING SEMANTIC MODELS

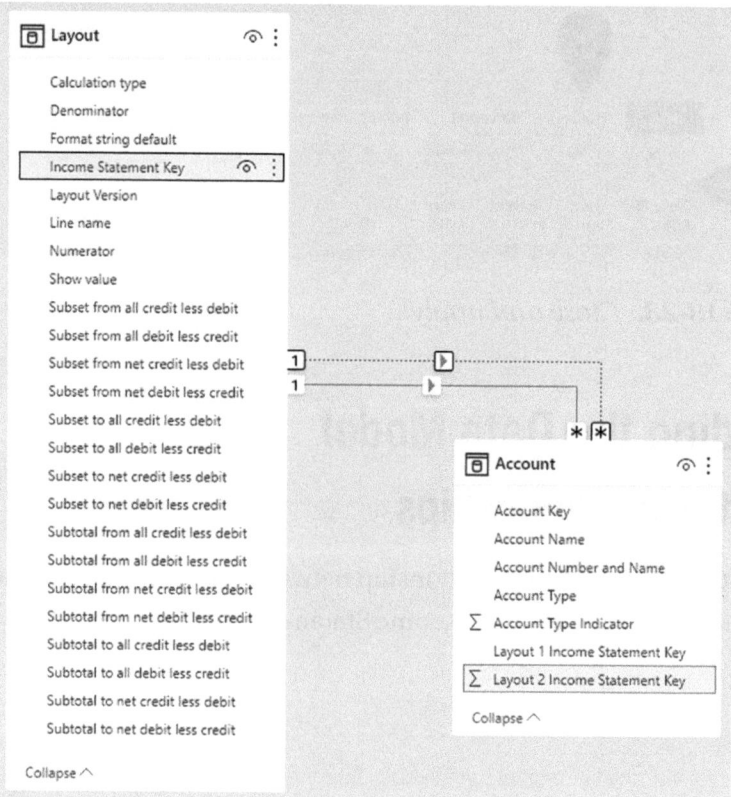

Figure 13-29. *Inactive relationship to account*

Step 2: Create a relationship between 'Effective Date'[Date] and 'Other Non-General Ledger Information'[Start of time period].

CHAPTER 13　INTERNAL REPORTING SEMANTIC MODELS

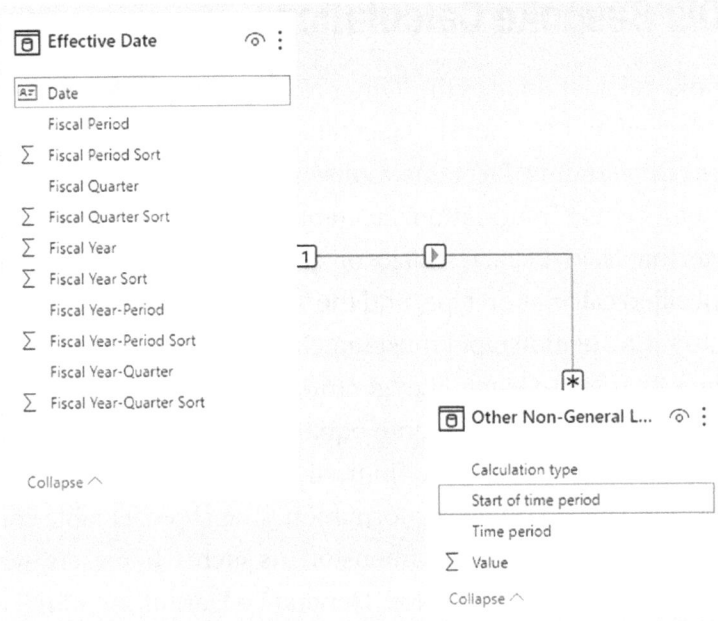

Figure 13-30. Relationship between effective date and other non-general ledger information

DAX Actuals Calculation

The calculations in steps 08 and 12 require amending for the semantic model to support the internal layout:

- **Step 08: Bespoke calculations**: Calculate FTE, FTE Attrition, Sales 50, and Sales 75.

- **Step 12: Bringing the calculation together**: Switch out to using the inactive relationship 'Layout'[Income Statement Key] → 'Account'[Layout 2 Income Statement Key] if the 'Layout'[Layout version] is internal.

397

CHAPTER 13　INTERNAL REPORTING SEMANTIC MODELS

Step 08: Bespoke Calculations

The bespoke calculation uses the 'Other Non-General Ledger Information' snapshot fact table. This snapshot fact table behaves non-additively like the 'Shares Outstanding' fact table. Consequently, each row in the 'Other Non-General Ledger Information' fact table is valid for the specified date range, that is, P1-2023, Q1-2023, or 2023. Each row is also only valid for the specified calculation type, and the 'Other Non-General Ledger Information'[Calculation type] must match the 'Layout'[Calculation type], that is, the 'Other Non-General Ledger Information'[Calculation type] and 'Layout'[Calculation type] must both equal *FTE*.

Unlike the 'Trial Balance' and 'Journal Entry' transactional fact tables, the 'Other Non-General Ledger Information' snapshot fact table contains no relationship to the 'Account' dimension. As such, when users evaluate the value by account, no 'Other Non-General Ledger Information'[Value] should be shown; there is no business logic which links the 'Other Non-General Ledger Information'[Value] to a given account.

The DAX for bespoke calculations is similar to the number of shares and is broken down into six parts:

- **Part 1**: Returns null if the 'Account' dimension or 'Effective Date'[Date] is filtered, else returns 1.

- **Part 2**: Determines the calculation type in the 'Layout' dimension.

- **Part 3**: Determines the time period in scope, either the

  - 'Effective date'[Fiscal Year-Period]
  - 'Effective date'[Fiscal Year-Quarter]
  - 'Effective date'[Fiscal Year] converted to a string

CHAPTER 13 INTERNAL REPORTING SEMANTIC MODELS

- **Part 4**: A calculated table variable for the 'Other Non-General Ledger Information' fact table where
    - 'Other Non-General Ledger Information'[Calculation Type] equals part 2
    - 'Other Non-General Ledger Information'[Time Period] equals part 3
- **Part 5**: The 'Other Non-General Ledger Information'[Value] is calculated based on the filter context from part 4 and multiplied by part 1 to return null if the accounts table or an individual date is filtered.
- **Part 6**: Returns the result from part 5.

```
Actuals Bespoke =
// Part 1
var Isaccountordatefiltered =
    if(
      or(
          ISFILTERED('Account'),
          ISFILTERED('Effective Date'[Date])
          ),
          blank()
       ,1)
// Part 2
VAR SelectedCalcualtionType = SELECTEDVALUE(
Layout[Calculation type] )
```

CHAPTER 13   INTERNAL REPORTING SEMANTIC MODELS

```
// Part 3

VAR SelectedTimePeriod =
        SELECTEDVALUE(
        'Effective Date'[Fiscal Year-Period],
            SELECTEDVALUE(
            'Effective Date'[Fiscal Year-Quarter],
                CONVERT (
                    SELECTEDVALUE( 'Effective Date'[Fiscal Year]
                ), STRING                                      )
            )
        )

// Part 4

VAR CalculateTableOtherNonGeneralLedgerInformation =
        CALCULATETABLE(
          'Other Non-General Ledger Information',
            'Other Non-General Ledger
            Information'[Calculation type]
            =SelectedCalcualtionType,
            'Other Non-General Ledger Information'[Time period] =
            SelectedTimePeriod
        )

// Part 5

VAR result =
   CALCULATE(
       SUM( 'Other Non-General Ledger Information'[Value] ),
       CalculateTableOtherNonGeneralLedgerInformation
       )
```

```
        x Isaccountordatefiltered
// Part 6
RETURN
        result
```

Step 12: Actuals

The actuals calculation currently combines steps 03–10 and multiplies the result by step 11. The updated actuals calculation is required to perform this calculation for the external or internal 'Layout'[Layout version] depending on which version is selected. To achieve this:

- The external calculation continues as before, following the active relationship 'Layout'[Income Statement Key] → 'Account'[Layout 1 Income Statement Key].

- The internal calculation follows the inactive relationship 'Layout'[Income Statement Key] → 'Account'[Layout 2 Income Statement Key].

The DAX for the actuals calculations is broken down into six parts:

- **Part 1**: Checks a single 'Layout'[Layout version] has been selected
- **Part 2**: Determines the 'Layout'[Layout version] selected
- **Part 3**: Combines steps 03–10
- **Part 4**: Combines steps 03–10 for the inactive relationship
- **Part 5**: Switches out the calculation and multiplies by step 11
    - If part 1 returns more than one value, null is returned.

CHAPTER 13　INTERNAL REPORTING SEMANTIC MODELS

- If external is selected, part 3 is returned.
- If internal is selected, part 4 is returned.
- **Part 6**: Returns the result from part 5

```
Actuals =

// Part 1
var layoutisfilteredtoonevalue = HASONEFILTER(Layout[Layout Version])

// Part 2
var selectedlayout = selectedvalue(Layout[Layout Version])

// Part 3
var ExternalLayout =
COALESCE(
    [Actuals Net Credit Less Debit],
    [Actuals Subtotal],
    [Actuals Subset],
    [Actuals Controlling and Non-Controlling Interest],
    [Actuals Bespoke],
    [Number of Shares],
    [Actuals Divide],
    [Actuals Blank]
)

// Part 4
var InternalLayout =
calculate(
    COALESCE(
        [Actuals Net Credit Less Debit],
        [Actuals Subtotal],
```

CHAPTER 13   INTERNAL REPORTING SEMANTIC MODELS

```
        [Actuals Subset],
        [Actuals Controlling and Non-Controlling Interest],
        [Actuals Bespoke],
        [Number of Shares],
        [Actuals Divide],
        [Actuals Blank]
    ),
    USERELATIONSHIP(Layout[Income Statement Key],Account[Layout
    2 Income Statement Key])
)
```

// **Part 5**:

```
var result =
switch(
    true(),
       layoutisfilteredtoonevalue = false, blank(),
       selectedlayout = "External", ExternalLayout,
       selectedlayout = "Internal", InternalLayout
)      × [Actuals Show Value]
```

// **Part 6**

```
return
      result
```

Summary

- To meet internal reporting requirements, the external reporting semantic models (Chapter 11) can be extended to include internal layouts and other non-general ledger information.

- DAX step 08 is updated to return values from the 'Other Non-General Ledger Information' snapshot fact table.

- DAX step 12 is updated to use the relationship:

    - Active relationship 'Layout'[Income Statement Key] → 'Account'[Layout 1 Income Statement Key] for the external layout
    - Inactive relationship 'Layout'[Income Statement Key] → 'Account'[Layout 2 Income Statement Key] for the internal layout

CHAPTER 14

Security and Self-Service Considerations

In this chapter, we will cover the semantic model security and self-service considerations. We firstly cover row-based and object-based security considerations, how these work and examples of these in practice. We then cover three key self-service considerations: what is relevant to end users, how the semantic model should be organized, and how the semantic model can be enriched.

In this chapter, there are two sections:

1. Security Considerations
2. Self-Service Considerations

Security Considerations

At the semantic model level, there are two security considerations:

1. **Row-level security:** Restricts access to rows of data, that is, restrict nonexecutive users from viewing any rows of data where the column 'Other Non-General Ledger Information' [Calculation type] equals "FTE attrition".

2. **Object-level security:** Restricts access to specific tables or columns, that is, for nonexecutive users, restrict access to the table 'Other Non-General Ledger Information' or the column 'Other Non-General Ledger Information'[Calculation type]

Each income statement semantic model can have its own unique security rules; these decisions are made according to the specifics of each case. Therefore, you should consider if you need to restrict access on a row or object basis for specific user groups.

In addition to restricting other non-general ledger information, examples include

- Restrict a geographical region, that is, users based in the UK can only view the income statement for the UK legal entity and any of its subsidiaries.

- Restrict lines on the income statement, that is, marketing users only viewing lines related to marketing expenses.

Note *The Microsoft documentation on setting up row-level and object-level security can be found at* https://learn.microsoft.com/en-us/power-bi/enterprise/service-admin-rls *and* https://learn.microsoft.com/en-us/power-bi/enterprise/service-admin-ols?tabs=table, *respectively. For Microsoft Fabric, at the time of writing the OneLake Security model for tables and folders is yet to go into general availability; however, you can follow any security updates at* https://learn.microsoft.com/en-us/fabric/onelake/onelake-security.

CHAPTER 14 SECURITY AND SELF-SERVICE CONSIDERATIONS

Self-Service Considerations

In Chapter 4, we covered how an income statement semantic model can help to explain the income statement, improve decision-making, improve data quality, increase understanding of the profitability drivers, and improve the month-end close process. To realize these benefits, the semantic model must be configured to enable end users to easily and intuitively access the information they need. To make optimal self-service decisions, it is important to

- **Have a deep understanding of end users' needs**: That is, do end users refer to products by their product code? If so, product code needs to be a selectable attribute.

- **Remain up to date with the latest product releases**: Semantic models have a vast array of options that can be adjusted, and the number of properties is constantly evolving.

Rather than focus on every technical property (which will be outdated by the time of this book's publication) or all permutations of end users' needs (which will be near limitless), this part focuses on three key considerations:

1. What is relevant to end users
2. How the semantic model should be organized
3. How the semantic model can be enriched

By focusing on just these three considerations, you can significantly improve the usability of your income statement semantic model.

CHAPTER 14   SECURITY AND SELF-SERVICE CONSIDERATIONS

Consideration 1: What Is Relevant to End Users

Removing Information

The temptation is to include everything "just in case" in the semantic model. However, this mindset is only adopted by junior developers; in practice, it leads to cognitive overload, and the important information gets lost in the noise. For instance, it is highly unlikely that end users will want to slice and dice the income statement by an 'Account'[Date created] or a 'Legal Entity'[Company code] attribute.

Wherever possible, information should be excluded. Not only does this help end users, but this also improves load performance as less data is brought into the semantic model.

Hiding Information

Information which is irrelevant to end users but needed in the semantic model can be hidden, that is, hiding all the measures in DAX steps 01–11 or the 'Account'[Layout 1 Income Statement Key]. There is also a Table.isPrivate property (available when using Power BI premium features), which means the table is only visible using developer tools (such as Tabular Editor). All measures can be moved to a secondary 'Hidden Measures' table with the Table.isPrivate property set to true. The same Table.isPrivate property can be set to true for the journal entry aggregations as report developers or end users do not need to be aware of their existence.

Consolidating Information

Where possible, multiple attributes should be consolidated, for instance, combining multiple address fields – address line 1, address line 2, country, etc. – into a single address attribute. Other examples include combining elements such as product code and product name or customer code and customer name. This helps to reduce the options end users have, making it easier to locate relevant information.

Consideration 2: How the Semantic Model Should Be Organized

Folders

Using folders makes it easier to locate information, that is, the five subtotal measures were grouped in the folder step 04 subtotals. The same can be done for fields in the tables. For instance, any attributes relating to geography can be grouped together. When folders are collapsed, end users have less information to navigate, and if they require information which is similar in nature, the folder can be expanded, and the similar fields are grouped together.

Hierarchies

Hierarchies enable end users to drill down on information contained within a single table from the highest level to a more granular detailed level. A common example is a fiscal year hierarchy; this starts at Fiscal Year, then drills to Fiscal Quarter, and finally the Fiscal Period. Within the StarSchema.co.uk example, there are four observable hierarchies (Table 14-1).

CHAPTER 14   SECURITY AND SELF-SERVICE CONSIDERATIONS

Table 14-1. StarSchema.co.uk observable hierarchies

Table Name	Hierarchy Name	Level 1	Level 2	Level 3
Effective Date	Fiscal Year Hierarchy	Fiscal Year	Fiscal Quarter	Fiscal Period
Posting Date	Posting Fiscal Year Hierarchy	Posting Year	Posting Quarter	Posting Period
Customer	Customer Group Hierarchy	Customer Group	Customer Name	NA
Product	Product Brand Hierarchy	Product Brand	Product Name	NA

By organizing information into hierarchies, end users do not have to remember each level and can select a single hierarchy rather than multiple attributes.

Consideration 3: How the Semantic Model Can Be Enriched

Here, we focus on two key ways the semantic model can be enriched. This is not an exhaustive list, and the importance of enrichments not covered – such as featured tables and perspectives – could be argued as vital depending on the use case. The main consideration is whether adjusting a property will improve the experience of end users. This is true for current properties and future properties which have arisen in the time elapsed between me writing this book and you reading it. That said, for income statement semantic models, the two enrichments covered are important now and for the foreseeable future.

Descriptions

Every measure, table, or column within the model can be given a description. For instance, 'Account' [Account Name] could be given the description "the name of the account in the general ledger." This can help end users as they have further information if they are unsure of the meaning of a given attribute.

Detailed Row Expressions

In Excel, it is possible to double-click a number and drill into the detail (see Chapter 4). For income statement semantic models, this is particularly important given the prevalence of spreadsheets in the finance community. This can be configured with Tabular Editor using detailed row expressions. The desired behavior is usually to

- Drill down from line-items, subtotals, or subsets to accounts
- Drill through from accounts to the journal entry detail

Line-items, subtotals, or subsets usually consist of at most a few hundred accounts. Therefore, it's possible to view this information on a single Excel sheet. However, accounts can consist of millions or billions of journal entries. Therefore, the drill through (detailed row expression) is usually configured for when users double-click accounts, and the number of records returned is, by default, the top 1,000; this ensures the volume of data returned from the semantic model does not exceed Excel's row limit.

StarSchema.co.uk Detailed Row Expression Example

Using Tabular Editor 2, click expand **Tables (1)**, expand **Measure (2)**, select the measure **Actuals (3)**, use the drop-down to select **Detail Row Expressions (4)**, and in the DAX window **(5)**, type

CHAPTER 14   SECURITY AND SELF-SERVICE CONSIDERATIONS

```
// Part 1
VAR ISK = MIN( Layout[Income Statement Key] )

// Part 2
VAR SubtotalFrom =
    MIN( Layout[Subtotal from net credit less debit] )
        + MIN( Layout[Subtotal from all credit less debit] )
        + MIN( Layout[Subtotal from net debit less credit] )
        + MIN( Layout[Subtotal from all debit less credit] )

// Part 3
VAR SubtotalTo =
    MIN( Layout[Subtotal to net credit less debit] )
        + MIN( Layout[Subtotal to all credit less debit] )
        + MIN( Layout[Subtotal to net debit less credit] )
        + MIN( Layout[Subtotal to all debit less credit] )

// Part 4
VAR SubsetFrom =
    MIN( Layout[Subset from net credit less debit] )
        + MIN( Layout[Subset from all credit less debit] )
        + MIN( Layout[Subset from net debit less credit] )
        + MIN( Layout[Subset from all debit less credit] )

// Part 5
VAR SubsetTo =
    MIN( Layout[Subset to net credit less debit] )
        + MIN( Layout[Subset to all credit less debit] )
        + MIN( Layout[Subset to net debit less credit] )
        + MIN( Layout[Subset to all debit less credit] )

// Part 6
VAR Accounttablefilter =
    CALCULATETABLE(
```

```
            Account,
                Account[Layout 1 Income Statement Key] = ISK ||
                Account[Layout 2 Income Statement Key] = ISK ||
                    (
                    Account[Layout 1 Income Statement Key] >=
                    SubtotalFrom &&
                    Account[Layout 1 Income Statement Key] <=
                    SubtotalTo
                    ) ||
                    (
                    Account[Layout 2 Income Statement Key] >=
                    SubtotalFrom &&
                    Account[Layout 2 Income Statement Key] <=
                    SubtotalTo
                    ) ||
                    (
                    Account[Account Key] >= SubsetFrom &&
                    Account[Account Key] <= SubsetTo
                    ),
            REMOVEFILTERS( Layout )
        )

//Part 7
VAR result =
    CALCULATETABLE(
        SELECTCOLUMNS(
            'Journal Entry',
            "Account Name and Number", RELATED( Account[Account
            Number and Name] ),
            "Journal Entry Number", 'Journal Entry'[Journal
            Entry Number],
```

CHAPTER 14   SECURITY AND SELF-SERVICE CONSIDERATIONS

```
            "Journal Entry Sequence ID", 'Journal
            Entry'[Journal Entry Sequence ID],
            "Journal Entry Effective Date", 'Journal
            Entry'[Effective Date],
            "Journal Entry Posted Date", 'Journal
            Entry'[Posting Date],
            "Journal Entry value", 'Journal Entry'[Journal
            Entry Value]
        ),
        REMOVEFILTERS( Layout ),
        Accounttablefilter
    )
// Part 8
RETURN
    result
```

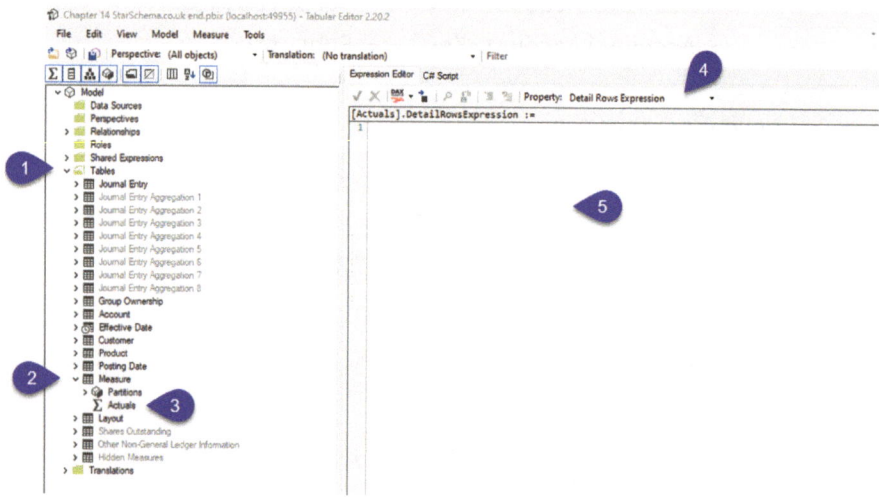

Figure 14-1. Tabular Editor 2 detailed row expressions

CHAPTER 14   SECURITY AND SELF-SERVICE CONSIDERATIONS

The DAX for the detailed row expression calculation is broken down into eight parts:

- **Part 1**: Calculates the min 'Layout'[Income Statement Key].

- **Part 2**: Calculates the income statement key for the subtotal from for the current income statement line. As only a maximum of one subtotal can be in scope for the detailed row expression, this is achieved by combining the four subtotal from fields, that is, 'Layout'[Subtotal from net credit less debit].

- **Part 3**: Calculates the income statement key for the subtotal to for the current income statement line. As only a maximum of one subtotal can be in scope for the detailed row expression, this is achieved by combining the four subtotal to fields, that is, 'Layout'[Subtotal to net credit less debit].

- **Part 4**: Calculates the account key for the subset from for the current income statement line. As only a maximum of one subset can be in scope for the detailed row expression, this is achieved by combiningthe four subset from fields, that is, 'Layout'[Subset from net credit less debit].

- **Part 5**: Calculates the account key for the subset to for the current income statement line. As only a maximum of one subset can be in scope for the detailed row expression, this is achieved by combining the four subset to fields, that is, 'Layout'[Subset to net credit less debit].

- **Part 6**: Calculates the 'Account' dimension, ignoring any filtering from the 'Layout' snowflake dimension, where

    - 'Account'[Layout 1 Income Statement Key] or 'Account'[Layout 2 Income Statement Key] equals part 1.

    - 'Account'[Layout 1 Income Statement Key] or 'Account'[Layout 2 Income Statement Key] is greater than or equal to part 2 and less than or equal to part 3.

    - 'Account'[Account Key] is greater than or equal to part 4 and less than or equal to part 5.

- **Part 7**: Selects columns from the 'Journal Entry' fact table filtered by part 6 and removing any filters from the 'Layout' dimension.

- **Part 8**: Returns the result from part 7.

The key to this calculation working is part 6 which results in the 'Account' dimension being filtered to only those accounts which appear

- In the line-item selected (part 1)

- Within the subtotal from (part 2) and subtotal to (part 3) range

- Within the subset from (part 4) and subset to (part 5) range

Given the 'Account' dimension is related to the 'Journal Entry' fact table, any filtering on the 'Account' dimension filters the 'Journal Entry' fact table.

CHAPTER 14   SECURITY AND SELF-SERVICE CONSIDERATIONS

Summary

- Row- and object-level security restricts the information certain groups of end users can see.
- When optimizing the income statement semantic model for self-service, consider
  - **What is relevant to end users**: Remove irrelevant information, hide technical information, and consolidate fields.
  - **How the semantic model should be organized**: Use folders and hierarchies.
  - **How the semantic model can be enriched**: Add descriptions and detailed row expressions.

CHAPTER 15

Review of the 16 Challenges

In this book, we have learned how to create an income statement semantic model based on the trial balance. We have also covered how to adapt this trial balance income statement semantic model to entity-specific requirements by adding dimensionality, aggregations, bespoke information, and multiple layouts.

In this chapter, we will review the 16 challenges outlined in Chapter 3, providing examples of how these challenges have been overcome.

In this chapter, there are three sections:

1. The Nine Calculation Challenges

2. The Four Presentation Challenges

3. The Three Analytical Challenges

The Nine Calculation Challenges

Challenges 1–6

Figure 15-1 shows how this income statement semantic modelling approach overcomes calculation challenges 1–6:

CHAPTER 15   REVIEW OF THE 16 CHALLENGES

- **Challenge 1**: Calculating line-items
- **Challenge 2**: Calculating subtotals
- **Challenge 3**: Calculating subsets
- **Challenge 4**: Calculating controlling and non-controlling interests
- **Challenge 5**: Calculating weighted average shares
- **Challenge 6**: Calculating earnings per share (EPS)

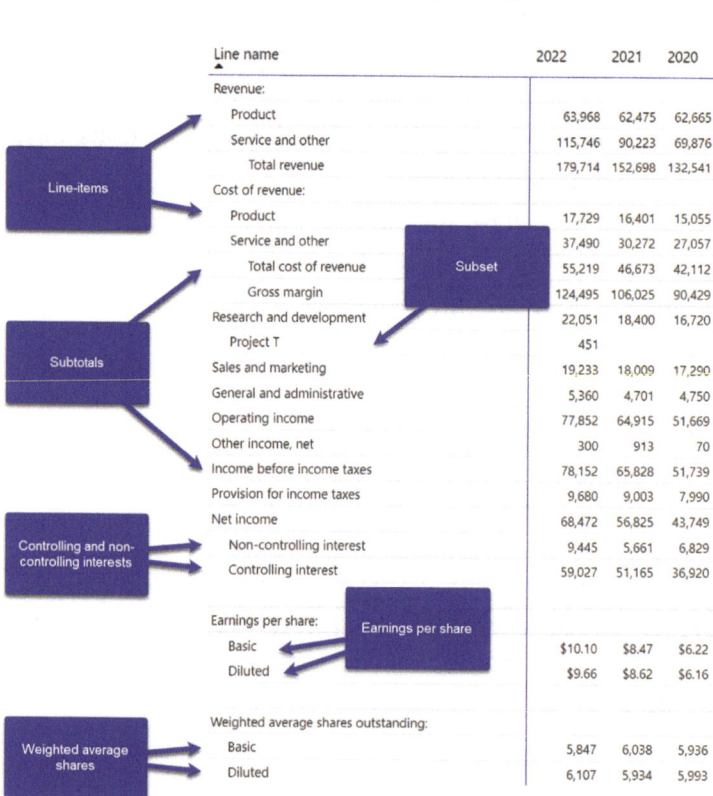

Figure 15-1. Tyrell Corp external semantic model Chapter 11 annotated with challenges 1–6

CHAPTER 15   REVIEW OF THE 16 CHALLENGES

Challenges 7–9

Figure 15-2 shows how this income statement semantic modelling approach overcomes calculation challenges 7–9:

- **Challenge 7**: Adding bespoke calculation
- **Challenge 8**: Calculating percentages
- **Challenge 9**: Blank lines

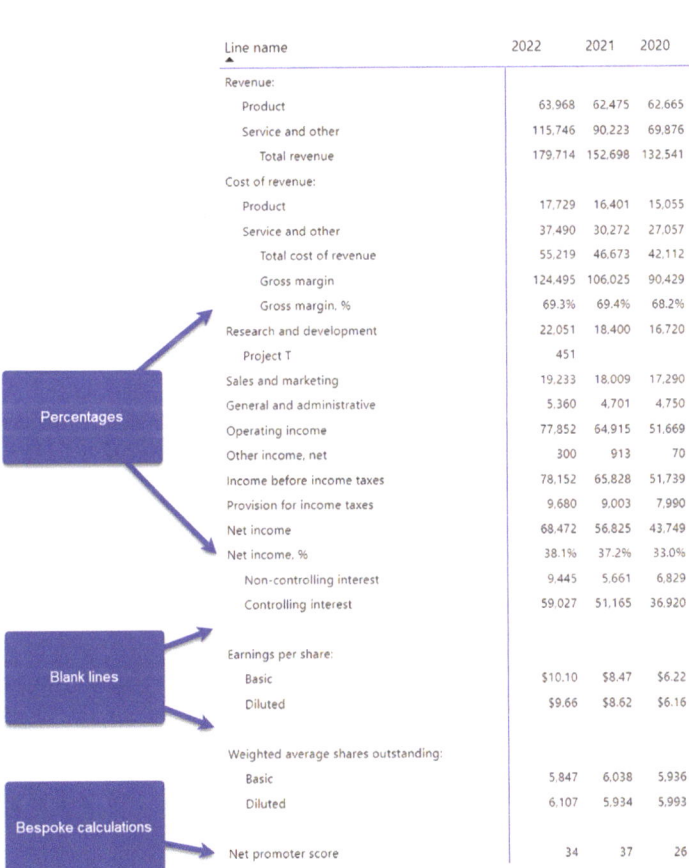

Figure 15-2. Tyrell Corp internal semantic model Chapter 13 annotated with challenges 7–9

CHAPTER 15   REVIEW OF THE 16 CHALLENGES

The Four Presentation Challenges
Challenges 10–12

Figure 15-3 shows how the income statement semantic modelling approach overcomes presentation challenges 10–12:

- **Challenge 10**: Hide lines
- **Challenge 11**: Sorting the hierarchy
- **Challenge 12**: Formatting income statement lines individually

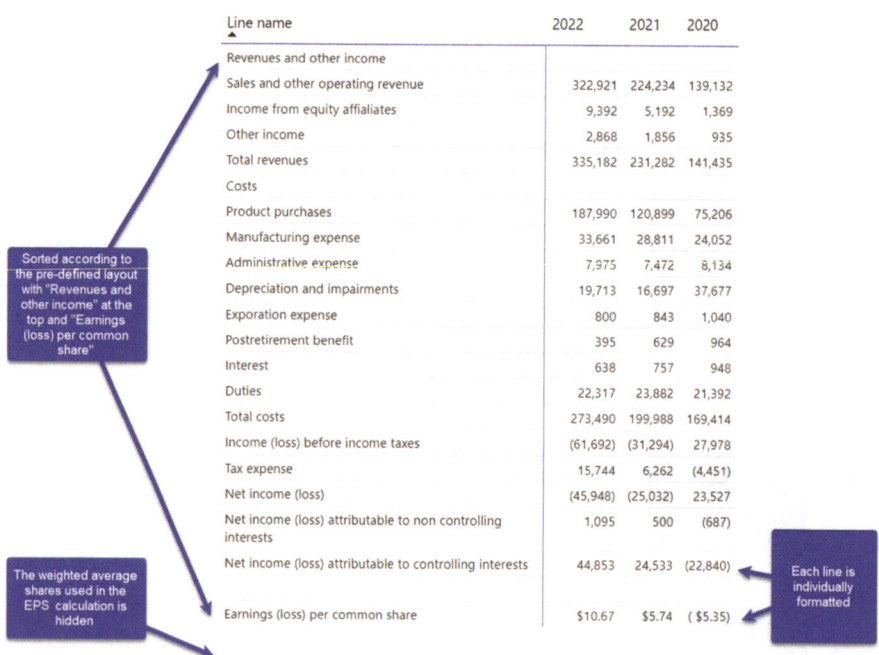

Figure 15-3. Weyland Industries external reporting semantic model Chapter 11 annotated with challenges 10–12

Challenge 13: Enabling Multiple Layouts

Figure 15-4 shows how a single semantic model can support multiple income statement layouts.

The Three Analytical Challenges
Challenges 14 and 15

Figure 15-5 shows the pivot table field list end users can select, all of which are ways the income statement for StarSchema.co.uk can be sliced and diced in Excel as well as Power BI overcoming

- **Challenge 14**: Enabling end users to build reports or conduct analysis in Excel or Power BI
- **Challenge 15**: Slice and dice the income statement

CHAPTER 15 REVIEW OF THE 16 CHALLENGES

Line name	2022	2021	2020		Line name	2022	2021	2020
Revenues and other income					Revenues and other income			
Sales and other operating revenue	322,921	224,234	139,132		Sales and other operating revenue	322,921	224,234	139,132
Income from equity affiliates	9,392	5,192	1,369		Income from equity affiliates	9,392	5,192	1,369
Other income	2,868	1,856	935		Other income	2,868	1,856	935
Total revenues	335,182	231,282	141,435		Total revenues	335,182	231,282	141,435
Costs					Costs			
Product purchases	187,990	120,899	75,206		Product purchases	187,990	120,899	75,206
Manufacturing expense	33,661	28,811	24,052		Manufacturing expense	33,661	28,811	24,052
Administrative expense	7,975	7,472	8,134		Administrative expense	7,975	7,472	8,134
Depreciation and impairments	19,713	16,697	37,677		Depreciation and impairments	19,713	16,697	37,677
Exporation expense	800	843	1,040		Exporation expense	800	843	1,040
Postretirement benefit	395	629	964		Postretirement benefit	395	629	964
Interest	638	757	948		Interest	638	757	948
Duties	22,317	23,882	21,392		Duties	22,317	23,882	21,392
Total costs	273,490	199,988	169,414		Total costs	273,490	199,988	169,414
Income (loss) before income taxes	(61,692)	(31,294)	27,978		Income (loss) before income taxes	(61,692)	(31,294)	27,978
Tax expense	15,744	6,262	(4,451)		Tax expense	15,744	6,262	(4,451)
Net income (loss)	(45,948)	(25,032)	23,527		Net income (loss)	(45,948)	(25,032)	23,527
Net income (loss) attributable to non controlling interests	1,095	500	(687)		Net income (loss) attributable to non controlling interests	1,095	500	(687)
Net income (loss) attributable to controlling interests	44,853	24,533	(22,840)		Net income (loss) attributable to controlling interests	44,853	24,533	(22,840)
Earnings (loss) per common share	$10.67	$5.74	($5.35)		Earnings (loss) per common share	$10.67	$5.74	($5.35)
					Barrels Produced	197	148	118

External and internal layout

Figure 15-4. *Weyland Industries internal reporting semantic model Chapter 13 side-by-side example*

CHAPTER 15   REVIEW OF THE 16 CHALLENGES

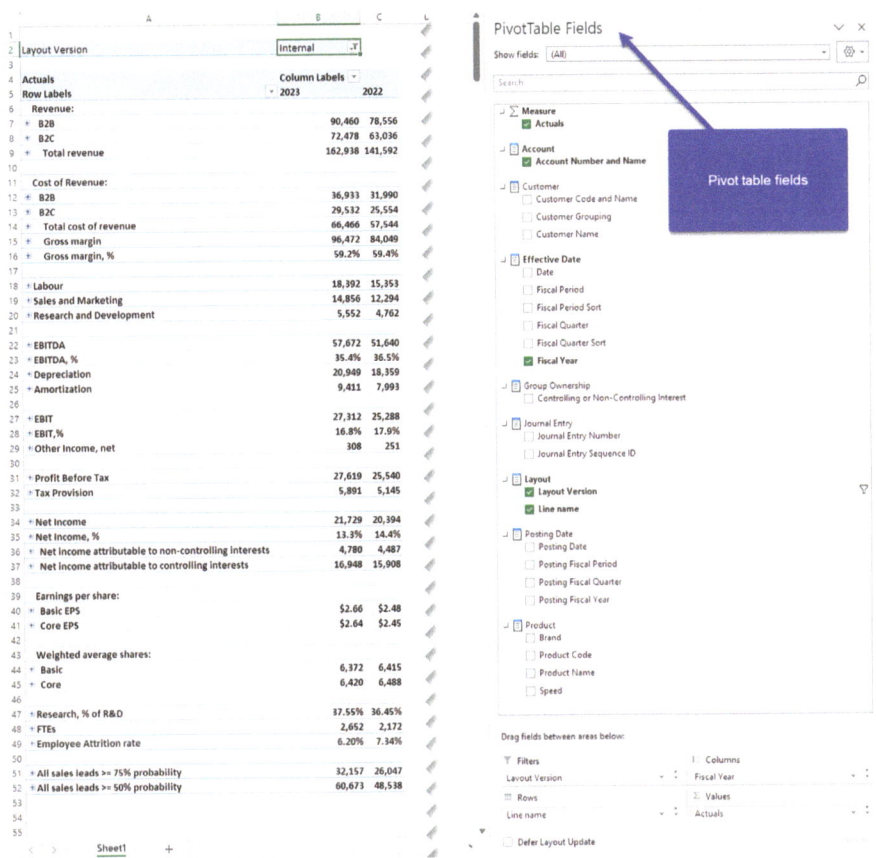

Figure 15-5. StarSchema.co.uk analyzed in Excel internal reporting semantic model Chapter 14

Challenge 16: Drilling from Income Statement Lines to Journal Entries

Figure 15-6 shows how end users can drill down on individual lines to the underlying accounts **(1)** and drill through by right-clicking a number **(2)** and selecting *show details* **(3)** to create a tab containing information about journal entries **(4)**.

425

CHAPTER 15   REVIEW OF THE 16 CHALLENGES

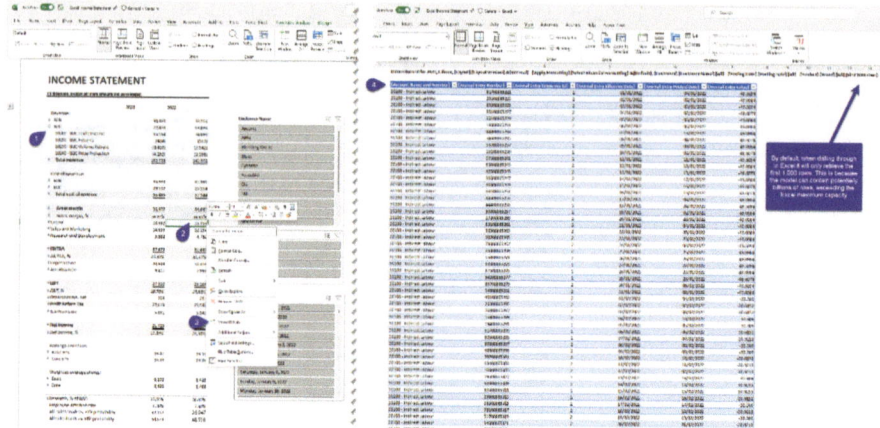

Figure 15-6.   StarSchema.co.uk drill down from subtotal to account to journal entry

Summary

- The approach outlined in this book overcomes the 16 challenges outlined in Chapter 3.

- Because entities abide by the rules of double-entry bookkeeping and outputs are tightly regulated, an approach based on the trial balance (the precursory step to building an income statement) is reusable.

CHAPTER 15   REVIEW OF THE 16 CHALLENGES

- Because of the unique nature of each entity, the base trial balance solution can be adapted adding in

    - **Dimensionality**: The ways an entity explains its income statement, that is, by legal entity

    - **Aggregations**: For each possible way end users can slice and dice the income statement

    - **Bespoke information**: Data from other sources and systems to further contextualize financial information

Index

A

Account balance, 15, 67
Account dimension, 149, 252
    account key, 252
    account name, 252
    account type, 201
    account type indicator, 193, 196, 252
    layout 1 Income Statement Key, 252
    layout 2 Income Statement Key, 364
Activity-based costing (ABC), 79

B

Bespoke calculations, 7, 218, 367, 421
    employee attrition rate, 7, 354
    full-time equivalent (FTE), 354
    potential future sales at 50% + probability, 7, 354
    potential future sales at 75% + probability, 7, 354

C

Calculation type, 217, 232, 348
Challenges, 35, 326
    four presentation challenges, 36, 419
    nine calculation challenges, 36, 419
    sixteen challenges, 35, 426
    three analytical challenges, 36, 419
Conceptual models, 69, 83
    journal entry conceptual model, 80
    trial balance conceptual model, 69

D

Data Analysis eXpressions (DAX), 1, 35, 107, 257, 371
    Actuals, 322
    Actuals Bespoke, 315
    Actuals Blank, 320
    Actuals Controlling and Non-Controlling Interest, 310

Data Analysis eXpressions (DAX) (*cont.*)
   Actuals Divide, 320
   Actuals Net Credit Less Debit, 144
   Actuals Net Credit Less Debit Indicator, 144
   Actuals Net Debit Less Credit, 144
   Actuals Net Debit Less Credit Indicator, 144
   Actuals Show Value, 321
   Actuals Subset, 309
   Actuals Subtotal, 304
   Actuals Sum, 144
   detailed row expressions, 411
   dynamic format strings, 257
   number of shares, 313
Data modelling, 1
Dimensional modelling, 11, 56
   aggregations, 83, 148
   attributes, 89
   data types, 85
   dimensions, 12
      degenerate dimensions, 89
      non-uniform dimensions, 22, 75
      uniform dimensions, 21, 75
   facts, 12
      snapshot fact table, 248, 311
      transactional fact tables, 311, 312
   field types, 84
   relationships, 3, 42, 76
      active relationship, 366
      inactive relationship, 364, 367
      role-playing dimension, 77
   snowflake schema, 11
   star schema, 11
Double-entry bookkeeping, 18, 50, 426
   accrual, 20
   credit, 17
   debit, 17
Drill down, 10, 425
Drill through, 10, 425
Dynamic format strings, 257

E

Earnings per share (EPS), 5, 15, 420
Effective Date, 149
Examples used throughout this book, xxxiii
   StarSchema.co.uk, xxxiii, 257, 258
   Tyrell Corp, xxxiii, 257, 258
   Weyland Industries, xxxiii, 257, 258
Excel, 3, 38
   cube formulas, 3
   pivot tables, 3, 423
Expense accounts, 72

F

Field types, 84
Financial Accounting Standards Board (FASB), 6
Format string default, 348

G, H

Generally Accepted Accounting Principles (GAAP), 6, 20
Granularity, 74, 77, 78
    atomic grain, 75
Group accounting, 5, 15, 37
    controlling interests, 5, 15
    non-controlling interests, 5, 15, 420
    subsidiaries, 5
Group Ownership, 149

I

Income Statement, 1, 3, 4, 15
    external income statement, 5
    internal income statements, 7, 326
    net income, 15, 50
Input-driven approach, 35, 258, 372
International Accounting Standards Board (IASB), 6
International Financial Reporting Standards (IFRS), 6, 20

J

Journal entry, 18
    adjusting journal entries, 17, 21
    compound journal entries, 19
    transaction journal entry, 19

K

Keys, 90
    composite keys, 89
    foreign keys, 89
    primary keys, 90
    surrogate keys, 89

L

Layout, 325
    external layout table, 327
    format string default, 219
    income statement key, 217
    internal layout table, 327
    is hidden, 217
    layout dimension, 213, 327
    layout version, 365
    line-items, 17, 420
    line name, 342
    multiple layouts, 326, 423
Layout table, 327
Logical models, 83, 327
    external reporting logical models, 327
        journal entry external reporting logical model, 255, 257
        trial balance external reporting logical model, 254, 257
    internal reporting logical models, 326, 371

INDEX

Logical models (*cont.*)
    journal entry internal reporting logical model, 368
    trial balance internal reporting logical model, 367

M, N

Microsoft Fabric, 108, 149
Multidimensional eXpressions (MDX), 35, 44, 225

O

Other non-general ledger information, 326, 354, 360, 371

P

Percentage, 7, 315, 421
    EBIT,%, 331
    EBITDA, %, 330
    gross margin, %, 7, 330
    net Income, %, 331
    research, % of R&D, 7, 333
Power BI, 1, 3, 38
    Building the Data Model, 107, 147, 295, 371
    mark as date table, 140, 193
    measure table, 143
    PBIX, 258

Power BI Desktop, 3
Power Query, 1, 149, 257, 371
    queries pane, 123
    shared expressions, 149, 259
Profit and loss, 4

Q

Qualitative characteristics, 6
    comparability characteristic, 6
    materiality characteristic, 6
    verifiability and understandability characteristics, 6

R

Revenue accounts, 72

S

Security, 326, 405
    object-level security, 406
    row-level security, 405
Self-service, 326, 405
    consolidating Information, 408
    descriptions, 411
    folders, 409
    hiding Information, 408
    hierarchies, 409
    removing Information, 408
    StarSchema.co.uk Detailed Row Expression Example, 411

Semantic model, 1, 3, 8, 13, 49, 258, 326
　external reporting semantic models, 326
　income statement semantic model, 9
　internal reporting semantic models, 326
　journal entry external reporting semantic model, 257, 371
　journal entry internal reporting semantic model, 371
　journal entry semantic model, 147
　Semantic Model Inputs, 257
　tabular object model (TOM), 45
　trial balance external reporting semantic models, 257
　trial balance internal reporting semantic model, 371
Shares outstanding, 213, 248
Sixteen challenges, 426
Slice and dice, 9, 95, 325, 423
Subtotal and Subset, 201
　all credit less debit, xxvii, 201, 202, 206, 211
　all debit less credit, xxvii, 201, 202, 209, 211
　net credit less debit, xxvii, 201, 202, 204, 211
　net debit less credit, xxvii, 201, 202, 207, 211
　subset, 17, 201, 420
　　subset ACLD, 232
　　subset ADLC, 232
　　subset NCLD, 232
　　subset NDLC, 232
　subtotal, 17, 201, 420
　　subtotal ACLD, 229
　　subtotal ADLC, 229
　　subtotal NCLD, 229
　　subtotal NDLC, 229

T, U

Trial balance, 15

V

Visual calculations, 56, 60–62, 64

W, X, Y, Z

Weighted average shares, 420